Introduction to
Theological Research

INTRODUCTION TO THEOLOGICAL RESEARCH

BY

CYRIL J. BARBER

MOODY PRESS

CHICAGO

For my former mentors:
  S. Lewis Johnson, Jr.
  J. Dwight Pentecost
  Bruce K. Waltke
who, in keeping with the apostle Paul's admonition in 1 Corinthians 3:10, laid a solid foundation for my present ministry, to each of them I owe a debt I can never repay.

ISBN: 0-8024-8625-8

Printed in the United States of America

CONTENTS

CHAPTER   PAGE

Abbreviations — 7

Foreword — 9

Preface — 11

Acknowledgments — 15

1. Introduction — 17

2. General Reference Works, Part 1 — 25

3. General Reference Works, Part 2 — 41

4. General Reference Works, Part 3 — 53

5. New Dimensions in Bible Study — 67

6. The Use of Concordances — 81

7. The Importance of Lexicons — 91

8. Word Studies, Part 1 — 103

9. Word Studies, Part 2 — 111

10. Specific Resource Tools: Books — 117

11. Specific Resource Tools: Indices and Abstracts, Part 1 — 131

12. Specific Resource Tools: Indices and Abstracts, Part 2 — 139

13. Bibliographies, Part 1 — 153

14. Bibliographies, Part 2 — 163

15. Unpublished Materials — 171

ABBREVIATIONS

ADD	*American Doctoral Dissertations*
BDB	*Hebrew and English Lexicon of the Old Testament,* edited by F. Brown, S. R. Driver and C. A. Briggs
BIP	*Books in Print*
BPI	*Business Periodical Index*
CDA	*Comprehensive Dissertation Abstracts*
CDAB	*Child Development Abstracts and Bibliography*
CIJE	*Current Index to Journals in Education*
CIM	*Cumulated Index Medicus*
CPI	*Christian Periodical Index*
DAB	*Dictionary of American Biography*
DAI	*Dissertation Abstracts International*
DNB	*Dictionary of National Biography*
ERIC	*Educational Resources Information Center*
Elenchus	*Elenchus Bibliographicus Biblicus*
Ephemerides	*Ephemerides Theological Louvanienses*
Hatch & Redpath	*Concordance to the Septuagint* . . . by E. Hatch and H. Redpath
HDAC	Hastings' *Dictionary of the Apostolic Church*
HDCG	Hastings' *Dictionary of Christ and the Gospels*
HDB	Hastings' *Dictionary of the Bible*
HERE	Hastings' *Encyclopedia of Religion and Ethics*
IB	*Interpreter's Bible*

ICC	*International Critical Commentary*
IDB	*Interpreter's Dictionary of the Bible*
IRPL	*Index to Religious Periodical Literature*
ISBE	*International Standard Bible Encyclopedia*
K & D	Keil & Delitzsch, *Biblical Commentary on the Old Testament*
KJV	King James (Authorized) Version
Köehler/ Baumgartner	*Lexicon in Veteris Testamenti libros,* by L. Köehler and W. Baumgartner
LC	Library of Congress
Liddell & Scott	*Greek-English Lexicon,* by H. G. Liddell and R. Scott
LXX	Septuagint
Moulton & Geden	*Concordance to the Greek Testament,* by W. F. Moulton and A. S. Geden
Moulton & Milligan	*Vocabulary of the Greek Testament,* by W. F. Moulton and G. Milligan
NASB	*New American Standard Bible*
NICNT	*New International Commentary on the New Testament*
NICOT	*New International Commentary on the Old Testament*
NIV	*New International Version*
NUC	National Union Catalog
PA	*Psychological Abstracts*
PAIS	*Public Affairs Information Service*
RIE	*Resources in Education*
RIO	*Religious Index One*
RIT	*Religious Index Two*
RSV	*Revised Standard Version*
RTA	*Religious and Theological Abstracts*
SA	*Sociological Abstracts*
SHERK	*New Schaff-Herzog Encyclopedia of Religious Knowledge*
SSCI	*Social Sciences Citation Index*
TDNT	*Theological Dictionary of the New Testament*
TDOT	*Theological Dictionary of the Old Testament*
TNTC	*Tyndale New Testament Commentaries*
TOTC	*Tyndale Old Testament Commentaries*
TWOT	*Theological Wordbook of the Old Testament*

FOREWORD

Easily one half of an education in any discipline in the humanities, such as biblical or theological studies, consists in knowing where to turn for the proper tools and how to use them once they are located. Professor Cyril Barber has opened up both those doors.

This volume had its origins in a course that the author prepared while he was librarian at Trinity Evangelical Divinity School. That course, entitled "Theological Research Methods," was designed to help master of arts and master of theology students gain bibliographical control over the whole range of theological literature while they prepared to investigate a selected topic for a graduate level thesis.

Many of those same procedures and principles of research are modified in this volume to provide the broadest foundation for the largest number of students of the Scriptures. Any student of the Bible who loves to explore its text and the various theological disciplines will bristle with delight as he or she is led by this master bibliographer and bibliophile through illuminating descriptions on general and specific reference tools. Especially useful will be the discussions on the use of concordances, the importance of lexicons, and the chapters on word studies.

Professor Barber has rightly earned a reputation as the evangelical Nestor of basic bibliography for ministers' libraries. In fact, his magnum opus in this area, *The Minister's Library*, was published in 1974. It has been periodically supplemented with additional titles in several paperback volumes, each of which maintains the annotated format and the eleven major divisions used in that first volume.

Therefore, it is a pleasure to commend *An Introduction to Theological Research* to all who truly aspire to enter into biblical and theological studies as fully as possible, given the tools at their disposal. Anyone who spends even a few hours with this guide will be richly repaid in many more profitable hours of happy research. Furthermore, we believe that the ministry of those researchers, whether they be behind the classroom lecturn, the congregational pulpit, or the scholarly pen, will be markedly more effective and penetrating. Their ministry also will be more alert to the issues involved in a given subject, the history of the discussion that has ensued, and the advances that have been achieved. Theological research need not be thought of as exotic or the domain of a few gifted academicians; rather, it is as ordinary and available as most of the books mentioned in these pages.

WALTER C. KAISER, JR.

PREFACE

Nothing aggravates students more during orientation week than being instructed in the use of the card catalog in the library, and nothing frustrates them more during the years of their studies than not being able to find the information they need. For the encouragement of those using this book, the approach here will *not* deal with those elementary issues. Instead, by building upon experience, we will seek to introduce those in college and seminary to a select few of the more important research tools.

Specific comments will be made in relation to each of the works mentioned. Not all of them are of equal value. Their usefulness will largely be dependent upon individual needs and the subject being researched. Our purpose is to eliminate as far as possible what William Wordsworth regarded as the "gloom of uninspired research." The best way to do that is to facilitate the collection of data. The result should be qualitatively better work and a greater sense of personal fulfillment.

Some who use this book will come from a strongly evangelical tradition and will have been taught to fear a "liberal" education. (The dictionary defines *liberal* as "favorable to progress or reform, as in religious or political affairs . . . favoring or permitting freedom of action, esp. with respect to matters of personal belief or expression . . . free from bigotry; tolerant." Theological liberalism differs radically from a truly liberal education and should not be confused with it.) They will be concerned lest they be led astray from the truth by unwittingly imbibing error. I can empathize with them, for I have experienced the same concerns. During my seminary studies at Dallas Theological Seminary, however, Dr. Howard G. Hendricks said something that has helped me considerably. "Men," he said (for those were the days before Dallas Seminary enrolled women), "all truth is God's truth, and truth in one discipline or area of investigation will not be found to be in conflict with truth in any other area." (For an explication of this principle see Arthur F. Holmes's *All Truth is God's Truth* [Grand Rapids: Eerdmans, 1977]. See also Frank E. Gaebelein, *The Pattern of God's Truth* [Chicago: Moody, 1968].)

I found that to be a liberating and stabilizing thought, particularly when culling truth from the writings of humanistic psychologists, secular historians, and pagan philosophers.

If you were to read only those books with which you were agreement then you would have to limit your study solely to the Bible, for only the Bible is entirely reliable and without error. All other books, this one included, contain imperfections.

In your studies, therefore, at no time should you feel that you are required to believe all you read. What you read should be read with discernment and in continuous subjection to the ministry of the Holy Spirit, for, as the apostle Paul said, "he who is spiritual appraises [discerns] all things" (1 Cor. 2:15), and it is the Holy Spirit Himself who acts as our guide and leads us into all truth (John 14:17; 16:13). So let Him be your real teacher! And as you adhere tenaciously to the teaching of the Scriptures, you will not need to fear interacting with the concepts of those who are theological liberals.

Some students view bibliographic research as if it should take the prize for being the most boring subject in the entire curriculum. In teaching theological research, I have tried to make the discussion of each of the areas interesting, practical, and relevant. *I believe that research can be exciting!*

Of course, it is easier to hold the attention of students in the classroom than to sense intuitively the needs of one's readers. In putting this material into print, I have tried to meet the needs of my readers as well. All I can hope is that those who use this book will be gracious with its (and my) shortcomings.

The illustrations I have used are factual and typify the numerous kinds of questions asked daily in the libraries of colleges and seminaries. I have used those typical questions as the basis of what will be discussed in later chapters.

A reader, however, might well raise the question, "Why go into so many areas of investigation? Why not confine the discussion solely to the Bible?" The question is a good one.

First, not every area of academic pursuit has been covered. Limitations have been imposed on this work. The criterion for the inclusion of a reference work or resource tool has been specifically those subjects most frequently associated with or impinging upon biblical and theological studies and the practice of the ministry. The needs of those in college or seminary who are not Bible majors have likewise been kept in mind.

Second, the Scriptures speak of the importance of the whole person (1 Thess. 5:23; Heb. 4:12), and Paul set an example in declaring to his converts the whole counsel of God (Acts 20:27). The needs of the Christian ministry extend beyond the preparation of gospel messages to the application of the truth of God's Word to the needs of the whole person. For that reason as well, reference tools and other specialized resource works have been included. If, however, reference be made to John A. Bollier's *The Literature of Theology,* readers will soon see how selective I have been. I have chosen for inclusion in this book only those works which experience has shown to be of greatest importance to students.

Although this book has been prepared with the needs of beginning researchers in mind, the procedure advocated also can be followed by those pursuing more advanced studies. Following a discussion of general reference works, the section on terminology will help one refine his topic (if such is necessary), and the discussion of subject catalogs will help one ascertain which published writings deal with the subject in question. The next chapters discuss indices and abstracts. They are designed to place the researcher in touch with journal articles on his subject. Computer terminals from which bibliographic printouts may be obtained are mentioned briefly. Finally, consideration is given to unpublished materials such as doctoral dissertations.

Progress, therefore, is purposeful and progressive and covers:

- General reference works
- Books
- Journal articles
- Unpublished materials.

In concluding this preface I would like to thank those who have helped in the preparation of this book. First, I would like to thank my wife, Aldyth, who graciously puts up with my writing ministry and unfailingly supports me in my work; second, my colleague, Janet Kobobel, who read the manuscript and corrected my misplaced modifiers, split infinitives, and dangling participles; third, two scholars whom I am privileged to call friends, Dr. James E. Rosscup of Talbot Theological Seminary, La Mirada, California, and Dr. John A. Witmer, librarian *par excellence* of Dallas Theological Seminary, Dallas, Texas, who read the manuscript and made practical suggestions for its improvement; and finally, my good friend and former colleague on the faculty of the Trinity Evangelical Divinity School, Deerfield, Illinois, and now its dean and vice-president for academic affairs, Dr. Walter C. Kaiser, Jr., for so kindly reading the manuscript and writing the Foreword.

ACKNOWLEDGMENTS

The author wishes to express his appreciation to the following publishers, who graciously gave permission for the reproduction of material currently under their imprints.

To Abingdon Press, Nashville, Tenn., for permission to reproduce material from James Strong's *Exhaustive Concordance of the Bible*.

To the Akademische Druck-U. Verlagsanstatt, Austria, for permission to reproduce material from Edwin Hatch's and Henry A. Redpath's *Concordance to the Septuagint*.

To the American Theological Library Association for permission to reproduce material from the *Index to Religious Periodical Literature*.

To Samuel Bagster, London, for permission to reproduce material from the *Englishman's Greek Concordance to the New Testament* and the *Englishman's Hebrew Concordance to the Old Testament*.

To T. and T. Clark, Edinburgh, for permission to reproduce material from James Hastings's *Dictionary of Christ and the Gospels*, *Dictionary of the Apostolic Church*, *Encyclopedia of Religion and Ethics;* and from W. F. Moulton's and A. S. Geden's *Concordance to the Greek Testament*.

To J. W. Edwards Publishers, Inc., Ann Arbor, Mich., for permission to reproduce material from the *Library of Congress—Books: Subjects* and the *National Union Catalog—Register of Additional Locations*.

To William B. Eerdmans Publishing Company, Grand Rapids, for permission to reproduce material from W. F. Moulton's and G. Milligan's *Vocabulary of the Greek Testament* and Robert Young's *Analytical Concordance to the Bible*.

To Walter de Gruyther, Berlin, for permission to reproduce material from the *Computer-Konkordanz zum Novum Testament.*

To William Heinemann, London, for permission to reproduce material from the Loeb Classical Library.

To the Library of Congress, Washington, D.C., for permission to reproduce material from the *Library of Congress Subject Headings.*

To Oxford University Press, New York, for permission to reproduce materials from the *Hebrew and English Lexicon of the Old Testament,* edited by F. Brown, S. R. Driver, and C. A. Briggs; G. H. W. Lampe's *Patristic Greek Lexicon,* and H. G. Liddell's and R. Scott's *Greek-English Lexicon.*

To the University of Chicago Press, Chicago, for permission to reproduce material from W. Bauer's *Greek-English Lexicon of the New Testament and Other Early Christian Literature,* translated and edited by William F. Arndt and F. Wilbur Gingrich.

To the University of Minnesota Press, Minneapolis, for permission to reproduce material from the *International Bibliography of Research in Marriage and Family, 1900-1964.*

To the H. W. Wilson Company, Bronx, N.Y., for permission to reproduce materials from the *Education Index,* the *Humanities Index,* and the *Social Sciences Index.*

To Xerox University Microfilms, Ann Arbor, Mich., for permission to reproduce materials from the *Comprehensive Dissertation Index.*

And to the Zondervan Publishing House, Grand Rapids, for permission to reproduce materials from the *Zondervan Pictorial Encyclopedia of the Bible.*

1

INTRODUCTION

What kind of questions do students ask librarians?

Recently, in preparing to write this book, I kept a record of the kinds of questions asked me in a single day. Here are some samples.

"Our evangelism class has been told to research the question, Does conversion involve the Lordship of Christ? for a debate on Wednesday. Where can I find this kind of information?"

"I'm doing a paper on the two natures of Christ for a Christology course. I've checked the card catalog, but cannot find any references to my topic. Does the library have any books dealing with this subject?"

"In church history we've been asked to familiarize ourselves with the beliefs and practices of the Arians, Monophysites, Montanists, Nestorians, and Pelagians. Where can I locate that information?"

"I'm a Christian ed major. Our prof thought it would be a good idea if we surveyed ten years of articles in a religious journal to observe different trends. He told us to avoid magazines. How does a journal differ from a magazine? And what journals can you recommend in my area?"

"We have a major paper due in two weeks on the names of God in the Old Testament. How does one go about researching the names of God? I haven't a clue where to begin. Furthermore, Dr. Smith warned us that in one of the most recent reference sources one of the names of God has been omitted by the contributor. Which source do you think he is referring to, and how can I know which name is missing?"

"I've been ill and now that I am back I've a lot of catching up to do. Our homiletics prof has assigned us Bible characters to preach on. Mine is

Balaam. He also stressed the importance of finding out all that the Bible has to say on a particular character before beginning our study. He explained that sometimes something in the New Testament will highlight an incident in the Old. Apart from the book of Numbers, where will I find references to Balaam in the Bible?"

"In Greek 303 we've been assigned a word study on *apostasia*. At first I thought this would be easy. I've consulted TDNT only to find that this word is not treated. What should I do?"

Does this sound familiar? These are the typical kinds of questions asked every day by students in the regular course of their research. Such questions invariably come after much futile searching and are frequently accompanied by frustration and embarrassment. The student, it seems, feels as if he should know where to find the information. He also seems to feel that having to ask a librarian for help is tacitly admitting failure. Such a view is definitely not true.

Nothing delights me more than to be able to assist students with their research. Those one-on-one contacts are stimulating and refreshing and make my duties most enjoyable. The larger the student body, however, the more numerous are the questions and the less time there is to spend with individuals. For this reason, in each of the institutions in which I have served, a special course in theological research has been developed.

The material to be found in the following pages was first developed to meet the needs of those preparing for the ministry at the Trinity Evangelical Divinity School, Deerfield, Illinois, and was later modified during the time I taught on the faculty of the Talbot Theological Seminary, La Mirada, California. It has now been further refined in order to meet the research needs of those studying in Christian colleges and seminaries across the country.

My aim in teaching this material was to accomplish three basic objectives:
1. To reduce each students' research time to about one-tenth of what he would normally spend looking for information
2. To enable each student to gain access to the kind of material that would help him or her produce qualitatively better work
3. To make each student happily independent of my services.

In this last area I have been guided by the mature wisdom of turn-of-the-century writer Elbert Hubbard who said, "The object of teaching is to enable the student to get along without his teacher." Education is not to be found in how much you have committed to memory, or even how much you know. It is being able to differentiate between what you know and what you do not. It is knowing where to go to find out what you need to know; and it is knowing how to use the information once you get it.

Hindsight has shown that those students who took the course in theological research experienced a greater sense of fulfillment from their studies, did better work even in the subjects that held little interest for them, and were possessed of a confidence they had never known before.

In placing the substance of those lectures in book form, I do so with the hope that I may be able to preserve something of the informality that characterized the classroom presentation. Bibliographic research is very demanding, but its rewards are great. Perhaps the greatest mistake anyone could make would be to conclude that it is easy and all it consists of is memorizing the titles of books. There is much, much more involved. Let me illustrate what I mean.

During my studies in library school, I was required to take a course entitled "Bibliography of the Social Sciences." It was taught by a man who had received two masters degrees in law, the one from Harvard and the other from Southern Methodist University. In addition, he held an M.S. in library science from Columbia University and had completed his education with a Ph.D. from the New School for Social Research in New York. As an instructor he knew his field thoroughly. In fact, it was a privilege to study under a person of such learning and experience.

After "ploughing through" the usual tomes supporting research in the various areas of the social sciences, we wrote the mid-term exam. Following the results of the examination, the number of students enrolled in the course dropped from forty-five to nineteen. Each student had met the same rigorous entrance requirements and had Graduate Record Exam scores proving his competence. Not all, however, were able to surmount the demands of graduate level bibliographical research.

In the years since then, I have found that research is not difficult if you are prepared to follow a simple plan. If you have little or no knowledge of a certain assigned subject, it is easy to begin with general reference works that will readily give you an overview of the material. Then it is easy for you to move to more specific sources of information. In other words, task number one is to become familiar with a few proved general reference works—works designed by their arrangement and treatment to be consulted for definite items of information rather than to be read consecutively (e.g., Bible encyclopedias, Bible dictionaries, etc.). By means of those you will be able to gain an overview of the subject you are researching. Then, once you have defined the boundaries of your topic, you can begin enlarging your understanding by reading more specialized materials.

In beginning your investigation of general reference works you should:

- Take note of the writer's outline; observe how he proceeds with the unfolding of the subject matter or deals with specifics that pertain to the topic under consideration
- Learn about those who have contributed in one way or another to the body of knowledge that has grown up around the subject
- Plot its historic development
- Ascertain the limitations and scope of the subject; check the bibliography at the end of the article to learn the representative works in this

area of study and when those contributions were made.

For example, the article on "Kenites" in *Zondervan's Pictorial Encyclopedia of the Bible* gives the etymology (both in Greek and Hebrew) of the word and traces the early history of the family from antedeluvian times to the era of Moses. After that the writer's treatment adheres, in broad outline, to the history of the Israelites. A brief but pertinent bibliography contains important works to which you may wish to refer in fleshing out your research.

But does this system of first researching general reference works really work?

Consider the situation of my son Stephen. A computer science major in his undergraduate work at the School of Engineering, University of Southern California, Stephen found himself compelled to take a history course to round out his program. The only one scheduled at a convenient time for him was medieval history. So, to make a long story longer, he signed up for it.

Imagine Stephen's surprise when, on the first day of class, his professor told him he had to write a paper on "The History of Banking in Baghdad in the Eighth Century" and present it to the class within three weeks.

Well, with ill-disguised disgust Stephen asked me if I would help him. I was "floored." To be truthful, I did not know that Arab countries had banking facilities in the eighth century. I agreed to help Stephen with his research in the same way I would help any other student—in the gathering of data only; after that, it was up to him.

In order to give myself time to think, I began by asking Stephen what he had done so far. I soon learned he was frustrated mainly because he had spent an entire afternoon walking from the card catalog to the stacks and back only to find, after checking every book on banking in the library, that he had failed to turn up a single reference to eighth-century practices in Baghdad.

I could readily empathize with him, for I had spent many fruitless hours engaged in the same kind of frustrating exercise. But what suggestions could I give him? My only recollection of Baghdad was from *Tales of the Arabian Nights,* and I did not think that would help.

"Stephen," I said at last, "let's back off a bit and see if a procedure I've followed before can be of any help to you in this instance. It has generally been found to be a good policy to check reference works first before proceeding on to specialized monographs." So I made a few suggestions.

A few days later a jubilant Stephen came into my study at home. His smile spoke volumes. He had checked in an encyclopedia under "Banking, History of," and had found some information. More important, a bibliography at the end of the article had listed a 1934 article entitled "Banking in 8th Century Baghdad" published by the Royal Asiatic Society. In checking a union list of periodicals he found that only two California libraries carried this journal: UCLA and Stanford. Stephen phoned UCLA and found that that issue had been stolen several years previously. A call to Stanford brought a photocopy of the article the next day.

KELAIAH kǐ lā′ yə (קְלָיָה). A Levite who had married a foreign wife and divorced her (Ezra 10:23; 1 Esd 9:23; KJV, ASV COLIUS). He was also called "Kelita" (1 Esd 9:23; KJV, ASV CALITAS). A Kelita appears in Nehemiah 8:7; 10:10; and 1 Esdras 9:48 (KJV, ASV CALITAS), but it is not certain that the two are the same.

S. BARABAS

KELITA kǐ lī′ tə (קְלִיטָא). See KELAIAH.

KEMUEL kĕm′ yŏŏ əl (קְמוּאֵל). 1. The father of Aram, and the son of Nahor the brother of Abraham (Gen 22:21).

2. Son of Shiphtan, and leader of the tribe of Ephraim, which it represented in the dividing of Canaan (Num 34:24).

3. A Levite, father of Hashabiah, a ruler of the Levites in the time of King David (1 Chron 27:17).

S. BARABAS

KENAN ke′ nən (קֵינָן). Son of Enosh and father of Mahalelel (Gen 5:9, 12; KJV CAINAN; 1 Chron 1:2).

KENATH ke′ năth (קְנָת). A city in Bashan, taken from the Amorites by Nobah who gave it his own name (Num 32:42). It was later recaptured by Geshur and Aram (1 Chron 2:23). It became one of the cities of the Decapolis under the name Kanatha. The Arabians defeated Herod the Great there (Jos. War I. xix. 2). It is usually identified with Qanawat, sixteen m. NE of Bostra, where there are many impressive ruins from Graeco-Roman times.

S. BARABAS

KENAZ ke′ năz (קְנַז, LXX Κενεζ, 1 below), Kenizzite, ken′ e zīt (קְנִזִּי, [KJV Kenezite], LXX Κενεζαιους, 2 below, meaning side, flank).

1. Singular form of the clan name Kenizzite.
a. Son of Eliphaz and grandson of Esau (Gen 36:11; 1 Chron 1:36), one of the chieftains of Edom (KJV Dukes) (Gen 36:15, 42; 1 Chron 1:53).

b. Younger brother of Caleb (Judg 1:13) and father of Othniel and Seraiah (Josh 15:17; Judg 3:9, 11; 1 Chron 4:13).

c. Son of Elah and grandson of Caleb (1 Chron 4:15, Heb. lit. "and the sons of Elah and Kenaz," KJV ". . . even Kenaz.")

2. Clan or family name. The Kenizzites are one of the S Palestinian tribes (listed between Kenites and Kadmonites) whose land God promised to Abraham's descendants (Gen 15:19). Unless predictive prophecy is involved here, this must be a different family from that of 1a above. Caleb is said to be the son of Jephunneh the Kenizzite (Num 32:12; Josh 14:6, 14). The exact meaning of the clan

name here is not clear. On the one hand, the Kenizzites are described as an alien people (Gen 15:19 above) and Caleb is promised a portion of the land because of faithfulness rather than birthright. On the other hand, the genealogies of 1 Chronicles 2 and 4 make him a grandson of Judah through Hezron (2:9, 18; yet cf. 4:15). Many scholars have seen the Chronicles genealogy as an attempt to give the descendants of Caleb legal status in postexilic Judaism. It is possible that the apparent discrepancy may be accounted for by duplicate names.

BIBLIOGRAPHY. H. L. Ginsberg and B. Maisler, "Semitized Hurrians in Syria and Palestine," JPOS, XIV (1934) 243-267; N. Glueck "Kenites and Kenizzites," PEQ, LXXII (1940) 22-24.

J. OSWALT

KENITES ken′ īts (קֵינִי, הַקֵּינִי, LXX Καιναιοι, Κιναιοι, meaning metalworkers, smiths). Clan or tribal name of semi-nomadic peoples of S Pal. and Sinai. The Aram. and Arab. etymologies of the root qyn show that it has to do with metal and metal work (thus the Heb. word from this root, "lance"). This prob. indicates that the Kenites were metal workers, esp. since Sinai and the Wadi 'Arabah were rich in highgrade copper ore. W. F. Albright has pointed to the Beni Hassan mural in Egypt (19th cent. B.C.) as an illustration of such a wandering group of smiths. This mural depicts thirty-six men, women and children in characteristic Sem. dress leading, along with other animals, donkeys laden with musical instruments, weapons and an item which Albright has identified as a bellows. He has further noted that Lamech's three children (Gen 4:19-22) were responsible for herds (Jabal), musical instruments (Jubal), and metal work (Tubal-Cain, or Tubal, the smith), the three occupations which seem most evident in the mural.

1. General references. It is clear that references to the Kenites are not to a tightly knit group living in a narrowly defined area. The name rather applies to a number of loosely related groups possessing common skills or perhaps claiming a common ancestor. At times the term is used quite narrowly in the Bible and at other times more widely, but at no time must it be applied to all Kenites. The land of the Kenites is promised to Abraham's descendants (Gen 15:19). This would be the territory of a certain Kenite clan, prob. S of Hebron. Similarly, it is a particular group of Kenites which is condemned in Baalam's oracle (Num 24:21, 22) while another group is praised for having been kind to the Hebrews in the wilderness (1 Sam 15:6). The exact cause for Baalam's condemnation is not given, but in the context it appears that these Kenites had allied themselves with Amalek against Moses.

Fig. 1. Page from the *Zondervan Pictorial Encyclopedia of the Bible.*

Of course, an introductory book such as this one must have certain limitations. Instead of covering the hundreds of reference works available today, it
will concentrate on only a few. *It will be highly selective and treat only those
publications that experience has shown to be most valuable.* Those desiring a
more comprehensive treatment are referred to the following sources: *The
Minister's Library* (Grand Rapids: Baker, 1974) and its biennial supplements; the excellent book by John A. Bollier of Yale Divinity School library
entitled *The Literature of Theology: A Guide for Students and Pastors*
(Philadelphia: Westminster, 1979); Frederick W. Danker's well-received
Multipurpose Tools for Bible Study (St. Louis: Concordia, 1970, rev. ed.);
and the handy work by Saul Galin and Peter Spielberg, *Reference Books:
How to Select and Use Them* (New York: Random House, 1969). All of those
should be available to you in your college or seminary library.

Second, this inquiry will primarily be limited to those works dealing with
biblical and theological topics. In this respect the scope will differ from some
broader treatments (e.g., W. Katz's *Introduction to Reference Work* [2 vols.,
1973-74]) that are general in nature.

In order to assist you to understand what we will be doing in the remainder of this book, let me diagram our approach.

PART 1	PART 2
General Reference Tools	*Special Resource Tools*
Bible encyclopedias	Books, monographs
Bible dictionaries	Periodicals
Yearbooks	a. Indices
Atlases	b. Abstracts
Concordances	Bibliographies
	Unpublished materials

Initially, we will look at those general reference works that will give you an
overview of the topic you have to research. Those reference tools will lay a
foundation for more specific investigation later on. Specific reference books
include those that will alert us to materials in books, journals, and unpublished theses or dissertations, which will add depth and insight to our study.

Once you have learned the art of research, you should be able to find
almost anything.

ASSIGNMENT

The purpose of this assignment is to enable you to become familiar with
the following reference works, their strengths and weaknesses, their
theological biases, and their abiding values. You will probably find these
books in the reference section of your school library:

- Hastings's *Encyclopedia of Religion and Ethics*
- McClintock's and Strong's *Cyclopedia of Biblical, Theological and Ecclesiastical Literature*
- *New Schaff-Herzog Encyclopedia of Religious Knowledge*
- Hastings's *Dictionary of the Bible*
- *International Standard Bible Encyclopedia*
- *Interpreter's Dictionary of the Bible*
- *Zondervan's Pictorial Encyclopedia of the Bible*.

For the sake of comparison, you may wish to consult articles on topics like "Baptism," "Ethics," "Hypostatic Union," "Marriage," "Prayer," "Titus, Epistle of," and "Zwingli." Do not be too surprised if you do not find all these topics in each of the works.

1. What is the nature and scope of each of these works (this is generally spelled out in the introduction or the preface)? How does this encyclopedia or dictionary differ from its predecessors? How comprehensive is it? Can you discern any strengths or weaknesses? Has it undergone revision (see the reverse of the title page)? Check on (a) the editor(s), and (b) the contributors. A list of the contributors will often be found either in the first volume or among the indices in the last volume. For writers from the era of the church Fathers to the present you may wish to consult Earle Cairns's *Wycliffe Biographical Dictionary of the Church*, the 1982 revised and enlarged edition of Elgin S. Moyer's *Who Was Who in Church History*. Another source for contemporary authors is the Marquis' *Who's Who in Religion*. Does an awareness of the theological training and denominational affiliation of the editor(s) and contributors give us any indication of the theological slant of this work, and the level of scholarship to be expected?

2. When focusing attention on specific articles(e.g., marriage, prayer, etc.), did you find them outlined? And if so, how (analytically, historically, topically, or some other way)? Does the article contain "See" or "See also" references, either in the body or at the end? Has the writer used any documentation (e.g., Scripture references, or citations from other writers)? How pertinent are those quotations?

3. How extensive is the bibliography? Is it truly representative (i.e., presenting all sides of the issue)? Which works cited do you feel warrant further investigation?

4. Compare articles of your choice in the *International Standard Bible Encyclopedia* (1915, 1929) and the newly revised *International Standard Bible Encyclopedia* (1979-present), edited by G. W. Bromiley. How do the articles compare biblically, theologically, and scholastically?

5. Take special note of the indices at the end of the encyclopedias and dictionaries listed above. How varied and comprehensive are they? Are Greek and Hebrew word studies included?

2

GENERAL REFERENCE WORKS PART 1

Tyson Bartlett sat in a church history class at the beginning of a new semester, listening half-heartedly as the professor droned on about the course. This faculty member had the reputation for believing that church history was dull, and he taught the subject as if it were his duty to perpetuate that tradition.

Ty vaguely remembers hearing, "Each of you will be required to prepare a documented research paper on a topic I will assign. It will be due the first class period following the Thanksgiving recess. I will now go through the register alphabetically and assign you your topic."

"Adams. I want you to write on 'Abjuration.'

"Anderson. Your topic is 'Adoptionism.'

"Aske. Your assignment is the 'Rise of the Bishopric.'

"Bartlett, you are to write on the 'Cluniacs.'"

Later Ty came to see me. "Who are the 'Kluniaks'?" he asked. "I've checked the card catalog and can't find a single reference to them!"

I sensed his frustration. Church history was not exactly his favorite subject. We began our search by consulting the index volume of James Hastings's *Encyclopedia of Religion and Ethics* and were referred to a lengthy article on monasticism. On closer examination we found an entire section devoted to the founding of the Cluniacs. That article, with other resources located through bibliographies, took no longer than twenty minutes to find, and the seemingly "Himalayan" task Ty had faced was reduced to size.

I tell this story out of the belief that bibliographic research can be exciting as well as timesaving. In fact, it can completely revolutionize a student's outlook toward his studies. From college freshmen to seniors, and even those in graduate school, many who once dreaded using the library suddenly loose their fear of "not being able to find what I'm looking for." They "come alive" when they find that research can be fun. As their outlook changes, their grades improve.

As mentioned in our first chapter, one proved way of researching a topic is to begin with general reference works and then move to specific ones. We begin our study, therefore, with encyclopedias and dictionaries. These are arranged in dictionary format, which means the topics are listed in alphabetical order (e.g., from "Aaron" to "Zuzim").

Even though we do not intend to slight or ignore the general encyclopedias like *Britannica III, Encyclopedia Americana,* and other fine reference works, our discussion will be devoted chiefly to works of a biblical and theological nature.

By definition an encyclopedia is usually a multivolume work containing a collection of articles that give essential information about all branches of knowledge. Its arrangement is almost always done alphabetically by subject. Specialized encyclopedias contain articles bearing on one specific field of knowledge.

As a general principle, a student should use an encyclopedia when he first begins to probe the limits of a topic, desires to refresh his memory on certain specifics, or wants to ascertain who the leaders were (or are) who contributed to the growth of knowledge in that particular area.

Encyclopedias have been prepared for different audiences. There are encyclopedias written for scholars and educated adults, and there are those designed specifically for laypeople; there are some prepared for young readers, whereas others are for children. Our focus will be on the more scholarly encyclopedias and dictionaries.

Although the primary purpose of an encyclopedia is to present information on all aspects of knowledge, each encyclopedia has its strong points. For example, Patrick Fairbairn's *Imperial Standard Bible Dictionary* (6 vols.; 1889, 1957) is particularly good when treating Bible characters. It would be excellent for researching material on Balaam, Deborah, Elihu, Fortunatus, Gershom, Hiram, Ittai, Jabez, and a host of others. On the other hand, the *Encyclopedia Biblica* (4 vols., 1899-1903) by T. K. Cheyne and J. S. Black is a scholary work evidencing a high degree of accuracy and completeness but marred by the adherence of the contributors to higher critical theories.

Information about biblical and theological encyclopedias and dictionaries may be found in *The Minister's Library,* pp. 42-44; Bollier's *The Literature of Theology,* p. 52; and Danker's *Multipurpose Tools for Bible Study,* pp. 151-62.

The question naturally arises, How can someone untrained in library science discern which encyclopedias or dictionaries are worthy of the investment of one's time (and perhaps money), and which are not? The answer can be outlined as follows:

- Is the encyclopedia or dictionary authoritative? Is the editor a person of repute? Have the articles been signed?* Are the contributors people of established reputation?
- Why was it written, and for whom was it intended? (This information is generally found in the introduction or preface.)
- What is its scope? Is the coverage comprehensive? Are the articles long or short? Is the thrust biblical or theological, denominational (e.g., Roman Catholic, Mennonite, etc.) or interdenominational, national or international?
- How up to date is it? Is it an entirely new work, or is it based on an earlier edition of the same or a different title? How reliable are the maps, charts, money conversions, et cetera?
- Are there any recognizable strong points? What features make this work superior to any others?

In using an encyclopedia or dictionary, you will want to know something about its contents, organization, arrangement (alphabetically letter-by-letter, or alphabetically word-by-word), indices, and general usefulness. We will discuss encyclopedias of religion before considering those dealing specifically with the Bible and related subjects. The scope of the former is broader than that of the latter.

ENCYCLOPEDIAS OF RELIGION

In this category we will focus our attention specifically on the following:
- Hastings's *Encyclopedia of Religion and Ethics*
- McClintock and Strong's *Cyclopedia of Biblical, Theological, and Ecclesiastical Literature*
- *New Catholic Encyclopedia*
- *New Schaff-Herzog Encyclopedia of Religious Knowledge*
- *Universal Jewish Encyclopedia.*

Encyclopedia of Religion and Ethics, edited by James Hastings (12 vols. and index, 1907-1927), is a comprehensive work with long, scholarly, signed articles dealing with "all the religions of the world and all the great systems of ethics," along with a wide variety of theological and philosophical topics. Extensive but dated bibliographies conclude most articles. A comprehensive index, a list of article titles, and an exhaustive subject index conclude this important work.

In keeping with all the multivolume works edited by Hastings, this one contains numerous "See" references interspersed throughout the major articles. The contributors were all scholars of renown and were considered

---

*Signed articles are regarded as being more thorough than unsigned ones because the contributor cannot hide behind the cloak of anonymity.

specialists in their respective fields. Each article is the product of mature reflection and good research. In fact, after consulting articles on topics like "Love," "Magi," "Marriage," "Mary," "Meekness," "Mercy," "Messiah," "Messiah (Pseudo)," "Mind," et cetera, it is not surprising that more recent works have relatively little new material to contribute.

Although dated in matters of history and archaeology and lacking information in some of the newer cults, HERE is still worth consulting. The subject index contains a valuable listing of topics that may well spark a student's interest whenever he is searching for a research topic.

The *Cyclopedia of Biblical, Theological, and Ecclesiastical Literature*, edited by James McClintock and James Strong (10 vols., 1867-81; supplement, 1894), is by far the most comprehensive and rewarding work to consult. It comprises a collection of articles ably compiled by two American scholars of a century ago. Using a team of the finest conservative theologians, McClintock and Strong assembled these well-researched articles covering all of Christendom and many of the major pagan religions. Rarely will a researcher find that his time spent consulting this work has been wasted.

Wilbur M. Smith, writing the introduction to the 1968-70 reprint by Baker Book House, said, "Even though a century has passed since the first volume was published, many articles in these pages are still superior to, and more comprehensive than, articles on the same subjects appearing in any other similar work."

This set is particularly strong in areas of biography, biblical geography, critical issues, customs and cultures, denominations and their growth, and a variety of other themes. "See" references are used in appropriate places, and extensive bibliographies conclude many of the longer essays. Articles on topics like "Abomination," "Antichrist," "Bible," "Confession," "Crucifixion," "Infallibility," "Messianic Hope," "Millennium," "Ring," "Sabbath," "Sacrament," "Samuel," "Sin," et cetera, are extremely well done.

The set was updated in 1894 with two supplemental volumes of approximately 1000 pages each.

New Catholic Encyclopedia, prepared by the editorial staff of the Catholic University of America, Washington, D.C. (15 vols. and index, 1967), is entirely new and, in spite of its title, bears no relation to the earlier *Catholic Encyclopedia* (17 vols., 1907-1922). Researchers who consult both works will find that this new one reflects the more tolerant views and policies of the post-Vatican II era.

Arranged alphabetically, the articles reflect maturity as well as reliability, and although manifesting a tendency to devote more space to the Catholic church in the United States and Latin America, cover virtually every aspect of Catholic history, theology, and ministry. Each of the 17,000 articles is signed, and helpful bibliographies are appended to many of them.

Among the plethora of articles of interest to Protestants are the following: Pagan religious rites (e.g., associated with the worship of Baal and the

become a *śrāvaka* and *pratyeka* by the mere understanding of the Four Truths or of dependent origination. Understanding of voidness (*śūnyatā*) is necessary.[1]

7. Technical details.—Many technical details are to be found in the Abhidharma and Vijñānavādin books—*e.g.*, the theory of the last incarnation of a future *pratyeka*.

The *chakravartin* (sovereign king) is conscious when descending into the maternal womb; then he becomes unconscious and is born unconscious. The future *pratyeka* remains conscious in the womb. The *bodhisattva* at his last birth is born conscious.

Literature.—1. *Mahāvyutpatti*, Bibl. Buddhica, xlii. [Petrograd, 1911] § 45 (p. 17); *Dharma-Saṃgraha*, Anec. Oxon., Aryan series, iii. v. [Oxford, 1885] ii.; *Mahāvastu*, ed. E. Senart, Paris, 1882, i. 301, iii. 271; *Madhyamakavṛtti*, Bibl.

Buddh. iv. [1913] 351, 353; *Divyāvadāna*, ed. E. B. Cowall and R. A. Neil, Cambridge, 1886, p. 293; *Madhyamakāvatāra*, Bibl. Budd. ix. [1912] 2 ff.

II. I. J. Schmidt, 'Über einige Grundlehren des Buddhismus,' *Mém. de l'Acad. de St. Pétersbourg*, 6th ser., 'Sciences politiques, histoire et philologie,' i. [1832] 241; A. Rémusat, *Fo'e koue ki*, Paris, 1836, p. 165; E. Burnouf, *Introd. à l'hist. du bouddhisme indien*, do. 1844 (reprint 1876), pp. 94, 297, 438, *Le Lotus de la bonne loi*, do. 1852, pp. 52, 315; S. Beal, *A Catena of Buddhist Scriptures from the Chinese*, London, 1871, p. 253; E. J. Eitel, *Handbook of Chinese Buddhism²*, do. 1888, p. 123; C. F. Köppen, *Die Religion des Buddha*, Berlin, 1857-59, i. 419, 426; W. Wassilieff, *Der Buddhismus*, Petrograd, 1860, pp. 13, 162, 289, 304; Sarat Chandra Das, *A Tibetan-English Dictionary*, Calcutta, 1902; R. Spence Hardy, *Eastern Monachism*, London, 1850, p. 290, *Manual of Buddhism²*, do 1880, p. 38; R. C. Childers, *Dictionary of Pali*, do. 1875, p. 309; H. Kern, *Manual of Indian Buddhism*, Strassburg, 1896, p. 611.   **L. DE LA VALLÉE POUSSIN.**

PRAYER.

Introductory and Primitive (E. N. FALLAIZE), p. 154.
American (H. B. ALEXANDER), p. 158.
Babylonian (S. LANGDON), p. 159.
Buddhist (M. ANESAKI), p. 166.
Chinese (J. DYER BALL), p. 170.
Christian—
    Theological (C. F. D'ARCY), p. 171.
    Liturgical (R. M. WOOLLEY), p. 177.
Egyptian (F. LL. GRIFFITH), p. 180.
Finns and Lapps (C. J. BILLSON), p. 181.

Greek (A. W. MAIR), p. 182.
Iranian (E. LEHMANN), p. 186.
Jain (M. STEVENSON), p. 187.
Japanese (M. REVON), p. 189.
Jewish (F. PERLES), p. 191.
Mexican (L. SPENCE), p. 196.
Muhammadan (TH. W. JUYNBOLL), p. 198.
Roman (J. B. CARTER), p. 199.
Teutonic (E. WELSFORD), p. 201.
Tibetan (L. A. WADDELL), p. 202.

PRAYER (Introductory and Primitive).—1. Origin and development.—In its simplest and most primitive form prayer is the expression of a desire, cast in the form of a request, to influence some force or power conceived as supernatural. Apart from the modern usage of the term, which connotes spiritual communion, it is usually understood to imply reverent entreaty. It must be said, however, that in the primitive mind reverence is usually obscured by fear—all spirits, whether good or bad, are regarded as dangerous—while the idea of entreaty, though the ostensible influence in determining the form, is largely coloured by a desire to compel or command. Genetically, prayer is related to the spell or charm, and it is frequently a matter of difficulty to determine whether a particular formula should be assigned to one category or to the other. Although the form of the address may be of assistance—some writers have endeavoured to distinguish between spell and prayer by assigning to the latter those formulæ which contain a vocative (see W. H. R. Rivers, *The Todas*, London, 1906, p. 272)—in the rudimentary forms the underlying psychological elements are hardly distinguishable. In performing a magical act the performer often supplements the mimetic action by indicating in a phrase or two what it is that he wishes to be done.

The Australian black-fellow who works magic against his enemy by pointing and stabbing with his spear says, 'Strike! Kill!' Here a simple command emphasizes the action. In another and more complex example the Maidu medicine-man inflicts disease on the neighbouring villages by burning certain roots and blowing smoke towards them saying, 'Over there! Over there! Not here! To the other place! Do not come back this way. We are good. Make these people sick. Kill them; they are bad people!' (R. B. Dixon, 'The Northern Maidu,' *Bull. Am. Mus. Nat. Hist.* xvii. pt. 3 [1905] 328 f.). In form this is a direct command, but in spirit it differs hardly, if at all, from supplication.

A familiar process of magic is to work evil against an enemy by performing a ceremony over some part of the body, such as hair or a piece of nail, or some object which has been in intimate contact with the body, such as earth impressed with a footprint. The ceremony is accompanied as a rule by some formula.

[1] *Aṣṭasāhasrikā*, Bibl. Indica (Calcutta, 1888), p. 379; *Madhyamakavṛtti*, p. 353 (a different opinion, p. 851).

The Maori priest was believed to be able to 'pray' mother and child to death by using the placenta in this way (G. Bennett, *Wanderings in New South Wales, Batavia, etc.*, London, 1834, i. 128).

The relation between formula and ceremony is shown in a Malay charm in which the nature and meaning of the treatment of the soil from the centre of a footprint were indicated by saying:

    'It is not earth that I switch,
    But the heart of So-and-so.'

But, while this instance merely illustrates the desire to make clear the intention of the charm (though it must be noted that it is an essential part in securing success), another charm from the same part of the world illustrates by a curious conjunction the primitive attitude of mind towards the powers to whom these invocations are addressed: in one of the ceremonies for bringing sickness, injury, or death upon an enemy by the mutilation or transfixing of a waxen image the operator, in the course of his address to the spirit, says:

    'Lo, I am burying the corpse of Somebody,

    Do you assist in killing him or making him sick:
    If you do not make him sick, if you do not kill him,
    You shall be a rebel against God,
    A rebel against Muhammad,'

which illustrates at once the request for help, the idea of compulsion involved in the charm, and a threat in case of non-compliance (W. W. Skeat, *Malay Magic*, London, 1900, pp. 569, 571). In some addresses to the dead, especially when the fear of the dead, however well disposed, has been much exaggerated by any peculiar or unusual circumstance, magical ceremony, entreaty, and command combine in much the same way.

The Orāons appear to regard the spirit of a woman who has died in childbirth or while pregnant as specially malignant. Not only is she buried with special precautions (the ankles are broken and the body is laid face downward with the bones of a donkey), but various invocations are addressed to her, such as, 'If you come back, may you turn into a donkey!' The roots of a palm-tree may be burned, while the mourners say, 'May you come home only when the leaves of the palm-tree wither!' (P. Dehon, 'Religion and Customs of the Orāons,' *Mem. As. Soc. Bengal*, i. 9 [1906], p. 139).

On the other hand, the Thonga formula at the *tjeba* ceremony of collective fishing by the community, which takes place when the lakes are

Fig. 2. Page from Hastings's *Encyclopedia of Religion and Ethics*.

Asherah); modern scholars (e.g., Martin Dibelius, Rudolf Otto); informative studies of cities now famous as a result of recent archaeological excavations (Mari, Nuzi, Ugarit); people of note in the history of the church (e.g., Gregory the Great, Hildebrand; however, Victor of St. Hugo and some other notable leaders have been omitted); champions of biblical exegesis (e.g., J. B. Lightfoot, B. F. Westcott); prominent missiologists (e.g., William Carey, Albert Schweitzer); American educators and theologians (e.g., Timothy Dwight, Jonathan Edwards, B. B. Warfield); and, of course, numerous articles on philosophers and their systems of thought.

The New Schaff-Herzog Encyclopedia of Religious Knowledge, edited by S. M. Jackson (12 vols. and index, 1908-1912), is based upon the third edition of the Herzog-Hauk *Realencyklopädie*. The articles that make up this English translation and expansion of the German original deal cogently and yet concisely with Protestant theology, church history, missions, philosophy, sects and isms, et cetera. They are written and signed by respected scholars. Biblical topics are also treated, but those do not measure up in quality to comparable articles in other encyclopedias. Biographical sketches of people who are otherwise difficult to research constitute a valuable addition, but in some instances the bibliographic sources cited are erroneous.

Readers are well advised to consult volume thirteen (index) when doing research.

Approximately forty years after the appearance of this English edition, two supplementary volumes entitled *Twentieth Century Encyclopedia of Religious Knowledge*, edited by Lefferts A. Loetscher (1950-55), were added. These supplements contain alphabetically arranged articles updating the original work. The articles, however, were not indexed.

Although some authorities regard SHERK as the "best known," "most authoritative," and "most widely used" of Protestant encyclopedias, the strength of this set lies more particularly in the familiarity of the contributors with German theology, European church history, and philosophical trends on the Continent up to and including the turn of the century. Its appeal also is more in keeping with those holding to a sacramental theology. Nevertheless, what is presented is worthy of consideration.

Universal Jewish Encyclopedia, edited by Isaac Landman et al (11 vols., 1939-44), is replete with information about the "Jews and Judaism since the earliest times." It consists of a compilation of 10,000 lengthy, signed articles on Jewish history, religion, culture, and customs, and is ideal for Bible character studies (e.g., Aaron, Barak, David, Elijah, Gehazi, Moses, Jonah) as well as an explanation of Jewish feasts (Trumpets, Purim) and fasts (Yom Kippur).

Although following an alphabetical sequence, the major articles are classified under seven headings: *History* (treating, among other topics, the era of the patriarchs; the construction and significance to Israel of the Tabernacle and its furnishings; the priesthood and its functions; David; the kingdom;

result of the efforts for a church alliance. The Church Diet was at first held every year, later every second year. In 1872 the last Diet was held at Halle. Although it did not bring about church alliance, it was for a quarter of a century a rallying-point of living church forces.

(WILHELM BAUR†.)

CHURCH DISCIPLINE.

I. In the Apostolic and Postapostolic Periods.
II. In the Roman Catholic Church.
III. In the Lutheran Churches.
  Methods and Results (§ 1).
  Modern Requirements (§ 2).
IV. In the Reformed Churches.
  The Zwinglian System (§ 1).
  Calvin's Basal Principles (§ 2).
  Genevan Ecclesiastical Tribunals (§ 3).
  In France (§ 4).
  In Great Britain (§ 5).
  In Holland and Germany (§ 6).
  Modern Modifications (§ 7).
V. In the United States.

Church discipline is a means of securing and maintaining the spiritual purity of the Christian Church. This exercise arises from the fact that the Church is a human institution, the members of which are subject to the limitations and weaknesses of humanity. The Christian congregation, therefore, like every other community, needs a means of self-protection in order to suppress or eliminate whatever might impair or destroy its life. But, from the constitution of the Church, the character of its discipline is purely spiritual. Therefore the only means which can properly be employed is exclusion, partial or total, of those whose acts jeopardize it.

I. In the Apostolic and Postapostolic Periods: The center of the Scriptural doctrine of ecclesiastical discipline is Matt. xviii. 15–18; and its practical application in the apostolical church is learned from I Cor. v. and II Cor. ii. 4–8. A member of the Corinthian congregation had married his stepmother, and the congregation had suffered the deed. Paul then wrote to the Corinthians that the offender should be excommunicated, and "delivered unto Satan." His words produced such an impression, not only on the congregation, but also on the offender, that, when he wrote again to the Corinthians, Paul could recommend mercy. It is, however, not only for such flagrant offenses as the above that Paul demands punishment, but also for minor failings by which a man is made a burden to his fellow men (II Thess. iii. 6); and he warns the congregations against heresy, for it eats like a canker (II Tim. ii. 17). A heretic, after admonishing him once or twice in vain, avoid (Tit. iii. 10); do not even bid him Godspeed (II John 10, 11). The punishment, however, must never be administered in a spirit of retaliation. Church discipline, though necessary for the self-protection of the church, has as its aim the reclamation and reconciliation of the offender; hence in the spirit of love it must dictate its punishments (II Cor. ii. 6–8). That the discipline is exercised by the Church is indicated in all the passages cited except that from Titus, where the direction is given for personal guidance alone (cf. verse 9). The

apostolical institutions of Excommunication (q.v.) and reconciliation lived on in the postapostolic church, and during the period of persecution became even more peremptory. Under Decius, whose goal seems to have been the total destruction of Christianity, there occurred, by the side of the most admirable examples of faithfulness, so frequent instances of defection that a special regulation for the reconciliation of the lapsed became a necessity. This regulation, which continued valid down to the fifth century, established a course of penance which ran through various stages, and comprised a period of several years; but its severity naturally called forth devices of evasion and subterfuge, such as the libelli of the confessors (see LAPSED), and church discipline became somewhat lax. A reaction toward greater severity followed, and the Montanists declared that the excommunicated ought to remain for their whole life in a state of penance, while the Novatians affirmed that the Church had no right at all to forgive the lapsed, though the Lord might be willing to do so. Meanwhile the developing organization of the Church had reached the department of discipline, and the penitents, who had been excommunicated and desired to be received back into fellowship, were divided into four classes and compelled to pass through as many stages of penance (see EXCOMMUNICATION).

II. In the Roman Catholic Church: The union of Church and State led to developments in discipline, the most important of which was the imposition of civil penalties for spiritual offenses. This was carried to the extreme of capital punishment, inflicted for heresy in the case of the Spanish bishop Priscillian and six companions, 385 A.D. The many sentences of deposition from office accompanied with exile during the controversial period attest the alliance of Church and State in the infliction of church discipline. Penitential discipline in its four grades was continued from the earlier period and was sanctioned by the councils of the fourth century. Yet the alliance of Church and State and the controversial activities produced a concentration of disciplinary attention upon heresy which allowed grave offenses against morals to go unpunished. A noteworthy exception to this was the refusal of Ambrose of Milan to administer the communion to Theodosius I. because of a massacre by the latter's soldiers in Thessalonica. In the early Middle Ages the extension of the Church among the barbaric races brought about further systematization. Discipline was administered by the bishops through synodical courts. The Penitential Books (q.v.), particularly the Liber pænitentialis of Halitgarius of Cambrai, were written for the guidance of confessors. Besides excommunication, the penalties of the Anathema and the Interdict (qq.v.) were developed. Penance (see PENANCE, REPENTANCE), including auricular confession (see CONFESSION OF SINS) and priestly absolution, became a sacrament, and the system of Indulgences (q.v.) was originated which later became so great a scandal and was one of the primary causes of the Reformation.   GEO. W. GILMORE.

III. In the Lutheran Churches: According to

Fig. 3. Page from *The New Schaff-Herzog Encyclopedia of Religious Knowledge*.

and races such as Syrians, Assyrians, Neo-Babylonians, and Persians); *Literature* (including the development and relationship of the different Semitic languages; hapax legomena; Hebrew lexicography; and analysis of Hebrew prose, poetry, and wisdom literature; the rise of the apocryphal and pseudepigraphal writings; allegorical interpretation); *Religion* (dealing with the rise of monotheism, a delineation of the various pagan deities encountered in the Old Testament, an assessment of Hebrew doctrine described as "Articles of Faith," ethical and social standards, spirituality, the names of God, the nature of man, and a discussion of customs and ceremonies); *Jewish Life* (including the family, the education of children, the place of the synagogue, and different legal procedures); the relationship of *Jews and Non-Jews* (describing the attitude of Jews toward other religions, including Christianity; their view of Christian doctrine; Gentile writers who have written on Jewish themes; anti-Semitism); *General* (archaeology and the Bible, folklore, symbolism, messianic movements, the messianic era, democracy, proselytes); and *Jewish Contributions to Civilization* (in and through art, architecture, the humanities, the sciences).

All things considered, this encyclopedia is one that Protestants should not neglect.

The earlier *Jewish Encyclopedia*, edited by Isidore Singer et al (12 vols., 1901-1906) has been completely superseded by Landman's work. The more recent *Encyclopedia Judaica*, edited by C. Roth et al (16 vols., 1972), was produced after the establishment of the state of Israel. It is a well-indexed reference tool and concentrates attention on Judaism since World War II. It has extensive cross-references, Hebrew words are transliterated, and bibliographies are up to date. Treatment of biblical and theological topics is generally most helpful. An index to pottery used in dating earthenware uncovered by archaeologists is in volume one.

ENCYCLOPEDIAS OF THE BIBLE

Having considered some of the strengths and weaknesses of encyclopedias of religion, we now refine our focus and consider seven of the more important multivolume biblical works. In this category we wish to consider:

- Hastings's *Dictionary of the Bible*
- Hastings's *Dictionary of Christ and the Gospels*
- Hastings's *Dictionary of the Apostolic Church*
- *Interpreter's Dictionary of the Bible*
- *International Standard Bible Encyclopedia*
- Smith's *Dictionary of the Bible*
- *Zondervan's Pictorial Encyclopedia of the Bible*.

Dictionary of the Bible, edited by James Hastings (5 vols., 1898-1904), is designed for those "entrusted with the responsibility of teaching the Word of God." This impressive work is the result of predominantly British scholarship and incisively treats biblical subjects from "A" (Aleph) to those descendants of Noah who dwelt in Him.

Each article is signed, and many of the longer ones have important bibliographies appended to them. "See" references are used in the body of some of the essays and at the end of others.

Although more moderate in its stance than the *Encyclopedia Biblica* by Cheyne and Black, readers will still find that many higher critical theories are espoused by the contributors. In spite of that weakness, HDB contains informative articles on all persons and places, ethnology and geology, natural history and biblical theology, and even deals with archaic words occurring in different English versions of the Bible.

Volume five contains thirty-seven extensive additional articles covering topics like the "Sermon on the Mount," "New Testament Times," the "Talmud," "Races of the Old Testament," "The Religion of Israel," et cetera. These are not arranged in alphabetical order. Invaluable indices to all articles, authors, Scripture texts, Hebrew and Greek terms, illustrations, and maps provide ready access to the wealth of material to be found in the dictionary.

Because recent archaeological finds have illuminated much of Bible history, geography, customs, and culture, a work of this nature obviously has its deficiencies. However, on those occasions when you wish to consult an article on a topic like "Roads and Travel," "Style of Scripture," "The Trinity," "Versions of the Bible," you immediately become impressed with the wealth of scholarship evidenced in each article. For this reason, HDB still is worth consulting.

A one-volume abridgment was issued in 1909. In 1963 it was reissued, having been revised and updated by F. C. Grant and H. H. Rowley. Certain new entries treating new items like the Dead Sea Scrolls and some biblical terms omitted from the earlier edition were included.

Dictionary of Christ and the Gospels, edited by James Hastings (2 vols., 1906), follows a similar format to HDB. HDCG is also primarily the product of British scholarship. It is designed to focus attention specifically on the Person, work, and teaching of Christ. In this respect it is "complementary to the *Dictionary of the Bible*." Its emphasis is "mainly with things biographical, historical, geographical, or antiquarian" as those areas of interest have a bearing on the ministry of Christ.

Replete with indices of subjects, Greek terms, and Scripture texts, this set will handsomely repay the researcher for his efforts. Excellent articles highlight the places of Christ's ministry, the traditions and practices of the Jews, the preaching style of the Lord Jesus, and topics like "Only Begotten" and "the Brethren of Our Lord," which are taken from the biblical record. In all, 2,000 topics have been covered.

A particular value are the biographical sketches—of people encountered for the first time in the gospel records and also of Old Testament per-

MEDIATOR.—*Introductory.*—The title 'Mediator' is applied to our Lord in the NT only by St. Paul (1 Ti 2⁵) and the author of Hebrews (8⁶ 9¹⁵ 12²⁴). In Gal 3¹⁹⁻²⁰ St. Paul's argument implies that there is an important sense in which Christ cannot be fitly called a mediator. Here Moses is described by this title, and the *mediator* (generic) is sharply distinguished from *God*. Moses was a person coming between two contracting parties, God and Israel, with the consequence that the law administered by Moses is apparently in opposition to the promises of God which depend upon God only. Obviously Christ is not such a mediator as Moses. He does not come between two contracting parties, for He Himself is the representative human receiver of God's promise, and the Divine Son through whom we receive that promise. He includes both parties in His own Person, instead of coming between them. He is not the instrument of a contract, but the embodiment of a Divine gift. This passage implies that Christ united God and man, two parties previously at variance, in a wholly unique manner. And the same truth is asserted in the verse which calls Him 'the one mediator between God and men' (1 Ti 2⁵). In what sense St. Paul calls Christ a mediator will be shown more fully in § 3.

1. The Synoptic Gospels.—Although these do not employ the title 'mediator,' they throughout imply that the teaching, life, and death of Jesus were mediatorial. The familiar old division of His mediatorial functions into those of Prophet, Priest, and King is roughly correct, though it may be better to designate them as those of Prophet, King, and Redeemer. By such a division we are able to find a more natural place for those passages in the Synoptic Gospels which speak of His atoning work, than if we use the word 'Priest.' We are also able to do more justice to the truth that He revealed Himself as already the Messiah during 'the days of his flesh,' and did not teach that His Messianic Kingdom was only an affair of the future.

(*a*) The 'wisdom' of our Lord impressed His hearers at Nazareth, and when they were offended at the difference which they noted between Him and His humble family, Jesus said, 'A prophet is not without honour, save in his own country, and in his own house' (Mt 13⁵⁴⁻⁵⁸). Here He seems in some way to claim the office of a *prophet*. And there are several passages which show that the ordinary people inclined to regard Him as a *Prophet*. See, fully, under art. PROPHET.

(*b*) He is also *King*. He claimed to fulfil the Jewish expectation of an ideal King, the Messiah. This cannot be reasonably disputed, in spite of the fact that this claim did not represent all that He was and all that He demanded. The confession of His Messiahship by St. Peter, the dispute between His disciples for places of honour, and especially the desire of the sons of Zebedee to sit on His right hand and His left, cannot be thrown aside as legendary inventions. Nor can we fail to see the Messianic meaning of His triumphal entry into Jerusalem, His trial and answer to the high priest (Mk 14⁶²), and the inscription 'The King of the Jews' upon the cross. Apart from His Messianic claim, His life and His death become unintelligible, although He used the actual title very seldom, and rather avoided it on account of the political associations which clung to it. See, further, artt. KING and KINGDOM OF GOD.

(*c*) Jesus, who is Mediator in revealing God, is also Mediator in *redeeming man*. He offered to the Father a sacrifice of perfect human obedience which effected a new relation between God and mankind. It was a reparation to God for the disobedience of man.

In dealing with the redemptive work of Christ, we have to consider as of primary importance the place occupied by His death in the theology as well as in the history of the Synoptics. It is frequently asserted or hinted that He did not foresee His death until an advanced period in His ministry, and that, when He found that it was inevitable, He did not attribute to it any power of obtaining the remission of sins. These two theories do not elucidate the Gospels, but simply contradict them. All the accounts of our Lord's baptism represent Him as hearing the words which declare that He is the Son in whom the Father is well pleased (Mt 3¹⁷, Mk 1¹¹, Lk 3²²). He was, therefore, from the first conscious that He fulfilled the Isaianic picture of the Servant of the Lord, who dies as a *guilt-offering* for the people. In submitting to baptism, He identified Himself with a race that has sinned ; in submitting to the subsequent temptation, He identified Himself with a race which suffers when Satan lures it to sin. He also predicted His death early in His ministry. He is the bridegroom who will be taken away in the midst of joy, and His disciples will fast at that day (Mk 2¹⁹⁻²⁰). Later, He tells how He has to submit to the baptism of His Passion, and feels anguish until it is accomplished. He dreads it ; but He desires it, because it is the necessary preliminary of His kindling a sacred fire on earth (Lk 12⁴⁹). With these words we must compare the question addressed to the ambitious sons of Zebedee, whether they can drink of His cup and be baptized with His baptism (Mk 10³⁸). The baptism and the cup represent the will of the Father with all the suffering which the doing of that will entailed. What that suffering was the story of Gethsemane tells us. It was there that He, with a final effort of His human will, identified Himself wholly with the Servant 'wounded for our transgressions.' But this identification had been outlined long before in the words, 'Whosoever would be first among you shall be servant of all. For verily the Son of Man came not to be ministered unto, but to minister, and to give his life a ransom for many' (Mk 10⁴⁵). This acceptance of death was not a mere example of perfect resignation. He had taught His disciples not to fear those who kill the body (Mt 10²⁸), He had assured them that 'he that findeth his life shall lose it ; and he that loseth his life for my sake shall find it' (10³⁹). But the disciple who loses his life for Christ's sake does not necessarily win any life except his own, whereas Christ's death avails 'for many.' With this prediction we must connect the words used at the institution of the Lord's Supper. Assuming that Christ did institute this sacrament, we may also assume that He who taught His own not to fear those who kill the body, did not mean that when His blood was shed 'for many' it was shed to save them from being killed by the Jews or Romans. Whether He did or did not add the words 'for the remission of sins,' He must have meant that a new covenant was being made between God and man. His death had some special value in itself, or else the Church would not have continued to show forth the Lord's death (1 Co 11²⁶). The special value which He attached to His own death is made plain by the account of the Lord's Supper contained in the Petrine Gospel of St. Mark no less than in the Pauline Gospel of St. Luke. The shedding of Christ's blood seals a covenant similar to the initial covenant made by Moses between God and the people (Ex 24³⁻⁸) ; it consecrates a new people to God. It also fulfils Jeremiah's prophecy of a new covenant, of which the very foundation was the forgiveness of sins (Jer 31³¹). And, like the blood of the Paschal lamb, the blood of Jesus saves His people from a destruction that comes from God. With this sacrifice of Jesus His disciples are

Fig. 4. Page from Hastings's *Dictionary of Christ and the Gospels.*

sonalities (e.g., Moses, Jonah, etc.) referred to by Christ.

Although manifesting the same theological tendencies as HDB, these volumes have achieved deserved praise from Bible scholars and may be consulted with profit.

Dictionary of the Apostolic Church, edited by James Hastings (2 vols., 1915), supplements HDCG and carries the history of Christianity through the period covered by the book of Acts to the close of the first century. Even though there is a greater representation of articles by American scholars, British contributors still predominate.

A careful perusal of this work shows that adequate attention is given extrabiblical source materials (e.g., the apocryphal writings) as well as less obvious topics like human emotions (anger, jealousy, love). Biographical articles are again prominent, and those vary in length from a few lines to several pages. Doctrinal issues likewise receive extensive treatment and are frequently linked with the teaching of the Old Testament (e.g., atonement).

Each book of the New Testament (the gospels excepted) is carefully outlined, introduced, and commented on in such a way as to bring out its primary purpose and message.

Perhaps the greatest single asset of this set is the manner in which historical events are used to highlight biblical teachings (e.g., adoption, emperor worship, the development of the law, etc.). In addition, the correlation of historical references with people and places, cities and events (e.g., Paul and Tarsus, John and Patmos, and the cities referred to in Revelation 2-3) all add such richness to the study of different New Testament passages.

In conclusion, although these volumes do not match the brilliance of those dealing with Christ and the gospels, they should be consulted whenever one is studying the expansion of the early church.

Interpreter's Dictionary of the Bible, edited by G. A. Buttrick et al (4 vols., 1962), is similar in range, scope, and purpose to Hastings's *Dictionary of the Bible.* IDB, however, aims at providing identifications and explanations of "all proper names, significant terms, and subjects in the Holy Scriptures, including the Apocrypha." Signed articles contributed by recognized scholars (most of them from the United States), and brief, up-to-date bibliographies for further study make this work a model publication. Numerous cross-references further enhance this resource tool; but there is no index.

In contrast to the other works cited in this chapter, IDB contains factual data about recent archaeological finds and, in some places, incorporates that information into the discussion of the biblical text. For the most part, however, the information is included as the development of a particular subject dictates but without attempting to show how it confirms or elucidates the teaching of Scripture.

IDB is also valuable for the pronunciation given different words at the beginning of some articles, the etymology of Hebrew, Aramaic, or Greek

out by Holtzmann, De Wette, and others (for a good summary of the facts see Moffatt, *op. cit.* pp. 375–381 ; Holtzmann's results are criticized by Sanday, art. 'Colossians' in Smith's *DB*[2] and by von Soden in *JPTh*, 1887 ; cf. his *Hist. of Early Christian Literature. The writings of the NT*). Results differ widely. Holtzmann's discussion went to show that neither Epistle could be regarded as wholly prior, and therefore he postulated a Pauline Col., expanded at a later date by a writer who also composed Eph. upon its basis. But the evidence for the division of Colossians has very largely broken down, with the wider view of the Pauline angelology (see art. COLOSSIANS). The tendency among scholars is now to assert the authenticity of Col. (so, among those who reject Eph., von Soden [in the main], Klöpper, von Dobschütz, Clemen, Wrede, Moffatt). This, if Holtzmann's results are accepted, proves the authenticity of Eph. also. The two Epistles must have been written by one author at about the same time. The alternative is to regard Eph., with De Wette, as a weak and tedious compilation from Col. and the earlier Epistles—a position which will appeal to few—or, more sympathetically, with Moffatt, 'as a set of variations played by a master hand upon one or two themes suggested by Colossians' (*op. cit.* p. 375). But this does no justice to the real independence of thought in Ephesians. The two main themes—the reconciliation of Jew and Gentile in the Church, and the fact of the Church as influencing Christian life—do not appear in Colossians at all, or only by allusion. The theology is the same, the application very different. Further, it is hard to think that so original a writer would have followed the very structure of Colossians. The rules for family life, *e.g.*, are an integral part of Eph., but have no very clear connexion with the rest of Colossians. It is most natural to suppose, *e.g.* in Col 3[18-21], that the writer is summarizing what he has written in Eph 5[22]-6[4], even at the risk of some obscurity. So, too, Col 2[19] has no clear connexion with its context, and must depend upon the fuller Eph 4[15, 16] for its explanation.

No parallel for the curious inter-connexion of language is to be found in the employment of sources by Matthew and Luke or of Jude by 2 Peter. There we have frank copying. Here there is nothing of the kind. Again and again phrases are used in Eph. to express or illustrate ideas with which they are not connected at all in Col. (cf. Eph. 2[15, 16] ‖ Col 2[14] 1[20], Eph. 3[19] 4[13] ‖ Col 2[9], Eph 2[16] 1[4] 5[27] ‖ Col 1[22]). The writer's mind is steeped in the language and thought of Col., but he is writing quite independently. The only probable psychological solution of the problem is that one writer wrote both Epistles, and at no great interval. And if so, that writer must have been St. Paul. It is quite likely, indeed, that Col. was composed while Eph. was still unfinished, since the latter is clearly the careful work of many hours, perhaps of many days.

(*b*) *Relation to 1 Peter.*—There is a considerable amount of resemblance in thought, structure, and language between Eph. and I Peter. This is especially obvious in the directions for family life (note the curious phrase 'your own husbands' in 1 P 3[1], which seems to depend on Eph 5[22]). Other parallels quoted are 1[3] with 1 P 1[3], 3[*bl.*] with 1 P 1[*loc.*]. (where it is quite unnecessary to argue that 1 Pet. is prior : the two passages may be independent), 1[4] with 1 P 1[19-20], 2[21] with 1 P 2[4], 1[14] with 1 P 2[9] (the use of περιποίησις in Eph. is not dependent on that in 1 Pet., being quite different ; the former is concrete, the latter not), 1[*loc.*] with 1 P 3[22]; 6[*loc.*] with 1 P 5[8, 9]; 4[9] with 1 P 3[19] 4[6]. These analogies are not unnatural, on the assumption that St. Peter knew Eph., and certainly do

not demand the priority of 1 Pet., as Hilgenfeld and others have argued.

(*c*) *Relation to the Lucan and Johannine writings.*—Numerous analogies, mainly of thought, have been found in Eph. to almost every book of the NT, but especially to those connected with the names of St. Luke and St. John. Parallels of language and idea have been seen in the farewell address at Miletus (Ac 20[18-35] ; cf. Moffatt, *op. cit.* p. 384) ; and Lock (*loc. cit.*) draws out the parallels of thought with the Eucharistic prayer in Jn 17. It is true that many of the conceptions of Eph. are found in the Fourth Gospel, but this is not at all unnatural. The parallels of language are by no means striking. The connexion with Rev., emphasized by Holtzmann, is very slight, and that with Heb. is not much more definite (details in Salmond, 'Ephesians,' in *EGT*, p. 212 ff.).

The general impression made on the present writer by the study of these various affinities is the outstanding resemblance in general thought, and even in expression, between Eph. and Romans—a resemblance which the difference of style does not obscure. This in itself is a strong witness to the authenticity of the Epistle.

LITERATURE.—The following is only a small selection from a very voluminous literature. I. *Commentaries.*—Besides the older Commentaries, such as E. W. E. Reuss (1878), H. Alford (1874), and C. J. Ellicott (1864), the most notable are those of A. Klöpper (1891), G. G. Findlay (*Expos. Bible*, 1892), H. von Soden (*Hand-Kommentar*, 1893, also artt. in *JPTh*, 1887, and *Hist. of Early Christian Literature. The Writings of the NT*, Eng. tr., 1906), T. K. Abbott (*ICC*, 1897, largely linguistic), E. Haupt (in Meyer's *Krit.-exeg. Kommentar über das NT*, 1902, very valuable exegetically), J. Armitage Robinson (1903, exegetical and philological, no introduction), S. D. F. Salmond (*EGT*, 1903), B. F. Westcott (1906), P. Ewald (in Zahn's *Kommentar zum NT*, 1910). Fundamental for modern critical studies is H. J. Holtzmann's *Kritik der Epheser- und Kolosserbriefe*, 1872.

II. *Against Pauline authorship.*—Besides Baur, Schwegler, Hitzig, are(S. Davidson, *Introd. to NT*[3], 1894 ; C. v. Weizsäcker, *The Apostolic Age*, Eng. tr., 1894-95 ; E. von Dobschütz, *Christian Life in the Primitive Church*, Eng. tr., 1904 ; O. Pfleiderer, *Primitive Christianity*, Eng. tr., 1906-11 ; R. Scott, *The Pauline Epistles*, 1909 ; J. Moffatt, *LNT*[3], 1912.

III. *For Pauline authorship.*—F., J. A. Hort, *Prolegomena to Romans and Ephesians*, 1895 ; A. Robertson, art. 'Ephesians' in Smith's *DB*[2], 1893 ; W. Lock, art. 'Ephesians' in *HDB*; T. Zahn, *Introd. to NT*, Eng. tr., 1909 (a storehouse of facts); A. S. Peake, *Crit. Introd. to NT*, 1909.

L. W. GRENSTED.

EPHESUS ('Eφεσος, a græcized form of a native Anatolian name).—The town of Ephesus was a little south of latitude 38° N., at the head of a gulf situated about the middle of the western coast of Asia Minor. It lay on the left bank of the river Cayster, at the foot of hills which slope towards the river. In ancient times the river reached to the city gates, but its mouth has gradually silted up so that the city is now some four to six miles from the sea. The effect of the river's action has been to raise the level of the land all over. The ruins, the most extensive in Asia Minor, give an idea of how large the ancient city was. The extent of the area covered by it cannot now be exactly estimated ; but, as the population in St. Paul's time was probably about a third of a million, and in ancient times open spaces were frequent and 'sky-scrapers' unknown, the city must have been large, even according to our standards. The temple of Artemis (see DIANA), the ruins of which were discovered by Wood, lies now about five miles from the coast, and was the most imposing feature of the city. Its site must have been sacred from very early times, and successive temples were built on it. Other notable features of the city were the fine harbour along the banks of the Cayster, the aqueducts, and the great road following the line of the Cayster to Sardis, with a branch to Smyrna. The heat in summer is very great, and fever is prevalent. The harvest rain-

Fig. 5 Page from Hastings's *Dictionary of the Apostolic Church.*

words, and an explanation of their meanings. The Bible text upon which this work is based is the RSV.

Most of the entries are short and vary in length from one paragraph to one page; some articles, however, are much longer and may run up to thirty pages or more in length (cf., "Versions of Scripture," "Jesus Christ," etc.).

A supplementary volume, edited by Keith Crim, was published in 1976.

Even though this set is claimed to be "excellent" for those "beginning research on a biblical subject," the theological orientation of many of the articles necessitates that IDB be used with discernment.

International Standard Bible Encyclopedia, edited by J. Orr et al (5 vols., 1915), is described by the editors as advocating a "reasonable conservatism." From the very first, ISBE was intended to provide a reliable guide to the history of peoples and religions encountered in both the Old and New Testaments as well as the ethnology, geography, topography, biography, arts and crafts, manners and customs, family life, natural history, agriculture, war, commerce, ritual, laws, sects, music, "and all else pertaining to the outer and inner life of the people of the Bible."

To accomplish this task, a team of international scholars was assembled, over one hundred of which were from the United States, about sixty from Great Britain and Europe, and the rest from other parts of the world. The result was an interdenominational work that soon achieved a deserved place on the bookshelf of pastors and teachers of all persuasions.

Although now sharing the same limitations as HDB and other older encyclopedias, ISBE nevertheless contains articles by some of the greatest scholars of Christendom, and that gives it a certain timeless quality. Those contributors include men of the calibre of W. F. Albright, T. Witton Davies, J. Garstang, A. S. Geden, M. G. Kyle, T. M. Lindsay, H. C. G. Moule, W. M. Flinders Petrie, A. T. Robertson, H. Strack, W. H. Griffith Thomas, and B. B. Warfield.

The articles are signed, and the longer ones contain "See" references and a bibliography listing books and articles representing all viewpoints. Volume five contains a "List of Contributors," a general index, index of Scripture texts, and two other valuable indices: an index to Hebrew and Aramaic words, and an index to Greek words.

In 1979 Eerdmans Publishing issued the first of a scheduled four volumes designed to revise and update ISBE. This new edition is under the general editorship of Geoffrey W. Bromiley. A list of the contributors appears in volume one, and readers are alerted to those contributors whose article(s) from the first edition have been retained. Although less conservative than the former edition, this new ISBE gives promise of meeting a real need, particularly in areas where older encyclopedias no longer are able to supply up-to-date information.

Dr. William Smith's Dictionary of the Bible, edited by H. B. Hackett and E. Abbott (4 vols., 1868-96), contains "by universal consent, the fruit of the ripest Biblical scholarship in England." In its unabridged form it lists places where information has been added to the American edition. The Scripture references used throughout this encyclopedic dictionary have all been verified, as have the cross-references. Obsolete expressions have been changed and this edition bears evidence of more American scholarship than was true of the first edition.

Well illustrated with black-and-white line drawings and containing numerous references to the original languages, Smith's famous dictionary may still be consulted with great profit, particularly in areas of Bible biography, doctrine, literature, word studies, and historical references. Lengthy initialed essays on topics like "Canon," "Dress," "Flood," "Genealogy," "Marriage," "Pentateuch" and books of the Bible invest this work with a unique quality. Obviously in matters of archaeology, geography, and sociology this set is dated. Researchers, however, will still find articles by men such as Henry Alford, C. J. Ellicott, H. B. Hackett, J. S. Howson, J. B. Lightfoot, J. J. Stewart Perowne, George Rawlinson, Philip Schaff, and many others well worth consulting.

The *Zondervan Pictorial Encyclopedia of the Bible*, edited by M. C. Tenney et al (5 vols., 1975), enlarges upon the one-volume *Zondervan Pictorial Bible Dictionary* (1963) and is in general the product of conservative theological scholarship. The list of contributors in the front of volume one gives evidence of the international and interdenominational scope of this important reference tool.

The articles vary in length from a few lines to book-length treatises (e.g., "Jesus Christ," "Paul," etc.). All the articles are signed, "See" references have been used to good effect, and the bibliographies reflect a wide range of literature. As is indicated by the title, this work is enhanced by the inclusion of numerous photographs, maps, and drawings.

Where necessary, articles being with the correct pronunciation of the word or name, followed by the Hebrew and/or Greek form together with an explanation of the etymology. Each essay is well outlined, clear and concise. Biblical references are numerous.

Articles like "Archaeology," "Biblical Theology," "Canon," "Education in Bible Times," "Herod," "Inspiration," "Interpretation," "Jerusalem," along with such features as a correlation of the history and chronology of Egypt with that of Israel, a defense of the integrity of Paul's Ephesian letter, and character studies of familiar and unfamiliar persons encountered on the pages of God's Word, place at the fingertips of the researcher a wide variety of factual material. There is no subject index or foreign word index.

Assignment

1. Familiarize yourself with Pfeiffer's *The Biblical World* and Avi-Yonah's *Encyclopedia of Archaeological Excavations*. As you consider the life of

Abraham (particularly as recorded in Genesis 12), to what extent do these reference works shed light on the life and times of the patriarch (i.e., by providing information on some of the cities he lived in or passed by, the route he followed from Ur in southern Mesopotamia to Hebron, and even the customs and culture of the people he encountered)?

2. Greek words and their meanings are handled in Brown's *New International Dictionary of New Testament Theology* and Kittel's *Theological Dictionary of the New Testament*. Assess the scope of each work by considering the way in which respective writers have handled words like "heal," *therapeuō* and its cognates; "heart," *kardia;* "king, kingdom," *basileus, basilia.*

3. *Compare the articles on "Kingdom," "Man," and "Pardon" in Baker's Dictionary of Theology* with those in Richardson's *Dictionary of Christian Theology.* What is the theological perspective of each writer? Is the article written from a biblical, historical, philosophical, or theological point of view? From which secondary sources does each writer draw his information? On a scale of one-to-ten, how would you rate each article for (a) general usefulness, (b) reliability, and (c) coverage of important issues?

3

GENERAL REFERENCE WORKS PART 2

Brenda was a senior. In college she had been a music major. Married for only a year, she was anticipating graduating with her husband and serving with him in a pastoral ministry. Although the most complex musical scores were seemingly "child's play" for her, theology held no interest whatever. It seemed too precise, too dogmatic. Her desires were to be with people, to minister to them. She wanted to engage in activities that gave her the opportunity to participate, give of herself, and bring pleasure to others.

It was not surprising, therefore, when in her last theology class she was required to obtain an overview of all the leading doctrines of the Christian church, Brenda rebelled. She had little patience with the theories of people long dead and was plainly disenchanted with the movements that had grown up around them. Consequently, when required to write on the "Biblical, Theological, and Historical Aspects of Redemption," she felt as if graduation and the ministry she so much desired were very far away.

I listened to Brenda's story as she sat across the desk from me. It was easy to sense her despair and to see the resentment she felt toward the assignment. But what should I do? It was early March and I had several theses to read and an oral defense of a dissertation to prepare for—all before the fifteenth.

For a moment I thought of sending her away with a few suggestions as to where she might find the information she needed. Then I recalled having been treated similarly by a librarian during my own student days, and I promptly changed my mind.

Pausing for a moment, I reflected on the best way to try to help Brenda. How could I show her that theology is not a lifeless science? Her topic was an easy one to research. Why had she developed such a mental block? Then, remembering some of the studies I had done in seminary, I reached for Adolf Deissmann's *Light From the Ancient East* on a nearby bookshelf and turned to a section that I had marked up many years earlier.

"Brenda," I said, "some archæologists, digging around at Delphi, in Greece, came across an inscription on one of the walls of the temple. It described the purchase of a female slave named Nicaea from her master by Amphissa for the purpose of setting her free.

"What do you think it was like for her to spend her youth as a slave, owned by someone else, and never able to go and do the things other girls did?

"Put yourself in her position. How would you have felt on the morning when you knew Amphissa would buy you for three-and-a-half minae, and set you *free*?

"What would freedom be like?"

I paused. Brenda had been following the story. Her eyes were now staring unseeingly at a spot on the wall behind me. Her sensitive nature made it easy for her to bridge the gulf of the centuries.

"That, Brenda," I continued, "is the experience of redemption."

When she again looked at me, I felt we could proceed. The steps were easy. We focused our attention first on the usage of the words for redemption in the Bible, and then the theological truths that emerge.

As we concluded, I remembered Brenda's interest in music.

"You may even wish to include in your paper a quotation or two from some hymns illustrating the experiential side of redemption," I said. I suggested the following example (italics added):

> Praise, my soul, the King of heaven,
>   To his feet thy tribute bring;
> *Ransomed,* healed, restored, forgiven,
>   Who, like me, His praise should sing?
>
> Henry F. Lyte

"You can always find additional sources in the *Judson Concordance to Hymns* by McDormand and Corssman."

She smiled. "Thank you, but I don't think that will be necessary."

And with that she left, and I returned to the theses on my desk.

I did not realize it then, but the procedure I had stumbled upon when trying to help Brenda with her research assignment is one that makes a lot of sense. In this chapter we shall consider first the historical setting and its bearing upon the study of Scripture. Then we shall look at the way in which the meaning of words in the lingua franca of the people enriches our understanding of biblical truth. Finally, we shall consider how all of this makes possible the confidence that should result from our study of theology.

ARCHAEOLOGICAL REFERENCE WORKS

Archaeology adds variety to our study. Its contribution is important. In previous sections, we frequently had occasion to remark that a certain work was dated archaeologically. New archaeological discoveries are being brought to the attention of readers with such frequency that it is difficult for anyone to stay fully abreast of all that is taking place in this burgeoning field. To assist researchers in ascertaining what has been done, reference can easily be made to *The Minister's Library*, pp. 76-77, 89-90, 134-35, and Bollier's *The Literature of Theology*, pp. 69-70 and 108-10.

Two primary works help us come to grips with relatively current information about the people and places of the ancient Near East. Those are:

- Avi-Yonah's *Encyclopedia of Archaeological Excavations in the Holy Land*
- Pfeiffer's *The Biblical World*.

The former is limited to Palestine and its environs, whereas the treatment of the latter work is broader, including the lands of the Fertile Crescent as well as the countries surrounding the Mediterranean.

Encyclopedia of Archaeological Excavations in the Holy Land, edited by M. Avi-Yonah and E. Stern (4 vols., 1976-78), was first published in both Hebrew and English. It gathers together information by the world's renowned biblical archaeologists (information that previously was dispersed in literally hundreds of books and journal articles). The data is grouped in alphabetical order according to the excavated sites. It then describes and, in many cases, provides illustrations of the numerous artifacts unearthed at those different locations.

Each site discussed treats the history behind its identification as well as the history of its occupation through prehistoric times, Bronze and Iron Ages, Persian and Hellenistic periods, and the era of the Crusades. Appropriate biblical references and supposed dates of occupancy are included in each article. Some questionable identifications (e.g., Ai, Debir) are not resolved.

The articles are signed, and brief bibliographies listing important books and essays are appended. A list of contributors is contained in volume four.

Beautifully illustrated with black-and-white and color photographs, drawings, maps and charts, this encyclopedia is of value to anyone interested in the history and geography, customs and culture of the peoples who have occupied the land of Palestine.

The Biblical World: A Dictionary of Biblical Archaeology, edited by Charles F. Pfeiffer (1966), is a popularly written, valuable reference tool that deserves repeated consultation. It treats the "lands of the eastern Mediterranean and the Fertile Crescent—the areas in which the events of Biblical history took place." It contains articles from "Abgar" to "Ziusudra," covering city mounds and the deciphering of texts, ancient law codes and books of wisdom, stories of God's people and records of military campaigns, hymns and religious epics, altars and temples. Biblical persons and places are included only if archaeology has added to one's knowledge of them.

Handsomely illustrated, this survey of biblical archaeology confirms time and again the integrity of the biblical record. Brief bibliographies conclude the more important essays, and "See" references alert the reader to articles listed under alternative names of places. An informative section traces the history of modern archaeology and provides a panoramic survey of the sites excavated by different archaeological teams.

THEOLOGICAL REFERENCE WORKS

Theological reference works are numerous. They fall into two primary categories, biblical and systematic. Within the former of those classifications, we will include dictionaries containing the study of words like *adoption, redemption, sanctification,* and many more.

In general, biblical theology may be said to have a distinctive task: it builds upon the labors of the exegete who is a philologist and historian. He analyzes and determines the value of words and notions in relation to their context, as well as their epochal and cultural setting. The biblical theologian is like the architect. He takes the material of the exegete and strives to erect a harmonious structure in which each element is seen in its correct perspective. One of the most important results of this has been the developing concentration upon lexical studies.

The benefits of lexical study include accuracy in handling the biblical text, a sense of authority in proclaiming it, and an inner quickening of the spirit as one begins to realize how much God, in Christ, accomplished for man's redemption. In addition, this approach helps expose unbiblical assumptions, recaptures the sense of unity of God's Word, and develops a norm by which we are able to measure past movements and present trends. All this has led to a new appreciation for biblical theology, which in turn lays an essential foundation for systematic theology.

Theology is intimately intertwined with the history of ideas. Its roots are deeply embedded in the civilizations of the ancient world, antedating even the time of Abraham. In the progress of revelation, however, theology became identified with the Judeo-Christian religion and, in the history of the early church, systematic theology began to emerge as a distinct dicipline. True theology, of necessity, should come from a study of the Bible itself. It should be grounded in exegesis and the teaching of Scripture, and come to fruition as it interacts with other disciplines.

There has always been a danger that philosophy, dealing as it does with topics closely allied to theology, will unduly influence the "queen of the sciences" instead of being influenced by it.

BIBLICAL THEOLOGY

Specific resources may be traced through *The Minister's Library,* pp. 131-32, and Bollier's *The Literature of Theology,* pp. 68-70.

In this section we will discuss the following works that are representative of the many volumes available on the subject:

- Allmen's *A Companion to the Bible*
- Leon-Dufour's *Dictionary of Biblical Theology*
- *New International Dictionary of New Testament Theology*
- *Sacramentum Verbi*
- Kittel's *Theological Dictionary of the New Testament*
- *Theological Dictionary of the Old Testament*
- *Theological Wordbook of the Old Testament.*

A Companion to the Bible, edited by Jean-Jacques von Allmen (1958), also appeared at one time under the title *Vocabulary of the Bible.* This book is the product of an evangelical Swiss Protestant theologian and a team of French and Swiss scholars. It was prepared to serve the needs of students, ministers, and laymen "seeking anew and rediscovering in the Holy Scriptures, the Word of the living God." In his Introduction to the English edition, H. H. Rowley remarked:

> In great periods of the history of the Church men knew what they believed, and a deeper theological interest today would lead to greater vitality in the Church. For theology is not something dull and remote, but something exciting and relevant. The Bible brings Good News to men, the stirring message of the wonder of God's love and the redemption whereby we can be lifted to share His life and power, and enter into His purpose for the world.

Within the scope of this volume we find alphabetically arranged articles, from "Adoption" to "Worship." Each essay is signed, but bibliographies have been omitted from the English translation. In spite of their general brevity, insightful material is to be found in most of these studies. Especially significant is the treatment of "Covenant," "Cross," "Fear" (including the "fear of God"), "Image," "Law," "Man," "Marriage," et cetera. Unfortunately articles on topics like atonement, propitiation, and theocracy are missing from this otherwise worthy compilation.

Dictionary of Biblical Theology, edited by X. Leon-Dufour (3rd ed. revised and enlarged, 1980), was first published in French in 1962 under the title *Vocabulaire de théologie biblique* and has since attained a reputation in Roman Catholic as well as Protestant circles for its succinct scholarship.

A Jesuit priest by training, Leon-Dufour describes the purpose behind this dictionary: "Sacred Scripture is the Word of God to man; theology seeks to be the word of man about God. When theology limits its study to the immediate content of the inspired books, eager to listen to them in their own terms, to penetrate into their langauge—in brief, to become the precise echo of the Word of God—then theology is biblical in the strict sense of the term."

Even though the editor speaks unashamedly of the divine inspiration of the Scriptures, many of the contributors hold to various documentary theories. Leon-Dufour also does not hesitate to say that the Bible possesses an amazing unity quite beyond the ability of man to develop. He goes on to say that this "unity comes from the person who is its very centre" (namely, Jesus Christ). Consequently, readers will find profound evangelical truths in these pages stated clearly and without ambiguity, and side by side other treatments of biblical truths that lamentably manifest a heavy reliance upon theologically liberal views.

As far as the articles are concerned, each subject is well outlined and initialed, contains numerous cross-references, and deals adequately with the broad boundaries of the topic. The treatment of "Day of the Lord," "Faith," "Justification," "Mediator," "Pardon," "Redemption," "Truth," "Worship," et cetera, is brief and helpful.

A table containing the abbreviations of books of the Bible (as found in the Douay Version) appears in the front of the book with a list of the contributors. An "Analytical Table" of subjects dealt with is found at the end of the book, together with a theological index.

New International Dictionary of New Testament Theology, edited by C. Brown (3 vols., 1975-78), is based upon the German *Theologisches Begriffslexikon zum Neuen Testament* by L. Coenen, E. Beyreuther, and H. Bietenhard. It brings within the grasp of the English reader a vast wealth of information. The purpose of this work takes the form of an invitation to enter into the labors of others and to begin to discover for oneself something of the limitless resources of God's inspired Word. The editor writes,

> A theological dictionary is not a collection of prepackaged sermons or an anthology of predigested devotion. It is more like an invitation to join in the collective enterprise of quarrying and building . . . (I Cor. 3: 10ff.). It is as one quarries among the mass of data and tries to build something out of it that the data becomes alive. What was perhaps previously flat and featureless takes on new perspective and meaning. One can go even further. The great revivals of the Christian church have come about when some individual here and there has been grasped by something that his predecessors and contemporaries have taken for granted.

Arranged alphabetically according to the English word (e.g., "Baptism," "Child," "Disciple," "Exhort"), each article also treats corresponding (and appropriate) Greek words and their cognates. In ascertaining the meaning of each word, the contributor traces its usage through the classical period, probes its meaning in the Septuagint (LXX), and then deals with its occurrence in the New Testament. From this premise he is then in a position to assess the theological significance of the word under consideration and relate the contribution of each biblical writer to the topic as a whole.

Each article is signed; and comprehensive, up-to-date bibliographies are at the end of most articles. Separate subject indices are provided for volumes one and two. A complete index to all the articles is at the end of volume three. Each volume contains a table of contents listing the words treated. This is followed by a list of contributors that cites the articles they wrote along with pertinent personal information. In addition, volume one contains a glossary of technical terms frequently encountered in theological literature. This glossary is at once accurate and reliable.

Designed for lay people, this set provides indispensable insights to all who will take time to dig into its truths.

Sacramentum Verbi: An Encyclopedia of Biblical Theology, edited by J. B. Bauer (3 vols, 1970), was prepared with the Catholic lay person in mind and contains articles designed to cover topics associated with biblical theology from the perspective of the biblical writers. In doing so, it also makes available to readers a synthesis of leading theologians' thinking from the time of the apostles to the present.

The contributors realize that "Dogmatic theology cannot be reduced to biblical theology," but rather must grow out of it. So in each article an attempt is made to allow the Scriptures to speak for themselves. It is interesting, therefore, for Protestants to see to what extent the writers have been successful in their aim. In the article on the "Brethren of Jesus," for example, the contributor begins appropriately enough by listing those passages of Scripture where reference is made to Christ's "brethren." He then discusses the linguistics involved and concludes, in keeping with Catholic dogma, that these "brethren" must have been cousins of Jesus, not brothers and sisters.

Although obviously slanted to the needs of Roman Catholics, this work should not be ignored by Protestants. The articles do manifest a theologically liberal stance, but that does not mean that discussions of topics like Abraham, *agapē*, authority, body, building up, conscience, conversion, day of Yahweh, and death are devoid of value.

Volume one lists the contents of all three volumes along with the author of each article.

G. Kittel and G. Friedrich have edited the *Theological Dictionary of the New Testament,* translated and edited by G. W. Bromily (9 vols. and index, 1964-76). The product of outstanding German scholarship, this series of studies aims at elucidating every word of religious or theological significance in the New Testament. Included in the treatment are many proper names of people of theological importance (e.g., Abel, Abraham, Adam), a discussion of some prepositions of value in theological discussion, and a handling of words by their root forms together with cognate terms.

Each article appears with the Greek term(s) to be discussed clearly identified in a rectangular box at the beginning. The word is then generally treated in keeping with its usage in the Old Testament (LXX), classical times, Judaism, the New Testament, and finally the apostolic and postapostolic periods. Because the words are handled in this way, the changes in nuance and meaning are clearly seen. Quotations from the Talmud, Midrash, Mishnah, or Greek writers of antiquity enhance the value of this work for research purposes.

All articles are signed, and a list of the contributors is found at the front of each volume. Extensive bibliographies conclude most essays.

Although the theological position of the majority of the contributors places them theologically left of center, these studies are of inestimable value and should not be ignored.

Volume ten contains indices of English key words, Greek key words, Aramaic and Hebrew words, and biblical references to both testaments and the Apocrypha. It concludes with a list of the contributors and co-workers.

Theological Dictionary of the Old Testament, edited by G. J. Botterweck and H. Ringgren, translated by J. T. Willis, (12 vols. scheduled, 1974—), is designed to be the companion of TDNT. Its discussion of key Old Testament words and concepts builds upon form-critical and traditio-historical methods of investigation and uses cognate languages (primarily Akkadian and Ugaritic) to bring to light the meaning of words whose etymology is often shrouded in antiquity.

Each article treats the Hebrew terminology, surveys the occurrence of the word under consideration in Hebrew as well as other Semitic languages, gives its equivalent in the Septuagint, and (where applicable) its use in the Qumran materials, pseudepigraphic, and rabbinic literature. The result is a comprehensive discussion of the theological significance of each word.

The signed articles contain extensive footnotes. Hebrew words are transliterated in order to make the text more readable, and in many cases the meaning of foreign words is provided in the context. When the verse numbers in the Masoretic Text differ from the verse numbers in the English Bible, the English verse is given in parenthesis.

Of real significance is the *Theological Wordbook of the Old Testament*, edited by R. L. Harris, G. L. Archer, and B. K. Waltke (2 vols., 1981). TWOT follows a similar format to TDOT, and although it is less extensive it is still complete and easier to use than TDOT.

The concise handling of each Hebrew word and its cognates in TWOT and the synthesis of all the relevant material into an easily digestible form makes this work one of the first that ought to be consulted by the busy pastor or earnest Christian worker. The explanation of the meaning of each word in its context and the explication of the word's theological concepts are designed to enrich our understanding. Each word, therefore, is treated in light of its etymology, cognate usage, and meaning in the lingua franca. The result is a highly usable dictionary to the literature of the Old Testament.

Even though some scholars will differ with the contributors on minor matters, little divergence of opinion is likely over the definition assigned a given word. Researchers will find that what is presented in TWOT is accurate and reliable.

To aid students the use of TWOT, an introductory section describes the arrangement of the dictionary and outlines the best method for tapping into its material. Every effort has been made by the editors to list alphabetically all the derivatives of a word whose consonants differ from the verbal roots. This feature alone is of particular help to the individual with limited facility in Hebrew and should eliminate the need to be overly reliant upon an analytical lexicon.

SYSTEMATIC THEOLOGY

In recent years the basis of true systematics has been eroded as a result of the decline in the study of the original languages. Today's theologians are seldom exegetes. As we evaluate reference tools in the broad area of theology, therefore, we need to do so in light of whether or not each article in a theological dictionary is based upon a demonstrated knowledge of the original languages and truly represents what the Bible has to say.

In this connection we will consider:
- *Baker's Dictionary of Theology*
- Richardson's *Dictionary of Christian Theology*
- *Sacramentum Mundi.*

Other theological works can be traced through *The Minister's Library,* pp. 189-96, and Bollier's *The Literature of Theology,* pp. 108-10.

Baker's Dictionary of Theology, edited by E. F. Harrison et al (1960), contains 874 articles by 138 international contributors. It has established itself as a generally evangelical work of value to lay people as well as students in colleges and seminaries.

Informative articles such as on the "Albergenses," "Montanists," and "Pelagians" make this an ideal work to consult when investigating the rise of sectarian groups and their beliefs and practices. Outstanding articles on "Christology," "God," "Law," "Paul and Paulinism," and "Word" give further indication of the excellence of this dictionary. No doctrine is neglected and yet nothing is superfluous. All the articles on the great doctrines pertaining to salvation (e.g., atonement, justification, propitiation, redemption, etc.) have been handled skillfully.

A *Theological Word Book of the Bible*, edited by Alan Richardson (1969), focuses the attention of the reader on contemporary theological issues. It leans heavily on the development of Christian ideas as it seeks to make relevant the contribution of history to the life of the church today.

First published in 1950, the early edition dealt mainly with words of doctrinal significance. Then, after nearly two decades, it was updated and expanded.

Listed in alphabetical order, the articles range from "*A Priori*" to "Zinzendorf" and "Zwingli." Articles are signed, and helpful bibliographies conclude most of them.

Although no effort has been spared to acquire the corroboration of some of the world's foremost scholars, few of them could be classified as either conservative or evangelical. But evidence of their scholarship abounds, particularly in the succinct, descriptive statements about the meaning of Greek words, the biographical sketches of leaders in the church from the era of the Fathers to the present, and evaluative critiques of sects and deviant religious movements.

For the student seeking help in philosophy, there are also articles dealing with all the leading thinkers and their systems of thought.

In spite of its merits this dictionary is deficient as a work on theology, mainly because theological tenets are not supported scripturally. However, it still must be admitted that this book shows a high standard of scholarship and is useful.

Sacramentum Mundi: An Encyclopedia of Theology, edited by K. Rahner et al (6 vols., 1968-70), was designed for Roman Catholic laity, and was issued simultaneously in English, Dutch, French, German, Italian, and Spanish. Its purpose is to articulate in modern terms changes that had taken place within Catholicism since Vatican II. The contributors are all theologians of established reputation; each article is signed; and bibliographies listing works in English, German, French, and occasionally Latin are appended to the longer essays.

Some of the articles are rather weak. "Temptation," for example, is not as well outlined as some of the others, yet the progression of thought is clear. Scripture references are numerous in the second part, but philosophical discussion predominates in the introduction and conclusion.

Important theologians (e.g., Abelard, K. Barth, J. Calvin), doctrines (e.g., Empiricism, Idealism, Phenomenology), papal encyclicals, systems of ethics, pastoral ministry, the "People of God," the "Roman Curia," and "Zen Buddhism," are all discussed.

Volume six provides a list of contributors and a general index.

ASSIGNMENT

1. In the following reference works trace as many articles as you can on the following topics: decision-making, leadership, legitimacy/illegitimacy, maturity, motivation, and the Puritans:
  • *Baker's Dictionary of Christian Ethics*
  • *International Encyclopedia of the Social Sciences*
  • *Encyclopedia of Education.*
How thorough is each article? What is the perspective of each writer (e.g., historical, philosophical, biblical, etc.)? Is the article well outlined? Signed? In comparing one article with another, apart from length, which do you prefer? Why?

2. Imagine that you are to research the lives and significant contribution(s) of each of the following: A. B. Bruce, J. B. Lightfoot, T. DeWitt

Talmage, and Roger Williams. A friend suggests that you consult the following works:
- *Dictionary of American Biography* (DAB)
- *Dictionary of National Biography* (DNB).

What report would you take back to your friend? How valuable were these works to you as you researched each person's life? Did you find any observable strengths and weaknesses in these reference works? Be specific.

3. Consider the influence of humanism, idealism, and naturalism on education as found in the following reference tools:
- *Westminster Dictionary of Christian Education*
- *Encyclopedia of Education*
- *International Encyclopedia of Philosophy.*

Who were the notable people involved in the spread of each theory? What was the contribution of each theory to education? How does each view differ from a distinctively Christian approach to education?

4. If you were to write a paper on the contribution of missions and missionaries to the education and sociology of a given ethnic group (one of your choice), what information could be derived from secular and Christian sources like:
- *Concise Dictionary of Christian World Mission*
- *Encyclopedia of Education*
- *International Encyclopedia of the Social Sciences?*

5. How influential have Origen, Augustine, John Knox, Thomas Arnold, and John Dewey been in shaping education trends (see Smith's *Dictionary of Christian Antiquities;* Smith's *Dictionary of Christian Biography, Literature, Sects and Doctrines;* DAC; and DNB).

4

GENERAL
REFERENCE WORKS
PART 3

We are living in an era in which it has become trite to speak of the "knowledge explosion." But a knowledge explosion has occurred. Educators, in dramatizing what has taken place and is continuing to take place, have sought to describe the contemporary scene in linear terms. They tell us, "If all of man's knowledge from the beginning of history to 1845 equalled one inch; and from 1845 to 1945, three inches; from 1945 to 1975 it would attain the height of the Washington Monument."

With this phenomenal growth of knowledge has come an equally important emphasis on interdisciplinary studies. Old "water-tight" compartments (e.g., law, medicine, philosophy, theology) are being compelled to interact with the social sciences and humanities, ethics and literature, history and psychology. Integration of subject matter can either be resisted or welcomed, but the fact remains, it is being done. Those who take theoretical truths and apply them to real life situations find the process exciting.

In this chapter we shall consider those reference tools that can enrich one's study of purely biblical, ecclesiastical, and theological themes. We shall treat a few areas as representative of the way in which one can engage in interdisciplinary study. The following subjects shall be considered:

- Education
- History and biography
- Missions
- Philosophy and ethics
- Practical theology.

EDUCATION

In building upon the Scriptures to form a truly biblical approach to education, you may wish to consult some of the works listed in *The Minister's Library*, pp. 321-33. Principles that "work" in secular education may or may not be biblical. Our need is to be cognizant of both effective secular principles and biblical standards and then apply that which is scriptural and relevant.

To integrate biblical and secular education principles effectively you will need to be familiar with *The Encyclopedia of Education*, edited by L. C. Deighton (9 vols. and index, 1971). This work comprises more than 1,000 scholarly, signed articles.

The Encyclopedia of Education covers a variety of themes pertaining to the institutions and people, processes and product, history and theory, research and philosophy of our teaching-learning institutions today.

Subjects included are: public as well as private systems of instruction, all levels of education from preschool through graduate programs, the nature and methods of instruction, governmental agencies and museums, libraries, and volunteer organizations.

Where appropriate, articles stress the *how to* of learning (the *is* as well as the *ought*) and the values to be acquired. No utopian models are suggested, but rather emphasis is laid upon the process of education, which should be lifelong.

Although the history of some institutions is given, stress is placed upon educational systems within the United States. Issues of importance to those institutions (e.g., accreditation, environment, library resources, etc.) are dealt with clearly and concisely. Matters of importance to those who teach within those institutions (e.g., academic freedom, tenure) are also discussed.

Of general interest to those earning degrees are articles like "Academic Regalia," "Accrediting Agencies," "Adult Education," "Role of the Library," "Degrees, Academic," et cetera. Other articles deal with the place of the emotions in education, ethics, the goals of education, studies in human potential, the classification of knowledge, and a multitude of other topics. Valuable treatments of "Libraries, Academic" and special resources (e.g., ERIC—Educational Resources Information Center), along with critiques of journals and biographical sketches of leading educators, make this a volume worthy of continual consultation. Bibliographies have been appended to most entries.

The Westminster Dictionary of Christian Education, edited by K. B. Cully (1963), grew out of a need for something more up to date than the 1915 *Encyclopedia of Sunday Schools and Religious Education*. The editor therefore selected a group of highly trained educators to collaborate with him in the production of this work.

Dealing with topics from "Administration" to "Zwingli," the dictionary provides articles on virtually every kind of program, person, department, task, activity, and country involved in the educational ministry of the church.

The articles are signed and indexed, and a lengthy bibliography (arranged under seven different subject headings) completes the work.

Although the contributors have been drawn from denominations not known for their evangelical stance, this dictionary may nevertheless be consulted with profit by those engaged in undergraduate as well as some graduate programs.

HISTORY AND BIOGRAPHY

An extra knowledge of who did what, and when and where, will go a long way toward infusing vitality into traditional courses in church history, historical theology, as well as in secular history courses. I have chosen the following encyclopedic works for consideration in historical and biographical study. (Additional information pertaining to primary source material as well as the history of denominations and the countries in which they have taken root may be found in *The Minister's Library*, pp. 337-60, and in Bollier's *The Literature of Theology*, pp. 114-32.)

The *Dictionary of American Biography*, edited by Allan Johnson (20 vols. and index, 1964), is the American counterpart of the British *Dictionary of National Biography*. Updated with five supplements (1935-55), this compilation of approximately 14,000 articles of noteworthy, deceased Americans includes both men and women and serves as a valuable resource tool for all who are studying the impact of individuals on social life and culture. Prominent people from all walks of life and all religious and nonreligious backgrounds are included (e.g., William Jennings Bryan, Robert Ingersoll, James Russell Lowell, Ira D. Sankey, etc.).

Many of the articles are of considerable length. They have all been contributed by noted scholars, are signed, and contain bibliographies.

DAB is ideal for researching religious leaders about whom separate biographies may not have been written. In a few instances, however, the biographer seems to lack empathy with his subject.

The more comprehensive *National Cyclopedia of American Biography* (57 vols., 1892-1977) is presently undergoing revision.

A *Dictionary of Christian Antiquities*, edited by Sir William Smith and Samuel 'Cheetham (2 cols., 1876), is fully in keeping with the many works of Sir William and gives evidence of the same painstaking scholarship that made his other publications famous. Intended to supplement the *Dictionary of Christian Biography, Literature, and Doctrines*, these volumes are designed to treat "the organization of the Church, its officers, legislation, discipline, and revenues; the social life of Christians; their worship and ceremonies, with the accompanying music, vestments, instruments and insignia; their sacred places; their architecture and other forms of art; their symbolism; their sacred days and seasons and the graves or Catacombs in which they were laid to rest."

While covering the period from the death of the apostles to the time of Charlemagne, these volumes provide informative insights into social life during those centuries (as seen in articles on "Actors and Actresses," "Books, Censure of," "Catacombs," "Contract of Marriage," "Dancing," "Divination," "Fasting"); church rites and practices ("Baptism," "Confession," [the rise of the office of] "Bishop," "Celibacy," "Council"); social attitudes and customs ("Adultery," "Betrothal," "Burial of the Dead," "Family," "Marriage"); events in the Christian year "Advent," "Ascension Day," "Calendar," "Easter," "Holy Week"); notable councils of the church (at Alexandria, Antioch, Chalcedon, Constantinople, Nicea, etc.); and much more.

The wealth and variety of information to be found in these volumes places the researcher forever in the debt of those whose assiduous studies and arduous labor made this work possible. All material is recorded with a completeness and precision that is without equal today.

Extensively documented, each article is initialed. A list of the contributors is found in volume one.

A Dictionary of Christian Biography, Literature, Sects and Doctrines, edited by W. Smith and H. Wace (4 vols., 1877), continues William Smith's famous *Dictionary of the Bible.* It contains "in the form of a Biographical Dictionary, a complete collection of materials for the History of the Christian Church from the time of the Apostles to the age of Charlemagne."

Many of the articles are long. They are all initialed, and brief bibliographies conclude some of the more important ones. Other references and quotations are frequently found in the body of an article. The contributors are all nineteenth-century theologians and historians and include in their number evangelicals such as C. J. Ellicott, E. Hatch, F. J. A. Hort, J. B. Lightfoot, W. Milligan, H. C. G. Moule, G. Salmon, A. P. Stanley, H. B. Swete, B. F. Westcott, C. Wordsworth, et cetera.

Important discussions of great leaders of antiquity include lengthy articles on persons such as "Athanasius," "Atilla," "Augustine," "Bar-Cochba," "Beda (Bede)," "Carpus," "Celsus," "Cerinthus," and of course, "Charlemagne"; doctrinal essays deal with "Antichrist," "Arianism," "Baptism," "Christology," "Church," "Confession," "Death and the Dead," "Demonology," and "Docetism"; and historical discussions include "Apologists," "Apostolic Fathers," "Balaamites," "Cabbalah," "Conscience," "Coptic Church," and "Church Creeds."

Without fear of contradiction, it can be said that these four volumes are a work of massive scholarship, and those who neglect them do so to their detriment.

The *Dictionary of National Biography,* edited by Leslie Stephen and

Sidney Lee (21 vols. and supplements, 1908-1909), is a work of such scholarship that it set the standard for dictionaries of its kind throughout the world. It includes notable Englishmen of the past, both in the United Kingdom and throughout the British Empire, including Americans of the colonial period.

Supplements issued between 1912 and 1971 have kept DNB up to date.

Although not all articles are of equal value, in many instances this is the only resource available when seeking reliable information about notable people; and where Christianity is concerned, DNB is inclined to be more objective than its American counterpart. DNB covers with consumate skill Thomas Arnold, John Brown of Haddington, John Brown of Whitburn, John Brown of Edinburgh, Frederick William Faber, John Knox, Andrew Melville, B. F. Westcott, and a host of other notable persons whose names are associated with Christ and His church.

A reprint, with additional entries up to 1950, is entitled *Dictionary of National Biography: The Concise Dictionary* (2 vols., 1953-61). It also contains an index to the larger work.

The New International Dictionary of the Christian Church, edited by J. D. Douglas (revised ed., 1978), is designed to give readers "a renewed sense of history; an identification and feeling of fellowship with those who have carried the torch before them . . . and most of all an appreciation of the priceless heritage which is ours in Christ."

The text has been compiled by a team of international scholars, and the researcher will find among the signed articles a treatment of subjects both old and new. In some instances, articles on well-known movements in church history have been treated concisely and fairly (e.g., the Clapham Sect, the ecumenical movement). In other instances, subjects have been discussed that have long been shrouded in the mists of obscurity (e.g., the Dyophysites, the Elkesorites, the Five Mile Act, etc.).

Biographical sketches have been provided for the better known as well as the lesser known people whose lives have made an impact for good or ill on the Christian church (e.g., Charles Hodge, Pope Joan, J. Kitto, R. Lull, E. B. Pusey). In some instances these sketches have been accompanied by an evaluative critique of their theology (e.g., J. W. Colenso, W. R. Inge, R. Kittel, G. Spalatin.)

Certain omissions are evident: for example, no mention is made of Charles G. Gordon, the famous British general who did so much to provide a foothold for the spread of the gospel in the lands in which he served; or Karl H. Graf who, with Julius Wellhausen, gave impetus to the "Documentary Hypothesis" of the Pentateuch; or John M. Gregory, one-time president of the University of Illinois and Christian educator par excellence.

Even though each essay is short, brief bibliographies have been appended to some of them, and these are sufficient to alert readers to other sources of information.

Other works of a similar nature that researchers may wish to consult include *The Oxford Dictionary of the Christian Church*, edited by F. L. Cross and E. A. Livingstone (1977), and *The Westminster Dictionary of Church History*, edited by J. C. Bauer (1971).

The first of those works is slanted more toward the history of the Anglican (Episcopal) Church in England, whereas the latter pays more attention to churches and church organizations in the United States. Neither work treats with any degree of adequacy the evangelical branches of the church or evangelical movements within the church. Only the most prominent of individuals (e.g., Jonathan Edwards, D. L. Moody, etc.) receive mention.

In the final analysis, however, Douglas's *New International Dictionary of the Christian Church* will probably be found to be the most satisfactory of the above-mentioned works.

MISSIONS

The carrying out of the Great Commission is the mission of the church. What has been done, as well as what remains to be done, may be gleaned from works cited in *The Minister's Library*, pp. 299-308, and in Bollier's *The Literature of Theology*, pp. 156-61. For those whose studies so incline them, each of those volumes also has a section on comparative religions.

As basic resources, however, you will find the following works helpful.

A Concise Dictionary of the Christian World Mission, edited by S. Neill, G. H. Anderson, and J. Goodwin (1971). The editors call upon a group of well-trained missiologists to treat the rise and progress of missions from 1492 to the present. Focusing specifically upon: (1) all the countries of the world, (2) biographies of notable leaders, and (3) dealing with topics ranging from acculturation to witchcraft, the contributors have provided a fine digest of missionary work and practice.

More than 200 persons contributed articles to this dictionary. Inasmuch as the contributors are from many countries and represent all denominations, the work is truly international and ecumenical.

Articles vary in length and are signed. The longer ones contain bibliographies. "See" references are in the body of an article, not at the end.

Statistical and cultural information may be obtained from the *World Christian Handbook* by H. W. Coxill and K. Grubb and the Europa publications *Africa South of the Sahara, The Far East and Australasia, The Middle East and North Africa*, et cetera.

The Encyclopedia of Modern Christian Missions: The Agencies, edited by B. L. Goddard et al (1967), has been produced by the faculty of the Gordon Divinity School (now Gordon-Conwell), Wenham, Massachusetts. It seeks to provide information (address, income, history, number of workers, nature of missionary enterprise, projects, and literature describing the work) about each of the 1,437 primarily Protestant agencies carrying on missionary work in all parts of the world. As such, it deals with missions in its widest sense.

Articles are all numbered and signed. They range from "Aoh Church of God" to the "Zurich Mission Für Süd—Und Osteuropa." Indices providing "Letter Designation of Agencies" (e.g., place, *Japan;* type, *Literature and Bible Distribution*) make this an ideal resource tool for students engaged in researching different kinds of missionary enterprise in different parts of the world.

For additional information see *The World Directory of Mission-Related Education Institutions,* compiled by R. B. Baker, Sr. and T. Ward (1972), and the latest edition of *Mission Handbook: North American Ministries Overseas,* prepared by the Missions Advanced Research and Community Center, Monrovia, California.

PHILOSOPHY AND ETHICS

Integration of knowledge is incomplete without the application of truth to life. Philosophy is man's attempt to uncover truth, and ethics is his attempt to provide a rational basis of conduct. Both of these disciplines are intimately related to theology, so much so that many contemporary exponents of morality are both philosophers and theologians. (But we should always bear in mind that a true theologian builds his system of knowledge upon the Word of God, and only then does he integrate the Word with truth from related disciplines.)

A discussion of philosophical and ethical themes will be found in the works listed in *The Minister's Library,* pp. 50-55, 228-29, and 233-36.

Of interest to the researcher will be the *Dictionary of Christian Ethics,* edited by C. F. H. Henry (1973). Produced in an era of moral ambivalence and confusion over values, this work seeks to lay a foundation for a biblically-based system of ethics. In doing so, it stresses the essential content of each system or practice, indicates accompanying impact upon man and society in the past, expounds upon the relevance of the problems affecting people today, and wrestles with the moral dilemmas that will have a direct bearing upon the future.

To accomplish his purpose, the editor gathered about him a team of 168 scholars from the United States, Great Britain, Europe, Canada, and Australia. Articles range from "Abandonment" to "Zwingli," are all signed, contain numerous "See" and "See also" references, and vary in length from a paragraph to several pages. Few articles have bibliographies.

Researchers will find adequate information on the human emotions, biographical sketches of biblical personalities, and subjects of sociological significance. The articles on "Kingdom," "Man," "Patriotism," et cetera, leave much to be desired. Essays on specific topics such as Pauline or Petrine ethics, free will, lying, lust, sex, sin, and worldliness are well done. Ironically, only passing mention is made of the "fear of the Lord," which from a biblical point of view is the basis of right conduct.

The Dictionary of Christian Ethics, edited by J. Macquarrie (1967), manifests concern over the evident lack of a realization of any moral obligation or consciousness of "sin." To meet a need, therefore, the editor solicited articles from leading Reformed scholars (mainly Episcopalian and Presbyterian) in the United States and Great Britain. Each contributor was required to deal realistically with the complexities of the subject assigned to him. The result is a "guide to Christian ethics not in the sense of laying down rigid norms, but in the sense of letting the reader see what the problems are, letting him know what the leading Christian moralists are thinking about the problems, and so enabling him to come to his own intelligent and responsible decisions."

The writers have drawn fine philosophical distinctions between beliefs and values, duty and desire, experience and practice, et cetera. In addition, excellent discussions of the leading philosophers and their systems of thought are to be found within these pages. Furthermore, Jewish, Buddhist, non-Christian sects, and even communist ethics have been treated with scholarly acumen. Each article is signed, and the major ones have bibliographies appended.

In the final analysis, however, little use had been made of the Scriptures as the revelation of the will of God to man. At best what is presented is an appeal for external norms as opposed to an internal dynamic that brings the individual into conformity with the truth of the Word of God.

The Encyclopedia of Philosophy, edited by Paul Edwards (8 vols., 1967), is a work that deals extensively with Eastern and Western philosophy; ancient, medieval and modern writers; and the theories of mathematicians, physicists, biologists, sociologists, moral reformers, and religious thinkers. The 1,500 articles are all well-outlined and signed, and they contain extensive bibliographies. Researchers will also find that this work abounds with information about philosophers (*e.g.,* Barth, Nietzsche, Tillich); philosophies (historical, metaphysical, pragmatic, religious); philosophical movements (Communism, Hegelianism, pragmatism); and religious ideologies and ideas (gnosticism, pietism). Of significance is that the articles include biographies as well as descriptions of different movements. The writings of the leading men and women discussed receive close, objective scrutiny; evaluative comments are included, and stimulus is provided for further research. (An article on "Philosophical Dictionaries and Encyclopedias" [6:170-99] alerts users to other source materials.)

Practical Theology

Few reference works of significance have been produced in the area of the pastoral ministry, yet monographs on church management, polity, and practice are being produced in ever increasing numbers.

A few works worthy of note are listed in *The Minister's Library*, pp. 247-77 (and its supplements). General reference works are as follows.

Baker's Dictionary of Practical Theology, edited by R. G. Trumbull (1967), is designed for pastors. It is composed of articles arranged under ten headings: "Preaching," "Homiletics," "Hermeneutics," "Evangelism-Missions," "Counselling," "Administration," "Pastoral," "Stewardship," "Worship," and "Education."

Each article is well-outlined and has been contributed by a person with experience in the field. The main criterion for being a contributor seems to have been practical experience and expertise in a particular field rather than academic training. Representative bibliographies have been included at the end of each section.

Articles vary in worth and biblical content. All, however, have been written with the busy pastor in mind. For example, in treating the subject of evangelism the writers deal first with its biblical basis, then with articles such as the "Great Awakening," "Evangelistic Movements," and "The Pastor as Evangelist." After describing the ways in which each minister of the gospel may contribute toward the fulfillment of the Great Commission, thirteen distinct kinds of outreach discuss the ways in which Christians may participate in an evangelistic ministry.

Indices to subjects and persons cited in each article complete this work.

The Westminster Dictionary of Worship, edited by J. G. Davies (1979), was originally published in England in 1972 under the title *A Dictionary of Liturgy and Worship*. It manifests a strong sacramental bias. Although some evangelicals (e.g., F. F. Bruce) have contributed articles to it, for the most part the contributors have long been identified with the ecumenical branch of the church and are not known for their orthodoxy.

As a reference work this book nevertheless has value, for it provides essential background information on the practices of all the major religious bodies throughout the world. Special emphasis is laid on the development of certain traditions, the use of vestments, the rise of ritual, the different forms of architecture, the use of candles, various symbolic ornaments, gestures and functions, and a host of other practices.

This book holds little of value to the student from an independent, baptistic background, but may perhaps have value to the student of comparative religion.

SOCIOLOGY AND PSYCHOLOGY

Accompanying the "relation revolution" has come an emphasis on ministering to the *whole* person. Such an approach is biblical. The "relational revolution," however, has minimized the need for biblical distinctions and emphasized instead mankind's existential need. As such, it has sown the seeds of its own demise and, in time will reap the results of its lack of biblical orthodoxy.

We would be negligent, however, if we failed to capitalize on the strengths of others and did not expand our ministry to meet people's needs. Lamentably, this is where many evangelicals fall short. The following general reference works are representative of the many scholarly books on psychology and sociology available at the present time.

International Encyclopedia of Psychiatry, Psychology, Psycho-Analysis, and Neurology, edited by B. B. Wolman (12 vols., 1977), contains much that pastors engaged in an extensive counseling ministry—or students pursuing the study of human nature and its needs—will find valuable. Over 1,500 authors contributed articles to this encyclopedia. Coverage includes an objective description on the present status of research followed by a discussion of the different methods of counseling. Frequent cross-references are found, and most articles contain bibliographies.

Obviously, a researcher is not expected to agree with the opinions expressed by those whose articles he consults. In this encyclopedia, however, there is such an abundance of information in such articles as "Adolescence," "Aged," "Cognition," "Communication," "Death," "Depression," "Emotions," "Family," "Father," "Group Dynamics," "Leadership," "Mass Media," et cetera, that a person will find his mental processes stimulated whether he agrees with the viewpoint of the writer or not.

Of significance is the extensive treatment given the subject of marriage. In addition to describing current aspects of contemporary marriages, there is also a discussion of the origins and development of marital conflict. Various theories of conflict resolution are outlined with an analysis of changing family roles. Helpful evaluations of each theory and method of counseling conclude each section.

Biographical sketches of deceased psychologists or psychiatrists enhance the overall usefulness of this work.

Volume twelve contains the indices. These include an alphabetical listing of the contents of volumes one through eleven, a name index indicating where a significant person's work is cited, and a helpful subject index.

The *International Encyclopedia of the Social Sciences,* edited by David L. Sills (17 vols., 1968), although similar in scope to the *Encyclopedia of the Social Sciences* (15 vols., 1930-35), is designed to complement rather than supplement its predecessor. Articles are arranged alphabetically by subject and cover all aspects of social studies, including anthropology economics, geography, history, law, political science, psychiatry, psychology, and statistics.

With articles arranged alphabetically by topic (as opposed to being arranged under each of the above-mentioned disciplines) and with specific articles that share the same general subject matter being grouped together, the use of the index (volume seventeen) is essential.

Biographical articles of approximately 600 scholars (including John Calvin, Martin Luther) have been included, together with sociological articles on all the major religions (e.g., Islam, Judaism), the role of monasticism, and the relationship of negativism to revivalism.

Other excellent articles include "Aging," "Leadership" (including psychological, sociological, and political aspects), "Loyalty," "Marriage," "Near Eastern Society," et cetera.

A list of the contributors along with an alphabetical list of articles, a classification of each article under broad headings, and a general index are in volume seventeen.

This is an indispensable work, and a few minutes spent perusing the index will be sufficient to spark the imagination of the alert reader to a variety of topics where secular research can be compared to biblical teaching.

The Harper Encyclopedia of Bible Life by Madeline S. Miller and J. Lane Miller (revised by B. M. Bennett, Jr., and D. H. Scott, 1978), is arranged topically under three major headings, "The World of the Bible," "How the People of the Bible Lived," and "How the People of the Bible Worked," and has received the praise of scholars of all persuasions.

The third edition differs from previous editions, which consisted of sections arranged alphabetically by topic. This latest revision, although more difficult to use, has the advantage of being more up to date. However it is not encyclopedic, and the lengthy essays bear more of a relationship to Roland de Vaux's *Ancient Israel* than to an "encyclopedia" of Bible life.

As with the previous editions, this work is beautifully illustrated. The theological bias of the authors is still present, although it is less obvious than in previous editions. (It still may be seen in their dating of specific events.) *The Harper Encyclopedia* is nevertheless of considerable value if used with discernment.

A related work by W. Corswant, *A Dictionary of Life in Bible Times* (translated by A. Heathcote, 1960), may also be consulted with profit.

ADDITIONAL NOTE—BIBLIOGRAPHIC RESEARCH

Bibliographic research (the term applied by librarians to the task of researching written records) involves the use of nearly all the library's resources. It is devoted almost exclusively to the examination of the published writings of others. It involves "seeking out again" what others have uncovered. The information is gleaned from a variety of sources, then subjected to fresh evaluation and verification. The factual data that remains is then analyzed and interpreted. That is done so that sound conclusions may be drawn from what past writers have left to posterity. The results are integrated with new information and eventually others will build upon our contribution.

The steps involved in research have been elaborated on in books specifically devoted to the writing of research projects.* The steps may be described as:

- Choosing a topic
- Gathering information
- Evaluating the data
- Organizing the ideas
- Writing, editing, and rewriting the material.

In assigning topics for research, professors may be either specific or general. They may provide you with specifics in the form of the broad limits of a subject (e.g., "Write on the tension between law and grace in Galatians"), or the assignment may be more flexible (e.g., "Write on some facet of Arian Christianity"). When this is done your task is comparatively easy. All you need to do is isolate some specific facet of the topic under consideration. That can be done quite easily by referring to a general reference works first and then to specialized research tools that will provide you with easy access to information in books, periodical articles, and unpublished essays or reports.

On the other hand, if the topic you are to research is stated in general terms (e.g., "Write on any subject covered in the syllabus") then your task is more difficult. In order to begin narrowing down a topic, you may wish to begin by reading encyclopedia articles that will give you some understanding of the breadth of the assignment. Then you should be able to discern trends and the people connected with them. Quite unconsciously you will have begun to narrow down the field of study while identifying possible themes for your paper. As soon as you come across something that excites you and gives promise of providing a fruitful field of investigation, you can begin gathering data on your topic.

Whether your topic is stated in specific or general terms, it is wise to write out as soon as possible exactly what you plan to do in your paper. To say "I've decided to write on 'Mackay of Africa' " (for your paper in missions), or "I want to write on 'the Influence of John Amos Comenius on American Christian education' " (for a paper in Christian education), is not good enough. You will need to isolate some more specific aspect of the topic that merits investigation.

You should also feel free to revise and refine the theme as new information is filtered through your mind. In refining your theme you may find it helpful to divide up the subject into logical parts. Ask yourself questions: *who* (the people involved); *what* (problems, ideas, things); *where* (place); *when* (time—past, present, impact on the future); *why* (causes, reason, conditions,

---

*T. Hillway, *Introduction to Research*, 2d ed. (Boston: Houghton Mifflin, 1964); R. Berry, *How to Write a Research Paper* (Elmsford, N.Y., Pergamon); L. Knowles, *A Guide for Writing Research Papers, Theses, and Dissertations* (Los Angeles: Tam's Books, 1973); K. L. Turabian, *Student's Guide for Writing College Papers*, 3d expanded ed. (Chicago: U. of Chicago, 1977).

results). In subsequent chapters additional ideas will be given on how to refine a topic.

Once you have some general knowledge of the area you wish to investigate and have narrowed your topic, you are in a position to begin gathering data. This may be done initially from bibliographies at the end of the encyclopedia articles or books you have consulted. *The cutting edge of research, however, is in journal articles and books of essays* (including Festschriften). These articles and essays can easily be located through the use of indices and abstracts (see Chapters 11 and 12).

As you gather information, it is important to keep a record (either on index cards or separate sheets of paper) of the bibliographic data to which you refer. This information consists of the name of the author, the title of the work, the date of publication, where the work was published, the publisher, and the pages involved. These cards or slips of paper may then be kept in alphabetical order and referred to as needed.

You may also wish to make brief notes to remind you of the strengths or weaknesses of the material, whether or not it contains quotable data, and what position is held by the writer.

Where insufficient information is cited in the bibliographies, take down as much as is given you. Additional information can nearly always be obtained by consulting the National Union Catalog of the Library of Congress (NUC) for American publications, or the General Catalog of the British Museum for British publications.

If done correctly, the method of collecting data advocated here and elsewhere in this book should provide you with more than enough information. You will then be in the happy position of being able to select from a surplus of material to produce qualitatively better research papers. The remainder of the task (namely, evaluating the information, organizing the ideas, allowing time for reflection, and writing the paper) can be more readily incorporated into your schedule.

Your final bibliography will reflect the breadth and depth of your research.

ASSIGNMENT

In preparation for the more specialized reference works to be covered in the next chapter, works dealing with: (1) places mentioned in the Bible, (2) commentaries expounding the Bible, and (3) concordances to the Bible, consider the following portions of Scripture:
- David's being forced to flee for his life from the presence of King Saul (1 Samuel 20-27)
- The statement of the Lord Jesus in Luke 4:18-19
- The apostle Paul's usage of the word *law*.

1. By consulting *Baker's Bible Atlas* and the *Macmillan Bible Atlas* trace: (a) David's journeys from Gibeah to Ramah, and eventually to Gath and Ziklag;

and (b) the footsteps of the Lord Jesus following His baptism by John back to Nazareth. Where is the traditional site of the temptation? Which of these atlases did you find most helpful? When would you use it? Which are the strengths and weaknesses of both works?

2. By consulting *law* in Strong's *Exhaustive Concordance of the Bible* and the *New American Standard Exhaustive Concordance of the Bible* determine how frequently the apostle Paul used the word in each of his epistles? Where is its usage most common? Is its meaning always the same? How would you distinguish between references to: (a) the moral law, (b) the law of Moses, and (c) the books of the law? As you compare these concordances, which do you prefer? Why?

3. The quotation from Isaiah appearing in the context of Luke 4:14-21 can be validly researched in both Testaments. Use the following reference works:
  • *Expositors's Bible Commentary*
  • *Interpreter's Bible*
  • Keil and Delitzsch's *Biblical Commentary on the Old Testament* for Isaiah 61:1-3, and R. C. H. Lenski's *Interpretation of the New Testament* for Luke 4:18-19.
Then ascertain: (a) what Christ omitted from Isaiah's quotation; (b) what the respective commentators have to say about each passage; and (c) the reasons they give for the omission. What do you believe to be the attitude of each commentator toward the integrity of Scripture?

5

NEW DIMENSIONS
IN BIBLE STUDY

In his introduction to the *Ryrie Study Bible* (p. v), Dr. Charles C. Ryrie comments, "The Bible is the greatest of all books; to study it is the noblest of all pursuits; to understand it, the highest of all goals."

Bible study should be exciting. For many, however, its message seems to be "sealed" (Dan. 8:26, RSV), and they lack the necessary knowledge and skill to unlock its treasures.

Certain basic reference tools can make all the difference in the world to the would-be Bible student. These include the use of a Bible atlas, a Bible concordance, and Bible commentaries. Each of these works will enhance one's study of God's Word and contribute toward the building of a solid, biblically-oriented approach to life.

BIBLE ATLASES

Bible atlases, it seems, are available in almost every bookstore. Each publisher has its own, and the differing nature and variety of those available is sufficient to boggle the mind of the researcher. Evaluations of different atlases have been provided in *The Minister's Library,* pp. 72-77; Bollier's *The Literature of Theology,* pp. 89-91; and Danker's *Multipurpose Tools for Bible Study,* pp. 222-23.

In our discussion we will limit ourselves to only three of the many Bible atlases available today:

- *Baker's Bible Atlas*
- *Macmillan Bible Atlas*

• *Westminster Bible Atlas.*

Baker's Bible Atlas, edited by C. F. Pfeiffer (2d ed., 1961), is the product of moderately conservative evangelical scholarship. The atlas surveys all of Bible history, is enhanced with color maps, contains numerous black-and-white pictures, and is accompanied by comments on the text that will richly reward the reader. Pfeiffer's chronology, particularly in the first edition, was faulty, but those errors have been rectified in the later edition.

The Macmillan Bible Atlas, edited by Y. Aharoni and M. Avi-Yonah (2 ed., 1977), was prepared by two Jewish scholars. It contains maps identifying biblical sites and events and follows the chronology of the Bible (though some of the dating is questionable). It may be used to good effect whenever one is studying a historical book of the Bible. Concentration is on the Holy Land, and so it lacks treatment of the expansion of the early church.

The Westminster Historical Atlas to the Bible, by G. E. Wright and F. B. Filson (revised ed., 1956), has been attractively produced, and at one time represented the epitome of liberal biblical scholarship. This work nevertheless is worth consulting because it includes a discussion of historical events, illustrates specific happenings with evidence from archaeology, and succeeds in illuminating the biblical text. It is well indexed and includes an index to Arabic names.

By means of an atlas you will be able to locate the places sacred to those living in Palestine (Shechem, Bethel, Shiloh, Mizpah, Zion), and you will be able to trace the movements of peoples and armies (e.g., the route of the Exodus; the settlement of the twelve tribes in Canaan; and attacks upon Jerusalem by Syrians, Assyrians, Babylonians, Egyptians). You will also come to understand the significance of events mentioned in the Bible (e.g., the routing of Sisera's army, Judges 4; the location of Joppa, Tarshish, and Nineveh in the book of Jonah; the proximity of Bethpage and Bethany to the Mount of Olives, Luke 19:29), and a host of other details.

BIBLE CONCORDANCES

There are Bible concordances to virtually every translation available: *A New Translation* (Moffat), *Revised Standard Version, The Living Bible,* and the *New American Standard Bible.* For an enumeration of some of these reference tools see *The Minister's Library,* pp. 47-48; Bollier's *The Literature of Theology,* pp. 78-80; and Danker's *Multipurpose Tools for Bible Study,* pp. 1-17.

Most people use a concordance when they are trying to locate a verse in the Bible. Concordances, however, have many other uses. They can be used in the following ways.

• Ascertain the usage of a word (e.g., compassion, constrain), because it is the usage of the word that determines its meaning.

• Learn the different shades of meaning of a word—nuances that are not

650 Man MAIN CONCORDANCE.

Ge 25: 9 the Hittite, which is before M': 4471
35: 27 came unto Isaac his father unto M'."
49: 30 Machpelah, which is before M'. "
50: 13 of Ephron the Hittite, before M'. "
man See also BONDMAN; CRAFTSMAN; DAYSMAN; FREEMAN; HARVESTMAN; HERDMAN; HORSEMAN; HUSBANDMAN; KINSMAN; MAN'S; MANSERVANT; MANSLAYER; MANKIND; MEN; NOBLEMAN; PLOWMAN; SPOKESMAN; WATCHMAN; WOMAN; WORKMAN.
Ge 1: 26 said, Let us make m' in our image, 120
27 So God created m' in his own image."
2: 5 there was not a m' to till the ground."
7 Lord God formed m' of the dust of "
7 of life; and m' became a living soul."
8 he put the m' whom he had formed. "
15 the Lord God took the m', and put "
16 the Lord God commanded the m', "
18 good that the m' should be alone; "
22 the Lord God had taken from m', "
22 woman, and brought her unto the m'."
23 because she was taken out of M'. 376
24 shall a m' leave his father and his "
25 both naked, the m' and his wife, 120
3: 12 the m' said, The woman whom thou "
22 m' is become as one of us, to know "
24 So he drove out the m'; and he "
4: 1 I have gotten a m' from the Lord. 376
23 I have slain a m' to my wounding, "
23 and a young m' to my hurt.
5: 1 In the day that God created m', in 120
6: 3 shall not always strive with m', "
5 that the wickedness of m' was great,"
6 repented the Lord...he had made m' "
7 will destroy m' whom I have created"
7 both m', and beast, and the creeping"
9 Noah was a just m' and perfect in 376
7: 21 upon the earth, and every m': 120
23 both m', and cattle, and the creeping"
9: 5 I require it, and at the hand of m'; "
5 brother will I require the life of m'. "
6 blood, by m' shall his blood be shed: "
6 for in the image of God made he m'. "
13: 16 if a m' can number the dust of the 376
16: 12 And he will be a wild m'; his hand*120
12 his hand will be against every m', and
17: 10 Every m' child among you shall *2145
12 every m' child in your generations,*"
14 the uncircumcised m' child whose* "
18: 7 good, and gave it unto a young m';*
19: 8 which have not known m'; 376
9 And they pressed sore upon the m', "
31 not a m' in the earth to come in unto"
20: 7 therefore restore the m' his wife; * "
24: 16 neither had any m' known her: "
21 m' wondering at her held his peace, "
22 the m' took a golden earring of half "
26 And the m' bowed down his head, "
29 and Laban ran out unto the m', unto"
30 saying, Thus spake the m' unto me; "
30 that he came unto the m'; and, "
32 And the m' came into the house: "
58 unto her, Wilt thou go with this m'? "
61 the camels, and followed the m': "
65 m' is this that walketh in the field "
25: 8 old age, an old m', and full of years;
27 a cunning hunter, a m' of the field; 376
27 and Jacob was a plain m', dwelling "
26: 11 He that toucheth this m' or his wife "
13 m' waxed great, and went forward, "
27: 11 is a hairy m', and I am a smooth m': "
29: 19 that I should give her to another m':"
30: 43 And the m' increased exceedingly, "
31: 50 my daughters, no m' is with us; "
32: 24 there wrestled a m' with him until "
34: 19 the young m' deferred not to do the
25 brethren, took each m' his sword, 376
37: 15 And a certain m' found him, and, "
15 and the m' asked him, saying, What "
17 And the m' said, They are departed "
38: 25 By the m', whose these are, am I "
39: 2 Joseph, and he was a prosperous m';"
40: 5 them, each m' his dream in one night,"
5 m' according to the interpretation "
41: 11 m' according to the interpretation "
12 there was there with us a young m', "
12 each m' according to his dream he "
33 look out a m' discreet and wise, "
38 a m' in whom the Spirit of God is? "
44 shall no m' lift up his hand or foot in"
42: 13 twelve brethren, the sons of one m' "
30 The m', who is the lord of the land, "
33 the m', the lord of the country, said "
43: 3 The m' did solemnly protest unto us,"
5 the m' said unto us, Ye shall not see "
6 as to tell the m' whether ye had yet a"
7 m' asked us straitly of our state, "
11 carry down the m' a present, a little "
13 and arise, go again unto the m': "
14 God...give you mercy before the m', "
17 And the m' did as Joseph bade; "
17, 24 m' brought the men into Joseph's"
27 well, the old m' of whom ye spake?
44: 11 took down every m' his sack to the 376
11 and opened every m' his sack, "
13 clothes, and laded every m' his ass, "
15 such a m' as I can certainly divine? "
17 but the m' in whose hand the cup is "
20 We have a father, an old m', and a "
45: 1 Cause every m' to go out from me. "
1 there stood no m' with him, while "
22 he gave each m' changes of raiment;"
47: 20 Egyptians sold every m' his field, "
49: 6 for in their anger they slew a m', "
Ex 1: 1 every m' and his household came "
2: 1 there went a m' of the house of Levi,"
Ex 2: 12 when he saw that there was no m', 376
20 why is it that ye have left the m'? "
21 was content to dwell with the m': "
7: 12 For they cast down every m' his rod, "
8: 17 it became lice in m', and in beast; 120
18 were lice upon m', and upon beast. "
9: 9, 10 forth with blains upon m', and "
19 for upon every m' and beast which "
22 hail in all the land of Egypt, upon m',"
25 was in the field, both m' and beast; "
10: 7 long shall this m' be a snare unto us?
11: 2 every m' borrow of his neighbour, 376
3 m' Moses was very great in the land "
7 a dog move his tongue, against m' or"
12: 3 shall take to them every m' a lamb, "
4 m' according to his eating shall * "
12 firstborn...both m' and beast; 120
16 save that which every m' must eat,5315
13: 2 both of m' and of beast: it is mine. 120
13 firstborn of m' among thy children "
15 of Egypt, both the firstborn of m', "
15: 3 The Lord is a m' of war: the Lord 376
16: 16 it every m' according to his eating, "
16 an omer for every m', according *1538
16 take ye every m' for them which are376
18 every m' according to his eating. "
19 no m' leave of it till the morning. "
21 every m' according to his eating: "
22 much bread, two omers for one m':*
29 m' in his place, let no m' go out of 376
19: 13 whether it be beast or m', it shall "
21: 7 And if a m' sell his daughter to be a "
12 He that smiteth a m', so that he die, "
13 And if a m' lie not in wait, but God
14 a m' come presumptuously upon his376
16 he that stealeth a m', and selleth "
20 And if a m' smite his servant, or his "
26 if a m' smite the eye of his servant, "
28 If an ox gore a m' or a woman, that "
29 that he hath killed a m' or a woman; "
33 And if a m' shall open a pit, or if "
33 a m' shall dig a pit, and not cover it, "
22: 1 If a m' shall steal an ox, or a sheep, "
5 If a m' shall cause a field or "
7 If a m'...deliver unto his neighbour "
10 If a m' deliver unto his neighbour "
10 hurt, or driven away, no m' seeing it:
14 And if a m' borrow ought of his 376
16 And if a m' entice a maid that is not "
23: 3 shalt thou countenance a poor m' in
24: 14 if any m' have any matters to do, *1167
25: 2 of every m' that giveth it willingly 376
30: 12 give every m' a ransom for his soul "
32: 1, 23 the m' that brought us up out of "
27 Put every m' his sword by his side, "
27 camp, and slay every m' his brother, "
27 and every m' his companion, "
27 and every m' his neighbour. "
29 every m' upon his son, and upon his "
33: 4 no m' did put on him his ornaments."
8 stood every m' at his tent door, and "
10 worshipped, every m' in his tent door."
11 as a m' speaketh unto his friend. "
11 the son of Nun, a young m', departed
20 face: for there shall no m' see me, 120
34: 3 And no m' shall come up with thee,376
3 neither let...m' be seen throughout "
24 neither shall any m' desire thy land, "
35: 22 every m' that offered offered an "
23, 24 every m', with whom was found "
29 every m' and woman, whose heart "
36: 1 every wise hearted m', in whom the "
2 and every wise hearted m', in whose "
4 came every m' from his work which "
6 Let neither m' nor woman make any"
8 every wise hearted m' among them
38: 26 A bekah for every m', that is, half*1538
Le 1: 2 m' of you bring an offering unto 120
5: 3 Or if he touch the uncleanness of m', "
3 be that a m' shall be defiled withal,*
4 a m' shall pronounce with an oath, 120
6: 3 of all these that a m' doeth, sinning "
7: 21 as the uncleanness of m', or any "
12: 2 conceived seed,...born a m' child: 2145
13: 2 a m' shall have in the skin of his 120
9 the plague of leprosy is in a m', then"
29 If a m' or woman have a plague 376
38 If a m' also or a woman have in the "
40 m' whose hair is fallen off his head, "
44 He is a leprous m', he is unclean: "
14: 11 present the m' that is to be clean, "
15: 2 When any m' hath a running issue "
18 The woman also with whom m' shall"
24 if any m' lie with her at all, and her "
33 of the m', and of the woman, and 2145
16: 17 shall be no m' in the tabernacle of 120
21 away by the hand of a fit m' in the 376
17: 3 What m' soever there be of the house"
4 shall be imputed unto that m'; he "
4 that m' shall be cut off from among "
8 Whatsoever m' there be of the house"
9 even that m' shall be cut off from "
10 whatsoever m' there be of the house "
13 And whatsoever m' there be of the "
18: 5 which if a m' do, he shall live in 120
19: 3 Ye shall fear every m' his mother, 376
32 honour the face of the old m', and
20: 3 I will set my face against that m', 376
4 ways hide their eyes from the m', "
5 I will set my face against that m', "
10 m' that committeth adultery with "
11 m' that lieth with his father's wife "
12 if a m' lie with his daughter in law, "
13 If a m' also lie with mankind, as he "
14 if a m' take a wife and her mother, "
15 And if a m' lie with a beast, he shall "
Le 20: 17 And if a m' shall take his sister, his 376
18 if a m' shall lie with a woman having"
20 if a m' shall lie with his uncle's wife,"
21 if a m' shall take his brother's wife, "
27 A m' also or woman that hath a "
21: 4 being a chief m' among his people,1167
18 m' he be that hath a blemish, he 376
18 a blind m', or a lame, or he that hath"
19 Or a m' that is brokenfooted, or "
21 No m' that hath a blemish of the "
22: 4 What m' soever of the seed of Aaron"
4 or a m' whose seed goeth from him; "
5 or a m' of whom he may take 120
14 And if a m' eat of the holy thing 376
24: 10 a m' of Israel strove together in the "
17 And he that killeth any m' shall5315,120
19 m' cause a blemish in his 376
20 he hath caused a blemish in a m', 120
21 he that killeth a m', he shall be put "
25: 10 return every m' unto his possession,376
10 return every m' unto his family: "
13 return every m' unto his possession. "
26 And if the m' have none to redeem it,"
27 restore the overplus unto the m' to "
29 And if a m' sell a dwelling house in a"
33 And if a m' purchase of the Levites,*
27: 2 a m' shall make a singular vow, the376
9 all that any m' giveth of such unto
14 when a m' shall sanctify his house 376
16 if a m' shall sanctify unto the Lord "
20 he have sold the field to another m', "
22 And if a m' sanctify unto the Lord a*
26 firstling, no m' shall sanctify it; 376
28 that m' shall devote unto the Lord "
28 that he hath, both of m' and beast, 120
31 m' will at all redeem ought of his 376
Nu 1: 4 there shall be a m' of every tribe; "
52 tents, every m' by his own camp, "
52 and every m' by his own standard, "
2: 2 Every m' of the children of Israel "
17 m' in his place by their standards. "
3: 13 in Israel, both m' and beast: 120
5: 6 m' or woman shall commit any sin 376
8 But if the m' have no kinsman to "
10 whatsoever any m' giveth the priest,"
13 a m' lie with her carnally, and it be "
15 the m' bring his wife unto the priest,"
19 If no m' have lain with thee, and if "
20 some m' have lain with thee beside "
31 the m' be guiltless from iniquity, "
6: 2 either m' or woman shall separate "
9 if any m' die very suddenly by him,
7: 5 every m' according to his service. 376
8: 17 Israel are mine, both m' and beast: 120
9: 6 defiled by the dead body of a m', "
7 are defiled by the dead body of a m':"
10 if any m' of you or of your posterity376
13 But the m' that is clean, and is not "
13 season, that m' shall bear his sin. "
11: 10 every m' in the door of his tent; "
27 there ran a young m', and told Moses,
12: 3 the m' Moses was very meek, above376
13: 2 of their fathers shall ye send a m', "
14: 15 shalt kill all this people as one m', "
15: 32 a m' that gathered sticks upon the * "
35 The m' shall be surely put to death: "
16: 7 the m' whom the Lord doth choose, "
17 take every m' his censer, and put "
17 before the Lord every m' his censer, "
18 they took every m' his censer, and "
22 shall one m' sin, and wilt thou be "
17: 9 looked, and took every m' his rod. "
18: 15 firstborn of m' shalt thou surely 120
19: 9 a m' that is clean shall gather up the 376
11 the dead body of any m' shall be 120
13 dead body of any m' that is dead, "
14 the law, when a m' dieth in a tent: "
16 or a dead body, or a bone of a m', "
20 But the m' that shall be unclean, 376
21: 9 if a serpent had bitten any m', "
23: 19 God is not a m', that he should lie; "
19 neither the son of m', that he should120
24: 3, 15 the m' whose eyes are open hath1397
25: 8 he went after the m' of Israel into 376
8 the m' of Israel, and the woman "
26: 64 there was not a m' of them whom "
65 there was not left a m' of them, save"
27: 8 If a m' die, and have no son, then ye "
16 flesh, set a m' over the congregation,"
18 a m' in whom is the spirit, and lay "
30: 2 If a m' vow a vow unto the Lord, or "
16 Moses, between a m' and his wife. "
31: 17 hath known m' by lying with 376,2145
18 not known a m' by lying with him, "
26 was taken, both of m' and of beast, 120
35 not known m' by lying with him. 2145
47 both of m' and of beast, and gave 120
49 and there lacketh not one m' of us. 376
50 what every m' hath gotten, of jewels"
53 taken spoil, every m' for himself.) "
32: 18 inherited every m' his inheritance. "
27 pass over, every m' armed for war,
29 every m' armed to battle, before the
35: 23 any stone, wherewith a m' may die,
36: 8 enjoy every m' the inheritance of his376
De 1: 16 between every m' and his brother, "
17 shall not be afraid of the face of m'; "
31 as a m' doth bear his son, in all the "
41 had girded on every m' his weapons "
3: 11 breadth of it, after the cubit of a m'."
20 return every m' unto his possession,"
4: 32 the day that God created m' upon 120
5: 24 that God doth talk with m', and he "
7: 24 shall no m' be able to stand before 375
8: 3 m' doth not live by bread only, but 120
3 the mouth of the Lord doth m' live. "

Fig. 6. Page from Strong's *Exhaustive Concordance of the Bible.*

apparent from the reading of the English text (e.g., Paul's use of "another" twice in Galatians 1:6-7, the first use implying another of the same kind, and the second insisting on its being another of a different kind).

- Trace a biblical writer's emphasis (e.g., Paul's use of "law" in Galatians; the emphasis on "Spirit" in Romans 8; the conflict between "light" and "darkness" and "belief" and "unbelief" in John's gospel and first epistle).
- Observe the growth of an idea or doctrine in the Old and New Testaments (e.g., the development of sacrificial worship, the typology of the Tabernacle, the rise of the monarchy—all of which prefigure truths developed as the Scriptures are unfolded. Some of these truths may point to Christ's Person and work. Such usage follows closely God's progressive revelation).
- Highlight references to places invested with importance in the Bible because of events that transpired in, on, or near them (e.g., Jacob's vow at Bethel, the Israelites frequent return to Gilgal, the Valley of Achor's becoming a, "door of hope," the destruction of the Temple at Shiloh, etc.).
- Develop a distinctively biblical theology through the study of specific words (e.g., reconciliation, redemption, resurrection, revelation, etc.), or through the study of Christ's claim to be the "Son of Man" (some have thought that this term refers to His humanity and that the term "Son of God" refers to His deity. From a study of all the passages in which this expression is used, we are led to conclude that "Son of Man" is a messianic term implying royalty, for Daniel speaks of His "everlasting dominion" and that "all the peoples, nations, and languages shall serve Him" [Dan. 7:27]).

The Bible student, therefore, should be like the scribe of Matthew 13:52, who having become a "disciple of the kingdom of heaven," is like a householder who brings forth out of his "treasure" (i.e., his knowledge of Scripture) things new and old.

In this connection, what concordances are deserving of serious consideration?

You will probably wish to use a concordance that is based on the Bible translation you most frequently use. Helpful ones include the *Analytical Concordance to the Bible* by Robert Young (reprint, 1955), the *Exhaustive Concordance of the Bible* by James Strong (1890), and the *New American Standard Exhaustive Concordance of the Bible* (1981).

Robert Young's *Analytical Concordance to the Bible* is based on the text of the King James Version and lists various Greek and Hebrew words under each English word. It also provides ready reference to each passage in which that word appears. This makes it easy to study words like *faith, love,* and *obedience* and to have listed concisely under each rendering the word or

FORGETFUL 367 FORMER

FORGETFUL, to be —
To forget also or besides, ἐπιλανθάνομαι *epilantha.*
Heb. 13. 2 Be not forgetful to entertain strangers

FORGETFULNESS —
Forgetfulness, נְשִׁיָּה *neshiyyah.*
Psa. 88. 12 thy righteousness in the land of forget.?

FORGIVE, to —
1. *To cover,* כָּפַר *kaphar,* 3.
Psa. 78. 38 But he..full of compassion, forgave (their)
Jer. 18. 23 forgive not their iniquity, neither blot out

2. *To lift up or away,* נָשָׂא *nasa.*
Gen. 50. 17 Forgive..the trespass..forgive the tresp.
Exod 10. 17 Now therefore forgive, I pray thee, my
32. 32 Yet now, if thou wilt forgive their sin
Num 14. 19 and as thou hast forgiven this people
Josh 24. 19 he will not forgive your transgressions
1 Sa. 25. 28 forgive the trespass of thine handmaid
Psa. 25. 18 Look upon..and forgive all my sins
32. 5 and thou forgavest the iniquity of my sin
85. 2 Thou hast forgiven the iniquity of thy p.
99. 8 thou wast a God that forgavest them
Isa. 2. 9 humbleth..therefore forgive them not

3. *To send away, let go,* סָלַח *salach.*
Num 30. 5, 8, 12 and the LORD shall forgive her
1 Ki. 8. 30 hear thou..and when thou hearest, forgive
8. 34 forgive the sin of thy people Israel
8. 36 forgive the sin of thy servants, and of thy
8. 39 in heaven thy dwelling-place, and forgive
8. 50 And forgive thy people that have sinned
2 Ch. 6. 21 hear..and when thou hearest forgive
6. 25 hear thou from the heavens, and forgive
6. 27 hear..and forgive the sin of thy servants
6. 30 forgive, and render unto every man acco.
6. 39 and forgive thy people which have sinned
7. 14 will forgive their sin, and will heal their
Psa. 103. 3 Who forgiveth all thine iniquities; who
Jer. 31. 34 I will forgive their iniquity, and I will re.
36. 3 that I may forgive their iniquity and
Dan. 9. 19 O Lord, forgive; O Lord, hearken and
Amos 7. 2 O Lord GOD, forgive, I beseech thee: by

4. *To loose away,* ἀπολύω *apoluō.*
Luke 6. 37, 37 forgive, and ye shall be forgiven

5. *To be gracious to,* χαρίζομαι *charizomai.*
Luke 7. 43 I suppose..(he) to whom he forgave most
2 Co. 2. 7 So that..ye (ought) rather to forgive (him)
2. 10 To whom ye forgive..for if I forgave
2. 10 any thing, to whom I forgave (it), for your
12. 13 not burdensome to you? forgive me this
Eph. 4. 32 tender-hearted, forgiving one another
4. 32 as God for Christ's sake hath forgiven
Col. 2. 13 quickened..having forgiven you all tres.
3. 13 forgiving one another..as Christ forgave

6. *To send or let off or away,* ἀφίημι *aphiēmi.*
Matt. 6. 12 And forgive us our debts, as we forgive
6. 14 For if ye forgive men their trespasses
6. 14 your heavenly Father will..forgive you
6. 15 if ye forgive not men their trespasses
6. 15 neither will your Father forgive your tr.
9. 2 Son, be of good cheer; thy sins be forgi.
9. 5 sins be forgiven thee; or to say, Arise
9. 6 hath power on earth to forgive sins
12. 31 All manner of sin..shall be forgiven
12. 31 the blasphemy..shall not be forgiven unto
12. 32 the Son of man, it shall be forgiven him
12. 32 it shall not be forgiven him, neither in
18. 21 Lord, how oft shall..I forgive him? till
18. 27 loosed him, and forgave him the debt
18. 32 I forgave thee all that debt, because thou
18. 35 [if ye from your hearts forgive not every]
Mark 2. 5 he said..Son, thy sins be forgiven thee
2. 7 who can forgive sins but God only?
2. 9 sins be forgiven thee; or to say, Arise
2. 10 hath power on earth to forgive sins
3. 28 All sins shall be forgiven unto the sons
4. 12 and (their) sins should be forgiven them
11. 25 forgive..that your Father..may forgive
11. 26 [do not forgive, neither will your F. f.]
Luke 5. 20 said..Man, thy sins are forgiven thee
5. 21 Who can forgive sins, but God alone?
5. 23 Thy sins be forgiven thee; or to say
5. 24 Son of man hath power..to forgive sins
7. 47 Her sins, which are many, are forgiven
7. 47 but to whom little is forgiven..loveth
7. 48 he said unto her, Thy sins are forgiven
7. 49 Who is this that forgiveth sins also?
11. 4 forgive us our sins: for we also forgive
12. 10 shall be forgiven him..it shall not be fo.
17. 3 Take heed..if he repent, forgive him
17. 4 saying, I repent: thou shalt forgive him
23. 34 [Then said Jesus, Father, forgive them]
Acts 8. 22 if perhaps the thought..may be forgiven
Rom. 4. 7 Blessed..they whose iniquities are forgi.
Jas. 5. 15 committed sins, they shall be forgiven
1 Jo. 1. 9 he is faithful and just to forgive us
2. 12 because your sins are forgiven you for

FORGIVE frankly, to —
To be gracious to, χαρίζομαι *charizomai.*
Luke 7. 42 nothing..he frankly forgave them both

FORGIVE, ready to —
Sending away, letting go, סַלָּח *sallach.*
Psa. 86. 5 thou, LORD, (art) good, and ready to forg.

FORGIVEN —
To lift up or away, נָשָׂא *nasa.*
Psa. 32. 1 (is he whose) transgression (is) forgiven
Isa. 33. 24 the people..(shall be) forgiven..iniquity

FORGIVEN, to be —
1. *To be covered,* כָּפַר *kaphar,* 7.
Deut 21. 8 And the blood shall be forgiven them

2. *To be sent away, let go,* סָלַח *salach,* 2.
Lev. 4. 20, 26, 31, 35 and it shall be forgiven
5. 10, 13, 16, 18 and it shall be forgiven him
6. 7 it shall be forgiven him for any thing
19. 22 the sin..he hath done shall be forgiven
Num 15. 25, 26, 28, and it shall be forgiven

FORGIVENESS —
1. *A sending away, letting go,* סְלִיחָה *selichah.*
Psa. 130. 4 But..forgiveness with thee, that thou
Dan. 9. 9 To the Lord our God..forgivenesses

2. *A sending away, letting go,* ἄφεσις *aphesis.*
Mark 3. 29 hath never forgiveness, but is in danger
Acts 5. 31 a Saviour..to give..forgiveness of sins
13. 38 is preached unto you the forgiveness of
26. 18 that they may receive forgiveness of sins
Eph. 1. 7 In whom we have..the forgiveness of
Col. 1. 14 In whom we have..the forgiveness of

FORGIVING —
1. *To lift up or away,* נָשָׂא *nasa.*
Exod 34. 7 forgiving iniquity and transgression
Num 14. 18 forgiving iniquity and transgression

2. *To be gracious to,* χαρίζομαι *charizomai.*
Eph. 4. 32 tender-hearted, forgiving one another
Col. 3. 13 Forbearing..and forgiving one another

FORGOTTEN —
To be forgotten, שָׁכַח *shakach,* 2.
Job 28. 4 forgotten of the foot: they are dried up

FORGOTTEN, to be —
1. *To be forgotten,* נָשָׁה *nashah,* 2.
Isa. 44. 21 O Israel, thou shalt not be forgotten of

2. *To be forgotten,* שָׁכַח *shakach,* 2.
Gen. 41. 30 the plenty shall be forgotten in the land
Deut 31. 21 shall not be forgotten out of the
Psa. 9. 18 the needy shall not alway be forgotten
31. 12 I am forgotten as a dead man out of
Eccl. 2. 16 that which now (is)..shall all be forgot.
9. 5 for the memory of them is forgotten
Isa. 23. 15 Tyre shall be forgotten seventy years
23. 16 thou harlot that hast been forgotten
65. 16 because the former troubles are forgotten
Jer. 20. 11 everlasting confusion shall never be forg.
23. 40 shame, which shall not be forgotten
50. 5 covenant (that) shall not be forgotten

3. *To be or become forgotten,* שָׁכַח *shakach,* 7.
Eccl. 8. 10 they were forgotten in the city where

FORGOTTEN, to cause to be —
To cause to forget, שָׁכַח *shakach,* 3.
Lam. 2. 6 hath caused the..sabbaths to be forgot.

FORK —
Triple fork, שְׁלֹשׁ קִלְּשׁוֹן *shelosh qilleshon.*
1 Sa. 13. 21 for the coulters, and for the forks, and

FORM —
1. *Sight, appearance, vision,* מַרְאֶה *mareh.*
Job 4. 16 I could not discern the form thereof

2. *Judgment, rule,* מִשְׁפָּט *mishpat.*
2 Ch. 4. 7 candlesticks..according to their form

3. *Face,* פָּנִים *panim.*
2 Sa. 14. 20 To fetch about this form of speech hath

4. *Form, sharp outline,* צוּרָה *tsurah.*
Eze. 43. 11 show them the form of the house, and the
43. 11 the forms thereof..all the forms thereof
43. 11 that they may keep the whole form ther.

5. *Image, shadow,* צֶלֶם *tselem.*
Dan. 3. 19 the form of his visage was changed against

6. *Appearance, sight,* רֵו *rev.*
Dan. 2. 31 image..and the form thereof (was) terri.
3. 25 form of the fourth is like the Son of God

7. *Form, visage,* תֹּאַר *toar.*
1 Sa. 28. 14 he said unto her, What form (is) he of?
Isa. 52. 14 and his form more than the sons of men
53. 2 For..he hath no form nor comeliness

8. *Pattern, form, building,* תַּבְנִית *tabnith.*
Eze. 8. 3 he put forth the form of an hand, and
8. 10 behold, every form of creeping things
10. 8 appeared..the form of a man's hand

9. *Form,* μορφή *morphē.*
Mark 16. 12 [he appeared in another form unto two]
Phil. 2. 6 Who, being in the form of God, thought
2. 7 took upon him the form of a servant

10. *Form, appearance,* μόρφωσις *morphōsis.*
Rom. 2. 20 which hast the form of knowledge and of
2 Ti. 3. 5 Having a form of godliness, but denying

11. *Type, impress,* τύπος *tupos.*
Rom. 6. 17 that form of doctrine which was delivered

12. *Under type, outline,* ὑποτύπωσις *hupotupōsis.*
2 Ti. 1. 13 Hold fast the form of sound words, which

FORM, to —
1. *To bring forth (in pain),* חִיל, חוּל *chil,* 3a.
Deut 32. 18 and hast forgotten God that formed thee
Job 26. 13 his hand..formed the crooked serpent
Psa. 90. 2 or ever thou hadst formed the earth and
Prov. 26. 10 The great (God), that formed all..both

2. *To form, fashion, frame, constitute,* יָצַר *yatsar.*
Gen. 2. 7 the LORD God formed man (of) the dust
2. 8 there he put the man..he had formed
2. 19 God formed every beast of the field
2 Ki. 19. 25 of ancient times that I have formed it?
Psa. 94. 9 he that formed the eye, shall he not see?
95. 5 and his hands formed the dry (land)
Isa. 27. 11 he that formed them will show them no
37. 26 Hast thou not heard..that I..formed it?
43. 1 thus saith..he that formed thee, O Israel
43. 7 I have formed him; yea, I have made
43. 21 This people have I formed for myself
44. 2 LORD that made thee, and formed thee
44. 10 Who hath formed a god, or molten a
44. 21 I have formed thee; thou (art) my servant
44. 24 he that formed thee from the womb
45. 7 I form the light, and create darkness
45. 18 God himself that formed the earth and
45. 18 he formed it to be inhabited: I (am) the
49. 5 And now, saith the LORD that formed me
Jer. 1. 5 Before I formed thee in the belly I knew
10. 16 [he (is) the former of all .. and Israel (is)]
33. 2 the LORD that formed it, to establish it
Amos 4. 13 For, lo, he that formeth the mountains
7. 1 he formed grasshoppers in the beginning
Zech. 12. 1 formeth the spirit of man within him

3. *To form,* μορφόω *morphoō.*
Gal. 4. 19 I travail in birth..until Christ be formed

4. *To shape, mould,* πλάσσω *plassō.*
Rom. 9. 20 say to him that formed (it), Why hast thou
1 Ti. 2. 13 For Adam was first formed, then Eve

FORM, without —
A ruin, vacancy, תֹּהוּ *tohu.*
Gen. 1. 2 And the earth was without form, and
Jer. 4. 23 and, lo, (it was) without form and void

FORMED, thing —
Thing moulded or shaped, πλάσμα *plasma.*
Rom. 9. 20 Shall the thing formed say..Why hast

FORMED, to be —
1. *To be brought forth (in pain),* חִיל, חוּל *chil,* 4a.
Job 26. 5 Dead (things) are formed from under

2. *To be formed, fashioned, framed,* יָצַר *yatsar,* 2.
Isa. 43. 10 before me there was no God formed

3. *To be formed, fashioned, framed,* יָצַר *yatsar,* 6.
Isa. 54. 17 No weapon that is formed against thee

4. *To be moved, kneaded, formed,* קָרַץ *qarats,* 4.
Job 33. 6 Behold..I also am formed out of the clay

FORMER —
1. *To form, constitute, fashion, frame,* יָצַר *yatsar.*
Jer. 51. 19 for he (is) the former of all; Jer. 10. 16

2. *Before, eastern, ancient,* קַדְמוֹנִי *qadmoni.*
Zech 14. 8 half of them toward the former sea
Mal. 3. 4 pleasant unto the LORD..as in former ye.

3. *First, former, foremost,* רִאשׁוֹן *rishon.*
Gen. 40. 13 after the former manner when thou wast
Num 21. 26 who had fought against the former king
Deut 24. 4 Her former husband, which sent her
1 Sa. 17. 30 answered him..after the former manner
2 Ki. 1. 14 the two captains of the former fifties with
17. 34 Unto this day they do after the former
17. 40 but they did after their former manner
Neh. 5. 15 But the former governors that (had been)
Psa. 79. 8 O remember not against us former iniqui.
89. 49 where (are) thy former loving kindnesses
Eccl. 1. 11 (There is) no remembrance of former
7. 10 that the former days were better than
Isa. 41. 22 let them show the former things, what
42. 9 the former things are come to pass
43. 9 who..can..show us former things? let
43. 18 Remember ye not the former things
46. 9 Remember the former things of old: for
48. 3 I have declared the former things from
61. 4 shall raise up the former desolations
65. 7 therefore will I measure their former
65. 16 because the former troubles are forgot.
65. 17 and the former shall not be remembered
Jer. 34. 5 the former kings which were before thee
36. 28 and write in it all the former words that
Dan. 11. 29 but it shall not be as the former, or as the
Hag. 2. 9 shall be greater than of the former, saith
Zech. 1. 4 unto whom the former prophets have
7. 7 LORD hath cried by the former prophets
7. 12 sent in his Spirit by the former prophets
8. 11 I (will) not (be)..as in the former days

4. *First, former,* רִישׁוֹן *rishon.*
Job 8. 8 enquire, I pray thee, of the former age

5. *Before, first,* πρότερος *proteros,* -ον.
Eph. 4. 22 concerning the former conversation, the
Heb. 10. 32 call to remembrance the former days, in
1 Pe. 1. 14 according to the former lusts in your ig.

6. *First, foremost,* πρῶτος *prōtos.*
Acts 1. 1 The former treatise have I made, O The.
Rev. 21. 4 for the former things are passed away

FORMER estate —
Former state or condition, קַדְמָה *qadmah.*
Eze. 16. 55, 55 shall return to their former estate
16. 55 shall return to your former estate

FORMER (rain) —
1. *Sprinkling rain,* מוֹרֶה *moreh.*
Joel 2. 23 given you the former rain..former rain

Fig. 7. Page from Young's *Analytical Concordance to the Bible.*

words used in the original languages. It is also interesting to note how different Hebrew and Greek words have been translated by a single English word (e.g., *lord, sleep, son, will*), demonstrating the flexibility as well as the precision of those biblical languages.

Included at the end of Young's work are handy lexicons to the words appearing in the Old and New Testaments.

James Strong's *Exhaustive Concordance of the Bible* is also based on the King James Version and has set a standard of excellence for accuracy and completeness. To the right of each entry is a number directing the researcher to an index at the back that contains information about the word used and its meaning(s) in the original Greek and Hebrew text. For example, under "offering" the number 4503 is indicated. Lower down, the number 8641 is given. How reference is made to 4053 and 8641 in the "Hebrew and Chaldee Dictionary" at the back of the concordance is shown in the accompanying illustrations.

With little technical knowledge of the biblical languages, a researcher may nevertheless avail himself of the scholarship of others.

The *New American Standard Exhaustive Concordance of the Bible* (1981) is patterned after Strong's *Exhaustive Concordance of the Bible*. It lists every word that may be used to locate a verse in the *New American Standard Bible* and also notes the Hebrew, Aramaic, or Greek word from which the English word is translated. More than ten years of work went into the preparation of this volume, and computers were used to compile an alphabetical listing of all English words and their frequency. More than 400,000 entries make up this useful resource tool.

The Hebrew-Aramaic and Greek dictionaries are particularly helpful, and have been arranged in such a way that those lacking a knowledge of the original language may nevertheless be appraised of the root form of the word, the frequency of its occurrence, and its meaning(s).

Having learned how to research biblical information through the use of Bible atlases and concordances, you are now in a position to investigate the viewpoints of others. Such information will generally be found in multivolume Bible commentaries.

BIBLE COMMENTARIES

So many sets of commentaries on the Scriptures have been published that it is hard to isolate the top twelve works with which each researcher should be familiar. Reference can always be made to *The Minister's Library*, pp. 44-47, 92-117, and 138-86; Bollier's *The Literature of Theology*, pp. 81-89; and Danker's *Multipurpose Tools for Bible Study*, pp. 239-73, for information about works not treated in this chapter.

For our purposes we will concentrate on the following multivolume works:

Le 7: 8 burnt offering which he hath o'. 7126
15 eaten the same day that it is o'; *7133
9: 15 slew it, and o' it for sin, as the 2398
16 and o' it according to the manner. 6213
10: 1 o' strange fire before the Lord. 7126
19 day have they o' their sin offering "
16: 1 when they o' before the Lord, and* "
Nu 3: 4 they o' strange fire before the Lord. "
7: 2 over them that were numbered, o': "
10 o' for dedicating of the altar in "
10 o' their offering before the altar. "
12 he that o' his offering the first day "
19 He o' for his offering one silver "
42 prince of the children of Gad, o': *
48 prince of the children of Ephraim, o':*
54 On the eighth day o' Gamaliel the*
60 prince of the children of Benjamin, o':*
66 prince of the children of Dan, o': *
72 prince of the children of Asher, o':*
78 prince of the children of Naphtali, o':*
8: 21 and Aaron o' them as an offering 5130
16: 35 and fifty men that o' incense. 7126
38 for they o' them before the Lord. "
39 they that were burnt had o'; and "
22: 40 And Balak o' oxen and sheep. *2076
23: 2 and Balaam o' on every altar a 5927
4 o' upon every altar a bullock and "
14, 30 o' a bullock and a ram on every "
26: 61 o' strange fire before the Lord. 7126
28: 15 offering unto the Lord shall be o'. 6213
24 o' beside the continual burnt "
31: 52 gold of the offering that they o' 7311
Jos 8: 31 they o' thereon burnt offerings 5927
J'g 5: 2 the people willingly o' themselves.
9 o' themselves willingly among the
6: 28 bullock was o' upon the altar 5927
13: 19 o' it upon a rock unto the Lord: "
20: 26 and o' burnt offerings and peace "
21: 4 and o' burnt offerings and peace "
1Sa 1: 4 the time was that Elkanah o'. *2076
2: 13 that, when any man o' sacrifice, "
6: 14 o' the kine a burnt offering unto 5927
15 of Beth-shemesh o' burnt offerings "
7: 9 lamb, and o' it for a burnt offering "
13: 9 And he o' the burnt offering. "
12 therefore, and o' a burnt offering. "
2Sa 6: 17 David o' burnt offerings and peace "
15: 12 from Giloh, while he o' sacrifices. 2076
24: 25 and o' burnt offerings and peace 5927
1Ki 3: 15 Lord, and o' up burnt offerings, "
15 o' peace offerings, and made a 6213
8: 62 him, o' sacrifice before the Lord. 2076
63 And Solomon o' a sacrifice of peace "
63 he o' unto the Lord, two and twenty "
64 there he o' burnt offerings, and 6213
12: 32 in Judah, and he o' upon the altar. *5927
33 So he o' upon the altar which he * "
33 he o' upon the altar, and burnt * "
22: 43 the people o' and burnt incense *2076
2Ki 3: 20 when the meat offering was o', *5927
27 o' him for a burnt offering upon "
16: 12 to the altar, and o' thereon. "
1Ch 6: 49 his sons o' upon the altar of the 6999
15: 26 they o' seven bullocks and seven *2076
16: 1 they o' burnt sacrifices and peace 7126
21: 26 and o' burnt offerings and peace 5927
29: 6 of the king's work, o' willingly,
9 rejoiced, for that they o' willingly,
9 with perfect heart they o' willingly
17 have willingly o' all these things:
21 o' burnt offerings unto the Lord, 5927
2Ch 1: 6 o' a thousand burnt offerings upon "
4: 6 such things as they o' for the *4639
7: 4 o' sacrifices before the Lord. 2076
5 And king Solomon o' a sacrifice of "
7 there he o' burnt offerings, and the 6213
8: 12 Solomon o' burnt offerings unto 5927
15: 11 o' unto the Lord the same time, *2076
17: 16 willingly o' himself unto the Lord;
24: 14 And they o' burnt offerings in the 5927
29: 7 incense nor o' burnt offerings "
Ezr 1: 6 beside all that was willingly o'.
2: 68 o' freely for the house of God to
3: 3 they o' burnt offerings thereon 5927
4 o' the daily burnt offerings by number,
5 o' the continual burnt offering, *
5 willingly o' a freewill offering 5068
6: 3 the place where they o' sacrifices, *1684
17 o' at the dedication of this house 7127
7: 15 freely o' unto the God of Israel, 5069
8: 25 all Israel there present, had o': 7311
35 o' burnt offerings unto the God of 7126
10: 19 they o' a ram of the flock for their
Ne 11: 2 willingly o' themselves to dwell at
12: 43 that day they o' great sacrifices, 2076
Job 1: 5 o' burnt offerings according to 5927
Isa 57: 6 thou hast o' a meat offering. "
66: 3 oblation, as if he o' swine's blood;* "
Jer 32: 29 they have o' incense unto Baal, 6999
Eze 20: 28 and they o' there their sacrifices, 2076
48: 12 this oblation of the land that is o' *8641
Da 11: 18 the reproach o' by him to cease;
Am 5: 25 Have ye o' unto me sacrifices and *5066
Jon 1: 16 o' a sacrifice unto the Lord, and 2076
Mal 1: 11 in every place incense shall be o' 5066
Ac 7: 41 and o' sacrifice unto the idol, and* 321
42 have ye o' to me slain beasts and *4374
8: 18 was given, he o' them money, "
15: 29 ye abstain from meats o' to idols, *1494
21: 25 themselves from things o' to idols, * "
26 until that an offering should be o' 4374
1Co 8: 1 as touching things o' unto idols, *1494
4 are o' in sacrifice unto idols, * "
7 eat it as a thing o' unto an idol; * "
10 those things which are o' to idols; * "
10: 19 o' in sacrifice to idols is any thing? * "
1Co 10: 28 This is o' in sacrifice unto idols, 1494
Ph'p 2: 17 and if I be o' upon the sacrifice 4689
2Ti 4: 6 For I am now ready to be o', and "
Heb 5: 7 when he had o' up prayers and 4374
7: 27 he did once, when he o' up himself.
9: 7 which he o' for himself, and for *4374
9 were o' both gifts and sacrifices,
14 o' himself without spot to God, 4374
28 once o' to bear the sins of many; "
10: 1 they o' year by year continually * "
2 they not have ceased to be o'? "
8 therein; which are o' by the law; "
12 he had o' one sacrifice for sins "
11: 4 By faith Abel o' unto God a more "
17 when he was tried, o' up Isaac: "
17 o' up his only begotten son, * "
Jas 2: 21 when he had o' Isaac his son upon 399

offereth

Le 6: 26 The priest that o' it for sin shall 2398
7: 8 that o' any man's burnt offering 7126
9 shall be the priest's that o' it. "
16 same day that he o' his sacrifice: "
18 it be imputed unto him that o' it: "
29 He that o' the sacrifice of his peace "
33 o' the blood of the peace offerings, "
17: 8 that o' a burnt offering or sacrifice, 5926
21: 8 for he o' the bread of thy God: he 7126
22: 21 o' a sacrifice of peace offerings unto "
Nu 15: 4 that o' his offering unto the Lord "
Ps 50: 23 Whoso o' praise glorifieth me: 2076
Isa 66: 3 he that o' an oblation, as if he 5927
Jer 48: 35 him that o' in the high places, and "
Mal 2: 12 that o' an offering unto the Lord 5066

offering See also OFFERINGS.

Ge 4: 3 the ground an o' unto the Lord. 4503
4 respect unto Abel and to his o': "
5 and to his o' he had not respect. "
22: 2 and offer him there for a burnt o'
3 and clave the wood for the burnt o',
6 took the wood of the burnt o', and
7 where is the lamb for a burnt o'?
8 himself a lamb for a burnt o': so
13 a burnt o' in the stead of his son.
35: 14 and he poured a drink o' thereon.
Ex 18: 12 took a burnt o' and sacrifices for
25: 2 Israel, that they bring me an o': 8641
2 with his heart ye shall take my o'. "
3 the o' which ye shall take of them; "
29: 14 without the camp: it is a sin o'.
18 it is a burnt o' unto the Lord: it is
18 an o' made by fire unto the Lord.
24 for a wave o' before the Lord.
25 them upon the altar for a burnt o',
25 an o' made by fire unto the Lord.
26 wave it for a wave o' before the Lord:
27 sanctify the breast of the wave o',
27 shoulder of the heave o', which is 8641
28 of Israel; for it is an heave o': "
28 be an heave o' from the children "
28 even their heave o' unto the Lord. "
36 every day a bullock for a sin o'
40 of an hin of wine for a drink o'.
41 to the meat o' of the morning, 4503
41 according to the drink o' thereof,
41 an o' made by fire unto the Lord.
42 This shall be a continual burnt o'
30: 9 nor burnt sacrifice, nor meat o'; 4503
9 neither shall ye pour drink o'
10 year with the blood of the sin o'
13 shekel shall be the o' of the Lord. 8641
14 shall give an o' unto the Lord. "
15 when they give an o' unto the Lord, "
20 minister, to burn o' made by fire
28 altar of burnt o' with all his vessels,
31: 9 the altar of burnt o' with all his
35: 5 among you an o' unto the Lord: 8641
5 let him bring it, an o' of the Lord; "
16 The altar of burnt o', with his
21 they brought the Lord's o' to the 8641
22 that offered offered an o' of gold
24 did offer an o' of silver and brass 8641
24 and brass brought the Lord's o': "
29 of Israel brought a willing o' unto
36: 3 they received of Moses all the o', 8641
6 work for the o' of the sanctuary. "
38: 1 altar of burnt o' of shittim wood:
24 holy place, even the gold of the o', 8573
29 the brass of the o' was seventy "
40: 6 set the altar of the burnt o' before
10 anoint the altar of the burnt o',
29 the altar of burnt o' by the door
29 offered upon it the burnt o' and the
29 and offered upon it...the meat o'; 4503
Le 1: 2 of you bring an o' unto the Lord. *7133
2 ye shall bring your o' of the cattle. * "
3 If his o' be a burnt sacrifice of the* "
4 upon the head of the burnt o';
6 he shall flay the burnt o', and cut
9 an o' made by fire, of a sweet
10 if his o' be of the flocks, namely, *7133
13 an o' made by fire, of a sweet
14 for his o' to the Lord be of fowls, *7133
14 he shall bring his o' of turtledoves, * "
17 an o' made by fire, of a sweet
2: 1 will offer a meat o' unto the Lord, 7133
1 Lord, his o' shall be of fine flour; * "
2 to be an o' made by fire, of a sweet
3 of the meat o' shall be Aaron's 4503
4 of a meat o' baken in the oven, "
5 be a meat o' baken in a pan, it "
6 pour oil thereon: it is a meat o'. "
7 be a meat o' baken in a fryingpan, "
8 thou shalt bring the meat o' that is "
9 priest shall take from the meat o' "
9 it is an o' made by fire, of a sweet
Le 2: 10 is left of the meat o' shall be 4503
11 No meat o', which ye shall bring "
11 in any o' of the Lord made by fire.
13 thy meat o' shalt thou season 4503
13 to be lacking from thy meat o': "
14, 14 offer a meat o' of thy firstfruits "
15 thereon: it is a meat o'. "
16 is an o' made by fire unto the Lord.
3: 1 oblation be a sacrifice of peace o', *
2 his hand upon the head of his o', *7133
3 offer of the sacrifice of the peace o', *
3 an o' made by fire unto the Lord;
5 it is an o' made by fire, of a sweet
6 if his o' for a sacrifice of peace *7133
6 sacrifice of peace o' unto the Lord*
7 If he offer a lamb for his o', then *7133
8 his hand upon the head of his o', * "
9 offer of the sacrifice of the peace o' *
9 an o' made by fire unto the Lord;
11 it is the food of the o' made by fire
12 if his o' be a goat, then he shall *7133
14 And he shall offer thereof his o', * "
14 an o' made by fire unto the Lord;
16 it is the food of the o' made by fire
4: 3 blemish unto the Lord for a sin o'.
7 bottom of the altar of the burnt o',
8 fat of the bullock for the sin o';
10 upon the altar of the burnt o'.
18 bottom of the altar of the burnt o',
20 did with the bullock for a sin o',
21 it is a sin o' for the congregation.
23 he shall bring his o', a kid of the *7133
24 where they kill the burnt o' before
24 before the Lord: it is a sin o'.
25 take of the blood of the sin o' with
25 the horns of the altar of burnt o',
25 bottom of the altar of burnt o'.
28 he shall bring his o', a kid of the *7133
29 hand upon the head of the sin o',
29 and slay the sin o' in the place of
29 in the place of the burnt o'.
30 the horns of the altar of burnt o',
32 And if he bring a lamb for a sin o', 7133
33 hand upon the head of the sin o',
33 and slay it for a sin o', in the
33 place where they kill the burnt o'.
34 blood of the sin o' with his finger,
34 the horns of the altar of burnt o',
5: 6 bring his trespass o' unto the Lord 817
6 or a kid of the goats, for a sin o';
7 one for a sin o', and the other
7 and the other for a burnt o'.
8 that which is for the sin o' first,
9 sprinkle of the blood of the sin o'
9 bottom of the altar: it is a sin o'.
10 offer the second for a burnt o',
11 that sinned shall bring for his o' 7133
11 an ephah of fine flour for a sin o';
11 thereon: for it is a sin o'.
12 fire unto the Lord: it is a sin o'.
13 shall be the priest's, as a meat o'. 4503
15 of the sanctuary, for a trespass o':
16 him with the ram of the trespass o',
18 thy estimation, for a trespass o', unto
19 It is a trespass o': he hath certainly
6: 5 in the day of his trespass o'. *
6 bring his trespass o' unto the Lord,
6 with thy estimation, of a trespass o',
9 This is the law of the burnt o':
9 It is the burnt o', because of the
10 with the burnt o' on the altar, and
12 lay the burnt o' in order upon it;
14 And this is the law of the meat o': 4503
15 the flour of the meat o', and of the "
15 which is upon the meat o', and "
17 it is most holy, as is the sin o',
17 most holy, as is...the trespass o'.
20 is the o' of Aaron and of his sons, *7133
20 fine flour for a meat o' perpetual, 4503
21 and the baken pieces of the meat o' "
23 every meat o' for the priest shall be "
25 saying, This is the law of the sin o':
25 place where the burnt o' is killed
25 the sin o' be killed before the Lord:
30 no sin o', whereof any of the blood
7: 1 this is the law of the trespass o':
2 place where they kill the burnt o'
2 shall they kill the trespass o': and
5 upon the altar for an o' made by fire
5 fire unto the Lord: it is a trespass o'.
7 As the sin o' is, so is the trespass
7 so is the trespass o': there is one
8 that offereth any man's burnt o',
8 the burnt o' which he hath offered.
9 meat o' that is baken in the oven, 4503
10 every meat o', mingled with oil, "
13 offer for his o' leavened bread *7133
14 for an heave o' unto the Lord, and 8641
16 if the sacrifice of his o' be a vow, *7133
16 or a voluntary o', it shall be eaten the
25 offer an o' made by fire unto the Lord,
30 waved for a wave o' before the Lord.
32 for an heave o' of the sacrifices of 8641
37 This is the law of the burnt o',
37 This is the law of...the meat o', 4503
37 This is the law of...the sin o',
37 This is the law of...the trespass o',
8: 2 and a bullock for the sin o', and
14 brought the bullock for the sin o':
14 head of the bullock for the sin o'.
18 brought the ram for the burnt o': 5930
21 an o' made by fire unto the Lord;
27 them for a wave o' before the Lord.
28 on the altar upon the burnt o':
28 an o' made by fire unto the Lord.
29 waved it for a wave o' before the Lord:

Fig. 8. From Strong's *Exhaustive Concordance.* (See middle column, under OFFERINGS.)

(prep.), *from* or *out of* in many senses (as follows):—above, after, among, at, because of, by (reason of), from (among), in, × neither, × nor, (out) of, over, since, × then, through, × whether, with.

4481. מִן **min** (Chald.), *min*; corresp. to 4480:—according, after, + because, + before, by, for, from, × him, × more than, (out) of, part, since, × these, to upon, + when.

4482. מֵן **mên**, *mane*; from an unused root mean. to apportion; a part; hence a musical chord (as parted into strings):—in [the same] (Psa. 68 : 23), stringed instrument (Psa. 150 : 4), whereby (Psa. 45 : 8 [*defective plur.*]).

4483. מְנָא **menâ'** (Chald.), *men-aw'*; or

מְנָה **menâh** (Chald.), *men-aw'*; corresp. to 4487; to count, appoint:—number, ordain, set.

4484. מְנֵא **menê'** (Chald.), *men-ay'*; pass. part. of 4483; *numbered*:—Mene.

4485. מַנְגִּינָה **mangîynâh**, *man-ghee-naw'*; from 5059; a satire:—music.

מִנְדָּה **mindâh**. See 4061.

4486. מַנְדַּע **manda'** (Chald.), *man-dah'*; corresp. to 4093; *wisdom* or *intelligence*:—knowledge, reason, understanding.

מְנֶה **menâh**. See 4483.

4487. מָנָה **mânâh**, *maw-naw'*; a prim. root; prop. to *weigh* out; by impl. to *allot* or constitute officially; also to *enumerate* or enroll:—appoint, count, number, prepare set, tell.

4488. מָנֶה **mâneh**, *maw-neh'*; from 4487; prop. a fixed *weight* or measured amount, i.e. (techn.) a *maneh* or *mina*:—maneh, pound.

4489. מֹנֶה **môneh**, *mo-neh'*; from 4487; prop. something *weighed* out, i.e. (fig.) a *portion* of time, i.e. an *instance*:—time.

4490. מָנָה **mânâh**, *maw-naw'*; from 4487; prop. something *weighed* out, i.e. (gen.) a *division*; spec. (of food) a *ration*; also a *lot*:—such things as belonged, part, portion.

4491. מִנְהָג **minhâg**, *min-hawg'*; from 5090; the *driving* (of a chariot):—driving.

4492. מִנְהָרָה **minhârâh**, *min-haw-raw'*; from 5102; prop. a *channel* or *fissure*, i.e. (by impl.) a *cavern*:—den.

4493. מָנוֹד **mânôwd**, *maw-node'*; from 5110; a *nodding* or *toss* (of the head in derision):—shaking.

4494. מָנוֹחַ **mânôwach**, *maw-no'-akh*; from 5117; *quiet*, i.e. (concr.) a *settled spot*, or (fig.) a *home*:—(place of) rest.

4495. מָנוֹחַ **Mânôwach**, *maw-no'-akh*; the same as 4494; *rest*; Manoäch, an Isr.:—Manoah.

4496. מְנוּחָה **menûwchâh**, *men-oo-khaw'*; or

מְנֻחָה **menûchâh**, *men-oo-khaw'*; fem. of 4495; *repose* or (adv.) *peacefully*; fig. *consolation* (spec. matrimony); hence (concr.) an *abode*:—comfortable, ease, quiet, rest (-ing place), still.

4497. מָנוֹן **mânôwn**, *maw-nohn'*; from 5125; a *continuator*, i.e. *heir*:—son.

4498. מָנוֹס **mânôwç**, *maw-noce'*; from 5127; a *retreat* (lit. or fig.); abstr. a *fleeing*:—× apace, escape, way to flee, flight, refuge.

4499. מְנוּסָה **menûwçâh**, *men-oo-saw'*; or

מְנֻסָה **menûçâh**, *men-oo-saw'*; fem. of 4498; *retreat*:—fleeing, flight.

4500. מָנוֹר **mânôwr**, *maw-nore'*; from 5214; a *yoke* (prop. for ploughing), i.e. the *frame* of a loom:—beam.

4501. מְנוֹרָה **menôwrâh**, *men-o-raw'*; or

מְנֹרָה **menôrâh**, *men-o-raw'*; fem. of 4500 (in the orig. sense of 5216); a *chandelier*:—candlestick.

4502. מִנְּזָר **minnezâr**, *min-ez-awr'*; from 5144; a *prince*:—crowned.

4503. מִנְחָה **minchâh**, *min-khaw'*; from an unused root mean. to apportion, i.e. bestow; a *donation*; euphem. *tribute*; spec. a sacrificial *offering* (usually bloodless and voluntary):—gift, oblation, (meat) offering, present, sacrifice.

4504. מִנְחָה **minchâh** (Chald.), *min-khaw'*; corresp. to 4503; a sacrificial *offering*:—oblation, meat offering.

מְנֻחָה **menûchâh**. See 4496.

מְנָחוֹת **Menûchôwth**. See 2679.

4505. מְנַחֵם **Menachêm**, *men-akh-ame'*; from 5162; *comforter*; Menachem, an Isr.:—Menahem.

4506. מָנַחַת **Mânachath**, *maw-nakh'-ath*; from 5117; *rest*; Manachath, the name of an Edomite and of a place in Moab:—Manahath.

מְנַחְתִּי **Menachtîy**. See 2680.

4507. מְנִי **Menîy**, *men-ee'*; from 4487; the *Apportioner*, i.e. Fate (as an idol):—number.

מְנִי **minnîy**. See 4480, 4482.

4508. מִנִּי **Minnîy**, *min-nee'*; of for. der.; *Minni*, an Armenian province:—Minni.

מְנָיוֹת **menâyôwth**. See 4521.

4509. מִנְיָמִין **Minyâmîyn**, *min-yaw-meen'*; from 4480 and 3225; *from* (the) *right hand*; Minjamin, the name of two Isr.:—Miniamin. Comp. 4326.

4510. מִנְיָן **minyân** (Chald.), *min-yawn'*; from 4483; *enumeration*:—number.

4511. מִנִּית **Minnîyth**, *min-neeth'*; from the same as 4482; *enumeration*; Minnith, a place E. of the Jordan:—Minnith.

4512. מִנְלֶה **minleh**, *min-leh'*; from 5239; *completion*, i.e. (in produce) *wealth*:—perfection.

מְנַסֶּה **menûçâh**. See 4499.

4513. מָנַע **mâna'**, *maw-nah'*; a prim. root; to *debar* (neg. or pos.) from benefit or injury:—deny, keep (back), refrain, restrain, withhold.

4514. מַנְעוּל **man'ûwl**, *man-ool'*; or

מַנְעָל **man'âl**, *man-ool'*; from 5274; a *bolt*:—lock.

4515. מַנְעָל **man'âl**, *man-awl'*; from 5274; a *bolt*:—shoe.

4516. מַנְעַם **man'am**, *man-am'*; from 5276; a *delicacy*:—dainty.

4517. מְנַעְנַע **men'ana'**, *men-ah-ah'*; from 5128; a *sistrum* (so called from its *rattling* sound):—cornet.

4518. מְנַקִּית **menaqqîyth**, *men-ak-keeth'*; from 5352; a sacrificial *basin* (for holding blood):—bowl.

מְנֹרָה **menôrâh**. See 4501.

4519. מְנַשֶּׁה **Menashsheh**, *men-ash-sheh'*; from 5382; *causing to forget*; Menashsheh, a grandson of Jacob, also the tribe desc. from him, and its territory:—Manasseh.

4520. מְנַשִּׁי **Menashshîy**, *men-ash-shee'*; from 4519; a Menashshite or desc. of Menashsheh:—of Manasseh, Manassites.

4521. מְנָת **menâth**, *men-awth'*; from 4487; an *allotment* (by courtesy, law or providence):—portion.

4522. מַס **maç**, *mas*; or

מִס **miç**, *mees*; from 4549; prop. a *burden* (as causing to *faint*), i.e. a *tax* in the form of forced labor:—discomfited, levy, task [-master], tribute (-tary).

4523. מָס **mâç**, *mawce*; from 4549; *fainting*, i.e. (fig.) *disconsolate*:—is afflicted.

4524. מֵסַב **mêçab**, *may-sab'*; plur. masc.

מְסִבִּים **meçibbîym**, *mes-ib-beem'*; or fem.

מְסִבּוֹת **meçibbôwth**, *mes-ib-bohth'*; from 5437; a *divan* (as *enclosing* the room); abstr. (adv.) *around*:—that compass about, (place) round about, at table.

מְסֻבָּה **mûçabbâh**. See 4142.

4525. מַסְגֵּר **maçgêr**, *mas-gare'*; from 5462; a *fastener*, i.e. (of a person) a *smith*, (of a thing) a *prison*:—prison, smith.

4526. מִסְגֶּרֶת **miçgereth**, *mis-gheh'-reth*; from 5462; *something enclosing*, i.e. a *margin* (of a region, of a panel); concr. a *stronghold*:—border, close place, hole.

4527. מַסַּד **maççad**, *mas-sad'*; from 3245; a *foundation*:—foundation.

מֹסָדָה **môçâdâh**. See 4146.

4528. מִסְדְּרוֹן **miçderôwn**, *mis-der-ohn'*; from the same as 5468; a *colonnade* or internal *portico* (from its *rows* of pillars):—porch.

4529. מָסָה **mâçâh**, *maw-saw'*; a prim. root; to *dissolve*:—make to consume away, (make to) melt, water.

4530. מִסָּה **miççâh**, *mis-saw'*; from 4549 (in the sense of *flowing*); *abundance*, i.e. (adv.) *liberally*:—tribute.

4531. מַסָּה **maççâh**, *mas-saw'*; from 5254; a *testing*, of men (judicial) or of God (querulous):—temptation, trial.

4532. מַסָּה **Maççâh**, *mas-saw'*; the same as 4531; *Massah*, a place in the Desert:—Massah.

4533. מַסְוֶה **maçveh**, *mas-veh'*; appar. from an unused root mean. to *cover*: a *veil*:—vail.

4534. מְסוּכָה **meçûwkâh**, *mes-oo-kaw'*; for 4881; a *hedge*:—thorn hedge.

4535. מַסָּח **maççâch**, *mas-sawkh'*; from 5255 in the sense of *staving off*; a *cordon*, (adv.) or (as a) *military barrier*:—broken down.

4536. מִסְחָר **miçchâr**, *mis-khawr'*; from 5503; *trade*:—traffic.

4537. מָסַךְ **mâçak**, *maw-sak'*; a prim. root; to *mix*, espec. wine (with spices):—mingle.

4538. מֶסֶךְ **meçek**, *meh'-sek*; from 4537; a *mixture*, i.e. of wine with spices:—mixture.

4539. מָסָךְ **mâçâk**, *maw-sawk'*; from 5526; a *cover*, i.e. *veil*:—covering, curtain, hanging.

4540. מְסֻכָּה **meçukkâh**, *mes-ook-kaw'*; from 5526; a *covering*, i.e. *garniture*:—covering.

4541. מַסֵּכָה **maççêkâh**, *mas-say-kaw'*; from 5258; prop. a *pouring over*, i.e. *fusion* of metal (espec. a *cast image*); by impl. a *libation*, i.e. *league*; concr. a *coverlet* (as if poured out):—covering, molten (image), vail.

4542. מִסְכֵּן **miçkên**, *mis-kane'*; from 5531; *indigent*:—poor (man).

4543. מִסְכְּנָה **miçkenâh**, *mis-ken-aw'*; by transp. from 3664; a *magazine*:—store (-house), treasure.

4544. מִסְכְּנֻת **miçkênûth**, *mis-kay-nooth'*; from 4542; *indigence*:—scarceness.

4545. מַסֶּכֶת **maççeketh**, *mas-seh'-keth*; from 5259 in the sense of *spreading out*; something *expanded*, i.e. the *warp* in a loom (as stretched out to receive the woof):—web.

4546. מְסִלָּה **meçillâh**, *mes-il-law'*; from 5549; a *thoroughfare* (as turnpiked), lit. or fig.: spec. a *viaduct*, a *staircase*:—causeway, course, highway, path, terrace.

4547. מַסְלוּל **maçlûwl**, *mas-lool'*; from 5549; a *thoroughfare* (as turnpiked):—highway.

4548. מַסְמֵר **maçmêr**, *mas-mare'*; or

מִסְמֵר **miçmêr**, *mis-mare'*; also (fem.)

מַסְמְרָה **maçmerâh**, *mas-mer-aw'*; or

מִסְמְרָה **miçmerâh**, *mis-mer-aw'*; or even

מַשְׂמְרָה **masmerâh** (Eccles. 12 : 11), *mas-mer-aw'*; from 5568; a *peg* (as *bristling* from the surface):—nail.

Fig. 9. From "Hebrew and Chaldee Dictionary" of Strong's *Exhaustive Concordance*. (See entry number 4503, top of center column.)

8605. תְּפִלָּה **tephillâh**, *tef-il-law'*; from 6419; *intercession, supplication;* by impl. a *hymn:*—prayer.

8606. תִּפְלֶצֶת **tiphletseth**, *tif-leh'-tseth;* from 6426; *fearfulness:*—terrible.

8607. תִּפְסַח **Tiphcach**, *tif-sakh';* from 6452; *ford; Tiphsach,* a place in Mesopotamia:—Tipsah.

8608. תָּפַף **tâphaph**, *taw-faf';* a prim. root; to *drum,* i.e. play (as) on the tambourine:—taber, play with timbrels.

8609. תָּפַר **tâphar**, *taw-far';* a prim. root; to *sew:*—(women that) sew (together).

8610. תָּפַשׂ **tâphas**, *taw-fas';* a prim. root; to *manipulate,* i.e. *seize;* chiefly to *capture, wield;* spec. to *overlay;* fig. to *use* unwarrantably:—catch, handle, (lay, take) hold (on, over), stop, X surely, surprise, take.

8611. תֹּפֶת **tôpheth**, *to'-feth;* from the base of 8608; a *smiting,* i.e. (fig.) *contempt:*—tabret.

8612. תֹּפֶת **Tôpheth**, *to'-feth;* the same as 8611; *Topheth,* a place near Jerus.:—Tophet, Topheth.

8613. תָּפְתֶּה **Tophteh**, *tof-teh';* prob. a form of 8612; *Tophteh,* a place of cremation:—Tophet.

8614. תִּפְתָי **tiphtay** (Chald.), *tif-tah'ee;* perh. from 8199; *judicial,* i.e. a *lawyer:*—sheriff.

תֹּצָאָה **tôtsâ'âh**. See 8444.

8615. תִּקְוָה **tiqvâh**, *tik-vaw';* from 6960; lit. a *cord* (as an *attachment* [comp. 6961]); fig. *expectancy:*—expectation ([-ted]), hope, live, thing that I long for.

8616. תִּקְוָה **Tiqvâh**, *tik-vaw';* the same as 8615; *Tikvah,* the name of two Isr.:—Tikvah.

8617. תְּקוּמָה **teqûwmâh**, *tek-oo-maw';* from 6965; *resistfulness:*—power to stand.

8618. תְּקוֹמֵם **teqôwmêm**, *tek-o-mame';* from 6965; an *opponent:*—rise up against.

8619. תָּקוֹעַ **tâqôwaʻ**, *taw-ko'-ah;* from 8628 (in the musical sense); a *trumpet:*—trumpet.

8620. תְּקוֹעַ **Teqôwaʻ**, *tek-o'-ah;* a form of 8619; *Tekoa,* a place in Pal.:—Tekoa, Tekoah.

8621. תְּקוֹעִי **Teqôwʻiy**, *tek-o-ee';* or

תְּקֹעִי **Teqôʻiy**, *tek-o-ee';* patron. from 8620; a *Tekoïte* or inhab. of Tekoah:—Tekoite.

8622. תְּקוּפָה **teqûwphâh**, *tek-oo-faw';* or

תְּקֻפָה **tequphâh**, *tek-oo-faw';* from 5362; a *revolution,* i.e. (of the sun) *course,* (of time) *lapse:*—circuit, come about, end.

8623. תַּקִּיף **taqqîyph**, *tak-keef';* from 8630; *powerful:*—mightier.

8624. תַּקִּיף **taqqîyph** (Chald.), *tak-keef';* corresp. to 8623:—mighty, strong.

8625. תְּקַל **teqal** (Chald.), *tek-al';* corresp. to 8254; to *balance:*—Tekel, be weighed.

8626. תָּקַן **tâqan**, *taw-kan';* a prim. root; to *equalize,* i.e. *straighten* (intrans. or trans.); fig. to *compose:*—set in order, make straight.

8627. תְּקַן **teqan** (Chald.), *tek-an';* corresp. to 8626; to *straighten up,* i.e. *confirm:*—establish.

8628. תָּקַע **tâqaʻ**, *taw-kah';* a prim. root; to *clatter,* i.e. *slap* (the hands together), *clang* (an instrument); by anal. to *drive* (a nail or tent-pin, a dart, etc.); by impl. to *become bondsman* (by handclasping):—blow ([a trumpet]), cast, clap, fasten, pitch [tent], smite, sound, strike, X suretiship, thrust.

8629. תֵּקַע **têqaʻ**, *tay-kah';* from 8628; a *blast of a trumpet:*—sound.

תְּקֹעִי **Teqôʻiy**. See 8621.

8630. תָּקַף **tâqaph**, *taw-kaf';* a prim. root; to *overpower:*—prevail (against).

8631. תְּקֵף **teqêph** (Chald.), *tek-afe';* corresp. to 8630; to *become* (caus. *make*) *mighty* or (fig.) *obstinate:*—make firm, harden, be (-come) strong.

8632. תְּקֹף **teqôph** (Chald.), *tek-ofe';* corresp. to 8633; *power:*—might, strength.

8633. תֹּקֶף **tôqeph**, *to'-kef;* from 8630; *might* or (fig.) *positiveness:*—authority, power, strength.

תְּקֻפָה **tequphâh**. See 8622.

תֹּר **tôr**. See 8447, 8449.

8634. תַּרְאֲלָה **Tarʼălâh**, *tar-al-aw';* prob. for 8653; a *reeling; Taralah,* a place in Pal.:—Taralah.

8635. תַּרְבּוּת **tarbûwth**, *tar-booth';* from 7235; *multiplication,* i.e. *progeny:*—increase.

8636. תַּרְבִּית **tarbîyth**, *tar-beeth';* from 7235; *multiplication,* i.e. *percentage* or *bonus* in addition to principal:—increase, unjust gain.

8637. תִּרְגַּל **tirgal**, *teer-gal';* a denom. from 7270; to *cause to walk:*—teach to go.

8638. תִּרְגַּם **tirgam**, *teer-gam';* a denom. from 7275 in the sense of *throwing over;* to *transfer,* i.e. *translate:*—interpret.

תֹּרָה **tôrâh**. See 8451.

8639. תַּרְדֵּמָה **tardêmâh**, *tar-day-maw';* from 7290; a *lethargy* or (by impl.) *trance:*—deep sleep.

8640. תִּרְהָקָה **Tirhâqâh**, *teer-haw'-kaw;* of for. der.; *Tirhakah,* a king of Kush:—Tirhakah.

8641. תְּרוּמָה **terûwmâh**, *ter-oo-maw';* or

תְּרֻמָה **terûmâh** (Deut. 12 : 11), *ter-oo-maw';* from 7311; a *present* (as offered up), espec. in *sacrifice* or as *tribute:*—gift, heave offering ([shoulder]), oblation, offered (-ing).

8642. תְּרוּמִיָּה **terûwmîyâh**, *ter-oo-mee-yaw';* formed as 8641; a *sacrificial offering:*—oblation.

8643. תְּרוּעָה **terûwʻâh**, *ter-oo-aw';* from 7321; *clamor,* i.e. *acclamation* of joy or a *battle-cry;* espec. *clangor* of trumpets, as an *alarum:*—alarm, blow (-ing) (of, the) (trumpets), joy, jubile, loud noise, rejoicing, shout (-ing), (high, joyful) sound (-ing).

8644. תְּרוּפָה **terûwphâh**, *ter-oo-faw';* from 7322 in the sense of its congener 7495; a *remedy:*—medicine.

8645. תִּרְזָה **tirzâh**, *teer-zaw';* prob. from 7329; a *species of tree* (appar. from its *slenderness*), perh. the *cypress:*—cypress.

8646. תֶּרַח **Terach**, *teh'-rakh;* of uncert. der.; *Terach,* the father of Abraham; also a place in the Desert:—Tarah, Terah.

8647. תִּרְחֲנָה **Tirchănâh**, *teer-khan-aw';* of uncert. der.; *Tirchanah,* an Isr.:—Tirhanah.

8648. תְּרֵין **treyn** (Chald.), *ter-ane';* fem.

תַּרְתֵּין **tarteyn**, *tar-tane';* corresp. to 8147; *two:*—second, + twelve, two.

8649. תָּרְמָה **tormâh**, *tor-maw';* and

תַּרְמוּת **tarmûwth**, *tar-mooth';* or

תַּרְמִית **tarmîyth**, *tar-meeth';* from 7411; *fraud:*—deceit (-ful), privily.

תְּרֻמָה **terûmâh**. See 8641.

8650. תֹּרֶן **tôren**, *to'-ren;* prob. for 766; a *pole* (as a *mast* or *flag-staff*):—beacon, mast.

8651. תְּרַע **teraʻ** (Chald.), *ter-ah';* corresp. to 8179; a *door;* by impl. a *palace:*—gate, mouth.

8652. תָּרָע **târâʻ** (Chald.), *taw-raw';* from 8651; a *doorkeeper:*—porter.

8653. תַּרְעֵלָה **tarʻêlâh**, *tar-ay-law';* from 7477; *reeling:*—astonishment, trembling.

8654. תִּרְעָתָא **Tirʻâthiy**, *teer-aw-thee';* patrial from an unused name mean. *gate;* a *Tirathite* or inhab. of an unknown Tirah:—Tirathite.

8655. תְּרָפִים **terâphîym**, *ter-aw-feme';* plur. per. from 7495; a *healer; Teraphim* (sing. or plur.) a family idol:—idols (-atry), images, teraphim.

8656. תִּרְצָה **Tirtsâh**, *teer-tsaw';* from 7521; *delightsomeness; Tirtsah,* a place in Pal.; also an Israelitess:—Tirzah.

8657. תֶּרֶשׁ **Teresh**, *teh'-resh;* of for. der.; *Teresh,* a eunuch of Xerxes:—Teresh.

8658. תַּרְשִׁישׁ **tarshiysh**, *tar-sheesh';* prob. of for. der. [comp. 8659]; a *gem,* perh. the *topaz:*—beryl.

8659. תַּרְשִׁישׁ **Tarshiysh**, *tar-sheesh';* prob. the same as 8658 (as the region of the stone, or the reverse); *Tarshish,* a place on the Mediterranean, hence the epithet of a *merchant* vessel (as if for or from that port); also the name of a Persian and of an Isr.:—Tarshish, Tharshish.

8660. תִּרְשָׁתָא **Tirshâthâ'**, *teer-shaw-thaw';* of for. der.; the title of a Pers. deputy or *governor:*—Tirshatha.

8661. תַּרְתָּן **tarteyn**. See 8648.

8661. תַּרְתָּן **Tartân**, *tar-tawn';* of for. der.; *Tartan,* an Assyrian:—Tartan.

8662. תַּרְתָּק **Tartâq**, *tar-tawk';* of for. der.; *Tartak,* a deity of the Avvites:—Tartak.

8663. תְּשֻׁאָה **teshuʼâh**, *tesh-oo-aw';* from 7722; a *crushing* or loud *clamor:*—crying, noise, shouting, stir.

תּוֹשָׁב **tôshâb**. See 8453.

8664. תִּשְׁבִּי **Tishbiy**, *tish-bee';* patrial from an unused name mean. *recourse;* a *Tishbite* or inhab. of Tishbeh (in Gilead):—Tishbite.

8665. תַּשְׁבֵּץ **tashbêts**, *tash-bates';* from 7660; *checkered* stuff (as *reticulated*):—broidered.

8666. תְּשׁוּבָה **teshûwbâh**, *tesh-oo-baw';* or

תְּשֻׁבָה **teshûbâh**, *tesh-oo-baw';* from 7725; a *recurrence* (of time or place); a *reply* (as *returned*):—answer, be expired, return.

8667. תְּשׂוּמֶת **tesûwmeth**, *tes-oo-meth';* from 7760; a *deposit,* i.e. *pledging:*—+ fellowship.

8668. תְּשׁוּעָה **teshûwʻâh**, *tesh-oo-aw';* or

תְּשֻׁעָה **teshuʻâh**, *tesh-oo-aw';* from 7768 in the sense of 3467; *rescue* (lit. or fig., pers., national or spir.):—deliverance, help, safety, salvation, victory.

8669. תְּשׁוּקָה **teshûwqâh**, *tesh-oo-kaw';* from 7783 in the orig. sense of *stretching* out after; a *longing:*—desire.

8670. תְּשׁוּרָה **teshûwrâh**, *tesh-oo-raw';* from 7788 in the sense of *arrival;* a *gift:*—present.

תַּשְׁחֵת **tashchêth**. See 516.

תּוּשִׁיָּה **tûshiyâh**. See 8454.

8671. תְּשִׁיעִי **teshîyʻiy**, *tesh-ee-ee';* ord. from 8672; *ninth:*—ninth.

תְּשֻׁעָה **teshuʻâh**. See 8668.

8672. תֵּשַׁע **têshaʻ**, *tay'-shah;* or (masc.)

תִּשְׁעָה **tishʻâh**, *tish-aw';* perh. from 8159 through the idea of a *turn* to the next or full number ten; *nine* or (ord.) *ninth:*—nine (+ -teen, + -teenth, -th).

8673. תִּשְׁעִים **tishʻîym**, *tish-eem';* multiple from 8672; *ninety:*—ninety.

8674. תַּתְּנַי **Tattenay**, *tat-ten-ah'ee;* of for. der.; *Tattenai,* a Persian:—Tatnai.

Fig. 10. From "Hebrew and Chaldee Dictionary" of Strong's *Exhaustive Concordance.* (See entry number 8641, middle of center column.)

- *Anchor Bible*
- *Expositor's Bible*
- *Expositor's Bible Commentary*
- *International Critical Commentary*
- Keil's and Delitzsch's *Biblical Commentary on the Old Testament*
- Lange's *Commentary on the Holy Scriptures*
- Lenski's *Interpretation of the New Testament*
- *New International Commentary on the New Testament*
- *New International Commentary on the Old Testament*
- *The Interpreter's Bible*
- *Tyndale New Testament Commentaries*
- *Tyndale Old Testament Commentaries.*

The Anchor Bible, edited by W. F. Albright and D. N. Freedman (1964-present), when completed will include all the canonical books and the Apocrypha. The philological scholarship undergirding these commentaries is unquestioned. The contributors have been drawn from Protestant, Catholic, and Jewish backgrounds. Although the purpose behind the publication is to make available to the general reader the benefits of modern biblical scholarship, some of the commentaries contributed to this series are highly technical and suited more to the needs of the theologue. Scholars will appreciate the excellent contributions by E. A. Speiser (Genesis), M. Dahood (Psalms), J. Bright (Jeremiah), F. I. Anderson (Hosea), R. Brown (John's gospel), and M. Barth (Ephesians), even though the theological perspective of the majority of the commentators is neither evangelical nor conservative.

The Expositor's Bible, edited by W. R. Nicoll, was originally published in England between 1887 and 1896 (49 vols.). It is a valuable work and contains some of the finest expository studies ever published (*e.g.*, Kellogg on Leviticus, Blaikie on Joshua and 1-2 Samuel, Maclaren on Psalms, Moule on Romans, and Edwards on Hebrews).

Not all the treatments are of equal value and there are some disagreements over interpretation. However, there still is a great deal in this set to merit the Bible student's attention.

The *Expositor's Bible Commentary*, edited by F. E. Gaebelein (1976-present) and scheduled for 12 volumes, is the product of international scholarship and is based on the text of the *New International Version*. Each contributor outlines clearly and concisely the book he intends to expound, reserves critical matters for the footnotes, and generally succeeds in providing an illuminating study of the biblical writer's thought. Volume one contains introductory articles covering a variety of biblical and theological themes.

The International Critical Commentary on the Holy Scriptures of the Old and New Testaments, edited by S. R. Driver, A. Plummer, and C. A. Briggs (1895-1951), deserves consultation. Since the appearance of the first volume the ICC has consistently maintained a high, if theologically liberal, standard of scholarship. Plummer on Luke and 2 Corinthians, Bernard on John's gospel, Sanday and Headlam on Romans, Robertson and Plummer on 1 Corinthians, and Burton on Galatians, have all established a mark of exegetical, philological, historical, and textual competence that has been hard to equal.

A new edition of the ICC under the editorial guidance of J. A. Emerton and C. E. B. Cranfield was begun in 1975 with the first of Cranfield's volumes on Romans. This pace-setting volume, like its predecessors, is a work that demands the attention of students of the Bible everywhere. It is hoped the other volumes will maintain the same high standard of scholarship.

The Interpreter's Bible, edited by G. A. Buttrick et al (12 vols., 1952-57), uses the text of the KJV and RSV, and aims at being both exegetical and expository. Volume one contains articles pertaining to the inspiration, canonicity, texts, history of transmission, et cetera of the Bible. Comments on each book of the Bible follow. The books are treated in the order in which they appear in our English Bibles.

Each writer provides a brief introduction to the book he expounds. Evidence of the liberal theological learning of the contributors abounds, and adherence to form-critical or redaction-critical theories mars the overall usefulness of this work. Of value, however, are some of the homiletic hints and helps. Unfortunately some, with the passing of time, they now appear hackneyed.

Volume twelve contains supplementary articles and indices.

Biblical Commentary on the Old Testament, by C. F. Keil and F. Delitzsch (25 vols., 1956 reprint), was produced by two evangelical German scholars during the last century and has now achieved landmark status. Issues involving the grammar and syntax of the text are dealt with fairly and impartially, and even though modern researchers may be inclined to disagree on points of interpretation and will readily notice the authors' moderate adherence to documentary theories, the fact remains that these Semitic scholars produced a work to which the whole world of Christian scholarship is indebted.

Commentary on the Holy Scriptures, Critical, Doctrinal and Homiletical, edited by J. P. Lange (translated by P. Schaff, 24 vols., 1960 reprint), is an extensive commentary that was first published in Germany between 1862 and 1876. It is prefaced with several important essays, all written from an evangelical, Reformed perspective. Each book of the Bible is carefully introduced, critical issues are handled with rare acumen, and the comments on the text are arranged under successive headings: "Exegetical and critical," "Doctrinal and ethical," "Homiletical and practical." Inasmuch as there is a paucity of commentaries on the Old Testament, this work is still worthy of consultation.

The Interpretation of the New Testament, by R. C. H. Lenski (14 vols., 1934-66), is based on the Greek text and contains Lenski's own translation.

Each volume bears mute testimony to its author's painstaking labors; historical details are carefully blended with perceptive comments on the text, and critical problems are handled judiciously. In spite of a rigidity in handling certain Greek tenses, these commentaries are deserving of careful consideration.

New International Commentary on the New Testament, edited by F. F. Bruce (1951-present), is generally representative of the best of modern Reformed scholarship from many countries and, when complete, will probably take its place among the most serviceable works for the minister and the more advanced Bible student.

Each expository study, although ostensibly based on the English text of 1881 Revised Version and the *American Standard Version* (1901), has in reality been established upon an exacting study of the original. Critical comments have been largely confined to footnotes. Elaboration on important issues, grammatical and textual factors highlighting some facet of the text, and historical details, will be found in special notes in the appendices.

Of particular significance to the researcher will be Lane's work on Mark, Morris's treatment of John's gospel, Bruce's expositions of Acts and Hebrews, Hughes's magisterial handling of 2 Corinthians, and Marshall's treatment of John's epistles.

New International Commentary on the Old Testament, edited by R. K. Harrison (1976-present), was originally under the editorship of E. J. Young (who contributed the book of Isaiah, the first three volumes in the series). Upon his death the editorial "mantle" fell on Harrison's shoulders.

This series, like its New Testament counterpart, is representative of the best of modern, evangelical scholarship. Each book is judiciously introduced and carefully expounded. Documentation is reserved for the footnotes. Extensive use is made of data from archaeological "digs" and philological comparisons are made between the Masoretic Text and information gleaned from the Dead Sea Scrolls or other Near Eastern sources.

Although varying in quality, the volumes produced thus far have added a new dimension to the study of the Old Testament.

Tyndale New Testament Commentaries, edited by R. V. G. Tasker (20 vols., 1957-74), is designed for lay people. These volumes are not overly technical—each work has been produced by a scholar who has brought to his exposition of the text a background rich in Greek literature and exegesis. The result is a series that is informative and suggestive of further study.

These commentaries are all based on the King James. Readers, however, will readily discern those instances in which the writer has felt free to provide his own translation of the text, with appropriate reasons for the change from KJV.

Outstanding contributions to this set include Cole on Mark, Morris on Luke, Bruce on Romans, Foulkes on Ephesians, Green on 2 Peter and Jude, and Stott on John's epistles.

Tyndale Old Testament Commentaries, edited by D. J. Wiseman (1974-present), is aimed at providing lay people with a useful, up-to-date commentary on each book of the Old Testament. The series has already distinguished itself for its able blending of extra-biblical information (history, archaeology, philology) with an explanation of the meaning of the text. Major critical questions are discussed in the introduction to each canonical book, and additional notes are included where needed. Cole's handling of Exodus evidences much wisdom in condensing all that might have been said into a concise commentary; Thompson's Deuteronomy is excellent; Harrison's Jeremiah/Lamentations, and more recently Leviticus, is deserving of the highest praise; Morris on Ruth is well done; and Kidner's Ezra/Nehemiah, Psalms (2 vols.), and *Proverbs* contain a wealth of information.

This series bears watching, particularly because new volumes are being added at regular intervals.

In this chapter we have looked briefly at Bible atlases, Bible concordances, and Bible commentaries. All of these resource tools have the potential of enriching your study of the Word of God. In our next chapter we will focus attention on those lexical aids (namely concordances) that will assist you to ascertain the meaning of Hebrew and Greek words.

ASSIGNMENT

Webster defines a concordance as an "alphabetical index to the principal words of a book, as of the Bible, with a reference to the passage in which each occurs and some part of the context." One of the uses of a concordance is the tracing of different words so that they can be studied in context.

By checking the entries in *Young's Analytical Concordance to the Bible* that list words for "anger," "child," "everlasting," identify both the Hebrew and Greek terms. Compare the entries found in *Young's Concordance* with those listed in the *Englishman's Hebrew and Chaldee Concordance* and the *Englishman's Greek Concordance of the New Testament*. More advanced students should use Mandlekern's *Veteris Testamenti concordantiae* and Moulton and Geden's *Concordance to the Greek Testament*.

How well does each of these reference works cover the usage of each word? What is the value of each of these works as a resource tool? How would you go about analyzing and summarizing the biblical data?

In recalling the student mentioned in Chapter 1 who had been assigned the task of researching the usage and meaning of the word *apostasia*, and by using a combination of the resources mentioned above, list (together with its possible meanings) those passages in the Bible where this word is used. To what extent does the context help you determine the meaning?

6

THE USE OF
CONCORDANCES

Have you ever wondered how someone such as William Barclay could find so many interesting and informative things to say about different words or terms used of people, places, or things in the Bible?

In the same vein, when was the last time you saw someone really become excited over something he had discovered as a result of studying Scripture?

Why is it that the things taught us from the Word of God frequently reflect a monotonous sameness that eventually deteriorates into a dry, pedantic rehearsal of the old, the familiar, and the bland?

For several years it was my privilege to teach a two-semester course in biblical studies to the first-year students of the Rosemead Graduate School of Professional Psychology, La Mirada, California. Each semester I would assign those in the class the project of writing on a Bible character of their choice. In the fall they would write on someone from the Old Testament, and in the spring they would write on someone from the New.

As each student began researching his or her Bible character, sooner or later they would come to the point of considering descriptive phrases or statements made about them. Rebekah, for example, is described with purposeful repetition as "a virgin" with whom no man had had sexual relations (Gen. 24:16). The significance of that may be traced to the culture of the people and the morality of the times.

David, one student found, had his entire life in relation to his people summed up by the word *servant* (Acts 13:36; see also 2 Sam. 7:5). Of course, other illustrations could be multiplied ad infinitum.

One spring a young man came to me obviously bubbling over with excite-

ment. In studying Nathanael he had been prompted to dig into some concordances and lexicons to trace the etymology of the word *guile* (John 1:47).
He had had no previous training in Greek, and the task was a difficult one.
Imagine his delight when he found that *guile* originally had been a word used
to describe the bait a fisherman would put on a hook. In time, this same
word came to be applied to people—con artists, we would call them
today—who deceived others. Appropriately, they were observed to "bait"
people into falling into their trap and were looked upon as being full of guile.

Word studies can be exciting. Their value can readily be seen in a book like
William Barclay's *Flesh and Spirit* (1962), which expounds the terms used by
the apostle Paul in Galatians 5:19-23.

The late Donald Grey Barnhouse, for thirty-three years pastor of the
historic Tenth Presbyterian Church, Philadelphia, and recipient of several
honorary degrees, told of his own practice of studying the Scriptures. He
travelled a great deal and always took with him suitcases containing Greek
and Hebrew texts of the Bible and about 22 concordances and lexicons. As he
studied a passage, he would trace the meaning of significant words throughout the entire Bible. Then, as he expounded the text, he would illustrate the
meaning of words or explain the significance of events from Genesis through
Revelation. Dr. Barnhouse's *Exposition of Bible Doctrine* (10 vols., 1952-63)
on Paul's letter to the church in Rome is illustrative of his approach.

Our initial interest lies in specific terms used in Scripture. (Chapters 8 and
9 will build on this chapter and deal specifically with word studies.) Some of
these terms are already well known to us (e.g., *justification, propitiation,
sanctification*). Illustrations of theological word studies done on these words
may be found in Leon Morris's *The Apostolic Preaching of the Cross* (1955).
Our concern here is with the methodology by which accurate ideas of words
and their meaning(s) may be obtained.

When we consider the resource tools available for biblical research, they
divide into two obvious groups: those dealing with the text of the Old Testament, and those dealing with the text of the New. The former can be expected to focus on the meaning of Hebrew and Aramaic words, and the latter
the Greek terms and expressions commonly used in the time of Christ and
the apostles.

A further resource is the Septuagint (LXX) translation of the Old Testament into Greek.

OLD TESTAMENT RESOURCES

Although students lacking an understanding of Hebrew will find Young's
Analytical Concordance to the Bible invaluable, they should also become
familiar with the word edited by George V. Wigram, *The Englishman's
Hebrew and Chaldee Concordance of the Old Testament* (5th ed., 1890).

KAL.—*Infinitive.*

Deu11:22. and to cleave unto him ;
   30:20. and that thou mayest cleave unto him:
Jos. 22: 5. and to cleave unto him,

KAL.—*Future.*

Gen19:19. lest some evil take me,
   34: 3. And his soul clave unto Dinah
Nu. 36: 7. of Israel shall keep himself to the inherit-
     ance (marg. cleave to)
   9. of Israel shall keep himself to his own
Deu10:20. to him shalt thou cleave,
   13: 4(5). and cleave unto him.
   17(18). there shall cleave nought of the
Jos. 23: 8. But cleave unto the Lord
Ru. 2: 8. abide here fast by my maidens:
   21. Thou shalt keep fast by my
   23. So she kept fast by the maidens
2Sa.23:10. and his hand clave unto the sword:
2K. 5:27. Naaman shall cleave unto thee,
   18: 6. For he clave to the Lord,
Ps.101: 3. shall not cleave to me.
   137: 6. let my tongue cleave to the
Jer. 13:11. as the girdle cleaveth to the loins of a man,
   42:16. shall follow close after you there in Egypt ;
   (marg. cleave)
Eze.29: 4. the fish of thy rivers shall stick

✳ PUAL.—*Future.* ✳

Job 38:38. the clods cleave fast together ?
   41:17(9). They are joined one to another,

✳ HIPHIL.—*Preterite.* ✳

Jud.20:42. but the battle overtook them ;
2Sa. 1: 6. horsemen followed hard after him.
Jer. 13:11. so have I caused to cleave
Eze.29: 4. and I will cause the fish of thy rivers to stick

HIPHIL.—*Future.*

Gen31:23. and they overtook him
Deu28:21. shall make the pestilence cleave
Iud.18:22. and overtook the children of Dan.
   20:45. and pursued hard after them
1Sa.14:22. even they also followed hard
   31: 2. And the Philistines followed hard upon
1Ch 10: 2. And the Philistines followed hard
Eze. 3:26. And I will make thy tongue cleave

✳ HOPHAL.—*Participle.* ✳

Ps. 22:15(16). my tongue cleaveth to my jaws ;

דְּבַק *[d'vak],* Ch.

✳ P'AL.—*Participle.* Active. ✳

Dan. 2:43. but they shall not cleave one to another,

דָּבֵק *dăh-vēhk',* adj.

Deu. 4: 4. But ye that did cleave unto the Lord
2Ch. 3:12. joining to the wing of the other
Pro.18:24. there is a friend (that) sticketh closer

דֶּבֶק *deh'-vek,* m.

1K. 22:34. between the joints of the harness:
2Ch 18:33. between the joints of the harness:
Isa. 41: 7. It (is) ready for the sodering : (marg. or, of the soder, It (is) good)

דָּבַר *[dăh-var'].*

✳ KAL.—*Infinitive.* ✳

Ps. 51: 4(6). be justified when thou speakest,

KAL.—*Participle.* Poel.

Gen16:13. the Lord that spake unto her,
Ex. 6:29. all that I say unto thee.
Nu. 27: 7. daughters of Zelophehad speak right:
   32:27. before the Lord to battle, as my lord saith.

Nu.36: 5. of Joseph hath said well.
Deu. 5: 1. I speak in your ears this day,
Est.10: 3. and speaking peace to all his seed.
Job 2:13. none spake a word unto him:
Ps. 5: 6(7). destroy them that speak leasing:
   15: 2. and speaketh the truth
   28: 3. which speak peace to their neighbours,
   31:18(19). which speak grievous things
   58: 3(4). as they be born, speaking lies.
   63:11(12). them that speak lies shall be
   101: 7. he that telleth lies
   109:20. and of them that speak evil
Pro.16:13. and they love him that speaketh
Isa. 9:17(16). and every mouth speaketh folly.
   33:15. and speaketh uprightly ;
   45:19. I the Lord speak righteousness,
Jer. 28: 7. that I speak in thine ears,
   32:42. the good that I have promised
   38:20. which I speak unto thee:
   40:16. thou speakest falsely of Ishmael.
Dan10:11. the words that I speak unto thee,
Am. 5:10. and they abhor him that speaketh
Jon. 3: 2. the preaching that I bid thee.
Mic. 7: 3. he uttereth his mischievous
Zec. 1: 9, 13, 19(2:2). the angel that talked with me
   14. the angel that communed with
   2: 3(7) & 4:1, 4, 5 & 5:5, 10 & 6:4. the angel that talked with me

KAL.—*Participle.* Paül.

Pro.25:11. A word fitly spoken

✳ NIPHAL.—*Preterite.* ✳

Ps.119:23. Princes also did sit (and) speak
Mal. 3:13. What have we spoken
   16. spake often one to another:

NIPHAL.—*Participle.*

Eze.33:30. still are talking against thee

✳ PIEL.—*Preterite.* ✳

Gen12: 4. as the Lord had spoken unto him ;
   17:23. as God had said unto him.
   18: 5. So do, as thou hast said.
   19. that which he hath spoken
   19:21. city, for the which thou hast spoken.
   21: 1. unto Sarah as he had spoken.
   2. which God had spoken to him.
   23:16. which he had named
   24: 7. which spake unto me,
   30. Thus spake the man unto me ;
   33. until I have told mine errand.
   51. as the Lord hath spoken.
   27:19. done according as thou badest me:
   28:15. which I have spoken to thee of.
   35:13, 14. where he talked with him.
   15. where God spake with him,
   39:19. which she spake unto him,
   41:28. the thing which I have spoken
   42:14. that I spake unto you,
   30. spake roughly to us,
   44: 2. the word that Joseph had spoken.
   45:15. after that his brethren talked with
   27. which he had said unto them:
   49:28. their father spake unto them,
Ex. 1:17. the king of Egypt commanded
   4:15. And thou shalt speak unto him,
   16. And he shall be thy spokesman (lit. and he shall speak for thee)
   30. which the Lord had spoken
   7:13, 22. as the Lord had said.
   8:15(11), 19(15). as the Lord had said:
   9: 1. Go in unto Pharaoh, and tell him,
   12, 35. as the Lord had spoken
   10:29. Thou hast spoken well,
   12:25. according as he hath promised,
   32. as ye have said,
   14:12. the word that we did tell thee
   16:23. which the Lord hath said,
   19: 8. All that the Lord hath spoken
   20:22. Ye have seen that I have talked
   24: 3. which the Lord said.
   7. All that the Lord hath said
   25:22. and I will commune with thee
   32:14. the evil which he thought to do
   34. of which I have spoken unto thee:
   33: 9. and (the Lord) talked with Moses.

Fig. 11. Page from *The Englishman's Hebrew and Chaldee Concordance of the Old Testament.*

(Edward W. Goodrick's *Do It Yourself Hebrew and Greek* [1980] is a helpful work for beginners.) Arranged by Hebrew word, this concordance lists passages in the Old Testament that contain the term, along with the word's KJV translation.

Because it is the usage of the word that determines its meaning, and because language is constantly changing, by using a concordance we can: (1) assess the general meaning of a given word, and (2) tie in its usage with different writers and/or eras of history (e.g., Mosaic era, united or divided monarchy, early or later prophets).

Two other concordances dealing with the Old Testament are indispensable to its study. These are:

- Mandelkern's *Veteris Testamenti concordantiae Hebraicae atique Chaldaicae*
- Lisowsky's *Konkordanz zum hebräischen Alten Testament.*

Most "non-language" students are intimidated by the titles of these two works, but their fear should begin to disappear as these books are used.

Solomon Mandelkern's *Veteris Testamenti concordantiae* (1955) contains citations according to sense, proper placement of entries misplaced under false roots, correction of grammatical confusions, and the addition of hapax legomena omitted in previous works. Even if the beginning student does little more than use the biblical references listed at the side of each citation, his study of Scripture will be immeasurably enhanced because of the accuracy of this important work. For the more advanced student, Mandelkern's now famous concordance not only gives him the accuracy his research requires, but also enables him to study words in relationship to important grammatical distinctions.

Of a similar nature is Gerhard Lisowsky's *Konkordanz zum hebräischen Alten Testament* (1958), which has been photographically reproduced from Lisowsky's handwritten manuscript. With emphasis placed upon nouns and verbs, this concordance is particularly helpful to the student engaged in word studies.

Of course, with the translation in the second century B.C. of the Old Testament into Greek, the zealous student will wish to compare the Greek words used to translate their Hebrew equivalent. A valuable resource in this area of study is *A Concordance to the Septuagint and Other Greek Versions of the Old Testament (Including the Apocryphal Books)* by Edwin Hatch and Henry Redpath (2 vols., 1892-1906). Each Greek word in the canonical and apocryphal books is listed with its Hebrew counterpart in a corresponding numerical sequence. Because the usage of a given word is crucial in determining its meaning(s), the inclusion in this instance of the Apocrypha is fortuitous. Were this not the case, we would have had to seek for another concordance that would alert us to word usage in those ancient, noncanonical writings.

O

ὁ, ἡ, τό, passim.

ὀβελίσκος. (1) חַדּוּדִים
Jb. 41. 21 (22). ἡ στρωμνὴ αὐτοῦ ὀβελίσκοι ὀξεῖς (1)
IV Ma. 11. 19. ὀβελίσκους ὀξεῖς πυρώσαντες

ὀβολός. (1) אֲגוֹרָה (2) גֵּרָה
Ex. 30. 13. εἴκοσι ὀβολοὶ τὸ δίδραχμον (2)
Le. 27. 25. εἴκοσι ὀβολοὶ ἔσται τὸ δίδραχμον (2)
Nu. 3. 47. εἴκοσι ὀβολοὺς τοῦ σίκλου [Α -οὶ ὅ σ.] (2)
18. 16. εἴκοσι ὀβολοί εἰσι (2)
I Ki. 2. 36. προσκυνεῖν αὐτῷ ὀβολοῦ ἀργυρίου (1)
Pr. 17. 6 (Α 4). τοῦ δὲ ἀπίστου οὐδὲ ὀβολός –
Ez. 45. 12. ὁ σίκλος εἴκοσι ὀβολοί (2)
[Aq., Th. Nu. 3. 47.]

ὀγδοήκοντα.
Ge. 5. 25†, 26†, 28 : 16. 16 : 35. 28.
Ex. 7. 7 bis.
Nu. 2. 9 : 4. 48†.
Jo. 14. 10.
Jd. 3. 30.
III Ki. 3. 1 (5. 29)† : 5. 15 (29) : 12. 21†.
IV Ki. 10. 24† : 19. 35.
I Ch. 7. 5 : 15. 9 : 21. 5† : 25. 7.
II Ch. 2. 2 (1), 18 (17) : 11. 1 : 14. 8 (7)† : 17. 15, 18 : 26. 17.
II Es. 8. 8, 14†.
Ne. 11. 18.
To. 14. 2†.
Es. 1. 4.
Ps. 89 (90). 10.
Ca. 6. 7 (8).
Is. 37. 36.
Je. 48 (41). 5.
I Ma. 7. 41.
II Ma. 4. 8 : 8. 19 : 11. 4 : 15. 22.
[Aq., Sm., Th. Ge. 5. 25, 26 : I Ki. 22. 18.]
[Heb., Sam. Ge. 5. 25, 26.]

ὀγδοηκοστός.
II Ma. 1. 10. R ἔτους ἑκατοστοῦ [Α om.] ὀ. καὶ ὀγδόου
[Aq., Sm. III Ki. 6. 1.]

ὄγδοος. (1) a. שְׁמִינִי b. שְׁמֹנַת c. שְׁמֹנֶה d. שְׁמֹנָה
Ge. 17. 14. τῇ ἡμέρᾳ τῇ ὀ.
21. 4. τῇ ἡμέρᾳ τῇ ὀ. (1 b)
Ex. 22. 30 (29). τῇ δὲ ὀγδόῃ ἡμέρᾳ [Α ἡ. τῇ ὀ.] ἀποδώσεις μοι (1 a)
Le. 9. 1. καὶ ἐγενήθη τῇ ἡμέρᾳ τῇ ὀ. (1 a)
12. 3. καὶ τῇ ἡμέρᾳ τῇ ὀ. περιτεμεῖ (1 a)
14. 10. τῇ ἡμέρᾳ τῇ ὀ. λήψεται δύο ἀμνούς (1 a)
– 23. προσοίσει αὐτὰ τῇ ἡμέρᾳ τῇ ὀ. (1 a)
15. 14. τῇ ἡμέρᾳ τῇ ὀ. λήψεται ἑαυτῷ (1 a)
– 29. τῇ ἡμέρᾳ τῇ ὀ. λήψεται (1 a)
22. 27. τῇ δὲ ἡμέρᾳ τῇ ὀ. (1 a)
23. 36. τῇ ἡμέρᾳ τῇ ὀ. κλητὴ ἁγία ἔσται (1 a)
– 39. τῇ ἡμέρᾳ τῇ ὀ. ἀνάπαυσις (1 a)
– 39. τῆς ἑορτῆς τὸ ἔτος τὸ ὀ. (1 a)
Nu. 6. 10. τῇ ἡμέρᾳ τῇ ὀ. οἴσει δύο τρυγόνας (1 a)
7. 54. τῇ ἡμ. τῇ ὀ. ἄρχων τῶν υἱῶν Μαν. (1 a)
29. 35. τῇ ἡμ. τῇ ὀ. ἐξόδιον ἔσται ὑμῖν (1 a)
III Ki. 6. 1 (38). οὗτος ὁ μὴν ὁ ὀ. (1 a)
8. 66. ἐν τῇ ἡμέρᾳ τῇ ὀ. (1 a)
12. 32, 33. ἐν τῷ μηνὶ τῷ ὀ. (1 a)
16. 29. Α ἐν ἔτει τριακοστῷ καὶ ὀ. τοῦ Ἀσά [Β al.] (1 c)
IV Ki. 15. 8. ἐν ἔτει τριακοστῷ καὶ ὀ. τῷ Ἀζ. (1 c)
22. 3. ἐν τῷ μηνὶ τῷ ὀ. [Α ἐβδόμῳ] (1 c)
24. 12. ἐν ἔτει ὀ. τῆς βασιλείας αὐ. (1 c)
I Ch. 12. 12. Ἰωανὰν ὁ ὀ. (1 a)
24. 10. τῷ Ἀβ. ὁ ὀ. (1 a)

i Ch. 25. 15. ὁ ὀ. Ἰωσ. (1 a)
26. 4. R Ἀβδεδὸμ ὁ ὄγδοος –
– 5. Α R Φ. ὁ ὄ. [Β om. ὁ ὄ.] (1 a)
27. 11. ὁ ὄ. τῷ μηνὶ τῷ ὀ. (1 a, 1 a)
II Ch. 7. 9. ἐν τῇ ἡμέρᾳ τῇ ὀ. †
16. 1. ἐν τῷ ὀ. καὶ τριακοστῷ ἔτει τῆς βασ. Ἀ. †
23. 1. ἐν τῷ ἔτει τῷ ὀ. [Α ἐβδόμῳ] (1 d)
29. 17. τῇ ἡμέρᾳ τῇ ὀ. τοῦ μηνὸς (1 d)
34. 3. ἐν τῷ ὀ. ἔτει τῆς βασ. αὐτοῦ (1 c)
Ne. 8. 18. καὶ [Sᵇ add. ἐν] τῇ ἡμέρᾳ τῇ ὀ. ἐξόδιον (1 a)
Ps. 6. tit. ὑπὲρ τῆς ὀγδόης ψαλμὸς τῷ Δαυίδ (1 a)
11 (12). tit. ὑπὲρ τῆς ὀγδόης ψαλμὸς τῷ Δαυίδ (1 a)
Si. prol. 19. ἐν γὰρ τῷ ὀ. καὶ τριακοστῷ ἔτει ἐπὶ τοῦ Εὐεργέτου βασιλέως
Za. 1. 1. ἐν τῷ ὀ. μηνὶ ἔτους δευτέρου (1 a)
[Α πέμπτῳ]
Je. 43 (36). 9. ἐγενήθη ἐν τῷ ἔτει τῷ ὀγδόῳ †
[Α πέμπτῳ]
Ez. 43. 27. ἀπὸ τῆς ἡμέρας τῆς ὀ. καὶ ἐπέκεινα (1 a)
I Ma. 4. 52. τοῦ [Sᵃ ἔτους] ὀ. καὶ τεσσαρακοστοῦ καὶ ἑκατοστοῦ ἔτους
II Ma. 1. 10. R ἔτους ἑκατοστοῦ [Α om.] ὀγδοηκοστοῦ καὶ ὀγδόου
11. 21, 33, 38. ἔτους ἑκατοστοῦ τεσσαρακοστοῦ ὀ.
[Aq., Th. Ps. 11 (12). 1.]

ὅδε. (1) אֵלֶּה (2) הָא (3) הִנֵּה (4) a. כֹּה b. כָּבָה (5) a. תָּדֶ כֹּה b. נְאֻם (6) κατὰ τάδε כֹּה (7) τάδε εἶπεν נְאֻם (8) τάδε λέγει נְאֻם
Ge. 25. 24 : 38. 27. καὶ τῇδε ἦν δίδυμα (3)
43. 21. καὶ τὸ ἀργύριον ἑκάστου (3)
45. 9. τάδε λέγει ὁ υἱός σου Ἰ. (4 a)
50. 18. οἵδε ἡμεῖς σοὶ οἰκέται (3)
Ex. 4. 22. τάδε λέγει κύριος (4 a)
5. 1. τάδε λέγει κ. ὁ θεὸς Ἰσρ. (4 a)
[Α τάδε λέγει Φ.
7. 17 : 8. 1 (7. 26), 20 (16). τάδε λέγει κύριος (4 a)
8. 29 (25). ὅδε ἐγὼ ἐξελεύσομαι ἀπὸ σοῦ (3)
9. 1, 13 : 10. 3. τάδε λέγει κ. ὁ θεὸς τῶν Ἑβρ. (4 a)
11. 4. τάδε λέγει κύριος (4 a)
14. 10. Α καὶ οἶδε [Β om.] οἱ Αἰγ. ἐστρατοπέδευσαν (3)
17. 6. ὅδε ἐγὼ ἕστηκα (3)
19. 3 : 20. 22. τάδε ἐρεῖς τῷ οἴκῳ Ἰ. (4 a)
32. 27. τάδε λέγει κ. ὁ θεὸς Ἰσρ. (4 a)
Le. 10. 16. καὶ ὅδε ἐνεπεπύριστο (3)
13. 55. καὶ ἥδε μὴ μετέβαλεν ἡ ἀφὴ τὴν ὄψιν (3)
Nu. 14. 40. οἵδε ἡμεῖς ἀναβησόμεθα (3)
16. 42 (17. 7). καὶ τήνδε ἐκάλυψεν αὐτὴν ἡ νεφ. (3)
20. 14. τάδε λέγει ὁ ἀδελφός σου Ἰσρ. (4 a)
22. 16. τάδε λέγει Β. (4 a)
23. 6. ὅδε εἱστήκει ἐπὶ τῶν ὁλοκαυτωμ. (3)
– 16. καὶ τάδε λαλήσεις (3)
– 17. ΑΒ² καὶ ὅδε ἐφειστήκει [Β¹ R al.] (3)
Jo. 7. 13. τάδε λέγει κ. ὁ θεὸς Ἰσρ. (4 a)
24. 2. τάδε λέγει κ. ὁ θεὸς Ἰσρ. (4 a)
Jd. 2. 1. τάδε λέγει κύριος [Α al.] –
6. 8. τάδε λέγει κ. ὁ θεὸς Ἰσρ. (4 a)
– 3. ὅδε πιλιορκοῦσίν με. (3)
11. 15. Α τάδε [Β οὕτω] λέγει Ἰ. (4 a)
19. 3. ὅδε εἰσήγαγεν αὐτὸν [Α al.] –
– 30. Α τάδε ἐρεῖτε πρὸς πάντα ἄνδρα Ἰσρ. –
Ru.1.17. τάδε ποιήσαι μοι κύριος καὶ τάδε προσθείη (4 a, 4 a)
I Ki. 2. 14. κατὰ τάδε [Α ταῦτα δὲ] ἐποίουν (4 b)
– 27. τάδε λέγει κύριος (4 a)
– 30. τάδε λέγει κ. ὁ θεὸς Ἰσρ. (7)
3. 17. τάδε ποιήσαι σοι ὁ θεός (4 a)
– 17. ΑΒ καὶ τάδε προσθείη (4 a)
9. 9. τάδε ἔλεγεν ἕκαστος –

I Ki. 10. 18. τάδε εἶπε κ. ὁ θεὸς Ἰσρ. (4 a)
11. 7. κατὰ τάδε ποιήσουσι τοῖς βουσὶν αὐ. (6)
– 9. τάδε ἐρεῖτε τοῖς ἀνδράσιν Ἰ. (4 a)
14. 9 (Β), 10. ἰδὲ τάδε εἴπωσι πρὸς ἡμᾶς (4 a)
– 41. ἰδὲ τάδε εἴπῃ [Α -ῃς] –
– 44. τάδε ποιήσαι μοι ὁ θεὸς καὶ τάδε προσθείη (4 a, 4 a)
15. 2. τάδε εἶπε κύριος σαβ. (4 a)
– 16. τάδε ἐρεῖτε τῷ Δαυίδ (4 a)
20. 7. ἐὰν τάδε εἴπῃ [Α -ῃς] (4 a)
– 13. τάδε ποιήσαι ὁ θεὸς τῷ Ἰων. καὶ τάδε προσθείη (4 a, 4 a)
– 22. ἐὰν τάδε εἴπω τῷ νεανίσκῳ (4 a)
25. 6. καὶ ἐρεῖτε τάδε (4 a)
– 22. τάδε ποιήσαι ὁ θ. τῷ Δ. καὶ τάδε προσθείη (4 a, 4 a)
27. 11. τάδε Δ. ποιεῖ (4 a)
– 11. τάδε [Α τόδε] τὸ δικαίωμα αὐ. (4 a)
II Ki. 3. 9. τάδε ποιήσαι ὁ θ. τῷ Ἀβ. καὶ τάδε προσθείη αὐτῷ (4 a, 4 a)
– 35. τάδε ποιήσαι μοι ὁ θ. καὶ τάδε προσθείη (4 a, 4 a)
7. 5. τάδε λέγει κύριος (4 a)
– 8. τάδε ἐρεῖς τῷ δούλῳ μου Δ. (4 a)
– 8. τάδε λέγει κύριος παντοκράτωρ (4 a)
11. 25. τάδε ἐρεῖς πρὸς Ἰ. (4 a)
12. 7. τάδε λέγει κ. ὁ θ. Ἰσρ. (4 a)
– 11. τάδε λέγει κύριος (4 a)
19. 13 (14). τάδε ποιήσαι μοι ὁ θ. καὶ τάδε προσθείη (4 a, 4 a)
24. 12. Β τάδε λέγει κύριος (4 a)
III Ki. 2. 23. τάδε ποιήσαι μοι ὁ θ. καὶ τάδε προσθείη (4 a, 4 a)
– 30. τάδε λέγει ὁ βασ. (4 a)
– 30. τάδε λελάληκεν Ἰ. καὶ τάδε ἀποκέκριταί μοι (4 a, 4 a)
11. 31. τάδε λέγει κ. ὁ θ. Ἰσρ. (4 a)
12. 10. τάδε λαλήσεις τῷ λαῷ τούτῳ (4 a)
– 10. τάδε λαλήσεις πρὸς αὐτούς (4 a)
– 24. τάδε λέγει κύριος (4 a)
– 24 sexiens. Β τάδε λέγει κύριος (4 a)
13. 2, 21. τάδε λέγει κύριος (4 a)
14. 7. τάδε λέγει κ. ὁ θεὸς Ἰσρ. (4 a)
19. 2. τάδε ποιήσαι μοι ὁ θ. καὶ τάδε προσθείη [Α al.] (4 a, 4 a)
20 (21). 19 bis. τάδε λέγει κύριος (4 a)
21 (20). 3, 5. τάδε λέγει υἱὸς Ἀδὲρ (4 a)
– 10. τάδε ποιήσαι μοι ὁ θ. καὶ τάδε προσθείη [Α al.] (4 a, 4 a)
– 13, 14, 28, 42 : 22. 11. τάδε λέγει κύριος (4 a)
22. 27. Α τάδε λέγει ὁ βασ. (4 a)
IV Ki. 1. 4, 6. τάδε λέγει κύριος (4 a)
– 11. τάδε λέγει ὁ βασ. (4 a)
– 16. 2. 21 : 3. 16, 17 : 4. 43. τάδε λέγει κύριος (4 a)
6. 8. εἰς τὸν τόπον τ. τινὰ ἐλμωνὶ παρεμβαλῶ –
– 31. τάδε ποιήσαι μοι ὁ θεὸς καὶ τάδε προσθείη (4 a, 4 a)
7. 1 : 9. 3. τάδε λέγει κύριος (4 a)
9. 6. τάδε λέγει κύριος ὁ θ. Ἰσρ. (4 a)
– 12. τάδε λέγει κύριος (4 a)
18. 19 : 18. 19, 29. τάδε λέγει ὁ βασ. (4 a)
19. 3. τάδε λέγει Ἐζ. (4 a)
– 3. τάδε ἐρεῖτε πρὸς τὸν κύριον ὑμῶν (4 a)
– 6. τάδε λέγει κύριος (4 a)
– 10. Α τάδε ἐρεῖτε πρὸς Ἐζ. (4 a)
– 20. τάδε λέγει ὁ θεὸς τῶν δυνάμεων (4 a)
– 32 : 20. 1. τάδε λέγει κύριος (4 a)
21. 12 : 22. 15. τάδε λέγει κ. ὁ θεὸς Ἰσρ. (4 a)
22. 16. τάδε λέγει κύριος (4 a)
– 15. τάδε ἐρεῖτε πρὸς αὐτὸν (4 a)
– 18. τάδε λέγει κ. ὁ θεὸς Ἰσρ. (4 a)

Fig. 12. Page from A *Concordance to the Septuagint and Other Greek Versions of the Old Testament (Including the Apocryphal Books)*, by Hatch and Redpath.

NEW TESTAMENT RESOURCES

Concordances to the New Testament, particularly in German, are legion. For this reason it is important to confine ourselves to only a few. Regardless of a researcher's knowledge of Greek, he should find at least one of the following helpful.

- *The Englishman's Greek Concordance of the New Testament*
- Moulton's and Geden's *Concordance to the Greek Testament*
- Schmoller's *Handkonkordanz zum griechischen Neuen Testament*
- *Computer-Konkordanz zum Novum Testamentum.*

G. K. Gillespie's *The Englishman's Greek Concordance of the New Testament* (edited by George V. Wigram, 1903) is arranged in the same way as its Old Testament counterpart. It is based on the text of the KJV and cites the Scripture references with brief quotations under alphabetically-listed Greek words. Included in the Scripture quotations are the English words translated from the Greek word under consideration. From this index the student will find, for example, a listing of the twenty-seven different English words used to translate *logos* ("word").

The *Concordance to the Greek Testament* by William F. Moulton and Albert S. Geden (1897) was revised by H. K. Moulton in 1978. Now complete with full citations even for particles like *apo, en, hoti, oun, sun,* this concordance has become one of the basic reference tools for students of the New Testament.

Based on the text of Westcott and Hort, this volume contains longer Scripture quotations than in most concordances of this kind. The work of Moulton and Geden is replete with grammatical hints, the usage of the word in the LXX and Apocrypha, and citations in Hebrew if the passage in question happens to be a quotation from the Old Testament.

Alfred Schmoller's *Handkonkordanz zum griechischen Neuen Testament* (14th ed., 1968), is based on the Nestle text, is smaller than Moulton and Geden, and is not as complete. It does contain symbols informing the reader of the usage of a given word in the LXX or Vulgate. A further limitation is found in the study of the synoptic gospels where parallel passages cited at the first mention of a word are not repeated.

Frederick W. Danker, whose wisdom is to be respected, has the following comment on Schmoller's handy concordance:

> The combination of Nestle's Greek text with Schmoller's 7th and following editions makes Nestle-Schmoller a most desirable travelling companion, whether to the conference hall or to the seashore. . . . At times, however, reliance on Schmoller can be frustrating, because he does not, on his own admission, include the entire New Testament vocabulary, and for a number of words he has only a representative listing.[*]

The valuable *Computer-Konkordanz zum Novum Testament* (1980) is an

---

[*]Frederick W. Danker, *Multipurpose Tools for Bible Study* (St. Louis: Concordia, 1966), p. 7.

THE

ENGLISHMAN'S GREEK CONCORDANCE.

A, *alpha.*

Rev. 1: 8. I am *Alpha* and Omega, the beginning
11. I am *Alpha* and Omega, the first and the
21: 6. I am *Alpha* and Omega, the beginning
22:13. I am *Alpha* and Omega, the beginning

ἀβαρής, *abarees.*

2Co.11: 9. kept myself *from being burdensome*

ἀββᾶ, *abba.*

Mar14:36. And he said, *Abba,* Father,
Ro. 8:15. whereby we cry, *Abba,* Father.
Gal. 4: 6. into your hearts, crying, *Abba,* Father.

ἄβυσσος, *abussos.*

Lu. 8:31. command them to go out into the *deep.*
Ro. 10: 7. Who shall descend into the *deep?*
Rev. 9: 1. the key of the *bottomless* pit.
2. And he opened the *bottomless* pit;
11. the angel of the *bottomless* pit,
11: 7. that ascendeth out of the *bottomless pit*
17: 8. shall ascend out of the *bottomless pit*
20: 1. having the key of the *bottomless pit*
3. cast him into the *bottomless pit,*

ἀγαθοεργέω, *agathoergeo.*

1Ti.6:18. *That* they *do good,* that they be rich in

ἀγαθοποιέω, *agathopoyeo.*

Mar. 3: 4. *to do good* on the sabbath days,
Lu. 6: 9. on the sabbath days *to do good,*
33. ye *do good* to them *which do good*
35. and *do good,* and lend,
Acts14:17. in that he *did good,* and gave us
1Pet 2:15. *with well doing* ye may put to silence
20. *when* ye *do well,* and suffer (for it),
3: 6. as long as ye *do well,* and are not afraid
17. ye suffer for *well doing,* than for evil
3 Joh. 11. He *that doeth good* is of God:

ἀγαθοποιΐα, *agathopoiya.*

1Pet.4:19. their souls (to him) in *well doing,*

ἀγαθοποιός, *agathopoyos.*

1Pet.2:14. for the praise of them *that do well.*

ἀγαθός, *agathos.*

Mat. 5:45. to rise on the evil and on the *good,*
7:11. give *good* gifts unto your children,
— which is in heaven give *good things*
17. every *good* tree bringeth forth good fruit;
18. A *good* tree cannot bring forth evil
12:34. ye, being evil, speak *good things?*
35. A *good* man out of the *good* treasure of the heart bringeth forth *good things :*
19:16. *Good* Master, what *good thing* shall I do,
17. Why callest thou me *good?* (there is) none *good*
20:15. Is thine eye evil, because I am *good?*
22:10. many as they found, both bad and *good :*
25:21. Well done, (thou) *good* and faithful
23. Well done, *good* and faithful servant;
Mar10:17. *Good* Master, what shall I do that I
18. Why callest thou me *good?* (there is) none *good*
Lu. 1:53. hath filled the hungry with *good things ;*
6:45. A *good* man out of the *good* treasure of his heart bringeth forth that which is *good ;*
8: 8. And other fell on *good* ground,
15. which in an honest and *good* heart,
10:42. Mary hath chosen that *good* part,
11:13. know how to give *good* gifts unto your
12:18. will I bestow all my fruits and my *goods.*
19. Soul, thou hast much *goods* laid up
16:25. thy lifetime receivedst thy *good things,*
18:18. *Good* Master, what shall I do to inherit
19. Why callest thou me *good?* none (is) *good,*
19:17. Well, thou *good* servant: because thou
23:50. (he was) a *good* man, and a just:
Joh. 1:46(47). Can there any *good thing* come out
5:29. they that have done *good,* unto the
7:12. some said, He is a *good* man: others
Acts 9:36. this woman was full of *good* works
11:24. For he was a *good* man, and full of the
23: 1. I have lived in all *good* conscience
Ro. 2: 7. by patient continuance *in well* doing
10. peace, to every man that worketh *good,*
3: 8. Let us do evil, that *good* may come?
5: 7. for a *good* man some would even dare
7:12. commandment holy, and just, and *good.*
13. Was then that which is *good* made death
— working death in me by that which is *good ;*
18. in my flesh, dwelleth no *good thing :*

Fig. 13. Page from Gillespie's *The Englishman's Greek Concordance of the New Testament,* edited by Wigram.

Re 2 17 ἐπὶ τὴν ψῆφον ὄνομα καινὸν γεγραμμένον
3 12 τὸ ὄνομα τ. πόλεως τ. Θεοῦ μου τ. καινῆς
     Ἱερουσαλήμ
  12 τὸ ὄνομά μου τὸ καινόν
5 9 ἄδουσιν ᾠδὴν καινήν
14 3 ᾄδουσιν ὡς ᾠδὴν καινὴν ἐνώπιον τ. θρόνου
21 1 εἶδον οὐρανὸν καινὸν κ. γῆν καινήν
  2 τ. πόλιν τ. ἁγίαν Ἱερουσαλὴμ καινὴν εἶδον
  5 ἰδοὺ καινὰ ποιῶ πάντα

ΚΑΙΝΟΤΗΣ

Ro 6 4 οὕτως κ. ἡμεῖς ἐν καινότητι ζωῆς περιπα-
  τήσωμεν
  7 6 ὥστε δουλεύειν ἡμᾶς ἐν καινότητι πνεύματος

ΚΑΙΠΕΡ

Phl 3 4 καίπερ ἐγὼ ἔχων πεποίθησιν κ. ἐν σαρκί
He 5 8 καίπερ ὢν υἱός
  7 5 καίπερ ἐξεληλυθότας ἐκ τ. ὀσφύος Ἀβραάμ
12 17 καίπερ μετὰ δακρύων ἐκζητήσας αὐτήν
II Pe 1 12 μελλήσω ἀεὶ ὑμᾶς ὑπομιμνήσκειν περὶ τού-
  των καίπερ εἰδότας

ΚΑΙΡΟΣ

(1) ἄχρι, πρὸ καιροῦ (2) πρὸς, κατὰ καιρόν
(3) καιροί (4) ὁ νῦν καιρός, καιρ. οὗτος,
ἐνεστηκώς

Mt 8 29 1 ἦλθες ὧδε πρὸ καιροῦ βασανίσαι ἡμᾶς
11 25 ἐν ἐκείνῳ τ. καιρῷ ἀποκριθεὶς ὁ Ἰησοῦς
12 1 ἐν ἐκείνῳ τ. καιρῷ ἐπορεύθη ὁ Ἰησοῦς
13 30 ἐν καιρῷ τ. θερισμοῦ ἐρῶ τ. θερισταῖς
14 1 ἐν ἐκείνῳ τ. καιρῷ ἤκουσεν Ἡρῴδης ὁ
  τετραάρχης
16 3 3 τὰ δὲ σημεῖα τ. καιρῶν οὐ δύνασθε
21 34 ὅτε δὲ ἤγγισεν ὁ καιρὸς τ. καρπῶν
  41 3 οἵτινες ἀποδώσουσιν αὐτῷ τ. καρποὺς ἐν
  τ. καιροῖς αὐτῶν
24 45 τοῦ δοῦναι αὐτοῖς τ. τροφὴν ἐν καιρῷ
26 18 ὁ καιρός μου ἐγγύς ἐστιν
Mk 1 15 πεπλήρωται ὁ καιρός
10 30 4 ἐὰν μὴ λάβῃ ἑκατονταπλασίονα νῦν ἐν τ.
  καιρῷ τούτῳ
11 13 ὁ γὰρ καιρὸς οὐκ ἦν σύκων
12 2 ἀπέστειλεν πρὸς τ. γεωργοὺς τ. καιρῷ
  δοῦλον
13 33 οὐκ οἴδατε γὰρ πότε ὁ καιρός ἐστιν
Lu 1 20 οἵτινες πληρωθήσονται εἰς τ. καιρὸν αὐτῶν
4 13 1 ὁ διάβολος ἀπέστη ἀπ' αὐτοῦ ἄχρι καιροῦ
8 13 2 οἳ πρὸς καιρὸν πιστεύουσιν,
  κ. ἐν καιρῷ πειρασμοῦ ἀφίστανται
12 42 τοῦ διδόναι ἐν καιρῷ τὸ σιτομέτριον
  56 4 τὸν καιρὸν δὲ τοῦτον πῶς οὐκ οἴδατε
  δοκιμάζειν
  τ. δὲ καιρ., TWH marg.
13 1 παρῆσαν δέ τινες ἐν αὐτῷ τ. καιρῷ
18 30 4 ὃς οὐχὶ μὴ λάβῃ πολλαπλασίονα ἐν τ.
  καιρῷ τούτῳ
19 44 ἀνθ' ὧν οὐκ ἔγνως τ. καιρὸν τ. ἐπισκοπῆς
  σου
20 10 καιρῷ ἀπέστειλεν πρὸς τ. γεωργοὺς δοῦλον
21 8 ὁ καιρὸς ἤγγικεν
  24 3 ἄχρι οὗ πληρωθῶσιν καιροὶ ἐθνῶν
  36 ἀγρυπνεῖτε δὲ ἐν παντὶ καιρῷ δεόμενοι

Jo 5 [4 2 ἄγγελος γὰρ Κυρίου κατὰ καιρὸν κατέβαινεν
  ἐν τ. κολυμβήθρα
  —h. v., TWHR non mg.
  7 6 ὁ καιρὸς ὁ ἐμὸς οὔπω πάρεστιν·
  ὁ δὲ καιρὸς ὁ ὑμέτερος πάντοτέ ἐστιν ἕτοιμος
  8 ὅτι ὁ ἐμὸς καιρὸς οὔπω πεπλήρωται
Ac 1 7 8 οὐχ ὑμῶν ἐστιν γνῶναι χρόνους ἢ καιρούς
3 20 3 ὅπως ἂν ἔλθωσιν καιροὶ ἀναψύξεως
7 20 ἐν ᾧ καιρῷ ἐγεννήθη Μωυσῆς
12 1 2 κατ' ἐκεῖνον δὲ τ. καιρὸν ἐπέβαλεν Ἡρῴδης
  . . . τ. χεῖρας
13 11 1 μὴ βλέπων τ. ἥλιον ἄχρι καιροῦ
14 17 3 οὐρανόθεν ὑμῖν ὑετοὺς διδοὺς κ. καιροὺς
  καρποφόρους
17 26 3 ὁρίσας προστεταγμένους καιρούς
19 23 2 ἐγένετο δὲ κατὰ τ. καιρὸν ἐκεῖνον τάραχος
  οὐκ ὀλίγος
24 25 καιρὸν δὲ μεταλαβὼν μετακαλέσομαί σε
Ro 3 26 4 πρὸς τ. ἔνδειξιν τ. δικαιοσύνης αὐτοῦ ἐν
  τ. νῦν καιρῷ
5 6 2 κατὰ καιρὸν ὑπὲρ ἀσεβῶν ἀπέθανεν
8 18 4 οὐκ ἄξια τὰ παθήματα τ. νῦν καιροῦ
9 9 2 κατὰ τ. καιρὸν τοῦτον ἐλεύσομαι
  שׁוֹב כָּעֵת אֵלֶיךָ אָשׁוּב כָּעֵת חַיָּה, Gen. xviii. 10
11 5 4 ἐν τ. νῦν καιρῷ λεῖμμα κατ' ἐκλογὴν
  χάριτος γέγονεν
12 11 τ. καιρῷ δουλεύοντες
  Κυρίῳ, TWHR non mg.
13 11 κ. τοῦτο εἰδότες τ. καιρόν
I Co 4 5 1 μὴ πρὸ καιροῦ τι κρίνετε
7 5 2 εἰ μήτι ἂν ἐκ συμφώνου πρὸς καιρόν
29 ὁ καιρὸς συνεσταλμένος
II Co 6 2 καιρῷ δεκτῷ ἐπήκουσά σου
  בְּעֵת רָצוֹן עֲנִיתִיךָ, Is. xlix. 8
  2 ἰδοὺ νῦν καιρὸς εὐπρόσδεκτος
8 14 4 ἐν τ. νῦν καιρῷ τὸ ὑμῶν περίσσευμα εἰς
  τὸ ἐκείνων ὑστέρημα
Ga 4 10 3 ἡμέρας παρατηρεῖσθε κ. μῆνας κ. καιρούς
6 9 καιρῷ γὰρ ἰδίῳ θερίσομεν μὴ ἐκλυόμενοι.
  10 ἄρα οὖν ὡς καιρὸν ἔχωμεν
Eph 1 10 3 εἰς οἰκονομίαν τ. πληρώματος τ. καιρῶν
2 12 ὅτι ἦτε τ. καιρῷ ἐκείνῳ χωρὶς Χριστοῦ
5 16 ὡς σοφοὶ ἐξαγοραζόμενοι τ. καιρόν
18 προσευχόμενοι ἐν παντὶ καιρῷ ἐν πνεύματι
Col 4 5 τ. καιρὸν ἐξαγοραζόμενοι
I Th 2 17 2 ἀπορφανισθέντες ἀφ' ὑμῶν πρὸς καιρὸν
  ὥρας
5 1 περὶ δὲ τ. χρόνων κ. τ. καιρῶν
II Th 2 6 εἰς τὸ ἀποκαλυφθῆναι αὐτὸν ἐν τ. αὐτοῦ καιρῷ
I Ti 2 6 3 τὸ μαρτύριον καιροῖς ἰδίοις
4 1 3 ἐν ὑστέροις καιροῖς ἀποστήσονταί τινες
  τ. πίστεως
6 15 3 ἣν καιροῖς ἰδίοις δείξει ὁ μακάριος κ.
  μόνος δυνάστης
II Ti 3 1 3 ἐν ἐσχάταις ἡμέραις ἐνστήσονται καιροὶ
  χαλεποί
  4 3 ἔσται γὰρ καιρὸς ὅτε τ. ὑγιαινούσης διδασκαλίας οὐκ ἀνέξονται
6 ὁ καιρὸς τ. ἀναλύσεώς μου ἐφέστηκεν
Tit 1 3 3 ἐφανέρωσεν δὲ καιροῖς ἰδίοις τ. λόγον αὐτοῦ
He 9 9 4 ἥτις παραβολὴ εἰς τ. καιρὸν τ. ἐνεστηκότα
  10 μέχρι καιροῦ διορθώσεως ἐπικείμενα
11 11 δύναμιν εἰς καταβολὴν σπέρματος ἔλαβεν
  κ. παρὰ καιρὸν ἡλικίας

Fig. 14. Page from *Concordance to the Greek Testament*, by Moulton and
Geden.

indispensable aid in the study of specific Greek words used in the New Testament. Based on the twenty-sixth edition of the Nestle-Aland text and the third edition of the United Bible Societies' *Greek New Testament,* this beautifully produced concordance lists every New Testament word and its frequency of occurrence. Each quotation is lengthy, and that enables the researcher better to assess the context in which the word appears.

As a general rule, words are arranged in accordance with their root form. In the case of some irregular verbs, however, the word is also listed under the different forms.

Words occurring in pericope are included with an asterisk following each entry. An appendix lists the appearance of conjunctions, particles, et cetera.

All things considered, this concordance is likely to become the standard resource tool for serious Bible students.

ASSIGNMENT

In preparation for a further discussion of words and their meaning, take special note of: (1) the way in which, *hesed,* "lovingkindness," is treated in the *Theological Wordbook of the Old Testament* by R. L. Harris, G. L. Archer, and B. K. Waltke; and (2) study carefully the article "Discipleship" in the *New International Dictionary of New Testament Theology,* edited by Colin Brown. Take special note of the sequence of thought, the sources from which the information is gleaned, and the movement from one historical period to the next.

Ψ

ψαλλω [5]

Rm	15 9	δια τουτο εξομολογησομαι σοι εν εθνεσιν και τω ονοματι σου ψαλω.
1Co	14 15	ψαλω τω πνευματι, ψαλω δε και τω νοι.
	14 15	ψαλω τω πνευματι, ψαλω δε και τω νοι.
Eph	5 19	αδοντες και ψαλλοντες τη καρδια υμων τω κυριω,
Ja	5 13	ευθυμει τις; ψαλλετω.

ψαλμος [7]

Lc	20 42	αυτος γαρ δαυιδ λεγει εν βιβλω ψαλμων· ειπεν κυριος τω κυριω μου·
	24 44	ουτοι οι λογοι μου ους ελαλησα προς υμας ετι ων συν υμιν, οτι δει πληρωθηναι παντα τα γεγραμμενα εν τω νομω μωϋσεως και τοις προφηταις και ψαλμοις περι εμου.
Ac	1 20	γεγραπται γαρ εν βιβλω ψαλμων· γενηθητω η επαυλις αυτου ερημος και μη εστω ο κατοικων εν αυτη,
	13 33	ως και εν τω ψαλμω γεγραπται τω δευτερω·
1Co	14 26	οταν συνερχησθε, εκαστος ψαλμον εχει,
Eph	5 19	λαλουντες εαυτοις [εν] ψαλμοις και υμνοις και ωδαις πνευματικαις,
Col	3 16	ψαλμοις υμνοις ωδαις πνευματικαις εν [τη] χαριτι αδοντες εν ταις καρδιαις υμων τω θεω·

ψευδαδελφος [2]

2Co	11 26	κινδυνοις εν ερημια, κινδυνοις εν θαλασση, κινδυνοις εν ψευδαδελφοις·
Ga	2 4	δια δε τους παρεισακτους ψευδαδελφους, οιτινες παρεισηλθον κατασκοπησαι την ελευθεριαν ημων ην εχομεν εν χριστω ιησου,

ψευδαποστολος [1]

2Co	11 13	οι γαρ τοιουτοι ψευδαποστολοι, εργαται δολιοι, μετασχηματιζομενοι εις αποστολους χριστου.

ψευδης [3]

Ac	6 13	εστησαν τε μαρτυρας ψευδεις λεγοντας·
Apc	2 2	και επειρασας τους λεγοντας εαυτους αποστολους και ουκ εισιν, και ευρες αυτους ψευδεις·
	21 8	τοις δε δειλοις και απιστοις και εβδελυγμενοις και φονευσιν και πορνοις και φαρμακοις και ειδωλολατραις και πασιν τοις ψευδεσιν το μερος αυτων εν τη λιμνη

ψευδοδιδασκαλος [1]

2Pt	2 1	εγενοντο δε και ψευδοπροφηται εν τω λαω, ως και εν υμιν

ψευδομαι [12]

Ja	3 14	ει δε ζηλον πικρον εχετε και εριθειαν εν τη καρδια υμων, μη κατακαυχασθε και ψευδεσθε κατα της αληθειας,
1Jh	1 6	εαν ειπωμεν οτι κοινωνιαν εχομεν μετ αυτου και εν τω σκοτει περιπατωμεν, ψευδομεθα και ου ποιουμεν την αληθειαν·
Apc	3 9	των λεγοντων εαυτους ιουδαιους ειναι, και ουκ εισιν αλλα ψευδονται·

ψευδομαρτυρεω [5]

Mt	19 18	το ου φονευσεις, ου μοιχευσεις, ου κλεψεις, ου ψευδομαρτυρησεις, τιμα τον πατερα και την μητερα, και αγαπησεις τον πλησιον σου ως σεαυτον·
Mc	10 19	μη φονευσης, μη μοιχευσης, μη κλεψης, μη ψευδομαρτυρησης, μη αποστερησης, τιμα τον πατερα σου και την μητερα.
	14 56	πολλοι γαρ εψευδομαρτυρουν κατ αυτου, και ισαι αι μαρτυριαι ουκ ησαν.
	57	και τινες ανασταντες εψευδομαρτυρουν κατ αυτου λεγοντες
Lc	18 20	μη μοιχευσης, μη φονευσης, μη κλεψης, μη ψευδομαρτυρησης, τιμα τον πατερα σου και την μητερα.

ψευδομαρτυρια [2]

Mt	15 19	εκ γαρ της καρδιας εξερχονται διαλογισμοι πονηροι, φονοι, μοιχειαι, πορνειαι, κλοπαι, ψευδομαρτυριαι, βλασφημιαι.
	26 59	οι δε αρχιερεις και το συνεδριον ολον εζητουν ψευδομαρτυριαν κατα του ιησου οπως αυτον θανατωσωσιν,

ψευδομαρτυς [2]

Mt	26 60	οι δε αρχιερεις και το συνεδριον ολον εζητουν ψευδομαρτυρων κατα του ιησου οπως αυτον θανατωσωσιν, και ουχ ευρον πολλων προσελθοντων ψευδομαρτυρων.
1Co	15 15	ευρισκομεθα δε και ψευδομαρτυρες του θεου,

ψευδοπροφητης [11]

Mt	7 15	προσεχετε απο των ψευδοπροφητων, οιτινες ερχονται προς υμας εν ενδυμασι προβατων,
	24 11	και πολλοι ψευδοπροφηται εγερθησονται και πλανησουσιν πολλους·
	24	εγερθησονται γαρ ψευδοχριστοι και ψευδοπροφηται,
Mc	13 22	εγερθησονται γαρ ψευδοχριστοι και ψευδοπροφηται και δωσουσιν σημεια και τερατα προς το αποπλαναν, ει δυνατον, τους εκλεκτους,
Lc	6 26	ουαι οταν καλως ειπωσιν υμας παντες οι ανθρωποι· κατα τα αυτα γαρ εποιουν τοις ψευδοπροφηταις οι πατερες αυτων.
Ac	13 6	διελθοντες δε ολην την νησον αχρι παφου ευρον ανδρα τινα μαγον ψευδοπροφητην ιουδαιον,
2Pt	2 1	εγενοντο δε και ψευδοπροφηται εν τω λαω,

Fig. 15. Page from *Computer-Konkordanz zum Novum Testament*.

7

THE IMPORTANCE
OF LEXICONS

Whereas concordances provide us with an alphabetical index of the principal words of a book (e.g., the Bible) or a writer (e.g., Paul), and a reference to the passage in which each mention of a word occurs (e.g., Galatians 1:4) along with some indication of the context, a lexicon may be described as a "wordbook or dictionary of a specific language, or the vocabulary of a particular people."

For a listing of the lexicographical tools available to the theological student, see *The Minister's Library*, pp. 79-80 and 123-24; Bollier's *The Literature of Theology*, p. 101; and Danker's *Multipurpose Tools for Bible Study*, pp. 97-150 (particularly pp. 123-32).

A lexicon is compiled to describe in succinct terms the meaning(s) of a given word. The etymology, traced through the successive stages of the history of the language, is important.

Hebrew Lexicons

Hebrew lexicography dates back to the ninth century A.D. More recently, however, there has been an upsurge of interest in Hebrew words and their meaning. Wilhelm Gesenius (1786-1842) produced the first modern dictionary under the title *Hebräisches-deutsches Handwörterbuch über die Schriften des Alten Testaments* in two volumes (1810-12). After seventeen editions and under the general editorship of Frants Buhl, this work appeared bearing the title *Hebräisches und aramaisches Handwörterbuch über das Alte Testament* (1922). A companion volume entitled *Thesaurus philologicus-criticus linguae Hebraeae et Chaldaeae Veteris Testamenti* was published posthumously (1829-58) and serves as a monument to Gesenius's tireless industry and thoroughness, as well as his extensive knowledge of Hebrew.

The value of Gesenius's work to us is that three British scholars, F. Brown, S. R. Driver, and C. A. Briggs, translated and edited Gesenius's dictionary and published their revision under the title *A Hebrew and English Lexicon to the Old Testament*. This outstanding work, frequently referred to as BDB, gives evidence of the real sensitivity of the editors to the nuances of the Semitic languages and remains *the* standard resource tool at the present time. The most recent corrections to the text were made in the 1962 edition.

A valuable *Index to Brown, Driver and Briggs Hebrew Lexicon* was compiled by B. Einspahr (1976). Containing nearly 140,000 references, this resource tool follows the text of the NASB and lists the words as they appear in the Bible. It provides the chapter and verse number, the unpointed Hebrew word as it occurs in the Masoretic Text, the word's meaning, with the page and section where it is discussed in BDB. Einspahr's *Index* must rank as one of the most valuable Old Testament study tools to be produced in many years.

Translations of the Talmud, Midrash, and Mishnah are now available in English.

Other important lexicographical works followed the publication of Gesenius's dictionary in 1810. It was not until 1876, however, that a comprehensive lexicon appeared dealing with the postbiblical Hebrew and Aramaic era. Jacob Levy's *Neuhebräisches und chaldäisches Wörterbuch Über die Talmudim und Midraschim* (1876-89; 2d ed., 1924) and *Chaldäisches Wörterbuch über die Targumim* (1881) provided access to the Talmudic and Midrashic literature of the Jews. These works bore some resemblance to Johann Buxtorf's *Lexicon Chaldaicum, Talmidicum et Rabbinicum* (1639) and Edmund Castell's *Lexicon Heptaglotton Hebraicum, Chaldaicum, Syriacum, Samaritanum, Aethiopicum, Arabicum et Persicum* (1669), but were more complete.

Prior to BDB, the renowned philologist S. P. Tregelles translated Gesenius's *Lexicon Manuale Hebraicum et Chaldaicum in Veteris Testamenti Libros* from Latin into English. This work still is in print under the title *Gesenius' Hebrew and Chaldee Lexicon to the Old Testament Scriptures* (n.d.), and deserves to be kept on the Bible student's desk. Another handy work is W. L. Holladay's *Concise Hebrew and Aramaic Lexicon of the Old Testament* (1971), which is up to date and easy to use.

Numerous other Hebrew lexicons have been published and, although these are in handy format and are ideal to keep at one's side, none have yet replaced BDB.

Of comparative significance to BDB is the *Lexicon in Veteris Testamenti libros*, edited by L. Köehler and W. Baumgartner (2 vols., 1951-53). This work, together with a supplement (1958), provides an English-German dictionary to words and their meanings in the third edition of Kittel's *Biblia Hebraica*. The order of the words is strictly alphabetical and not by root as in BDB. Usage is also made of Ugaritic sources not available to Brown, Driver, and Briggs. This lexicon is presently undergoing revision.

By means of a lexicon, the eager and inquiring researcher will be able to verify speedily and easily the results of his investigation via the numerous concordances of Hebrew words and their meaning.

It now remains for us to consider Greek works paralleling these Hebrew resources.

GREEK LEXICONS

The history of Greek literature may conveniently be classified into five broad periods of time. Obviously, these eras are capable of further subdivision. For convenience they are tabulated as follows:

- *The early period* (second millennium to c. 950 B.C.), consisting of hymns to the gods, harvest songs, war songs, dirges—all of which provided resource material for writers in the classical period
- *The classical period* (c. 950 to 330 B.C.), which included the writings of Homer, Hesiod, Euripedes, Xenophon, Thuycidides, Aristophenes, Herodotus, Aristotle, Demosthenes
- *The Hellenistic period* (330 B.C. to c. A.D. 325), during which the lingua franca of the people was essentially the same as the Koine Greek of the New Testament. This era included Plutarch, Philo, Josephus, Polybius, the writers of the New Testament, Clement, Origen, Irenaeus
- *The Byzantine period* (c. A.D. 325 to 1435)—a period that lies outside the realm of our discussion
- *The modern period* (1453—present).

Our interest will be primarily with the Hellenistic period. However, because many of the words used by the writers of the New Testament have their roots in the classical period, information from those writers will provide fertile ground for lexicographical research.

The most important resource tool to the classical period of Greek literature is the unabridged edition of H. G. Liddell's and R. Scott's *Greek-English Lexicon* (1897). A revised and updated edition was prepared for publication by H. S. Jones (1940), and a supplement by E. A. Barber was issued in 1968.

At the beginning is an index to the Greek authors and their works. It provides a key to the abbreviations used in the body of the lexicon (e.g., D. H. is Dionysius of Halicarnassus; J. *Vit* is Josephus, *Vita*; Plu. *Galb* is Plutarch(us), Lives (Galba); etc.).

The references cited in Liddell and Scott appear formidable to the student until he realizes that the famous Loeb Classical Library, published simulta-

ἀπόσκοπος, *erring from the mark*; met., of man as erring from the way, Hesych.H.*Ps.tit.*17(M.27.708D).

ἀποσκοραπισμός, ὁ, *rejection*, Eus.*Is.*66:16(M.24.520D); τὸν...ἀ. 'ἐπιτίμησιν' ἐκάλεσαν οἱ λοιποί Thdt.*Is.*66:15(p.260.19; cf.2.400).

*ἀποσκορακιστέον, *one must reject utterly*, Clem.*paed.*2.12(p.230.3; M.8.544B); *ib.*3.11(p.276.20; 649B); τοὺς...λέγοντας τὸ μίαν φύσιν τοῦ θεοῦ λόγου σεσαρκωμένην ἀ. Leont.H.*monoph.*(M.86.1812D).

ἀποσκυβαλίζω, *throw away as vile rubbish, excrete*, Dion.Al.ap.Eus. *h.e.*7.22.10(M.20.689B); Synes.*calv.*7(p.203.19; M.66.1180C); Melet. *nat.hom.*18(M.64.1220B); met., Gr.Naz.*ep.*88(M.37.161C); λογισμὸν ...ῥυπαρὸν τῆς ψυχῆς ἀ. Mac.Aeg.*elev.*13(M.34.901A); ἀ. τὰς αἱρέσεις, ὡς ἄχυρα Procl.CP or.18.2(M.65.820C); *treat as worthless* εἰ...τις ὡς μικροπολίτιν τὴν ἐκκλησίαν ἀποσκυβαλίσει Synes.*ep.*58(M.66.1401D); *cat.Apoc.*7:4(p.287.11).

ἀπόσμηξις, ἡ, *cleansing* ῥύπου παντὸς ἀ. Proc.G.*Is.*60:1ff.(M.87.2621A).

ἀποσμήχω, *clean*; of spiritual purification; 1. *purge away*; a. act., Meth.*symp.*1.1(p.9.9; M.18.40A); ἀ. τοῦ βίου τὴν θεοστυγίαν Eus.*h.e.*10.9.9(M.20.904C); Chrys.*hom.*80.1 *in Mt.*(7.765D); id.*hom.*4.6 *in 2Cor.*(10.463C); *ib.*15.5(10.551A) cit. s. ἐκκλησία; οὐδὲν οὕτως ἀ. τὰ ἁμαρτήματα, ὡς δάκρυα id.*hom.*12.4 *in Col.*(11.417D); b. med., Hipp.*Dan.*1.33; Chrys.*David* 3(4.770B); id.*hom.*1.3 *in Philm.*(11.778E); οὐ γὰρ ἦν ἑτέρως ~εσθαι τῆς τῶν πλανωμένων ψυχῆς τὴν...κηλῖδα, μὴ οὐχὶ διὰ τοῦ ἁγίου βαπτίσματος Cyr.*Is.*2.4(2.283B); of Jewish ritual washings μολυσμούς...δι' ὑδάτων καὶ λουτρῶν ἀ. Epiph. *haer.*15.1(p.209.8; M.41.244A); 2. med., *wipe off on oneself*; met., *acquire by contact* τούτου τὴν σκληραγωγίαν τέτρασιν ἀποσμηξάμενος ἔτεσιν Jo.D.*hom.*11.8(M.96.769C); 3. *cleanse, purify*; a. act., Ath. *inc.*57.3(M.25.196C); τὴν στολὴν τῆς ψυχῆς ἀ. Chrys.*hom.*2.1 *in Mt.* (7.19A); id.*hom.*23.4 *in Heb.*(12.218B); †Jo.D.B.J.20(M.96.1041B); b. med., fig. μηδενὸς...μολέμου...ἐν θαλάττῃ ἀ. Chrys.*hom.*3.4 *in 1Thess.* (11.446A); c. pass., Meth.*symp.*1.1(p.8.12; M.18.37B); ψυχὰς θείῳ λουτρῷ...~θείσας Eus.*h.e.*10.4.64(M.20.876A); Max.*ep.*8(M.91.441D); 4. *reveal, make plain*, Cyr.*hom.pasch.*6(5ª.61B).

ἀποσοβ-έω, 1. *scare away, drive off*; insects διάκονοι...~είτωσαν τὰ μικρὰ τῶν ἱπταμένων ζῴων, ὅπως ἂν μὴ ἐγχρίμπτωνται εἰς τὰ κύπελλα Lit.ap.Const.*App.*8.12.3; heretics from the flock of Christ, Eus.*h.e.*4.24(M.20.389B); τῆς κοινωνίας ἀ. Chrys.*grat.*2 (2.660A); Satan τὸν διάβολον ἀ. id.*hom.*22.6 *in Mt.*(7.283D); Cyr.*Ps.* 80:7(M.69.1204C); Christ οἱ Φαρισαῖοι...ἀπεσόβουν μὲν αὐτῆς [sc. τῆς συναγωγῆς] τὸν ἐξ οὐρανοῦ νυμφίον id.*Os.*3(3.66A); sins ὅταν πλεονεξίαν ~ήσωμεν τῆς ψυχῆς Chrys.*hom.*19.2 *in Eph.*(11.136B); Χριστὸν ἐνδεδυμένοι τὸν πᾶσαν ἔξωθεν προσβάλλουσαν ~οῦντα ἐπήρειαν Nil.*Magn.*43(M.79.1021C); 2. *dissociate* τοῦ μὲν θεοῦ λόγου τὰς τοιάσδε φωνὰς ~εῖσθαι δεῖν Cyr.*apol.Thdt.*4(p.125.5; 6¹.218E); ref. Nestorian view ἐκβάλλετε τοῦ εἶναι θεὸν...τὸν ἐκ τῆς ἁγίας παρθένου, τὸ παθεῖν αὐτῷ προσνίμοντες μόνῳ, καὶ ~οῦντες αὐτὸν τοῦ θεοῦ λόγου id.*ep.*55(p.61.3; 5ª.190E).

ἄποσος, *without quantity*; of God, Gr.Naz.*or.*41.9(M.36.441B); ἐπὶ γὰρ τοῦ ἀ. μέτρον οὐκ ἔστιν Gr.Nyss.*v.Mos.*(M.44.405B); id.*beat.*3 (M.44.1225B); Cyr.*ep.Calos.*(6ª.384A); ref. Creation πῶς τὸ ποσὸν ἐκ τοῦ ἀ.; Gr.Nyss.*hex.*7(M.44.69C); of Trin., Gr.Nyss.*Eun.*3(2 p.35.20; M.45.601C); ‡Caes.Naz.*dial.*18(M.38.873); of Logos ποσοῦται ὁ ἀ. ‡Jo.D.*hom.*5(M.96.653B); ‡Jo.D.*ep.Thphl.*3(M.95.349D); ref. false visions φυλάττου τὰς παγίδας τῶν ἐναντίων...τοῦ τὸ ἀθροὺς ἐκκαλυφθέν σοι, ποσὸν τὸ θεῖον εἶναι πείσῃ. ἄποσον δὲ τὸ θεῖον Evagr.Pont. *or.*67(M.79.1181B).

*ἀποσφίζομαι, *argue subtly, display ingenuity*, Mac.Mgn.*apocr.* 3.14(p.91.3).

ἀποσπαίρω, *quiver convulsively*, Bas.*hom.*8.3(2.65C; M.31.312C).

ἀπόσπαραγμα, τό, *fragment*, Anast.S.*hod.*23(M.89.296D).

ἀποσπαργαν-όω, *take off wrappings*; pass., be stripped ἐσπαργανωθὴ μέν, ἀλλ' ~οῦται τὰ τῆς ταφῆς ἀνιστάμενος Gr.Naz.*or.*29.19 (p.103.9; M.36.100B).

ἀποσπάω, *drag away; detach*; 1. *pull up* a plant, Meth.*res.*1.41 (p.285.15; M.18.269A); Dor.*doct.*11.2(M.88.1737A); 2. *seduce*, Arist. *apol.*10.8; met., pass., from God, Herm.*sim.*6.2.3; and from good, Isidorus Gnost.ap.Clem.*str.*3.1(p.196.2; M.8.1101A); Eus.*d.e.*1.9(p.40.29; M.22.77D); 3. *rescue* ἀπὸ τῶν εἰδώλων ἀ. *2Clem.*17.1; ἐξ ὧν... ἀ. ἡμᾶς Ἰησοῦς Just.*dial.*116.2(M.6.744C); Clem.*exc.Thdot.*67.4(p.129.10; M.9.692A); 4. reflex., *withdraw* for contemplation πάντων ἑαυτοὺς ἀ. προσέχοντι τοῖς λεγομένοις Thdr.Mops.*Nah.*1:11(M.66.401D).

ἀποσπερμαίνω, *beget*, Dion.Al.ap.Eus.*p.e.*14.26(778D; M.21.1281B).

ἀποσπινθηρίζω, *emit in sparks* φλογῶν ἀ. Rom.Mel.(*AS* 1 p.192).

ἀποσπογγίζ-ω, *wipe away as with a sponge*; liturg., *wipe, cleanse*

τά τε ἴδια χείλη καὶ τὸ ἱερὸν ποτήριον τῷ...καλύμματι ἀ. Lit.Chrys. (p.359.14ff.); met., *wipe out, extinguish* ψαλμός. ~ει τὰ πάθη Procl. CP *or.*2.1(M.65.692C); of the holy name σκιαῖς πυρετοὺς ἀ. Leont. B.*mesopent.*(M.86.1989C).

ἀποσπουδάζ-ω, 1. *despise, reject*; pass., Cyr.*Juln.*5(6ª.177B); *ib.*6 (193A); 2. *shun, be averse from* τὸ παρεῖναι [sc. ἡμᾶς] ἀ. Gr.Naz.*ep.*43 (M.37.89B); τοὺς...τοῖς φαύλοις προσκεκλιμένους, ~οντας δὲ τὸ ἀγαθόν Cyr.*Mich.*30(3.417C); ~ειν κελεύει μᾶλλοι δὲ ἀποστρέφεσθαι παντελῶς...τὸ θύειν εἰδώλοις id.*ador.*6(1.178B); med., id.*apol.Thdt.*3 (p.120.19; 6¹.214B).

ἀποστασία, ἡ, 1. *revolt, defection*, esp. spiritual; a. of fallen angels ἀγγέλους...ἐν ἀ. γεγονότας Iren.*haer.*1.10.1(M.7.552A); of Devil and demons ὑπόθεσις δὲ αὐτοῖς τῆς ἀ. οἱ ἄνθρωποι γίνονται Tat.*orat.*8 (p.8.4; M.6.821A); Clem.*str.*6.8(p.465.9; M.9.288B); Hermias *irris.*1 (M.6.1169A); b. of man, by original sin, Cyr.II.*catech.*19.4; by sin in gen. ὁ κατακλυσμὸς ἐγένετο διὰ τὴν ἀ. Iren.*haer.*5.29.2(M.7.1202C); ἡ ἀπὸ τοῦ εὐαγγελίου ἀ. Clem.*str.*7.14(p.62.23; M.9.521B); ἡ τῆς ὄντως ἀγαθότητος ὀλέθριος ἀ. Dion.Ar.*e.h.*3.3.11(M.3.440C); *ib.*2.3.3 (400B); from truth, †Bas.*bapt.*2.10.1 cit. s. σκάνδαλον; 2. *apostasy*; from paganism προσνείμαντες ἑαυτοὺς τῷ τῆς ἀ. πνεύματι Juln.ap. Cyr.*Juln.*7(6ª.237D); from Judaism, an accusation against S. Paul, ‡Ath.*dial.Trin.*1.5(M.28.1124D); from Christianity, under persecution τῶν ἐν στρατείας ἐξεταζομένων τινὲς ἠπατήθησαν εἰς ἀ. Chron. *Pasch.*p.296(M.92.744A); of Julian, *ib.*p.295(740A); 2 Thess.2:3, of antichrist, Just.*dial.*110.2(M.6.729A); Iren.*haer.*5.28.2 ap.Or. *Apoc.*38(p.41); Chrys.*hom.*3.2 *in 2Thess.*(11.525B); from orthodoxy of Theodotus the cobbler, †Hipp.*Artem.*ap.Eus.*h.e.*5.28.6(M.20.513A); of Arians, Ath.*decr.*27(p.24.8; M.25.465D); of Eunomius, Gr.Nyss.*Eun.*2(2 p.362.6; M.45.541A); from the Church, *secession, schism* σχίσματα καὶ ἀ. ὅλων ἐκκλησιῶν γεγονέναι Dion.Al.ap.Eus. *h.e.*7.24.6(M.20.696A); ἄνδρες παράνομοι καὶ Χριστομάχοι διδάσκοντες ἀ., ἦν...ἀν τις πρόδρομον τοῦ ἀντιχρίστου...καλέσειεν Al·x.Al. *ep.encycl.*1(p.7.1; M.18.572B); of Novatian, Eus.*h.e.*6.45.1(633B); of Meletians, Ath.*v.Anton.*68(M.26.940B); 3. *divorce* τὸν νόμον τοῦ τῆς ἀ. βιβλίου νόμον Or.*comm.in Mt.*14.22(p.338.32; M.13.1214B); A.Xanthipp.66(p.62.8); 4. *departure*; a. *removal* τήν...ἀ. εἰς Ἱεροσαλήμ Dorm.BMV 33(p.105); b. *defection* from a monastery, †Bas. *const.*34(2.581A; M.31.1425B); 5. s.v.l., *standing aloof* (ref. Mt.11:16-19) ἐφαίνων ἐπὶ τῆς αὐτῶν ἀπειθείας Chrys.*hom.*37.4 *in Mt.*(7.420B, v.l. ἀ.).

*ἀποστασιάζω, *stir up in revolt*, Synes.*ep.*67(M.66.1413B); Pall. *h.Laus.*21(p.65.6; M.34.1073D).

ἀποστάσιον, τό, 1. *divorce* τὴν τοῦ ἀ. ῥῆσιν [sc. in Mt.5:32] Clem. *str.*3.6(p.219.11; M.8.1153A); βιβλίον τοῦ ἀ. Or.*comm.in Mt.*14.22 (p.338.26; M.13.1214B); Chrys.*hom.*17.4 *in Mt.*(7.227A); also bill of *divorce*, Or.*Jo.*13.9(p.233.24; M.14.412C); 2. *legal alienation, renunciation*, Sophr.H.*v.Anast.*(M.92.1684B).

ἀπόστασις, ἡ, 1. *departure* ἑκάτερος [sc. ὕπνος καὶ θάνατος]... δηλοῖ τὴν ἀ. τῆς ψυχῆς Clem.*str.*4.22(p.310.20; M.8.1352A); 2. *defection, revolt; apostasy* φθοράν...ἡ ἀπὸ τῆς τοῦ θεοῦ γνώσεως ἀ. παρέχει *ib.*5.10(p.369.3; M.9.97B); Gr.Naz.*carm.*1.2.34.247(M.37.963A); τῆς ἀ. τῆς ἀπὸ τοῦ θεοῦ διὰ τῆς παρακοῆς προηγήσατο [sc. Eve] Gr.Nyss.*Eun.*12(2 p.280.3; M.45.892A); Cyr.*Is.*3.2(2.420C); *defection* from a monastery, †Bas.*const.*34(2.581B; M.31.1425C); 3. *giving up, renunciation* διὰ τὴν θείαν σπουδὴν ἡ τοῦ γένους ἀ. Vict.*Mc.*10:31 (p.382.24); 4. *absence* μηδὲ ἀ. σημαινέτω τοῦ χείρονος τὴν ἀφαιρετικὴν σημασίαν (e.g. in ἄφθαρτος) Gr.Nyss.*Eun.*12(2 p.382.13; 1109D); 5. *separation, distinction* ὑπόστασιν ὑποστάσει ἡνωμένη εἶναι οὐ δύναται σωζομένων ἄμφω τῶν ὑποστάσεων· εἴτουν ἀποστάσεων Leont. H.*Nest.*2.7(M.86.1552B); 6. *divorce* ἀποστάσεως βιβλίον Or.*comm.in Mt.*14.22(p.338.22; M.13.1214A); τὴν ἀ. τῆς μισουμένης γυναικὸς Vict.*Mc.*10:3ff.(p.374.4).

ἀποστατ-έω, 1. *stand aloof from. fail* οὐδενὸς τῶν ὄντων ~εῖ [sc. God] Dion.Ar.*d.n.*5.5(M.3.820A); 2. *fall away* ἀ.ριστός...εἰς φίλαν εἰσάγων τὰ τῆς προσάλληλα κοινωνίας ~ήσαντα τουτέστιν, ἄνθρωπον καὶ θεόν Cyr.*thes.*33(5¹.296C); *reject* the scriptures, Hom.Clem.2.39; *apostatize*, Meth.*res.*1.32(p.268.15; M.4?.1144C); †Bas.*Is.*269(1.584B M.30.552B); by sin, *ib.*270(585B; M.593B); Cyr.*thes.*33(5¹.292D); ἀ. τῆς ἰδίας ποίμνης Const.*App.*2.20.5; from Christ, Or.*Jo.*28.7(6; p.397.33; M.14.669A).

ἀποστάτης, ὁ, 1. *rebel* against God; a. of Devil ὁ ἄγγελος οὗτος καὶ ἐχθρός, ἀφ' ὅτε ἐξήλωσε τὸ πλάσμα τοῦ θεοῦ Iren.*haer.* 4.40.3(M.7.1113C); Clem.*str.*1.17(p.55.12; M.8.800C); ὁ δράκων ὁ ἀ. Cyr.*Ps.*36:32(M.69.945D); ἐπ' ἐκείνου οὐκ ἐξ ἀρχῆς ἦν [sc. ἡ πονηρία] ἀλλὰ μετὰ ταῦτα ἐπεγένετο, διὸ καὶ ἀ. λέγεται Chrys.*diab.*2.2(2.262E); as adj. τὸν ἀ. δράκοντα Gr.Nyss.*Eun.*12(2 p.280.10; M.45.892B);

Fig. 16. Page from *Greek-English Lexicon*, by Liddell and Scott.

longer easy for them to bring it back under cultivation, inasmuch as it had suffered both from the desertion of slaves and the loss of animals with which they were to cultivate it, and, as few of the husbandmen had any store of grain on hand for the next year for either seed or food. The senate, being informed of this, sent ambassadors to the Tyrrhenians and to the Campanians and also to the Pomptine plain, as it is called, to buy up all the corn they could, while Publius Valerius and Lucius Geganius were sent to Sicily; Valerius was a son of Publicola, and Geganius was brother to one of the consuls. Tyrants ruled in the various cities at that time, and the most illustrious was Gelon, the son of Deinomenes, who had lately succeeded to the tyranny of Hippocrates,[1]—not Dionysius of Syracuse, as Licinius and Gellius and many others of the Roman historians have stated, without having made any careful investigation of the dates involved, as the facts show of themselves, but rashly relating the first account that offered itself. For the embassy appointed to go to Sicily set sail in the second year of the seventy-second Olympiad,[2] when Hybrilides was archon at Athens, seventeen years after the expulsion of the kings, as these and almost all the other historians agree; whereas Dionysius the Elder, having made an uprising against the Syracusans in the eighty-fifth year after this, possessed himself of the tyranny in the third year of the ninety-third Olympiad,[3]

---

[1] Gelon became tyrant of Gela in 491, and from 485 to his death in 478 was tyrant of Syracuse.
[2] 490 B.C.   [3] 405 B.C.   He reigned from 405 to 367.

DIONYSIUS OF HALICARNASSUS

τοῖς γεωργοῖς ἀναλαβεῖν αὐτὴν ἔτι ῥᾴδιον εἶναι δούλων τε ἀποστάσει καὶ κτηνῶν ὀλέθρῳ μεθ' ὧν αὐτὴν ἔμελλον ἐργάζεσθαι κεκακωμένην, ἀφορμῆς τε οὐ πολλοῖς[1] εἰς τὸν ἐπιόντα ἐνιαυτὸν

3 ὑπαρχούσης οὔτε σπερμάτων οὔτε τροφῆς. ταῦτα ἡ βουλὴ μαθοῦσα πρέσβεις διεπέμπετο πρὸς[2] Τυρρηνοὺς καὶ Καμπανοὺς καὶ τὸ καλούμενον Πωμεντῖνον πεδίον σῖτον ὅσον ἂν δύναιτο πλεῖστον ὠνησομένους· Πόπλιος δὲ Οὐαλέριος καὶ Λεύκιος Γεγάνιος εἰς Σικελίαν ἀπεστάλησαν, Οὐαλέριος μὲν υἱὸς ὢν Ποπλικόλα, Γεγάνιος δὲ

4 θατέρου τῶν ὑπάτων ἀδελφός. τύραννοι δὲ τότε κατὰ πόλεις μὲν ἦσαν, ἐπιφανέστατος δὲ Γέλων ὁ Δεινομένους νεωστὶ τὴν Ἱπποκράτους[3] τυραννίδα παρειληφώς, οὐχὶ Διονύσιος ὁ Συρακούσιος, ὡς Λικίνιος γέγραφε καὶ Γέλλιος καὶ ἄλλοι συχνοὶ τῶν Ῥωμαίων συγγραφέων οὐθὲν ἐξητακότες τῶν περὶ τοὺς χρόνους ἀκριβῶς, ὡς αὐτὸ δηλοῖ τοὔργον,

5 ἀλλ' εἰκῇ τὸ προστυχὸν ἀποφαινόμενοι. ἡ μὲν γὰρ εἰς Σικελίαν ἀποδειχθεῖσα πρεσβεία κατὰ τὸν δεύτερον ἐνιαυτὸν τῆς ἑβδομηκοστῆς καὶ δευτέρας ὀλυμπιάδος ἐξέπλευσεν ἄρχοντος Ἀθήνησιν Ὑβριλίδου, ἑπτακαίδεκα διελθόντων ἐτῶν μετὰ τὴν ἐκβολὴν τῶν βασιλέων, ὡς οὗτοί τε καὶ οἱ ἄλλοι σχεδὸν ἅπαντες συγγραφεῖς ὁμολογοῦσι· Διονύσιος δ' ὁ πρεσβύτερος ὀγδοηκοστῷ καὶ πέμπτῳ μετὰ ταῦτα ἔτει Συρακουσίοις ἐπαναστὰς κατέσχε τὴν τυραννίδα κατὰ τὸν τρίτον ἐνιαυτὸν τῆς ἐνενηκοστῆς καὶ τρίτης ὀλυμπιάδος ἄρχοντος

---

[1] πολλοῖς B: πολλῆς R.
[2] διεπέμπετο πρός R: διέπεμπεν εἰς B.

Fig. 17. Facing pages from *Dionysius of Halicarnassus* (Loeb Classical Library).

many to do so against their will, marched out with all his followers and set fire to the villages, belonging to Gadara and Hippos, which lay on the frontiers of Tiberias and of the territory of Scythopolis.

(10) Such was the position of affairs at Tiberias ; [(iii.) Gis-chala.] at Gischala the situation was as follows. John, son of Levi, observing that some of the citizens were highly elated by the revolt from Rome, tried to restrain them and urged them to maintain their allegiance. His earnest efforts, however, proved unavailing ; for the inhabitants of the neighbouring states, Gadara, Gabara, Sogane and Tyre, mustered a large force, stormed and took Gischala, burnt and razed it to the ground, and returned to their homes. Incensed at this outrage, John armed all his followers, made a determined attack on the aforesaid peoples and defeated them. He then rebuilt Gischala on a grander scale than before and fortified it with walls as a security for the future.

(11) Gamala remained loyal to Rome under the [(iv.) Gamala and Philip] following circumstances. Philip, son of Jacimus, King [King ben Jaci-mus.] Agrippa's lieutenant, after miraculously escaping with his life from the royal palace at Jerusalem, when it was besieged, was exposed to the further peril of being slain by Menahem and his brigands.[a] The latter were, however, prevented from accomplishing their purpose by some Babylonian kinsmen of Philip, who were then in Jerusalem. Here he remained for four days and on the fifth escaped, disguised by a wig, and reaching one of the villages under his

---

[a] *Cf. B.* ii. 556 f.; 433 ff.

λοὺς δὲ καὶ μὴ θελήσαντας ἀναγκάσας, ἐξελθὼν σὺν πᾶσιν τούτοις ἐμπίμπρησιν τάς τε Γαδαρηνῶν καὶ Ἱππηνῶν κώμας, αἱ δὴ μεθόριοι τῆς Τιβεριάδος καὶ τῆς τῶν Σκυθοπολιτῶν γῆς ἐτύγχανον κείμεναι.

43 (10) Καὶ Τιβεριὰς μὲν ἐν τοιούτοις ἦν, τὰ περὶ Γίσχαλα δὲ εἶχε τὸν τρόπον τοῦτον. Ἰωάννης ὁ τοῦ Ληουεί, τῶν πολιτῶν τινας ὁρῶν διὰ τὴν ἀποστασίαν τὴν ἀπὸ Ῥωμαίων μέγα φρονοῦντας κατέχειν αὐτοὺς ἐπειρᾶτο καὶ τὴν πίστιν ἠξίου

44 διαφυλάττειν. οὐ μὴν ἠδυνήθη καίτοι πάνυ προθυμούμενος. τὰ γὰρ πέριξ ἔθνη, Γαδαρηνοὶ καὶ Γαβαρηνοί, Σωγαναῖοι καὶ Τύριοι, πολλὴν ἀθροίσαντες δύναμιν καὶ τοῖς Γισχάλοις ἐπεισπεσόντες λαμβάνουσι τὰ Γίσχαλα κατὰ κράτος, καὶ πυρπολήσαντες εἶτα δὲ καὶ προσκατασκάψαντες εἰς τὴν

45 οἰκείαν ἀνέζευξαν. Ἰωάννης δὲ ἐπὶ τούτῳ παροξυνθεὶς ὁπλίζει πάντας τοὺς μετ' αὐτοῦ καὶ συμβαλὼν τοῖς προειρημένοις ἔθνεσιν κατὰ κράτος εὔκρος, τά τε Γίσχαλα κρείττονα πάλιν ἀνακτίσας τείχεσιν ὑπὲρ ἀσφαλείας τῆς εἰς ὕστερον ὠχύρωσεν.

46 (11) Γάμαλα δὲ πίστει τῇ πρὸς Ῥωμαίους ἐνέμεινε δι' αἰτίαν τοιαύτην. Φίλιππος ὁ Ἰακείμου παῖς, ἔπαρχος δὲ τοῦ βασιλέως Ἀγρίππα, σωθεὶς παρὰ δόξαν ἐκ τῆς ἐν Ἱεροσολύμοις βασιλικῆς αὐλῆς πολιορκουμένης καὶ διαφυγὼν εἰς ἕτερον

47 ἐνέπεσε κίνδυνον, ὥστε ὑπὸ Μαναήμου καὶ τῶν Βαβυλωνίων τινὲς συγγενεῖς αὐτοῦ ἐν Ἱεροσολύμοις ὄντες πρᾶξαι τοὺς λῃστὰς τὸ ἔργον. ἐπιμείνας οὖν ἡμέρας τέσσαρας ὁ Φίλιππος ἐκεῖ τῇ πέμπτῃ φεύγει περιθετῇ χρησάμενος κόμῃ τοῦ μὴ κατάδηλος γενέσθαι, καὶ παραγενόμενος εἴς τινα

18

---

[1] Emended. The mss. in lieu of the two latter names, have ἱαραγανέοι or the like.

Fig. 18. Facing pages from *Josephus* (Loeb Classical Library).

neously in England and the United States, makes available the finest translations of the Greek classics mentioned in this lexicon. The books in the Loeb Classical Library are arranged with the Greek text on one page and an English translation on a facing page. This makes it easy for the researcher to study the word in its context and thereby determine its usage. An illustration of how usage determines meaning may be found in T. J. Conant's *The Meaning and Use of Baptizein* (1977).

Although Liddell's and Scott's *Lexicon* primarily is valuable for the classical information provided, literature is also cited through to the sixth century A.D. and includes the Septuagint and Apocrypha. The closer the reference is to the New Testament era, therefore, the greater will be its bearing on the meaning of the term during the time of Christ and the period of the apostolic church.

The Hellenistic period of Greek literature witnessed: (1) the translation of the Old Testament and the Apocrypha into Greek; (2) the penning of the canonical books of the New Testament; (3) the writings of Jews such as Philo of Alexandria and Josephus; (4) the flourishing of Greek as the lingua franca of the Egyptians (as is evidenced by archaeological discoveries there); and (5) the era of the early church Fathers. Sources providing the inquiring student with access to this data include:

- Bauer's *Greek-English Lexicon of the New Testament*
- Moulton's and Milligan's *Vocabulary of the Greek Testament*
- Lampe's *Patristic Greek Lexicon*.

The history behind the production of Walter Bauer's *Greek-English Lexicon of the New Testament and Other Early Christian Literature* (translated and edited by W. F. Arndt and F. W. Gingrich, revised and augmented by F. W. Gingrich and F. W. Danker, 1979) has been told by Danker in *Multipurpose Tools for Bible Study* (pp. 124-27).

Often referred to as "Arndt and Gingrich," this lexicon is based on an extensive examination of Greek literature, including New Testament words still in use in Byzantine times. An incredible amount of material was mastered and then reduced to succinct, descriptive statements about each word and its meaning during different eras of Greek literary history. The true value of this lexicon can only be appreciated as one reads through the prefatory material, and particularly the introduction by Bauer (pp. xi-xxviii).

The coverage is excellent, the meaning(s) given each word is judicious, grammatical hints are of the utmost importance, and the references to literature outside the New Testament are well-chosen and representative.

Researchers, therefore, will find Bauer's lexicon to be indispensable whether in an academic setting, in the pastorate, or on the mission field.

A second source of philological illumination comes from papyri discovered in Egypt. The terminology found in those papyrus fragments, letters and ostraka, parallels the Greek of the New Testament. Much of it, therefore, may be used to add new insights into the meaning of words employed by the writers of the New Testament.

ἀπορρέω fut. ἀπορυήσομαι (trag., Hdt.+; Eudoxos-Pap. [=PPar. 1] 14, 17 [II вс]; LXX) flow down fig., of leaves (Demosth. 22, 70) fall down B 11: 6, 8 (Ps 1: 3).*

ἀπορφανίζω 1 aor. pass. ptc. ἀπορφανισθείς (Aeschyl.; Bull. de corr. hell. 46, '22, 345; Philo [Nägeli 25]) make an orphan of someone, fig., of the apostle separated fr. his church ἀπορφανισθέντες ἀφ' ὑμῶν made orphans by separation fr. you 1 Th 2: 17.*

ἀποσκευάζω 1 aor. ἀπεσκευασάμην (mostly mid.; Polyb.+; cf. Dit., Syll.³ 588, 54 [196 вс]; 633, 68; Lev 14: 36; Philo, Deus Imm. 135) lay aside, get rid of τὶ (Jos., Bell. 1, 260; 618) τ. συνήθειαν lay aside the habit Dg 2: 1. Ac 21: 15 t.r., ἀ. prob. means pack up and leave. M-M.*

ἀποσκίασμα, ατος, τό (Aëtius [100 AD] 2, 30, 3: Dox. Gr. 361b, 21.—ἀποσκιασμοί Plut., Pericl. 6, 5) shadow τροπῆς ἀ. a shadow cast by variation (in position of heavenly bodies) Js 1: 17 (Theopomp. [?]: 115 fgm. 400 Jac. τὸ ἀποσκίασμα τῆς τοῦ ἡλίου ἀνταυγείας). JH Ropes, ICC ad loc. and Gdspd, Probs. 189f prefer the rdg. of B אּ* POxy. 1229 et al. (παρ.) ἡ τροπῆς ἀποσκιάσματος '(no variation) of changing shadow'. MDibelius, Meyer⁷ '21 ad loc. would emend to put both nouns in the genitive and transl. the clause 'who is without change and knows neither turning nor darkness'. M-M.*

ἀποσπάω 1 aor. ἀπέσπασα, pass. ἀπεσπάσθην (Pind., Hdt.+; pap., LXX) draw or pull away.
    1. lit., draw out ἀ. τ. μάχαιραν draw a sword Mt 26: 51. ἀ. τοὺς ἥλους ἀπὸ τ. χειρῶν draw out the nails fr. the hands GP 6: 21.
    2. fig., of pers. draw or tear away, attract (cf. Artem. 5, 43 τινά τινος someone from someone; Josh 8: 6; Jer 12: 14; Jos., Vi. 321, Ant. 8, 277 ἀπὸ τ. θεοῦ) ἀπὸ τ. εἰδώλων fr. idols 2 Cl 17: 1 (cf. Polyaenus 8, 51 of the bringing out of one who has fled to a temple for refuge; cf. ἀπὸ τ. ἁμαρτιῶν ἀποσπασθῆναι Third Corinthians 3: 9). ἀ. τοὺς μαθητὰς ὀπίσω ἑαυτῶν draw away the disciples after them (and thereby alienate them) Ac 20: 30 (cf. Aelian, V.H. 13: 32; Diog. L. 2, 113 ἀ. τινὰ ἀπό τινος alienate pupils from someone; PPetr. III 43[3], 12; BGU 1125, 9 [13 вс] οὐκ ἀποσπάσω αὐτὸν ἀπὸ σοῦ).
    3. pass. ἀ. ἀπό τινος be parted fr. someone Ac 21: 1; Hs 6, 2, 3.—Withdraw (Diod. S. 20, 39; POxy. 275, 22 [66 AD]; Job 41: 9; Jos., Bell. 2, 498; 6, 379) ἀπό τινος Lk 22: 41. M-M.*

ἀποσταλῶ, ἀποσταλείς s. ἀποστέλλω.

ἀποστασία, ας, ἡ (a form quotable since Diod. S. outside the Bible [Nägeli 31] for class. ἀπόστασις [Phryn. 528 L.]) rebellion, abandonment in relig. sense, apostasy (Josh 22: 22; 2 Ch 29: 19; 1 Macc 2: 15) ἀπό τινος (Plu., Galb. 1, 9 Z. v.l. ἀπὸ Νέρωνος ἀ.; Jos., Vi. 43) ἀποστασίαν διδάσκεις ἀπὸ Μωϋσέως you teach (Jews) to abandon Moses Ac 21: 21. Of the rebellion caused by the Antichrist in the last days 2 Th 2: 3. M-M.*

ἀποστάσιον, ου, τό a legal t.t. found as early as Lysias, Hyperid. [fgm. Or. 17] and Demosth., and freq. in pap. since PHib. 96, 3 [258 вс]; PSI 551, 9 [III вс] (cf. Wilcken, APF 2, '03, 143 and 388f; 4, '08, 183 and 456f; Preisigke, Fachwörter '15) in the sense of relinquishment of property after sale, abandonment, etc. The consequent giving up of one's claim explains the meaning which the word acquires in Jewish circles: δοῦναι βιβλίον ἀποστασίου (Jer 3: 8) give (one's wife) a certificate of divorce Mt 19: 7. διδόναι ἀποστάσιον, w. the same mng. 5: 31. For this γράφειν β.

ἀ. (Dt 24: 1, 3) Mk 10: 4.—S. lit. on ἀπολύω 2a and Tractate Gittin (Certificates of Divorce). M-M.*

ἀποστάτης, ου, ὁ (Polyb.+; Dit., Syll.³ 705, 50 [112 вс]; PAmh. 30, 33ff; Witkowski p. 96, 12; LXX; Berosus in Jos., Ant. 10, 221=C. Ap. 1, 136) deserter, apostate w. ἔθνη Hv 1, 4, 2; w. προδότης s 8, 6, 4; w. βλάσφημος and προδότης s 9, 19, 1. W. obj. gen. (Polyb. 5, 57, 4 and Diod. S. 15, 18, 1 τ. βασιλέως) νόμου from the law (2 Macc 5: 8 τ. νόμων ἀ.) Js 2: 11 v.l.*

ἀποστεγάζω 1 aor. ἀπεστέγασα (rare and in var. mngs.; Jer 49: 10 Sym.) unroof τ. στέγην remove the roof Mk 2: 4 (so Strabo 4, 4, 6; 8, 3, 30; Artem. 2, 36 p. 137, 26; Dit., Syll.³ 852, 30 στοὰ ἀπεστέγασται ὅλη).—S. lit. on στέγη.*

ἀποστέλλω fut. ἀποστελῶ; 1 aor. ἀπέστειλα; ἀποστείλω Ac 7: 34 (Ex 3: 10) is perh. not hortat. subj. but pres. ind. as in the Pontic dial. (Thumb 18, cf. M-M); pf. ἀπέσταλκα, pass. ἀπέσταλμαι; 2 aor. pass. ἀπεστάλην (Soph., Hdt.+; inscr., pap., LXX, Ep. Arist., Philo, Joseph., Test. 12 Patr.).
    1. send away or out τινά someone.
        a. w. the obj. given alone Mt 13: 41; Mk 11: 1; 12: 5 al.
        b. more exactly defined—α. w. indication of the pers. to whom someone is sent: by the dat. (PPar. 32, 20) Mt 22: 16; Ac 28: 28. εἴς τινα Mt 15: 24; Lk 11: 49; Ac 26: 17. πρός τινα (Epict. 3, 22, 74; Jos., Ant. 7, 334) Mt 21: 34, 37; 23: 34, 37; 27: 19; Mk 3: 31; 12: 4, 6; J 1: 19 al.
        β. w. indication of the place to which someone is sent, w. εἰς: Mt 14: 35; 20: 2; Mk 8: 26; Lk 1: 26; 10: 1; J 3: 17 al. W. ἐν (4 Km 17: 25; 2 Ch 7: 13) ἐν μέσῳ λύκων Mt 10: 16; Lk 10: 3 (cf. Jer 32: 27). ἔξω τ. χώρας outside the country Mk 5: 10. W. ὧδε here Mk 11: 3. ἀ. πρεσβείαν ὀπίσω τινός send an embassy after someone Lk 19: 14 (cf. 4 Km 14: 19). ἀ. ἐμπροσθέν τινος (cf. Gen 45: 5, 7; 46: 28) send before someone J 3: 28; cf. ἀ. ἄγγελον πρὸ προσώπου σου Mt 11: 10; Mk 1: 2 (Ex 23: 20; cf. Mal 3: 1); cf. Lk 9: 52; 10: 1.
        γ. w. the purpose of the sending indicated by ἵνα (Gen 30: 25) Mk 12: 2, 13; Lk 20: 10; J 1: 19; 3: 17; 7: 32; Hv 5: 2 al. By ὅπως (1 Macc 16: 18) Ac 9: 17. By the inf. (Num 21: 32—4) Mt 22: 3; Mk 3: 14; 11: 1; 19; 4: 18a (Is 61: 1); 9: 2; 14: 17; J 4: 38; Ac 5: 21; 1 Cor 1: 17; Rv 22: 6; B 14: 9 (Is 61: 1); Hm 12, 6, 1. By ἐπί w. acc. (Apollon. Paradox. 1; PFlor. 126, 8; Sb 174 [III вс] ἀ. ἐπὶ τ. θήραν τ. ἐλεφάντων) ἐπὶ τοῦτο for this purpose Lk 4: 43. εἰς διακονίαν to render service Hb 1: 14 (cf. Jdth 11: 7; Gen 45: 5). By the simple acc. τοῦτον ἄρχοντα καὶ λυτρωτὴν ἀπέσταλκεν this man he sent as leader and deliverer Ac 7: 35. ἀ. τὸν υἱὸν αὐτοῦ ἱλασμόν 1 J 4: 10. ἀ. τ. υἱὸν σωτῆρα vs. 14.
        δ. in pass. ἀποστέλλεσθαι παρὰ θεοῦ (Vi. Aesopi I c. 31 p. 295, 1 ed. Eberh. ἀπεστάλην παρὰ τ. θεοῦ μου; cf. Sir 15: 9; 34: 6) J 1: 6. ἀπὸ τ. θεοῦ (Epict. 3, 22, 23 ἀπὸ τοῦ Διός; Vi. Aesopi P. I c. 119: the prophets of Heliupolis say ἡμεῖς ἀπεστάλημεν ἀπὸ τοῦ θεοῦ) Lk 1: 26; cf. 1 Cl 65: 1. ἀπὸ Κορνηλίου πρὸς αὐτόν Ac 10: 21 v.l. ἀπὸ Καισαρείας 11: 11 (cf. 1 Macc 15: 1). ἀπ' οὐρανοῦ 1 Pt 1: 12.
        c. esp. of the sending out of the disciples by Jesus Mt 10: 5; Mk 3: 14; 6: 7; Lk 9: 2; J 4: 38; 17: 18, as well as the sending forth of Jesus by God (of the divine mission, esp. of prophets, very oft. in LXX; on the Heb. שׁלח see LKopf, Vetus Testamentum 7, '58, 207-9.—Philo, Migr. Abr. 22. The Cynic ἀπὸ τ. Διὸς ἀπέσταλται Epict. 3, 22, 23; cf. 46.—Cornutus 16 p. 30, 19 ὁ Ἑρμῆς ὁ λόγος ὤν, ὃν ἀπέστειλαν πρὸς ἡμᾶς ἐξ οὐρανοῦ οἱ θεοί) Mt 15: 24;

The *Wörterbuch der griechischen Papyrusurkunden mit Einschluss der griechischen Inschriften, Aufschriften, Ostraka, Mumienschilder usw. aus Ägypten*, by F. Preisigke and E. Kiessling (3 vols., 1925-31), deals exclusively with the vocabulary of the papyri unearthed by archaeologists in Egypt.

A work of related importance by J. H. Moulton and G. Milligan entitled *Vocabulary of the Greek Testament, Illustrated from the Papyri and Other Non-literary Sources* (1929) is presently available in one volume. It is based on articles published as "lexical notes" in *The Expositor* (1908-1911). Part 1 of the book appeared in 1914 and part 2 in 1915. Following Moulton's death in 1917, Milligan carried on the work alone, finally finishing this important resource tool in 1929.

Within the pages of Moulton and Milligan the student will find numerous parallels to the terminology of the New Testament. Furthermore, investigation of the source material offered in the concise format of this volume will not only enrich his study but also provide numerous illustrations of word usage in the lingua franca of the people of the New Testament period.

Finally, the *Patristic Greek Lexicon*, edited by G. H. W. Lampe (1961), places the researcher in touch with the writings of the early church Fathers. Based on the material contained in Milne's *Patrologia Graeca*, this work took more than half a century to bring to completion. Its object was to make available the theological and ecclesiastical vocabulary of the Greek Christian authors from Clement of Rome to Theodore of Stadium, so that researchers could trace easily and efficiently the development of Christian thought. Informative coverage, therefore, is given terms like *apostolos*, *episkopos*, *presbuteros*, et cetera.

The values of using a lexicon like this one are many.

First, as far as the development of doctrine is concerned, we can trace by example as well as precept either the early church's adherence to "sound doctrine" or its departure from it. The reasons for the latter frequently parallel trends in our own time, for although we tend to be more sophisticated, human nature remains the same and the origin of our defection is often merely clothed in more acceptable terms.

Second, in the course of history, changes in the usage of words and their meaning were inevitable. It is interesting to note that the term *disciple*, used so extensively in the gospels of one who had counted the cost of following Christ, in the era of the early church came to be applied futuristically to those whose manner of life would permit this term to be connected with their name. Often death by martyrdom was regarded as the criterion for calling one a "disciple." Such usage is a far cry from the meaning given the word by Christ.

In keeping with the format adopted by Liddell and Scott, this work by Lampe also begins with a list of the authors and their writings (e.g., Iren. *haer* is the abbreviation for Irenaeus Lugdunensis, *Adversus Haereses*

Δ

δαιμονίζομαι—δακρύω

δαιμονίζομαι

in its NT sense of being possessed with demons seems to occur only in later Greek. For a form δαιμονιάζω, otherwise unknown, see the Paris Great Magical Papyrus, Leaf 33³⁰⁰⁷ (*c.* A.D. 300) πρὸς δαιμονιαζομένους Πιβήχεως δόκιμον, "for those possessed by demons, an approved charm by Pibechis" (cited by Deissmann *LAE*, p. 251). The normal form occurs in P Leid Wᵛⁱ·³⁰ (ii/iii A.D.) ἐν (*l.* ἐὰν) δαιμονιζομέν(ῳ) εἴπῃς τὸ (ὄνομα), προσάγων τῇ ῥεινὶ αὐτοῦ θεῖον καὶ ἄσφαλτον, εὐθέως λαλήσει (*sc.* τὸ δαιμόνιον) κ(αὶ) ἀπελεύσεται. In MGr the act. δαιμονίζω appears, = "drive mad": cf. Abbott *Songs*, p. 224 (no. 47). The derived noun δαιμονισμός occurs in Vettius Valens, p. 2¹⁸.

δαιμόνιον.

The old adj. may be seen in *OGIS* 383¹⁷⁵ (i/B.C.) where Antiochus of Commagene dedicates temple slaves κατὰ δαιμόνιον βούλησιν.

Syll 924 ¹⁴ (B.C. 210-5) τὰς εἰς τὸ δαιμόνιον εὐσεβείας, and similarly 279¹⁶ (*c.* B.C. 193) τῆς συναντωμένης ἡμεῖν εὐμενίας διὰ ταῦτα παρὰ τοῦ δαιμονίου (following τῆς πρὸς τοὺς θεοὺς εὐσεβείας, and succeeded by τὴν ἡμετέραν εἰς τὸ θεῖον προτιμίαν) are witnesses to the growing sense in later Hellas of the unity of the Divine. Paul's solitary τὸ θεῖον in Ac 17²⁹ is the only NT passage which recalls this impersonal conception. The "Septuagint Memorial" from Hadrumetum of iii/A.D., published by Deissmann *BS*, p. 271 ff., opens with an adjuration to the demonic spirit of the tomb on which the spell was laid—ὁρκίζω σε, δαιμόνιον πνεῦμα τὸ ἐνθάδε κείμενον, τῷ ὀνόματι τῷ ἁγίῳ Αωθ κτλ., where the editor refers to the belief of post-biblical Judaism that the δαιμόνια stay beside the grave, and compares the Gospel idea that the demons reside in lonely and desert regions (Mt 12⁴³: cf. Mk 5³ and see Baruch 4³⁵). The magic papyrus P Lond 46¹⁹⁰ (iv/A.D.) (= I. p. 69 f.) has εἰσάκουσόν μου καὶ ἀπόστρεψο[ν] τὸ δαιμόνιον τοῦτο, and later ¹⁶⁴ ὑπόταξόν μοι πάντα τὰ δαιμόνια ἵνα μοι ᾖ ὑπήκοος πᾶς δαίμων οὐράνιος καὶ αἰθέριος καὶ ἐπίγειος καὶ χερσαῖο[ς] καὶ ἔνυδρος. That a magic document by a writer who knows Judaism, perhaps even Christianity, should use δαιμόνιον of an evil spirit is, of course, not strange. The noun may be quoted from Vettius Valens: thus p. 67⁵ ὑπὸ δαιμονίων καὶ φαντασίας εἰδώλων χρηματισθήσονται, where it is clearly something weird. Elsewhere he uses it much as τὸ θεῖον, as p. 355¹⁶ δυνάμενος τυχεῖν ὧν μὴ ἐβούλετο τὸ δαιμόνιον παρέχειν.

It may be noted that in Lk 4³⁵ D δαιμόνιον has a masc. predicate—ῥείψας αὐτὸν τὸ δαιμόνιον, and that in 9¹ D it is feminine—ἐπὶ πᾶσαν δαιμόνιον: see Wellhausen *Einleitung*, p. 12.

δαίμων.

The word is used in its old sense in P Leid Wˣˡᵛ·⁹ (ii/iii A.D) δαίμων δαιμώνων, in a spell addressed to a divinity. It answers often to the Latin *Genius*. Thus in a notification of the accession of Nero, P Oxy VII. 1021⁹ (A.D. 54) the Emperor is described as ἀγαθὸς δαίμων δὲ τῆς οὐκουμένης (*l.* οἰκ—"the good genius of the world." Similarly *OGIS* 666 Νέρων] Κλαύδιος . . . ὁ ἀγαθὸς δαίμων τῆς οἰκουμένης σὺν ἅπασιν οἷς εὐεργέτησεν ἀγαθοῖς: cf. *ib.* 672⁷ (A.D. 80 with reference to the Nile—ὡρύγη Ἀγαθὸς Δαίμων ποταμός ἐπὶ τὰ τρία στερεά κτλ. In a private letter of iii/A.D. th combination occurs as a proper name, P Strass I. 7, Ἀγαθὸς Δαίμων σύν σοι εἰσελθὼν διεπέμψατο: cf. BGU II. 494¹⁴ (ii/A.D.), *al.* For the word in a bad sense, see th magical incantation, P Par 574¹²²⁷ ((iii/A.D.) (= *Selections* p. 113) πρᾶξις γενναία ἐκβάλλουσα δαίμονας, "a notabl spell for driving out demons," and the Christian amulet i which the wearer prays, ὅπως διώξῃς ἀπ' ἐμοῦ τοῦ δούλου σου τὸν δαίμονα προβασκανίας, "that Thou mayst dri from me Thy servant the demon of witchcraft"—BGU III 954⁹ (*c.* vi/A.D.) (= *Selections*, p. 133). In P Grenf II. 76 (A.D. 305-6) two νεκροτάφοι from Kusis agree to a forma divorce, seeing that "owing to some evil deity" they hav renounced their wedded life=ἐπὶ (*l.* ἐπεὶ) ἐκ τινος πονηρο δαίμονος συνέβη αὐτοὺς ἀποζεύχθαι ἀλλήλων τὴν κοινὴ αὐτῶν συνβίωσιν. So P Cairo Preis 2¹² (A.D. 362) ὡς τῇ γυναικός μου πῖραν λαβοῦσαν (for λαβούσης) δέμονος, "i the belief that my wife had had experience of a demon."

δάκνω

survives in MGr δαγκάνω, also δάκνω, with noun δάγκαμα "a bite," which puts it among words which have no changed in 3000 years. But we cannot quote from Κοιν documents. ~~Vettius Valens p. 127²⁹~~ has the noun, θηρίω δακετῶν αἰτίαις.

δάκρυον.

P Petr II. 1⁴ (*c.* B.C. 260) μετὰ δακρύων, which Mayse Gr. p. 268, notes must not be assigned to δάκρυ, despite th heteroclite δάκρυσιν in NT. BGU IV. 1141²⁷ ᵗ (*c.* B.C. 14 οἴαν γὰρ ὕβριν μοι πεποήκεν ἐν τῷ κήπῳ καὶ ἐν τῇ οἰκί . . . ., ἢ ἦν δάκρυα σοὶ γράφειν, γεγραφήκειν ἂν ἀπὸ τῶ δακρύων, "wenn Thränen ein Brief wären" (Ed.). Th noun survives still.

δακρύω

survives as δακρύζω to-day, with ptc. δακρυσμένος = "re with weeping." It may be quoted from *Preisigke* 373, a undated tombstone, Μάγνα, [σὲ] θανοῦσ[αν] πᾶσα γ δακρυσά[τω.

Fig. 20. Page from *Vocabulary of the Greek Testament, Illustrated from the Papyri and Other Non-literary Sources*, by Moulton and Milligan.

[*Against Heresies*]; Tat. *orat* is Tatian(us)'s *Oratio ad Graecos;* and Clem. *str.* is Clement of Alexandria's *Stromateis*).

Each of these references can be traced in the appropriate volumes of the Loeb Classical Library.

For those desirous of pursuing their study beyond the era of the church Fathers, there is E. A. Sophocles's *Greek Lexicon of the Roman and Byzantine Periods* (2 vols., 1957).

Concordances and lexicons are indispensable reference tools and are available for people at all levels of attainment. Sooner or later, however, some expertise in biblical languages becomes a necessity.

A study of material referred to in a concordance should precede the consultation of a lexicon. After tracing the sources mentioned in a concordance and studying the usage of the word in light of the context, a lexicon can be consulted either to validate or correct the work you have done. And because lexicons synthesize material, you may well uncover something passed over by the concordance editors because they were dealing with broader issues than the one you have found.

A knowledge of the use of concordances and lexicons, however, should prepare you for engaging in one of the most exciting of pursuits—word studies. How to do a word study will be the focus of the next chapter.

Assignment

1. In tracing the meaning of words found in the Old Testament, consider the meanings assigned *perish, way,* and *word* in BDB's *A Hebrew and English Lexicon of the Old Testament,* and in Köehler's and Baumgartner's *Lexicon in Veteris Testamenti libros.* (You may wish to use Young's *Analytical Concordance to the Bible* first to identify the Hebrew and Greek words.) How well has the meaning of each word been analyzed? In what ways does the approach of each of these reference tools differ? Which approach do you prefer? Why?

2. By using Bauer's *Greek-English Lexicon to the New Testament,* trace the different Greek words for *prayer* mentioned in the New Testament. How do they differ from each other? In what contexts have these words been used in the different periods of Greek history? (Where the meaning in classical literature is given in Bauer, check two or three references listed by Bauer in the Loeb Classical Library.)

3. By using Hatch's and Redpath's *Concordance to the Septuagint,* trace the historical references to *Gilgal* and *Shiloh.* (Again, you may wish to use Young's.) Probe the significance of these places in the history of God's people and identify the era of each biblical author.

8

WORD STUDIES
PART 1

Several years ago, while teaching a course in bibliographic research in a local seminary, I gave the students an assignment that required them to research a particular word in both the Old and New Testaments as well as in extra-biblical literature.

During the semester I had endeavored to foster an atmosphere of open discussion, and the students felt free to share their reactions to the assignment with me.

One, who was "rearing to go," could hardly wait for the buzzer to sound so that he could go over to the library and begin work.

The response of the other students, however, was more typical of the attitudes of many toward this kind of exercise.

"Why can't we just read up on this word in TDNT?" objected one.

"Because TDNT omits this word," I replied.

"But I'm interested in people," stated another. "They couldn't care less about Greek and Hebrew words and their etymology. The meaning of some obscure word won't make any difference to the way they live!"

"True," I replied, "but that is where you come in. It's your responsibility to make the Bible come alive, and word studies are one way of doing it."

"I'm not good at the study of the original languages," responded a third student. "The assignment you have given us intimidates me. What happens if we [really, 'I'] get stuck?"

The question was stated honestly and probably represented the feelings of most of the class. None had ever taken a course in bibliographic research before and so they may have felt overwhelmed.

Introduction to Theological Research

"I appreciate your candor," I replied. "Perhaps this is a good place to assess what we have been doing so far and review the resources that will help you with the assignment."

That assessment consisted of a review of the general reference works that we also have covered in this book. It would be well for us to go back over those as follows.

- The whole subject of religion (e.g., McClintock and Strong's *Cyclopedia of Biblical, Theological and Ecclesiastical Literature*). These works, you will remember, follow a dictionary format in that they are arranged alphabetically by topic. The better encyclopedias contain articles based on the original languages, and philological matters are considered at the beginning of the longer, more scholarly articles.
- Bible dictionaries and encyclopedias (e.g., *Zondervan Pictorial Encyclopedia of the Bible*). Some of these works contain word studies, and some have Hebrew and Greek indices where each word is treated.
- Encyclopedias relating to specific disciplines (e.g., theology [biblical and systematic], history, philosophy, sociology). Some of those works contain philological studies.
- Bible atlases, Bible concordances, and Bible commentaries. Sometimes technical commentaries contain helpful information about the nuances of different words. To find out where these words appear in Scripture, you may wish to use a concordance (e.g., Strong's *Exhaustive Concordance to the Bible* and Young's *Analytical Concordance* or the *New American Standard Exhaustive Concordance of the Bible*) and then check biblical reference in one or more of the commentaries.
- Hebrew and Greek concordances and lexicons were covered in the previous two chapters.

I concluded by telling the students, "The assignment gives you the opportunity to fall back on the material covered this semester—as far back as you need to go—and then begin working forward until you come to those technical language tools, that is, concordances and lexicons, which are essential to a study of the derivation and meaning of words."

Further discussion did not reveal any additional objections, so we proceeded with some specifics.

HEBREW WORD STUDIES

Recognizing the limitations of students with only a beginner's knowledge of Hebrew, this section will deal with the rudiments of

- *Etymology*, in which we trace the origin and development of a word historically
- *Usage*, in which we analyze the occurrences of the word in a given body of literature (e.g., the Old Testament) and seek to lay bare the categories of meaning

- *Verification,* in which we check our findings against reference materials produced by specialists in the field.

In doing a Hebrew word study, it is important: (1) to focus on the root form of the word; and then (2) to consider the usage of the word in the Semitic family of languages, of which Hebrew is a part. Broadly speaking, Semitics may be divided into East Semitic (Akkadian, with its subdialects of Babylonian and Assyrian), South Semitic (Arabic and Ethiopic), and North Semitic (Canaanite, including Ugaritic, Sinaitic, Phoenecian, and Aramaic with its later offshoot, Syriac). Hebrew belongs to the North Semitic group.

ETYMOLOGY

The etymology of a given word not only considers the derivation and history of that word but also its meaning in the cognate Semitic languages. To trace properly the historical development of a given Hebrew term, the researcher should have access to the following:

- *Hebrew and English Lexicon to the Old Testament,* edited by F. Brown, S. R. Driver, and C. A. Briggs
- *Lexicon in Veteris Testamenti libros,* by L. H. Köehler and W. Baumgartner
- *Konkordanz zum hebräischen Alten Testament,* by G. Lisowsky
- *Veteris Testamenti concordantiae,* by S. Mandelkern
- *Concordance to the Septuagint,* by E. Hatch and H. A. Redpath.

It will readily be seen in the accompanying illustration of the root *dabar* from BDB that the editors have gone to considerable lengths to provide the equivalent meaning of a given Hebrew word in related Semitic languages. (Because this is an introduction to theological research, a lengthy discussion of the merits of philological research in Akkadian, Ugaritic, and Aramaic, et cetera, will not be given. More advanced students will wish to consult Rosenthal's *Aramaic Handbook;* Wehr's *Arabic Dictionary;* the Assyrian Dictionary [CAD], published by the Oriental Institute, University of Chicago; J. P. Smith's *Comprehensive Syriac Dictionary;* Moscati's *Introduction to the Comparative Grammar of the Semitic Languages;* Donner's and Rollig's *Kanaanaische und aramaische Inschriften;* Gordan's *Ugaritic Textbook;* and even von Soden's *Akkadisches Handwörterbuch.* Also of value is the *Dictionnaire des Inscriptions Semitiques de l'Quest* and Jean and Hoftijzer.) Building upon what the lexicographers have supplied the researcher can write down their dictionary definitions of the word. This should then be compared with the definition(s) given in Köehler-Baumgartner's *Lexicon.* Differences of meaning should be noted and reflection given as to the possible reasons for the changes. In tracing the possible common origin of a word, the lowest common denominator (or common idea behind the historical development and meaning) of the word should be sought.

Caution needs to be exercised to prevent the inexperienced researcher from too readily adopting opinions based upon inadequate data. In this

5^{27}; sq. אַחֲרֵי Je 42^{16}; sq. acc. Gn 19^{19} (J); subj.
sin ψ 101^3 (sq. בְּ pers.) **Pu.** *Impf.* 3 mpl.
יְדֻבָּקוּ pass. of Hiph. **1** sq. בְּ, of crocodile's scales,
they are joined together Jb 41^9 (|| יִתְלַכָּדוּ); abs.
of earth-clods Jb 38^{38}. **Hiph.** *Pf.* 3 fs. sf.
הִדְבִּיקָתְהוּ Ju 20^{42}; 3 pl. sf. הִדְבִּיקֻהָ 2 S 1^6; 1 s.
הִדְבַּקְתִּי Je 13^{11}; וְהִדְבַּקְתִּי Ez 29^4; *Impf.* juss. יַדְבֵּק
Dt 28^{21}; וַיַּדְבֵּק Gn 31^{23}; אַדְבִּיק Ez 3^{26}; וַיַּדְבִּקוּ
Ju 18^{22} 20^{45}; וַיַּדְבְּקוּ 1 S 14^{22}+2 t. (cf. Ges $^{§53 R 4}$
Kö $^{I. 220}$). **1.** *cause to cling* or *cleave* to, sq. acc.
+ אֶל, lit. וּלְשׁוֹנֲךָ אַדְבִּיק אֶל־חִכֶּךָ Ez 3^{26}; v. also 29^4
(sq. acc. +בְּ; lit.,but in metaph.); fig. of causing
to cleave to ל Je 13^{11} (sq. acc. + אֶל); cf. further
Dt 28^{21} (subj. ל, sq. acc. of disease +בְּ). **2.**
pursue closely, sq. אַחֲרֵי Ju 20^{45} 1 S 14^{22} 1 Ch
10^2= 1 S 31^2 (sq. acc.); so also 2 S 1^6 (sq. acc.).
3. *overtake*, sq. acc. Gn 31^{23} (E), Ju 18^{22}; cf. 20^{42}
(subj. הַמִּלְחָמָה). **Hoph.** *Pt.* וּלְשׁוֹנִי מֻדְבָּק מַלְקוֹחָי
ψ 22^{16} *and my tongue is made to cleave (to) my
gums;* cf. sub **Qal 1.**

†דָּבֵק **adj.** clinging, cleaving (to), ל fabs.
דִּבְקָה ל Pr 18^{24}; וְיֵשׁ אֹהֵב דָּבֵק מֵאָח 2 Ch 3^{12} (of
cherub's wing); of cleaving to בְּ י הַדְּבֵקִים Dt 4^4.

†דֶּבֶק **n.m.** $^{Is 41, 7}$ joining, soldering, appendage—**1.** ד' *joining, soldering* Is 41^7. **2.**
pl. הַדְּבָקִים *appendages* of breastplate (?) 1 K 22^{34}
= 2 Ch 18^{33} בֵּין הַדְּ וּבֵין הַשִּׁרְיָן. (The Be al. cf.
VB: the jointed *attachment* or *appendage* to
the rigid breast-armour, which covered the
abdomen; >Klo prop. appendage of helmet;
Thes suggests armpits, lit. *joints* (cf. מַדְבְּקֵי יָד
Je 38^{12} 𝔗); Ew the soft muscles etc. *connecting*
the chest with the bottom of the back.)

[דבר] $_{III.}$ **vb.** speak (original mng. dub.;
range in order Thes is conjectural and not
comprehensive enough; *treiben* MV does not
explain Ar. or Heb. usage, but only Aram.
A mng. *go away,* sustained by Ar. ذَبَرَ go
away with it, would best explain the four
branches of usage:—(1) Ar. ذَبَرَ *depart, perish,*
IV. *retreat,* fig. *retrograde, decline;* ذَبَرَ *passing
away, death;* As. *dabâru,* Pi. *drive away,* Bez
$^{Orient. Diplom. Vocab.}$, *Dibbara,* pest-god, Hpt. in
KAT$^{2.500}$, דֶּבֶר *pestilence.* (2) Ar. دَبَرَ *follow
behind,* in time, place, or station; دُبُرٌ *part
behind,* دَبِيرٌ *back,* דְּבִיר *hindmost chamber of
temple.* (3) Syr. ܕܒܰܪ *lead, guide,* cattle, sheep,
government, *take a wife,* = Aram. דְּבַר; Syr.
ܕܰܒܳܪ, Aram. דַּבָּר *leader;* Syr. ܡܰܕܒܰܪ, Aram.
דַּבְרָא *guidance;* Syr. ܕܒܰܪ, Aram. דַּבְרָא Heb.
דֶּבֶר; Syr. ܡܰܕܒܪܳܐ, Aram. מַדְבְּרָא, Heb. מִדְבָּר *pas-
ture, wilderness;* Ar. دَبَرَ, Syr. ܕܒܰܪ, Aram.

דְּבוֹרָה, Heb. דַּבְּרְתָּא *swarm of bees,* may be in
this line, as led by their queen, so Thes. (4)
Ar. دَبَرَ *consider the end* or *issue* (of an affair),
relate (a story or tradition); دَبَّرَ فِي *consider,*
دَبَّرَ عَلَى *plan against;* Ph. דבר *speak;* Heb.
דִּבֵּר etc. Syn. of אָמַר *say,* as Aram. מַלֵּל with
אָמַר; Gk. λαλεῖν, λέγειν; Lat. *loqui, dicere;*
Germ. *reden, sagen*)—†**Qal** $_{41}$ only inf. (once ?)
& pt.: *Inf.* sf. בְּדָבְרְךָ (by attraction to בְּשָׁפְטֶךָ
for usual Piel) ψ 51^6; *Pt.* דֹּבֵר Ex 6^{29} + 30 t.;
pl. דֹּבְרִים Nu 36^5 ψ 109^{20}; cstr. דֹּבְרֵי ψ 5^7 + 3 t.;
f. דֹּבְרוֹת Nu 27^7 ψ 31^{19}; pass. דָּבֻר Pr 25^{11};—*speak,*
abs. Nu 27^7 32^{27} 36^5 (P) ψ 51^6 (?); דָּבַר דָּבָר *word
spoken* Pr 25^{11}; with acc. rei דֹּבֵר דָּבָר *speaking
a word* Jb 2^{13}; אֱמֶת ψ 15^2, חֲמָס Am 5^{10},(מ)שָׁרִים
Pr 16^{13} Is 33^{15}, צֶדֶק Is 45^{19}, שָׁלוֹם Est 10^3 ψ 28^3,
רָע ψ 5^7 58^4, כָּזָב ψ 63^{12} 101^7 Je 40^{16},(י)שְׁקָרִים
109^{20}, נְבֵלָה Is 9^{16}, הַיַּת נַפְשׁוּ Mi 7^3; with אֶל of
person, *unto* Gn 16^{13} (J) Ex 6^{29} (P) Je 38^{20} 40^{16}
Dn 10^{11} Jon 3^2; בְּאָזְנֵי *in the ears of* Dt 5^1 Je
28^7; עַל *concerning, about* ψ 31^{11} 109^{20} Je 32^{42}
(sometimes rendered *against,* but dub.); עִם
with ψ 28^3; הַמַּלְאָךְ הַדֹּבֵר בִּי *the angel that spake
with me* (as a prophet, an instrument of com-
municating with Israel) Zc $1^{9.13.14}$ $2^{2.7}$ $4^{1.4.5}$ $5^{5.10}$
6^4 (vid. prep. בְּ **III. 2** Ew $^{§27 f. (3)}$). †**Niph.**,
Pf. נִדְבְּרוּ Mal 3^{16}, נִדְבְּרוּ ψ 119^{23}, נִדְבַּרְנוּ Mal 3^{13};
Pt. הַנִּדְבָּרִים Ez 33^{30}; reciprocal sense, *speak
with one another, talk,* abs. Mal 3^{16}; with בְּ,
against ψ 119^{23} Ez 33^{30}; with עַל, *concerning,
about* Mal 3^{13} (RV *against,* vid. Ew $^{§217l.}$) **Pi.**
$_{1089}$ *Pf.* דִּבֶּר Gn 12^4+, דִּבֶּר Gn 21^1+ (on
Ex 12^{25} Dt 26^{19} v. Bö $^{§1021 d (1)}$ Kö $^{L 188}$); *Impf.*
יְדַבֵּר Gn 44^7 +, יְדַבֵּר Gn 44^{18} +; תְּדַבְּרוּן Gn 32^{20},
תְּדַבְּרֵן ψ 58^2; *Imv.* דַּבֵּר Gn 24^{33} +, דַּבֵּר Ex
11^2 +; *Inf.* דַּבֵּר Gn 24^{50} +, דַּבֵּר Is 59^{13} +;
Pt. מְדַבֵּר Gn 27^6 +; f. מְדַבֶּרֶת 1 S 1^{13} +;—(הַדַּבֵּר
Je 5^{13}, inf. Ki ^{48}, prob. Ol ^{§182a} Kö $^{§23 (5)}$, perhaps
MV; but more prob. a noun, as Ges $^{§52 (2), Anm. 3}$
Ew ^{§156a}, dub. pf. as Sta ^{§222}; בְּיוֹם דִּבֶּר Ex 6^{28}
Nu 3^1 Dt 4^{15}; תְּחִלַּת דִּבֶּר Ho 1^2, inf. Ki ^{48} Bö
$^{§987 (7)}$ Kö $^{§23 (5)}$; but more prob. pf., as Ges $^{§52 (2),}$
$^{Anm. 3)}$;—*speak,* **1.** abs. Dt 18^{17} + (throughout
the literature) usu. with לֵאמֹר, less freq. וַיֹּאמֶר:
2 K 18^{28} +, cf. the phrases †דברתי (י)אֲנִי Ez 5^{13}
+18 t. Ez; †דבר כי Is 1^2 21^{17} 22^{25} 24^3 25^8 Je
13^{15} Jo 4^8 Ob ^{18}; †דבר פי כי Is 1^{20} 40^5 58^{14} Mi
4^4; †דבר פי ψ 49^4; (י)דבר פי ψ 66^{14} 145^{21};
†הֹשַּׁכֵם וְדַבֵּר Je 7^{13} 25^3 35^{11}; עוֹד זֶה מְדַבֵּר וְדַבֵּר Jb
$1^{16.17.18}$. **2.** with acc. rei, very frequently, ד'
אֶת הַדְּבָרִים הָאֵלֶּה Ex 20^1 Dt 5^{19}+; לָמָּה תְּדַבֵּר
עוֹד דְּבָרֶיךָ *why speakest thou any more of thy
affairs?* 2 S 19^{30}; עַד אִם־דִּבַּרְתִּי דְּבָרָי *until I*

connection, the warning given as well as the example set by James Barr in *Comparative Philology of the Text of the Old Testament* (1961) is important.

Now, turning to our illustration of *dabar,* we find at the beginning of the discussion a listing of the meanings of this word in Arabic (Ar.), Aramaic (Aram.), Alexandrine manuscript of the Septuagint (A), Assyrian (As.), and Syriac (Syr.), et cetera. Because Ras Shamra (ancient Ugarit) has been discovered in more recent times, the important contribution of Ugaritic studies to Old Testament literature will not be found in BDB and will have to be obtained from other sources (e.g., Gordan's *Ugaritic Textbook*).

With some idea of the meaning of the word under consideration, it will be of value to the researcher if he takes note of the derived terms that may illustrate the basic idea; the occasions when the word is used; the people involved; the synonyms, antonyms, or homonyms employed in different forms of Hebrew parallelism; and the situations given rise to the word's usage. Then, having examined as thoroughly as possible the dictionary definition of the word and its meaning in cognate Semitic languages, it is appropriate to consider in depth and detail its usage in the canonical Scriptures of the Old Testament.

USAGE

The usage of a term is of the utmost importance in determining its meaning, and to survey its usage we need to use one or more concordances. Those lacking a sufficient knowledge of Hebrew to permit them to use the more technical reference works will find Strong's *Exhaustive Concordance to the Bible* or the *New American Standard Exhaustive Concordance of the Bible* helpful, particularly if the number listed opposite each entry is checked with the brief definition of the word in the index at the back. Likewise, Young's *Analytical Concordance to the Bible* will be found valuable. However, because a study of a word must be undertaken in accordance with its root, those lacking a knowledge of Hebrew may find it necessary to resort to the *Englishman's Hebrew and Chaldee Concordance of the Old Testament.* All of those works are based on the text of the KJV, with the exception of the *New American Standard Exhaustive Concordance of the Bible.*

Indispensable tools to the student with a knowledge of Hebrew include:
- Lisowsky's *Konkordanz zum hebräischen Alten Testament,* with the meaning of each word given in Latin, German, and English. The value of this work lies in its listing of every Scripture verse in which a particular Hebrew word is found.
- Mandelkern's *Veteris Testamenti concordantiae Hebraicae atque Chaldaicae,* which lists each distinct form separately and provides the researcher with references for each root of a word.
- Hatch and Redpath's *Concordance to the Septuagint,* a work that makes available parallel references to the Greek text of the LXX.

The procedure to be followed is to look up each occurrence of the word, evaluate its usage in light of the context, and decide upon its precise meaning. When that has been done, the different usages may be grouped together into semantic categories for further study.

For example, the verb *bahan* is found to mean "to examine, to try, to prove." Its derivatives include "testing," "watchtower," "siege towers," and "assayer."

The occurrence of *bahan* is chiefly in the books of Job, Psalms, and Jeremiah, though its usage is not confined to those writings. In addition, it occurs in parallelism with *nasa* ("to put to the test, to tempt") and *sarap* ("to smelt, to refine"). Its meaning, therefore, seems to denote examination with a view to determining the essential qualities or integrity of a person, people, place, or thing. On closer examination, the usage of *bahan* generally has God as the subject, whereas *nasa* almost always has a man as the subject, and *sarap* is used exclusively in a religious sense with God as the subject and man as the object. Three of the references to *bahan* reverse the general order and have God as the One being tested (e.g., Psalm 95:9; Malachi 3:10, 15) by the attitude or conduct of His people.

A further observation of the usage of *bahan*, which may be made on the basis of an investigation of the text, is that *nasa* and *sarap* seem to denote the attainment of knowledge through testing, whereas *bahan* seems to denote the acquisition of knowledge through learning or intuition.

Similar studies may be done of key Hebrew words like *hesed*, "lovingkindness"; *qadosh*, "holy"; *tselem*, "image"; *tsedeq*, "righteousness"; *gibbor*, "man of valor, mighty man." Each word will be found to possess a fascination all its own, and the insights derived from such a study will readily lend themselves to homiletic subdivision, sermon illustration, and practical application.

Of further interest is the comparison of the Hebrew text with the LXX. For this you will need Hatch's and Redpath's *Concordance to the Septuagint*. In this connection it is interesting to compare the Greek translation of Isaiah 7:14 with the Hebrew original. Attention, of course, is focused on the word *'almah*, "young woman," and we are told that if Isaiah had intended us to understand "virgin" he would have used the term *bethulah*. With this judgment most lexicons agree.

But how did the Jews who translated their own Scripture into Greek understand the usage of *'almah* in this passage?

It is interesting that the Greek text of Rahlfs's *Septuagint, id est, Vetus Testamentum Graece iuxta LXX interpretes* (2 vols., 3d ed., 1965) uses the word *parthenos* as the Hellenistic equivalent of *'almah*, and *parthenos* unequivocally means "virgin." Further corroboration of this comes from another Jew named Levi (or Matthew). He was a learned man and a former employee of Rome. When quoting Isaiah's prophecy he unashamedly used *parthenos* to describe Christ's miraculous conception by Mary (Matthew 1:23).

Reference to the Septuagint provides many such sidelights on the terms employed by the writers of Scripture. Its use, therefore, should not be neglected.

VERIFYING YOUR FINDINGS

Because the most valuable lexicons may, on occasion, be misleading (e.g., as in the case of 'almah referred to above), we need to verify our findings as well as the accuracy of each lexical entry. In doing so, reference may be made to a variety of source materials alluded to in earlier chapters. Those include:

- Commentaries, and particularly exegetical ones like *International Critical Commentary*, which, although not conservative, may prove helpful to the researcher in either broadening his perspective on the usage of a word or providing insights into the way the meanings of a word may be analyzed. Other suggestions may be obtained by consulting *The Minister's Library* (pp. 92-117).
- *Theological Wordbook of the Old Testament*, by Harris, Archer, and Waltke, is a thoroughly conservative and scholarly resource tool and should be consulted repeatedly.

By regularly evaluating the material contained in reference tools, you will be able to verify the results of your own research. The product of your investigation will enrich your own life and ministry. It will be evidenced by the assurance you bring to your exposition of the text, the interest that you are able to generate in the study of the Old Testament, and the way in which seemingly irrelevant issues suddenly take on contemporary significance.

ASSIGNMENT

By utilizing English and Greek concordances, study the usage of the words *poroō, pōrōsis* ("to become hard, dull") in the New Testament as well as the Septuagint. Seek to ascertain its basic meaning as well as its spiritual significance.

9

WORD STUDIES
PART 2

A preacher cannot minister effectively without having an in-depth under-standing of the meaning of words and terms used in the Bible. John 3:16, for example, requires at the very least a working definition of *agapē* love. The Beatitudes that begin the Sermon on the Mount (Matthew 5:1-12) require a knowledge of the meaning of "discipleship," "blessed," "poor in spirit," "kingdom of heaven," "mourn," "comfort," "gentle (or humble or meek)," "righteousness," et cetera, if they are to be properly interpreted and prop-erly understood. The great teachings of the Christian faith—justification, forgiveness, redemption, reconciliation, propitiation, sanctification, glorification—require of each believer an understanding of their meaning.

The late Dr. William Barclay, the Scot who earned deserved praise for his many commentaries on the books of the New Testament, once said:

> The more I study words, the more I am convinced of their basic and funda-mental importance. On the meaning of words everything depends. No one can build up a theology without a clear definition of the terms which are to be used in it. No one can construct a Christian ethic without a close study of the ethical terms of the New Testament. Christian belief and Christian action both depend upon a clear understanding of the meaning of words.*

A study of specific words used in the New Testament may be expected to do the following for us:

- Aid in providing an enriched perspective and an in-depth understand-ing of the theological and practical importance of the word in question

---

*William Barclay, *More New Testament Words* (New York: Harper, 1958), p. 9.

- Serve as a check on the lexical aids that we all must use
- Reveal to us the many-faceted riches of God's Word.

The procedure for doing a study of a New Testament word is essentially the same as for the Old Testament. (Those with little prior experience in Greek word studies are advised to read Edward W. Goodrick's *Do It Yourself Greek,* no. 6-10.)

GREEK WORD STUDIES

ETYMOLOGY

In undertaking a study of a New Testament word, the first prerequisite is that it be historical. In Chapter 7 we outlined tentatively five eras of Greek literary history: (1) *the early period* from the second millennium to about 950 B.C.; (2) *the classical period* from c. 950 B.C.—c. 330 B.C.; (3) *the Hellenistic period* from c. 330 B.C.—A.D. 325, (4) *the Byzantine period* from A.D. 325-1453; and (5) *the modern period.* Our Interest, of course, is primarily with the Hellenistic period.

During the course of time, words change in meaning. A historical approach, therefore, will alert us to those changes. For example, in the New Testament, *eritheia* is the word for "strife" or "selfish ambition." This, however, was not always its meaning. In the process of time its original meaning degenerated so that in each of its seven occurrences in the New Testament it is used of contention or the abuse of ambition that undermines the cause of Christ and impedes the word of the church.

Eritheia originally came from the word *eris* ("day laborer"—specifically, one associated with the wool industry), and meant "labor," or more precisely, "labor for wages." It involved doing a day's work well in order to receive a day's pay.

How then did *eritheia* come to mean "contention, strife, or selfish ambition?"

The point of departure from the healthy to the unhealthy connotation of the term seems to be in the motive of the laborers. In the course of time, emphasis was no longer placed on *honest* labor. Instead, the attitude of the workers seemed to be, What can I get out of this situation? Less and less quality work was done, and more and more was demanded. That, of course, led to squabbles, power struggles between an employer and a united band of employees, and "political games." It is not surprising, therefore, that eventually the word came to be applied to one who would exploit a situation for his own advantage.

Quite obviously, a historical approach to the meaning of a term can bring to New Testament study a fascination all its own. It can also make the application of truth to life most interesting.

CONTEXT

Second, the word we choose to investigate must be studied inductively before its meaning in a particular context, or in a particular period of time, or use by a particular author, can be deduced.

In an earlier chapter, we made reference to T. J. Conant's famous work *The Meaning and Use of Baptizein* (1977) in which Dr. Conant examined each occurrence of the word in classical and Hellenistic Greek to determine its meaning. This seems to be appropriate for a term that has caused division in the church for almost two thousand years. Quite apart from its meaning when considered as an ordinance of the church, Dr. Conant found that in literature outside the New Testament *baptizein* was used of ritual washing, a ship that sank, a person whose head was held under water until he drowned, and union with a person quite apart from any sacramental association.

What then did Thomas Conant find to be the common denominator of all these meanings?

An inductive study of the word *baptizein* leads us to conclude that its basic meaning is "identification." When applied to the New Testament, this "working definition" of the word is found to be consistent. The ancient Israelites were identified with Moses in the events of the exodus (1 Cor. 10:2); proselytes to Judaism immersed themselves, signifying their identification with the people of Israel; the Jews of John's day identified themselves with the message he proclaimed by being baptized; the Lord Jesus, by baptism, identified Himself with those whom He came to save; and the people who believed the message of the coming of the Kingdom, which He preached as being "at hand," showed their identification with it by being baptized.

Once the meaning of baptism has been established, we are then free to consider the mode of baptism and the subjects. Its mode, however, should not be confused with its basic meaning!

ROOT FORM

Third, as in our study of Hebrew words, the study of Greek terms must also be in accordance with the root form of the word. (See again Figure 12, p. 85).

It is at this juncture that, depending on the word to be studied, a problem may arise. Some Greek terms have an obscure origin, and the root may be hard to trace. Three works for the study of the New Testament are parallel to Einspahr's *Index to Brown, Driver and Brigg's Hebrew Lexicon*. Those are *A Parsing Guide to the Greek New Testament* (1971), compiled by N. E. Han; the two-volume *Linguistic Key to the Greek New Testament* by F. Rienecker (translated and edited by C. L. Rogers, Jr.), published in English in 1976 and 1980; and the *Analytical Greek Lexicon* (revised ed., 1972).

The works by Han and Rienecker follow the biblical text and the former provides the root form of the word. Both works supply the parsing and the latter gives suggestions as to the meaning of words. The *Analytical Greek Lexicon* lists words (with their prefixes, suffixes, or infixes) in alphabetical order and then refers readers to those places where the term is treated in accordance with its basic root. Frequently regarded as a "crutch" by Greek professors, it is not always reliable and its meanings as well as suggested roots should in cases of doubt be checked against the standard lexicons or J. Stegenga's *Analytical Corcordance of the Greek-English New Testament* (1963).

USAGE

Once the root form of the word has been identified, you are then free to begin tracing the meaning of the word through the classical and Hellenistic periods of Greek literature. This can be achieved with relative ease by using

- Liddell's and Scott's *Greek-English Lexicon* for the classical period and by checking references to specific words in the Loeb Classical Library
- Hatch's and Redpath's *Concordance to the Septuagint*
- Moulton's and Geden's *Concordance to the Greek Testament* or the *Computer-Konkordanz zum Novum Testament* for word usage in the New Testament
- Moulton's and Milligan's *Vocabulary of the Greek Testament* for the usage of words occurring in the New Testament found in the papyri
- Lampe's *Patristic Greek Lexicon* for illustrations of the meaning attached to words after the period of the apostles.

Such a review of above-listed reference books, in which each reference to a word is carefully checked, will enable you to research its meaning before, during, and immediately after the era of the New Testament. Obviously, the nearer the occurrence of a word chronologically and contextually to the writing of the period of Christ and the apostles, the more likely it will reflect the meaning of the word in its biblical setting.

In each study of a word and its meaning(s), you will need to analyze its usage and then study the different nuances in order to uncover the basic meaning common to each usage of the word. When this has been done, your findings can then be verified by consulting other scholarly sources.

VERIFICATION

Because even the finest of lexicons may be misleading, it is wise to verify the results of your inductive research by consulting such works as exegetical commentaries (examples of which may be found in *The Minister's Library*, pp. 141-85); Kittel's and Friedrich's *Theological Dictionary of the New Testament*; and Brown's *New International Dictionary of New Testament Theology*.

By evaluating the critical data contained in these reference works, or the comments by the author of a technical commentary, you will be able to verify

Mon.inc.2(M.86.3316B); τὴν μητέρα [sc. the font] τῆς υἱ. Dion.Ar.
e.h.2.2.7(M.3.396C); hence as synonym for baptism οἱ τῆς υἱ. ἠξιω-
μένοι Thdt.Ps.57:6(1.985); d. in gen. τὸν ἑκόντα μετὰ ἀσκήσεως καὶ
διδασκαλίας τὴν γνῶσιν τῆς ἀληθείας ἐπανηρημένον εἰς υἱ. καλεῖ, τὴν
μεγίστην πασῶν προκοπὴν Clem.str.2.16(p.152.25; M.8.1013B); Mac.
Aeg.ep.(M.34.413A); οἱ γὰρ πνευματικῶς πολιτευόμενοι, τοῦ τῆς υἱ.
μεταλαγχάνουσιν ἀξιώματος Thdt.Rom.8:14(3.85); μήποτε...ἐκπέσω-
μεν τῆς τοιαύτης υἱ. ὁ δὲ ταύτης ἐκπίπτων, ὁμοίος γίνεται 'Ιούδα Ant.
Mon.hom.129(M.89.1840C); e. implying immortality τὴν υἱ. τὴν
ἀθανασίαν καλῶν, ἐπειδὴ υἱὸν εἶναι νομίζει θεοῦ ἀθανάτους εἶναι Thdr.
Mops.Rom.8:19(p.138.33; M.66.825D); Gennad.fr.Rom.1:7(p.352.
22); cf. ἠγέρθη Χριστὸς ἐκ νεκρῶν εἰς υἱ. ib.6:3f.(p.365.28; M.85.
1673C); to be completed in the future, ref. Rom.8:23 νῦν μὲν ὡς ἐν
ἀπαρχῇ λαμβάνουσα [sc. Church] τῆς υἱ. τὸν ἀρραβῶνα, καὶ τὴν τῆς
ἀναστάσεως ἐλπίδα Or.schol.in Cant.7:1(M.17.280D); Diod.Rom.8:23
(p.95.9); εἶπεν ὅτι ἐλάβομεν πνεῦμα υἱοθεσίας· ἀλλ' ὅμως διδάσκει
σαφέστερον, ὅτι τὸ μὲν ὄνομα νῦν ἐλάβομεν, τοῦ δέ γε πράγματος τότε
μεθέξομεν, ὅταν ἡμῖν ἀπαλλαγῇ τὰ σώματα τῆς φθορᾶς Thdt.Rom.
8:23(3.89); ref. 1Cor.15:28 υἱοὶ δὲ θεοῦ ἔσονται [sc. οἱ ἅγιοι] τῷ τῆς
υἱ. πνεύματι σφραγισθέντες Eus.e.th.3.15(p.173.6; M.24.1029C).
  B. not applicable to Son τῶν γὰρ ἑτεροδόξων οἱ μὲν...ἄνθρωπον
εἶναι αὐτὸν...ὑποθέμενοι ἐξ ἀνθρώπου, υἱοθεσίᾳ τετιμῆσθαι αὐτὸν
ἔφασαν Eus.Marcell.2.1(p.33.13; M.24.780B); οὐκ ἐκ δουλείας εἰς
προκοπὴν υἱοθεσίας ἐλθόντα, ἀλλὰ υἱὸν ἀεὶ γεννηθέντα Cyr.H.catech.11.
4; αὐτὸς ἄλλου υἱοῦ τοῦ χαριζομένου αὐτῷ τὴν υἱ. οὐκ ἐπιδέεται, ἀλλ'
ὅπερ ἐστὶ κατὰ φύσιν, καὶ ὀνομάζεται Gr.Nyss.Eun.3(2 p.41.20; M.45.
609A); Didym.(‡Bas.)Eun.4(1.287D; M.29.692A).
  II. sonship, of Son ὑπὲρ δὲ τῆς αὐτοῦ καταρτισθείσης υἱοθεσίας,
υἱοπρεπῶς μὲν διὰ τὴν φύσιν,...προσάγων εὐχαριστήρια τῷ πατρὶ
†Diad.Ar.7(M.65.1161C).
  υἱοθετ-έω, adopt as a son; 1. men by God; a. through Christ
ἡ υἱότης αὐτοῦ διαφέρει τῶν δι' αὐτοῦ θέσει ~ηθέντων Alex.Al.ep.
Alex.7(p.24.11; M.18.557C); b. through H. Ghost in baptism, Bas.
ep.105(3.200B; M.32.513B) cit. s. ~ἀναθανατίζω; Gr.Nyss.bapt.(M.46.
425B); διὰ τοῦ λουτροῦ παλιγγενεσίᾳ καὶ ἀνακαινώσεως πνεύματος
ἁγίου ~ούμεθα Didym.(‡Bas.)Eun.5(1.303A; M.29.728A); Jo.D.
f.o.4.8(M.91.1117A); c. in gen., Or.exp.in Pr.17:20(M.17.201A); of
Israel θέσει...καὶ χαρακτῆρί τινι...~ούμενοι ἀπὸ τοῦ ἀληθινοῦ
θεοῦ Didym.(‡Bas.)Eun.5(1.313B; M.752A); Max.ep.19(M.91.592A);
2. pass., of Church, opp. Israel ~εῖται...δι' ἀγάπης ἁγιαζομένη
Didym.(‡Bas.)Eun.5(1.309B; M.29.741B); 3. met., soul by wisdom,
Proc.G.Cant.6:8(M.87.1756B).
  υἱοθετέω, adopted as a son; of Christ into Gnost. Pleroma, Clem.
exc.Thdot.33(M.117.19; M.9.676B).
  *υἱοπατερία, ἡ, v. ~υἱοπατορία.
  *υἱοπατήρ, ὁ, v. ~υἱοπάτωρ.
  υἱοπατορία (-τερία), ἡ, doctrine of the identity of Son and
Father, as taught by Sabellians μήτε ἀπαλλοτριώσῃς τοῦ πατρὸς
τὸν υἱόν, μήτε συναλοιφὴν ἐργασάμενος υἱ. πιστεύσῃς Cyr.H.catech.4.8;
ib.15.9; Ammon.Jo.1:1(M.85.1392C); CCP(381)can.7; ‡Acac.CP ep.
Petr.(p.19.20; -τερία H.2.845A); ‡Caes.Naz.dial.3(M.38.861).
  υἱοπάτωρ (-πατήρ), ὁ, 1. divine Person who is both Father and
Son οὐδ' ὡς Σαβέλλιος τὴν μονάδα διαιρῶν υἱ. εἶπεν Ar.ep.Alex.(p.12.
12; M.26.709A); υἱ. τὸν θεὸν κατὰ τὸν Σαβέλλιον, υἱ. καὶ γυμνῷ τῷ
λόγῳ, τῷ γοῦν ἀληθείᾳ εἰσάγων [sc. Marcellus] Eus.e.th.1.1(p.62.33;
M.24.829C); οὔτε υἱ. φρονοῦμεν, ὡς οἱ Σαβέλλιοι λέγοντες μονοού-
σιον καὶ οὐχ ὁμοούσιον †Ath.exp.fid.2(M.25.204A); εἴ τις ὁ ἄχρονον
τῆς τοῦ μονογενοῦς Χριστοῦ ἐκ πατρὸς ὑποστάσεως ἐπὶ τὴν ἀγέννητον
τοῦ θεοῦ οὐσίαν ἀναφέρει, ὡς υἱ. λέγων, ἀνάθεμα ἔστω CAnc.(358)
anath.17; Μοντανιστὰς...τὸν αὐτὸν υἱοπατέρα ὁμοῦ καὶ παράκλητον
νοοῦντας Didym.Trin.3.18(M.39.881B); Νόητος...υἱ. τὸν Χριστὸν ἐδί-
δηξε, τὸν αὐτὸν εἶναι (λέγων) πατέρα καὶ υἱὸν καὶ πνεῦμα Epiph.
anac.57(p.213.4; M.41.848D); αὐτὸν θεὸν τὸν πατέρα ἕνα ὄντα δυσὶν
ὀνόμασι γεραίροντα αὐτὸν υἱ. προσαγορεύουσι [sc. Sabellians]
‡Gr.Nyss.Ar.et Sab.1(M.45.1281A); 2. one who holds such a doctrine, Filiopatrian τὴν τῶν υἱοπατόρων λεγομένων ἀπάτην Gr.Nyss.
Eun.12(1 p.227.16; M.45.924A).
  υἱοποι-έω, A. adopt as a son, Adam.dial.2.19(p.104.26); met., of
Christ βασιλείας ~οῦντές τινες, οὐχ ἡγοῦνται διδόναι ἀφθόνῳ ἢ λαμ-
βάνειν. ~ησαι σὺ τὸν Χριστόν, καὶ ἕξεις πολλὴν ἀσφάλειαν Chrys.
hom.1.4 in Phil.(11.200F); ‡Chrys.caec.Zacch.4(8.126C).
  B. make into a son of God; 1. men, ref. Ps.81:6 σχέσει γὰρ τῇ
πρὸς θεὸν υἱοποιηθέντες παρ' αὐτὸ θεοποιούμεθα Cyr.thes.4(5¹.25A);
through Christ υἱοποίησεν ἡμᾶς τῷ πατρὶ Ath.Ar.1.38(M.26.92B);
συγκαταβάντος τοῦ λόγου, ~εῖται καὶ αὕτη ἡ κτίσις δι' αὐτοῦ ib.2.64
(384B); τοῦ υἱοῦ μετέχοντες ~ούμεθα δι' αὐτοῦ Cyr.thes.13(5¹.131A);

id.Ps.83:6(M.69.1209A); through H. Ghost τοῦ Χριστοῦ ὄντος ἀληθινοῦ υἱοῦ, ἡμεῖς τὸ πνεῦμα λαμβάνοντες, ~ούμεθα Ath.ep.Serap.1.19
(M.26.576A); Cyr.Nest.2.4(p.40.39; 6¹.42E); in baptism βαπτιζόμενοι
φωτιζόμεθα, φωτιζόμενοι ~ούμεθα, ~ούμενοι τελειούμεθα Clem.paed.
1.6(p.105.20; M.8.281A); ~ούμεθα καὶ ἡμεῖς ἀληθῶς Ath.decr.31(p.27.
25; M.25.473C); ἐκ ποιημάτων ὄντες, ~ούμεθα λοιπὸν id.Ar.1.34(M.26.
84A); Const.App.2.33.1 cit. s. δεξιός; 2. of Christ (heret.) τὸν φύσει
υἱὸν θεοῦ, θέσει καὶ χάριτι υἱοποιηθέντα λέγουσι Didym.(‡Bas.)Eun.5
(1.314A; M.29.753A); Cyr.Arcad.(p.66.13; 5².49A); εἰ οὖν οὕτως καὶ ὁ
λόγος καὶ ὁ Χριστὸς μεταλήψει κοινοῦ τινος ἑτέρου...~οῦνται θεῷ
Leont.H.Nest.4.12(M.86.1648D); orthodox ἵν' ὡς ἄνθρωπος ~ηθείς,
καίτοι κατὰ φύσιν υἱάρχων θεός, ὁδοποιήσῃ δι' ἑαυτοῦ τῇ ἀνθρωπίνῃ
φύσει τῆς υἱοθεσίας τὴν μέθεξιν Cyr.Heb.1:1(p.365.23).
  *υἱοποίησις, ἡ, making into sons, ref. Heb.1:6 τῆς δὲ κτίσεως
πρωτότοκον διὰ τὴν τῶν πάντων υἱ. Ath.Ar.2.64(M.26.284C); ib.3.9
(340C); τὸ πνεῦμα, ἐπείπερ ἐστὶ τοῦ υἱοῦ, ἐνεργήσει...τὴν υἱ. Cyr.dial.
Trin.3(5¹.492C).
  υἱοποίητος, adopted as a son, Chrys.hom.5.2 in Eph.(11.34B);
‡Chrys.caec.Zacch.4(8.126C).
  υἱοποιΐα, ἡ, making into a son, ref. Ps.2:7 τῷ ἔργῳ τῆς πρὸς αὐτὸν
[sc. θεὸν] υἱοποιΐας αὐτοῦ [sc. τοῦ κατὰ Χριστὸν ἀνθρώπου] Leont.H.
Nest.3.5(M.86.1616A).
  *υἱοποιός, son-making, Leont.B.Nest.et Eut.1(M.86.1301A) cit. s.
θεοποιός; γεννήσεως υἱ. Leont.H.Nest.4.19(M.86.1661A).
  *υἱοπρεπής, filial, befitting a son υἱ. ἰδιώματα [sc. τῆς τοῦ λόγου
θείας φύσεως] Leont.H.Nest.2.21(M.86.1584A).
  *υἱοπρεπῶς, as befits a son, †Diad.Ar.7(M.65.1161C) cit. s.
ἀρχιερατικῶς.
  υἱός, ὁ, son [voc. υἱός, T.Sal.20.1(p.60.6); plur. υἱεῖς, Athenag.
leg.20.2(M.6.932A); Disp.Phot.(M.88.565D); poet. acc. υἱέα, Gr.Naz.
carm.1.1.2.1(M.37.401A); υἱῆα, Nonn.par.Jo.13:22(M.43.865A)].
  A. in Hebraisms τὰς υἱ. τῶν ἀνθρώπων 1Clem.61.2; υἱοὶ τῆς
ἀνομίας Herm.vis.3.6.1; τοῦ μέλλοντος αἰῶνος ὄντες υἱ. Hom.Clem.2.
15; γενόμενοι διὰ τὸν 'Ιησοῦν υἱ. τῆς εἰρήνης Or.Cels.5.33(p.35.28; M.
11.1232B); ἀπειθείας υἱοὺς ὀνομάζει τοὺς ἀπειθεῖς, οἱονεὶ τῆς κατὰ τὴν
ἀπείθειαν κακίας μητρὸς (γινομένης καὶ γεννώσης αὐτοὺς ἔχοντας τὸν
τῆς μητρὸς χαρακτῆρα id.comm.in Eph.5:6(p.561).
  B. of a spiritual son, Barn.1.1; Clem.str.1.1(p.3.23; M.8.689A);
Thdt.haer.prooem.(4.280A); etc.
  C. υἱὸς θεοῦ; 1. of Israel, Eus.Ps.81:6-7(M.23.988B); υἱοὺς ἔλεγε
τοὺς πάλαι λαοὺς ὁ θεὸς Ath.Ar.1.39(M.26.92C); Juln.Imp.ap.Cyr.
Juln.9(6².290D); 2. of Christian believers ὡς πρέπει υἱοῖς θεοῦ
ἀντιστῶμεν Barn.4.9; υἱοὶ ὑψίστου πάντες δύνασθαι γενέσθαι κατηξίω-
ται Just.diol.124.4(M.6.765B); τίς δὲ υἱ. εἶναι δυνάμενος τοῦ θεοῦ
δουλεύειν ἤδεται; Clem.prot.10(p.68.3; M.8.205A); οἱ τῆς ἀνομίας υἱ.
ποτε διὰ τὴν φιλανθρωπίαν τοῦ λόγου υἱοὶ...γεγόναμεν τοῦ θεοῦ ib.2
(p.20.14; 97B); υἱ. θεοῦ καὶ μαθητὴς θεοῦ ὁμοῦ καὶ φίλος καὶ συγγενὴς
id.str.7.16(p.66.17; M.9.529B); διὰ τὴν ὁμοιότητα υἱ. λέγεται εἶναι
λογιωθέντες πάντων δεσπότας ἀποκαταστῆναι δυνήσεσθε Hom.Clem.10.
6; οὐ μόνον υἱ. θεοῦ ἀλλὰ καὶ θεοὶ θνητοὶ τὴν φύσιν ἄνδρες ἐκλήθησαν
[i.e. in scripture] Eus.e.th.1.20(p.84.23; M.24.857B); υἱ. δὲ θεοῦ
ἔσονται τῷ τῆς υἱοθεσίας πνεύματι κοσμηθέντες ib.3.15(p.173.5; 1029C);
υἱοὶ θεοῦ κατὰ μετοχὴν τῆς τοῦ μονογενοῦς αὐτοῦ κοινωνίας ἀποτε-
λεσθέντες μετουσίᾳ τῶν τῆς θεότητος αὐτοῦ μαρμαρυγῶν ib.3.18(p.179.
34; 1041C); οὐκ ἄρα μισθὸν ἔσχε τὸ λέγεσθαι υἱὸς καὶ θεός, ἀλλὰ μᾶλ-
λον αὐτὸς υἱοποίησεν ἡμᾶς τῷ πατρί, καὶ ἐθεοποίησε τοὺς ἀνθρώπους
γενόμενος αὐτὸς ἄνθρωπος Ath.Ar.1.38(M.26.92B); γινόμεθα καὶ ἡμεῖς
υἱ., οὐχ ὡς ἐκεῖνος φύσει καὶ ἀληθείᾳ, ἀλλὰ κατὰ χάριν τοῦ καλέσαντος ib.
3.19(361C); ἄνθρωπος...υἱ. θεοῦ γίνεται διὰ τῆς πνευματικῆς γεννήσεως
Χριστῷ συναπτόμενος· ὁ δὲ τὸν ἄνθρωπον διὰ Χριστοῦ θεοῦ υἱὸν ποιῶν
αὐτὸς θέλων τὴν τοῦ χαριζομένου αὐτῷ τὴν υἱοθεσίαν οὐκ ἐπιδέεται Gr.
Nyss.Eun.3(2 p.41.17; M.45.609A); ἡμεῖς ὡς ἐν αὐτῷ τε καὶ δι' αὐτοῦ
υἱ. θεοῦ φυσικῶς τε καὶ κατὰ χάριν, φυσικῶς μὲν ὡς ἐξ αὐτοῦ... τε καὶ
μόνῳ, μεθεκτῶς δὲ καὶ κατὰ χάριν υἱεῖς δι' αὐτοῦ ἐν πνεύματι Cyr.
Thds.30(p.61.31; 5².27A); αὐτὸς μὲν κατὰ φύσιν υἱ. ἡμεῖς δὲ
κατὰ χάριν Justn.conf.(p.76.23; M.86.999B); ref. Rom.8:19-
21 κτίσιν καλῶν ἐνταῦθα τοὺς ἀγγέλους, υἱ. δὲ θεοῦ τοὺς ἀνθρώπους
Cosm.Ind.top.2(M.88.120B); υἱοὶ δέ, οἱ μήτε φόβῳ τῶν
ἠπειλημένων, μήτε πόθῳ τῶν ἐπηγγελμένων, ἀλλὰ τρόπῳ καὶ ἕξει τῇ
πρὸς τὸ καλόν...τῆς ψυχῆς ῥοπῆς...μηδέποτε τοῦ θεοῦ χωριζόμενοι
Max.myst.(M.91.712A); Χριστιανὸς ὀρθόδοξος καὶ υἱ. τοῦ θεοῦ χάριτι
Lit.Jac.proem.(NBP 10² p.39); Gnost., of followers of Prodicus
υἱοὺς μὲν φύσει τοῦ πρώτου θεοῦ λέγοντες αὐτοὺς Clem.str.3.4(p.200.31;
M.8.1136A); Basilidean υἱ. δέ, φησίν, ἐσμὲν ἡμεῖς οἱ πνευματικοί Hipp.
haer.7.25(p.202.26; M.16.3311D); αὐτοὺς εἶναι υἱ. φασιν, οἱ τούτου
χάριν εἰσὶν ἐν κόσμῳ, ἵνα...ἅμα τῇ υἱότητι ἀνέλθωσι πρὸς τὸν ἄνω

Fig. 22. Page from Lampe's *Patristic Greek Lexicon.*

your own research. Only by following the process described above will a new generation of Bible students be able to modify and advance the work of those who have preceded them.

Having concluded our study of general reference works, we are now in a position to consider two related topics: (1) the further collection of data from books, periodicals, and unpublished materials, and (2) the process by which topics can be refined.

In preparation for the next chapter, research the standard systematic theologies and consider all the subdivisions of Christology. How would you go about researching the two natures of Christ? Make a list of the resources you would consult. Add to your list works cited in the footnotes of the treatises on theology. As far as possible, ascertain the perspective of each writer (i.e., his theological position [liberal, conservative, Calvinistic, Arminian]), and then his denominational background, level of scholarship, evident strengths, and weaknesses.

10

SPECIFIC RESOURCE TOOLS: BOOKS

In the preceding chapters we covered general reference works—those research tools that will enable you to explore the limits of virtually any topic. From these resources you should be able to ascertain who has made a contribution to the advancement of knowledge and in a particular area, when and where that was done, and obtain some evaluation of the strengths and weaknesses of each contributor.

If the topic of your research is either biblical or theological, the reference works you use should also treat the Greek and Hebrew terms upon which a discussion of the topic must be based. Without such a foundation, the value of the material to you is reduced considerably and accuracy is lost.

We are now ready to explore those resources that will help you find out what books have been written on the topic you are researching. In doing so, we will be moving from the general to the specific. Our focus now will be on books and specialized monographs.

REFINING YOUR TOPIC

In moving from a consideration of general reference works to special resource tools, there is an important step that is often overlooked. It involves refining your terminology and perhaps narrowing the focus of your topic.

117

Because books in libraries are cataloged according to their content, it is important for us to know something about the subject categories that have been assigned to them by the library. Two primary resources are available to librarians in the United States who are responsible for providing *approved* subject heading for each book. These are *The Library of Congress Subject Headings* (2 vols., 9th ed., 1980) and the *Sears List of Subject Headings,* edited by Barbara M. Westby (11th ed., 1977). The former is used in most academic libraries, whereas the latter is more suited to public libraries.

The subject heading relating to the content of a given book is typed on a card (or entered into a computer) and then reproduced so that for each book in the library there are multiple entries in the catalog: author (or main entry), title, and subject(s). We are primarily interested in the subject headings appearing at the bottom of a card, with the subject typed in capital letters on the top. The subject heading cards are then filed alphabetically.

BT
262
M867   Morris, Leon L
1965   The cross in the New Testament.   Grand
                  Rapids, Eerdmans, 1965.
                  454 p.   24cm.

                  Bibliographical notes.

                  1.   Atonement—Biblical teaching.
              I.   Title.

Fig. 23. Sample of library card catalog author and title card. (Note subject heading at the bottom.)

In some libraries, author and title cards are filed together, but subject cards are filed separately. Librarians call this a divided catalog, and it is the easiest for the researcher to use. A dictionary catalog has all the cards together in a single sequence. In this arrangement subject cards are interfiled alphabetically either word-by-word or letter-by-letter with author and title cards. Subject cards are distinguished from author and title cards because the subject headings at the top are typed in capital letters.

Now take for example the subject of Christology. The student who was asked to research the two natures of Christ (see Chapter 1) and checked the card catalog under "CHRISTOLOGY" was tempted to conclude that the library did not have holdings in this area. Had he checked the *Library of Congress Subject Headings* he would have found an entry in light type under "Christology" advising him to check under "Jesus Christ."

BT
262
M867
1965

ATONEMENT—BIBLICAL TEACHING

Morris, Leon L
    The cross in the New Testament.   Grand
Rapids, Eerdmans, 1965.
    454p. 24cm.

Bibliographical notes.

    1. Atonement—Biblical teaching.
  I. Title.

Fig. 24. Sample of library card catalog subject card.

Under **Jesus Christ** he would have found general Library of Congress classification numbers *(BT198-590)*, and that would have alerted him to the area of the library where these books are located. **Jesus Christ** is in boldface type, meaning that this is an approved subject heading. Subdivisions under this general heading occupy the next four pages, enabling a researcher to refine his topic while sharpening the focus of his terminology.

In addition, under most headings there are these symbols:
    sa (see also)   indicates a reference to a related or subordinate topic

    x (see from)   indicates a reference from an expression not itself used as a heading

    xx (see also from)   indicates a related or broader heading from which a "see also" reference is made.

These are most helpful in alerting researchers to other places where approved subject headings may be found.

For example, under "**Jesus Christ**—Natures" there is also an *sa* (see also) reference directing the researcher to additional areas: "**Hypostatic Union**" and "**Jesus Christ**—Person and offices." He then has three areas to investigate:

    Jesus Christ—Natures
    Hypostatic Union (including Hypostatic Union—History of doctrines)
    Jesus Christ—Person and offices.

And under **Hypostatic Union** a single classification number is given *(BT 205)*. This is more specific than the ones assigned for Christology *(BT 198-590)*.

— Siege, 86 B.C.
    xx Jews—History—953-586 B.C.
— Siege, 701 B.C.
    xx Jews—History—953-586 B.C.
— Siege, 1948
    xx Israel-Arab War, 1948-1949
        Palestine—History—1929-1948
Jerusalem. Temple
    sa Tabernacle
    Example under Architecture, Jewish: Archi-
        tecture, Oriental
— Symbolism
        See Temple of God
Jerusalem artichoke (SB211.J)
    x Topinambur
    xx Artichokes
Jerusalem in art
Jerusalem in Islam
    xx Islam
        Palestine in Islam
Jerusalem in Judaism
    xx Jews—Restoration
        Judaism
        Palestine in Judaism
        Zionism
Jerusalem in literature
    sa Jerusalem in the Bible
        Jerusalem in the Midrash
Jerusalem in the Bible
    xx Bible—Theology
        Jerusalem in literature
        Religion and geography
Jerusalem in the Midrash (BM518.J4)
    xx Jerusalem in literature
        Midrash
Jeshan
    See Independence Day (Afghanistan)
Jesness inventory
    xx Criminal behavior, Prediction of
        Personality tests
Jessamine
    See Jasmine
Jesson family
    See Jessup family
Jessopp family
    See Jessup family
Jessup family
    x Jessop family
        Jessopp family
        Jesup family
Jest-books
    See Chap-books
        Wit and humor
Jesters
    See Fools and jesters
Jests
    See Wit and humor
Jesuats (BX3760)
Jesuit architecture
    See Architecture, Jesuit
Jesuit art
    See Art, Jesuit
Jesuit artists
    See Artists, Jesuit
Jesuit drama
    xx Drama
Jesuit drama, French, [etc.] (Indirect)
Jesuit War, 1754-1759 (South America)
    See Seven Reductions, War of the,
        1754-1756
Jesuits (Indirect) (Men, BX3701-3755;
        Women, BX4371-4376)
    sa Bollandists
    x Jesus, Society of
        Society of Jesus
    xx Counter-Reformation
        Monasticism and religious orders
— Bibliography
— Bio-bibliography (Z7840.J4)
— Biography (BX3755)
— Controversial literature

— Dictionaries
— Education (LC493)
        Example under Education
— Heraldry
— History (BX3706-3749)
— Missions (BV2290)
        sa Catholic Church—Missions
        xx Indians of North America—Missions
        Example under Missions; Monasticism
            and religious orders—Missions
— Necrology
        Example under Necrologies
— Occupations
        Example under Monasticism and reli-
            gious orders—Occupations
— Portraits
— Prayer-books and devotions
— Rules (BX3704)
        Example under Monasticism and reli-
            gious orders—Rules
— Spiritual life (BX3703)
        Example under Monastic and religious
            life
— England
        sa Archpriest controversy, 1598-1602
            Popish Plot, 1678
— Paraguay
        sa Seven Reductions, War of the,
            1754-1756
Jesuits' bark
    See Cinchona
Jesuits in literature
Jesup family
    See Jessup family
Jesus, Society of
    See Jesuits
Jesus Christ (BT198-590)
    sa Antichrist
        Atonement
        Christianity
        Crosses
        Incarnation
        Logos
        Lord's Supper
        Mercersburg theology
        Messiah
        Millennium
        Redemption
        Salvation
        Second Advent
        Trinity
    x Christ
        Christology
    xx Christianity
        God
        Theology, Doctrinal
        Trinity
— Addresses, essays, lectures
        Afro-American interpretations
        xx Afro-Americans—Religion
— Agrapha
        See Jesus Christ—Words—
            Extra-canonical parallels
— Anthroposophical interpretations
— Apparitions and miracles (Modern)
        (BT580)
        xx Apparitions
— Appearance
        See Jesus Christ—Physical appearance
— Appearances (BT490)
        Here are entered works dealing with
            the appearances of Jesus Christ
            after His resurrection.
        sa Theophanies
        xx Jesus Christ—Forty days
            Jesus Christ—Resurrection
            Theophanies
— Appreciation
        Art (N8050-8054)
            sa Bible—Picture Bibles

Botticelli, Sandro, 1447?-1510.
    Nativity
Buonarroti, Michel Angelo,
    1475-1564. Pietà
Christian art and symbolism
Essen. Cathedral. Grablegung
Fazzini, Pericle, 1913-
    Resurrection
Fish (in religion, folk-lore, etc.)
Foppa, Vincenzo, fl. 1459-1490.
    Processional banner of Orzinuovi
Giorgione, Giorgio Barbarelli, known
    as, 1477-1511. Nativity
Gozzoli, Benozzo, 1420-1497.
    Adoration of the Magi
Icons
Jesus Christ—Iconography
Magi—Art
Mary, Virgin—Art
Second Advent in art
Tiziano Vecelli, 1477-1576.
    Madonna and Child with rabbit
Tiziano Vecelli, 1477-1576.
    Resurrection altarpiece
Veit, Philipp, 1793-1877. Mainz
    Cathedral frescoes
    x Jesus Christ—Burial—Art
        Jesus Christ—Family—Art
        Jesus Christ—Nativity—Art
        Jesus Christ—Passion—Art
        Jesus Christ—Pictures, illustrations,
            etc.
        Jesus Christ—Resurrection—Art
        Jesus Christ in art
    xx God—Art
        Mary, Virgin—Art
        Example under Bible—Illustrations;
            Christian art and symbolism
— Ascension (BT500)
        sa Ascension Day
        x Ascension of Christ
— — History of doctrines (BT500)
— Atonement
        See Atonement
— Attitude towards Jewish dietary laws
        xx Jesus Christ—Attitude towards
            Jewish law
            Jews—Dietary laws
— Attitude towards Jewish law (BT590.J)
        sa Jesus Christ—Attitude towards
            Jewish dietary laws
        xx Jesus Christ—Attitude towards the
            Old Testament
            Jewish law
— Attitude towards the Old Testament
        sa Jesus Christ—Attitude towards
            Jewish law
        xx Jesus Christ—Knowledge and
            learning
— Attitude towards women (BT590.W6)
— Baptism (BT350)
— Beatitudes
        See Beatitudes
— Betrayal (BT435)
        x Betrayal of Christ
        xx Jesus Christ—Biography—Passion
            Week
            Jesus Christ—Passion
— Biography (BT298-500)
        sa Mysteries of the Rosary
        x Jesus Christ—Life
— — Apocryphal and legendary literature
        (BT520)
        xx Christian literature, Early
— — Juvenile literature
— Devotional literature (BT306.28-5)
— Drama
        See Jesus Christ—Drama
— Early life (BT310-330)
        sa Jesus Christ—Childhood
            Jesus Christ—Flight into Egypt

Fig. 25. Page from *Library of Congress Subject Headings.* (See entry **Jesus Christ**, top of right column.)

ndriasis
Hypochon ria
ic mic anemia (RC641.7.H9)
li on deficiency anemia
Anemia. Microcytic hypochromic
icrocytic hypochromic anemia
mia
eales (QK623.P9)
Fungi
y (Ethics. BJ1535.H8. Theolo,.
BV4627.H8)
nduct of life
E:hics
praemia
yocupremia
emia
Copper deficiency disease
lvpocupraemia
ypocuprosis
Copper in body
ficiency diseases in domestic animals
a is
Hypocupremia
oids
cycloids and hypoc ds
mic injections
ctions, Hypodermic
nic jet injectors
njectors. Hypodermic jet
injectors, Hypodermic
ctions, Hypoderm i.
Medical instruments and apparat
mic needles
podermic syringes
njections, hypodermic
under Medical instruments a p-
paratus
mic syringe
Hypodermic eedles
ctiors. Hypodermic
ptic differ equations
ifferent quations. Hypoellipti.
anemia
on deficiency anemia
ic acid (QD305.A2. Botanical
chemistry, QK866.)
umaglobulinemia
Agammaglobulinemia
ric plexus
y
ossal nerve
rvus hypoglossus
erves, Cranial
vcemia (Disease, RC857)
kery for hypoglycem
ypoglycem agents
sulin sho
poglycemosis
B ood sugar
Endocrine glands--Diseases
poglycemic agents
oglycin A
lin
reas--Diseases
emia. Acute toxic
Hypoglycem Toxicology
emia in children (K 520.H94
w blood sugar in children
Metabolic disorders in children
mic agents (RC661.A1)
benclamide
Hypoglycemia
poglycemic sulphony reas
ypoglycin A
Insulin
Phenformin
olbutamide
Antidiabetics
Diabetes
rugs
Hypoglyce

Hypoglycemic sulphonylureas (Indirect)
(RM666.H)
  sa Chlorpropamide
     Glibenclamide
     Tolbutamide
   x Sulphonylureas, Hypoglycemic
  xx Hypoglycemic agents
     Sulphonamides
     Urea
Hypoglycemosis
  See Hypoglycemia
Hypoglycin A
  sa Hypoglycemia
   x Aminomethylenecyclopropanepropionic
     acid
  xx Aceraceae
     Amino acids
     Cyclopropane
     Hippocastanaceae
     Hypoglycemic agents
     Poisons
     Propionic acid
     Sapindaceae
  — Toxicology
     x Acute toxic hypoglycemia
       Akee poisoning
       Hypoglycemia, Acute toxic
       Jamaica vomiting sickness
       Vomiting sickness of Jamaica
Hypogonadism
  sa Klinefelter's syndrome
  xx Sexual disorders
Hypoid gearing
  See Gearing, Hypoid
Hypokalemia
  See Hypokalemia
Hypokalemia (Indirect) (RC632.P)
   x Hypokalaemia
     Hypokaliaemia
     Hypokaliemia
  xx Potassium metabolism
     Water-electrolyte imbalances
Hypokaliaemia
  See Hypokalemia
Hypokaliemia
  See Hypokalemia
Hypokinesia
   x Hypoactivity
     Inactivity, Physical
     Physical inactivity
     Underactivity
  xx Movement disorders
Hypoleucemia
  See Leucopenia
Hypoleucia
  See Leucopenia
Hypoleucocytosis
  See Leucopenia
Hypolimnas (QL561.N9)
  xx Nymphalidae
Hypolimnas macarthuri (QL561.N9)
Hypolipaemia
  See Hypolipemia
Hypolipemia (Indirect) (RC632.H)
   x Hypolipidaemia
     Hypolipidemia
  xx Blood lipids
     Lipid metabolism disorders
Hypolipidemia
  See Hypolipemia
Hypomesus olidus
  See Pond smelt
Hyponatremia
  xx Sodium metabolism disorders
     Water-electrolyte imbalances
Hyponomeutidae
  See Yponomeutidae
Hypopharynx (Comparative anatomy.
     QL861; Human anatomy, QM331)
  sa Pharyngoesophageal sphincter
   x Laryngopharynx

  xx Pharynx
  -- Diseases
     sa Hypopharynx—Diverticula
     Diverticula (RF497.H96)
        x Diverticula of the hypopharynx
          Pharyngoesophageal diverticula
       xx Hypopharynx—Diseases
Hypophosphatasia
  xx Phosphorus metabolism disorders
Hypophosphatemia, Familial
   x Familial hypophosphatemia
  xx Familial diseases
     Metabolism, Inborn errors of
     Renal tubular transport, Disorders of
Hypophosphites (Therapeutics. RM666.H9)
  xx Materia medica
Hypophyseal dwarfism
  See Dwarfism, Pituitary
Hypophysectomy
   x Pituitary body--Excision
Hypophysis cerebri
  See Pituitary body
Hypoptyalism (Indirect) (RC815.5)
   x Hyposialosis
  xx Salivary glands--Diseases
Hyporhina (QE862.L2)
  xx Hyporhinidae
Hyporhina tertia (QE862.L2)
Hyporhinidae (QE862.L2)
  sa Hyporhina
  xx Lizards, Fossil
Hyposensitization therapy
  See Allergy desensitization
Hyposialosis
  See Hypoptyalism
Hypospadias
  sa Chordee
  xx Penis
     Urethra
Hypostatic union (BT205)
  sa Jesus Christ:--Natures
   x Union, Hypostatic
  xx Jesus Christ—Natures
     Jesus Christ—Person and offices
  — History of doctrines
Hypostomus
  xx Loricariidae
Hyposulphites (QD181.S1)
Hypotension
  sa Hypotension, Orthostatic
     Hypotension in pregnancy
   x Blood pressure, Low
     Low blood pressure
  xx Blood--Circulation, Disorders of
Hypotension, Controlled
   x Controlled hypotension
     Hypotension, Induced
     Induced hypotension
  xx Analgesia
     Anesthesia
Hypotension, Induced
  See Hypotension, Controlled
Hypotension, Orthostatic (Internal medicine.
     RC685.H; Pediatrics. RJ426.H94)
   x Orthostatic hypotension
     Postural hypotension
  xx Hypotension
     Standing position
Hypotension in pregnancy (RG580.H95)
  xx Hypotension
     Pregnancy, Complications of
Hypotensive agents
  sa Hydralazine
     Kinins
     Saralasin
     Sodium nitroferricyanide
     Vasodilators
   x Antihypertensive agents
  xx Cardiovascular agents
     Hypertension

Fig. 26. Page from *Library of Congress Subject Headings.* (See entry **Hypostatic union,** bottom of right column.)

DATA COLLECTION

With a clearer idea of the approved library terminology relating to your topic, you are now in a position to proceed to the next stage of your investigation—finding out who has written on the subject you have selected. In this connection, two basic resource tools will help you survey the contribution of others to the theme you are researching: (1) *Library of Congress Catalog—Books: Subjects;* (2) *Subject Guide to Books in Print.*

The *Library of Congress Catalog—Books: Subjects* is a most useful quinquennial cumulation of books cataloged by the Library of Congress or one of its participating libraries. Begun in 1950, it arranges alphabetically *by subject* those books whose contents deal with the topic you have chosen. Books covering more than one subject area will appear under each subject heading. For example Martin Chemnitz's *The Two Natures of Christ* is found under **"Hypostatic Union"** and **"Jesus Christ**—Person and office." Helpful "see also" references are included following most major headings.

The value of this work for research is that it enables the researcher to review the most important scholarly publications on any subject from 1950 to within the last few years. This is done easily and efficiently. The time saved as well as the overview obtained amply reward one's efforts. And those engaged in dissertation research will find numerous entries to books in French, German, and other European and Asian languages.

The second work, *Subject Guide to Books in Print* (1957-present), is an annual. It arranges the titles of books listed in *Books in Print* by subject following the headings assigned by the Library of Congress The latest volume(s) take over from where the last quinquennial cumulation of *Library of Congress Catalog—Books: Subjects* left off. By consulting the *Subject Guide to Books in Print,* you can locate those publications too recent to have been included in the *Library of Congress Catalog.* Furthermore, by using both the *Library of Congress Catalog* and *Subject Guide to Books in Print,* you can achieve excellent bibliographic control of all important works published since 1950. Such control assures you that the most strategic works pertaining to your subject have come under your purview. For works not included in the *Library of Congress Catalog* you may wish to consult *The Minister's Library,* and J. F. Hurst's *The Literature of Theology* (1896).

LOCATING BOOKS NOT IN YOUR LIBRARY

But what about that dilemma that faces all aspiring theologues—the fact that your library may not have a copy of the book you need for your research?

Let us take as an illustration of a hard-to-find book, W. R. Inge's *Studies of English Mystics,* a work first published in 1905 and then reissued in a limited printing in 1969. And let us assume that you have become aware of this book through a footnote in another book, but that the footnote gave *only* the year of publication.

HYPOGASTRURIDAE

Thibaud, Jean Marc.
Biologie et écologie des Collemboles Hypogastruridae édaphiques et cavernicoles [illegible] M. Thibaud. [illegible] Éditions du Muséum [illegible]
[illegible]

HYPOGLOSSAL [illegible]

Aldskogius, H
Indirect and direct Wallerian degeneration in [illegible] [illegible] nerve: an electron microscopical study [illegible] Aldskogius. [illegible] New York, [illegible] Verlag. [illegible]
[illegible]
QL801.E67 [illegible]

HYPOGLYCEMIA

Bastenie, P
[illegible] hypoglycémie [illegible] traitement [illegible] direction de [illegible] A. [illegible] Malaisse. Bruxelles, Presses [illegible] Paris, Libr. [illegible]
[illegible]

Blevin, Margo.
The low blood sugar cookbook, by Margo Blevin and Geri Ginder [illegible] by Herman [illegible] Goldman. [illegible] Doubleday [illegible]
[illegible]
RM [illegible]

Davis, Francyne.
The low blood sugar cookbook. Foreword by Carlton Fredericks. [illegible] New York, Grosset & Dunlap [illegible] 1973.
[illegible]

Fredericks, Carlton.
[illegible] blood sugar and you, by Carlton Fredericks and [illegible] Goodman. New York, Constellation International [illegible]
[illegible]

Genes, Semen Grigor'evich, [illegible]
[illegible]

Hurdle, J [illegible] **Frank,** 1927-
Low blood sugar; a doctor's guide to its effective control, by J. Frank Hurdle. West Nyack, N. Y., Parker Pub. Co., 1969,
[illegible]

Laurent, Jean.
Hypoglycemic tumours, by [illegible] G. [illegible] and J. [illegible] Amsterdam, Excerpta Medica, 1971.
[illegible]

Métabolisme glucidique et sa régulation (par R. Assan et al.) Paris, Masson, 1973.
5, 287 p. illus. 24 cm. (Actualités de physiologie pathologique, 4. sér.) F***
At head of title: École pratique des hautes études.
Includes bibliographies.
1. Glucose metabolism. 2. Insulin—Physiological effect. 3. Hypoglycemia. I. Assan, R. II. Series.
RC660.M48 616.4'62 72-87697
ISBN 2-225-36222-5 MARC

Steincrohn, Peter Joseph, 1899-
Low blood sugar (by) Peter J. Steincrohn. Chicago, Regnery (1972)
xii, 160 p. 22 cm. $5.95
1. Hypoglycemia. I. Title.
RC662.2.S74 616.4'66 72-8004
MARC

—CONGRESSES

International Symposium on Hypoglycaemia and Diazoxide Venice, 1971.
Hypoglycaemia and diazoxide. Proceedings of the International Symposium on Hypoglycaemia and Diazoxide. Venice, Fondazione G. Cini, Isola di S. Giorgio Maggiore, October 15-16th 1971. Edited by M. Austoni (and others) Padova, CEDAM, 1972.
xi, 428 p. illus. 24 cm. L12000 It 73-Aug
English, French, or Italian.
Includes bibliographies.
1. Hypoglycemia—Congresses. 2. Diazoxide—Therapeutic use—Congresses. I. Austoni, M., ed. II. Title.
(DNLM: 1. Diazoxide—Therapeutic use—Congresses. 2. Hypoglycemia—Drug therapy—Congresses. WK880 I 61h 1971)
[RC662 [illegible] 1971] 616.4'66'061 73-595534
Shared Cataloging with DNLM

HYPOGONADISM

see also Klinefelter's syndrome

Conti, Carlo.
Gli ipogonadismi maschili. Aspetti strutturali e funzionali del testicolo umano normale e patologico ... Relazione al 69. Congresso della Società italiana di medicina interna. Roma, ottobre 1968. Roma, L. Pozzi, 1968.
172 p. illus., col. plate. 26 cm. [illegible] It***
[RC [illegible]] 77-451461
Shared Cataloging with DNLM

A Psychiatric-psychological study of 50 severely hypogonadal male patients, including 24 with Klinefelter's syndrome 47, XXY By Johannes Nielsen (and others) København, Universitetsforlaget i Aarhus og Munksgaard, 1969.
[illegible] p. diagrs. 25 cm. (Acta Jutlandica, 41:3. Skrifter fra Aarhus Universitet) [illegible] D 70-2
AS281.A34 vol. 41, pt. 3 616.6 78-480531
MARC

Thomas, Jack Ward.
Studies in hypogonadism in white-tailed deer of the central mineral region in Texas, by Jack Ward Thomas, R. M. Robinson (and) R. G. Marburger. (Austin) Texas Parks & Wildlife Dept., 1970.
iv, 50 p. illus. 23 cm. (Texas Parks and Wildlife Dept. Technical series no. 5)
Bibliography: p. 45-50.
1. White-tailed deer. 2. Hypogonadism. I. Robinson, Richard Michael, joint author. II. Marburger, R. G., joint author. III. Title. IV. Series.
SF997.5.D4T [illegible] 599'.7357 75-634532
MARC

Tronchetti, Fabio.
[illegible] ipogonadismi maschili. Fisiopatologia, clinica e terapia [illegible] Relatori: F. Tronchetti, V. Marescotti (con la collaborazione di) M. Luisi [illegible] Franchi, A. Carnicelli, ... P. [illegible] Roma, L. Pozzi, 1968.
[illegible] p. illus. 26 cm. (Atti [illegible] congresso della Società italiana di medicina interna, 69. congresso, Roma 13-16 ottobre 1968. Relazione, 2) [illegible] It 69-Jan
[RC [illegible]] 75-500041
Shared Cataloging with DNLM

HYPOLEUKOCYTOSIS see Leukopenia

HYPOMNESTICON

Chisholm, John Edward.
The Pseudo-Augustinian Hypomnesticon against the Pelagians and Celestians. [illegible] The University Press, 1967-
v. [illegible] cm. (Paradosis, [illegible] to the history of early Christian [illegible] and theology [illegible] 25.00 (v. 1)
BT1450 [illegible] 71-491130
MARC

HYPOPHOSPHATASIA

Rasmussen, Karsten.
Phosphorylethanolamine and hypophosphatasia. Studies on urinary excretion, renal handling and elimination of endogenous and exogenous phosphorylethanolamine in healthy persons, in carriers of and in patients with hypophosphatasia. (Translated from Danish by Hanne Ejsing Jørgensen) Virum, Centers Bogtrykkeri, 1968.
112 p. 25 cm. D***
RC632.H93R313 77-400927
MARC

HYPOPHYSECTOMY

Hardy, Jules.
Transsphenoidal operations on the pituitary. (New York, Audiovisual Education in Neurosurgery, 1972)
39 p. illus. 26 cm.
"Designed to supplement the surgical demonstration in Dr. Jules Hardy's video cassette."
1. Hypophysectomy. 2. Pituitary body—Tumors. I. Title.
RD594.H37 617'.481 73-77397
MARC

Mitchell, James Boswell.
Experimental studies of the bird hypophysis; I. Effects of hypophysectomy in the brown leghorn fowl, by James Boswell Mitchell, Jr. 1928.
[illegible]
QP188.P58M57 74-399128

Ray, Bronson S
Intracranial operations on the pituitary (by) Bronson S. Ray. New York, Audiovisual Education in Neurosurgery, 1972
[illegible] p. illus. 26 cm.
Designed to supplement the surgical demonstration in the author's video cassette.
1. Pituitary body—Surgery. 2. Hypophysectomy. I. Title.
RD594.R38 617'.481 77- [illegible] 141
MARC

HYPOPHYSIS CEREBRI see Pituitary body

HYPOSPADIAS

Bosio, Leopoldo.
Ipospadia. Illustrazioni di A. Bertolasi. (Torino), Minerva medica, (196-)
235 p. illus. 23 cm. (Collana monografica di chirurgia plastica)
RC882.B66 70-466518

HYPOSTATIC UNION

Chemnitz, Martin, 1522-1586.
The two natures in Christ; a monograph concerning the two natures in Christ, their hypostatic union, the communication of their attributes, and related questions, recently prepared and revised on the basis of Scripture and the witnesses of the ancient church. With a pref. by Nicolaus Selnecker. Translated by J. A. O. Preus. Saint Louis, Concordia Pub. House (1971)
542 p. 24 cm.
BT200.C4313 232'.8 74-115465
MARC

—HISTORY OF DOCTRINES

Lafont, Ghislain.
Peut-on connaître Dieu en Jésus-Christ? Problématique. Paris, les Éditions du Cerf, 1969.
[illegible] 22 cm. (Cogitatio fidei, 44) 30.00 F 70-620
[illegible] 78-540304

Patfoort, A
L'unité d'être dans le Christ d'après S. Thomas; à la croisée de l'ontologie et de la christologie, par A. Patfoort. Paris, New York, Desclée (1964)
326 p. 23 cm. (Bibliothèque de théologie. Théologie dogmatique, série 1, v. 4)
Bibliography: p. 321-324.
BT213.P35 75-250616

HYPOTENSION

Arbeitskreis für Neurovegetative Therapie.
Hypo- und Hypertonie. Bericht über die 12. Arbeitstagung des Arbeitskreises für Neurovegetative Therapie. Hrsg. von D. Gross, in Zusammenarbeit mit O. H. Arnold (et al.) Stuttgart, Hippokrates (1973)
271 p. illus. 21 cm. (Therapie über das Nervensystem, Bd. 11) GFR***
Includes bibliographies.
1. Hypertension. 2. [illegible] tension. I. Gross, Dieter, ed. II. [illegible] III. Series.
(DNLM: 1. Hypertension. 2. Hypotension. W1 TH645 Bd. 11 1973/WG 340 A664h 1973)
[RC685.H8A65 1973] 73-595121
ISBN 3-7773-0263-1
Shared Cataloging with DNLM

Fig. 27. Page from *Library of Congress Catalog–Books: Subjects.* (See entry HYPOSTATIC UNION, right column.)

JESUS CHRIST
—PERSON AND OFFICES
(Cont nued)

Boyall, Charles Spurgeo.
The man for us . . . by Charle· S. Boyall. Sydney.
Alpha Books, 1973.
x 145 : 18 cm 81.37
Index.
1. Jesus Christ—Pe··· ··· 2 Jesus Cri·te- Person and off···.
I. Title.
FT901.2.B65   232   73-178347
ISBN ··· 33-123-7 ··· ···rted in ··· ·ok   MA···

Boyd, Malcolm, 1923-
The runner. Waco. Tex.. Word ..ooks ,1974,
206 p 23 cm $5.95
1. Jesus · · · ·· · ·· of ··· ·es 2. ·· ·stian life-Anglican
authors. I Tith
BT202.B67 ·····   ··· ··   75-91012
MARC

Braun, Herbert, 1903-
Jes·· Der Mann aus Nazareth ·nd sein· Zeit. Stutt
gart, Berlin, Kreuz-Verlag (1969).
175 p . 20 cm. ···· ·· ·· (Thenl·· Pt 1) unpriced
BT202.B68   70-436440

Brien, André.
J·· Christ, ma l'berté. ···   Éditions de Centurion,
19·.
187 p. 20 cm. (3 / 54/·····/ ·./ ··/ ··) 18.50F F···
1 J·eus ····-Pe··· ··· ··· ··· I. Title.
B··· 1974   72-319635

Brunner Rudolf, 18··-
Ch····· ·ra Abl · V · ··um···· ··· dem Glauben.
Frei·weilen-Zürich, ··· ··teli·V··· ·· 1963-
v. 23 cm.
BT··· ···78   74-264517

Brunotti, Manlio.
C · · cape della C···so nella ··log'a contemporanea
Ro·· Is,··ta p·· ··· R·· ··, 1972.
··· ···· · 17 cm. ··· ···· ·· ···· 7t 22···
1933 graph·, p ·,··· ·
d··· ··· ··· ···· d ch···m · ··· Jesu· Christ History of
do···· ···· ···· I Title.
B··· ·· ·· ···   73-340602

Bur··, ··· 1960
··· ··· ·eatokrasor: Uatologio ·n·· Eschatologia a's Grun
··ge · ·· Le··re ro G···. Hurzhucg·S··r·stedt, R. Reic.,
1969.
17·· · ··· ··· cm ··· ·· ·· gisete Form une · ···wschaftliche Bei-
rage ··· ·· ·· ·· ··· ··· rion le···
BT···· ·   77-175600

Bushnell, Horace, 180·-1878
God in Christ ·T ··· ·liscourses · ·· ··· ·nd at New Haven,
Cambridge, an ·· ·nd·ver, with · · ·· Pre···ry dissertation
on l·· ·uage. Hartford Brown a: Parsons ? 49 Nev
York. MS Press, 19?9.
290 p 23 cm.
1 Jesus Christ—·· ·· ·· ··· 2. Language and ····· 3. Degr·a.
I Language and ling·· ·· I. Title.
BT202.·'·85 1972   932   76-305-58
ISBN: 404-0245-0   MARC

Butler, Samuel, ··-1902
The ··r li· on. ·h· AMS ed N·· York. AMS P··s
··· 1974,
··· xviii, 258 p, ···nt. ··· (The Sh··· ··· ·rs edi··n of the w·rt··
of Sacred R·li·· ·· ·· 2
Repr·· t of the 1923 ed.
··· ·e·us Chr·· ·· P·r··ces ·n· off···· ··· ··· · rist · Miracles.
3. Jesus Christ— Resurr··n · ·· ·Histor· and criticism. 4 Str···
De b) · ··rideb·h ····· 3. A fi·· ·· ··· 1910 :·8?
Title.
PR4349.R7 1974,v···   ·92° ··33'4   72-1869.4
(r)·96·   MARC

Casci··n. José Mari·.
··esu·r··o y la ·· ··· pol·ica. 2 ··· Madrid, Edic·
··· Pr··l··· ,1972,
·· ··· ··· ·· · ··· P·lom··· ·
·· · ··· ··· · · ··· ·· ·· ·· ···ch. I. Title.
BT202.C·· 197· ···   74-319190
ISBN 54-7114 ···1 ·

Castelnuovo, Elias.
Jesucristo, montanero de Ju·es. Buenos Aires ,Tall.
Gráf. La Técnica Impresora, 1971.
137 p. 20 cm.
1. Communism and Christianity 2. Jesus Christ—Person and offices. I. Title.   LACAP 71-4752
HX536.C855   72-316109

Cegielka, Francis A
Handbook of ecclesiology and Christology; a concise, au-
thoritative review of the mystery of the church and the
Incarnation in the light of Vatican II ,by, Francis A.
Cegielka. Staten Island, N. Y., Alba House ,1971,
ix, 179 p. 21 cm. $1.90
BX1746.C4   230.2   77-158569
ISBN 0-8189-0201-9   MARC

Chalendar, Xavier de.
Mort sous Ponce Pilate. ,Paris, Fayard ,1971,
ix, 194 p. 22 cm. 22.50F   F···
BT431.C46   72-889169

Chemnitz, Martin, 1522-1586.
The two natures in Christ; a monograph concerning the
two natures in Christ, their hypostatic union, the communication of their attributes, and related questions, recently
prepared and revised on the basis of Scripture and the witnesses of the ancient church. With a pref. by Nicolaus
Selnecker. Translated by J. A. O. Preus. Saint Louis,
Concordia Pub. House ,1971,
542 p. 24 cm.
BT200.C4513   232.8   74-115465
MARC

Christ, faith and history: Cambridge studies in Chri·tology;
edited by S W. Sykes and J. P. Clayton. London, Cam-
bridge University Press, 1972.
x, 303 p . 24 cm. $4.20   B 72-22009
Papers presented to a graduate Christology sevinar, Cambridge.
Includes bibliographical references.
1. Jesus Christ—Person and offices I. Sykes, Stephen, ed.
II. Clayton, John Powell, ed.
BT202.C5   232'.08   73-176257
ISBN 0-521-0-451-2   MARC

Christ, Felix.
Jesus Sophia. Die Sophia-Christologie bei den Synopti-
kern. Zürich, Zwingli-Verlag (1970).
196 p. 23 cm. (Abhandlungen zur Theologie des Alten und Neuen
Testaments, Bd. 57) 24.90   Sw 70-A-4044
BT202.C5··   77-832704

Christ and humanity. Ivar Asheim, editor. Foreword by
Mikko Juva. Philadelphia, Fortress Press ,1970,
xiii, 186 p. 21 cm. 3.50
BT763.C49   73-101426
MARC

Christus, das Heil der Welt: 2. Theol. Gespräch zwischen d.
Ökumen. Patriarchat Konstantinopel u. d. Evang. Kirche
in Deutschland vom 4.-8. Okt. 1971/ hrsg. vom Kirchl.
Aussenamt. Mit e. Vorw. von Adolf Wischmann. - Stutt-
gart: Ev·· ·elischer, Missio··verlag, 1972.
127 p. 22 cm. — (Ökumeni·che Rundschau. Beiheft; Nr. 22)
DM19.80   GFR 73-A25
Includes bibliographical references.
1. Jesus Christ—Person and offices. 2. Constantinople (Patri-
archate) II. Evangelische Kirche in Deutschland. III. Evangelische
Kirche in Deutschland. Kirchliches Aussenamt.
BT202.C545   74-347583
ISBN 3-7714-0170-4   MARC

Combrink, Hans Jacob Bernardus.
Die diens van Jesus, 'n Ek·egetiese beskouing oor Markus
10:45, Groningen, V. R. B.-Offsetdrukkerij ,Kleine der
A 3-4) 197·
viii, 288 p. 23; cm. unpriced   N·B·68-June
BS2555.2.C6   78-474118

Conant, Ruth Sanger, 1905-
Jesus Christ the Liberator. ·t ed., Brooklyn, N. Y.,
Pageant-Poseidon ,1971,
80 p. map, 21 cm. $3.95
Bibliography: p. 82-86.
1. Jesus Christ—Person and ·ff·· I. Title.
BT20·.C5·   35·   77-149064
ISBN ·· ·· -0181-4   MARC

Conzelmann, Hans.
Je··s; the classic article f·· RGG expanded and updated. Translated by J. R·· ·nd Lorl. Edited with an
introd. by John Reumann. Philadelphia, Fortress Press
,1973.
xii 11 p. 24 cm. $2.95
"A translation of Jesus Christus ·· ·lished in the 3d ed. of, Die
Religion in Geschichte und Gege·· ··· Handwörterbuch für Theologie und Religi·onswesen ·· ·· (1959)"
Bibliography: p. 97-1(·)
1. Jesus Christ—Person and ·· I. Title.
BT202.C713   73-79011
ISP? 0-8006-1000-5   MARC

Cornelius, Friedrich.
Jesus der Mensch: in seinem religionsgeschichtl. Zusam-
menhang/ Friedrich Cornelius. — Asken: Scientia-Verlag,
1973.
221 p.; 23 cm. DM45.00   GFR 74-A
Includes bibliographical references.
1. Jesus Christ—Person and offices. 2. Christianity and other
religions. 3. Church history—Primitive and early church, ca. 30-
600. I. Title.
BT202.C68   74-324447
ISBN 3-511-00120-X

Cullmann, Oscar.
Die Christologie des Neuen Testaments. 4. Aufl. Unver-
änderter Nachdruck der 3., durchgesehenen Aufl. Tübingen,
Mohr (Siebeck) 1966.
xii, 352 p. 24 cm. 25.00   GDB 67-A3-10
BT198.C8 1966   76-458853
***

Cullmann, Oscar.
Jesus and the revolutionaries. Translated from the Ger-
man by Gareth Putnam. ,1st ed., New York, Harper &
Row ,1970,
xi, 84 p. 22 cm. 3.95
BT202.C8413   232   75-124710
MARC

Cullmann, Oscar.
Jesus und die Revolutionären seiner Zeit. Gottesdienst,
Gesellschaft, Politik. Tübingen, Mohr (Siebeck) 1970.
82 p. 19 cm. DM5.80   GDB 70-A25-7
BT202.C84   74-545141

Cullmann, Oscar.
Royauté du Christ et l'Église, selon le Nouveau Testament.
(Neuchâtel.) ,elachaux et Niestlé, 1971.
82 p. 18 cm. (Foi vivante, 140) 5.50F   Sw 71-A-4044
Issued from label monograf ·n t. p. title covered by label: La
royauté du Christ et de l'Église selon le 3·· veau Testament.
Includes bibliographical references.
1. Jesus Christ—Person and offices. 2. Church. I. Title.
BT202.C86 1971   232   74-179500
MARC

Davis, Ralph Marshall.
The woods; the ·uman self and the realism ·f Jesus,
wi·· a brief, restructured Gospel ,by P. M. Davis, Staun-
ton. Va. ,c1971,
79 p. 18 cm.
1. Jesus Christ—Person and offices. 2. Jesus Christ—T·· ·tings.
I. Title
BT202.D34   232   72-183344
MARC

Dewailly, L   M
Jésus-Christ, parole de Dieu ,par, L.-M. Dewailly 4d.
refundue. Paris, Éditions du Cerf ,1969,
202 p. 20 cm. 18.00
BT202.D47 1969   70-523707

Dixon, Jeane.
The call to glory. Jeane Dixon speaks of Jesus. New
York, Morrow, 1972 ,c1971,
192 p. 22 cm. $4.00
BF1283.D48A53   232   78-187805
MARC

Dodd, Charles Harold, 1884-
The founder of Christianity ,by, C. H. Dodd. ,New
York, Macmillan ,1970,
xi, 181 p. 22 cm.
BT202.D57   232   78-90222
MARC

Dor, Prosper.
Solution au problème de Jésus. ·ed., Nîmes, Éditions
de la Maison carrée ,1944,
412 p. 20 cm.
Includes bibliographical references.
1. Jesus Christ—Person and offices. I. Title.
BT9··.D57 1944   74-218127

Du Plessis, Isak Johannes.
Christus as hoof ·· kerk en kosmos; 'n eksegetiese-teolo-
giese studie van Christus se hoofskap veral in Efesiërs en
Kolossense. Gron·· en, Druk: V. R. B., 1962.
13·p. 24 cm.
Proefschrift—Theologische Hoogeschool van de Gereformeerde Ker-
ken in Nederland.
Summary in English.
Includes bibliographical references.
1. Jesus Christ—Person and offices. 2. Church—Biblical teaching.
3. Bible. N. T. Ephe·· Theology. 4. Bible. N. T. Colossians—
Theology. I. Title.
BT202.D78   72 .2968

397

Fig. 28. Page from *Library of Congress Catalog–Books: Subjects*. (See entry
Chemnitz, Martin, center column.)

JESUS CHRIST
—PASSION (Continued)

Tessitori, Tiziano, 1895–
Cristo: processo, condanna, resurrezione. ¡Milano, Istituto tip. editoriale ¡1963¡
145 p. illus. 22 cm.
BT431.T47 — 76-422214

Thöny, Wilhelm, 1888–1949.
Bilder zur Passion. (Graz, Wien, Köln, Styria, 1965)
28 p., 2 leaves. 40 cm. S 395.–
N8053.T47 1965 — 759.36 — 66-66823

Trens, Manuel.
Les majestats catalanes. Barcelona, Editorial Alpha ¡1967, *1966¡
161 p. 94 plates (part col.) 32 cm. (Monumenta cataloniae. Materials per a la història de l'art à Catalunya, v. 13)
N7109.C3M6 vol. 13 — 68-130504

Zoals er gezegd is over het kruis. Door J. van Goudoever, Th. de Kruijf, H. van Praag ¡e. a.¡ Hilversum, W. de Haan; Antwerpen, Standaard-Boekhandel, 1968.
160 p., 40 p. of photos. 19 cm. (Phoenix bijbelpockets. 2. reeks, deel 23¡ fl 4.25
BT431.Z6 — 75-350517

—PASSION—ART see Jesus Christ
—ART

—PASSION—DEVOTIONAL
LITERATURE

Liguori, Alfonso Maria de', Saint, 1696–1787.
The Passion of Jesus Christ, by St. Alphonsus Maria de Liguori. Translated from the Italian. Baltimore, Helicon ¡1968¡
xii, 230 p. 22 cm. (His Ascetical works, v. 8)
BT430.L633 — 242 — 65-3753

Smith, Bernie, 1920–
Journey to Calvary. Grand Rapids, Baker Book House ¡1967, *1966¡
88 p. 21 cm.
BT431.S68 — 242.3'5 — 67-15766

—PASSION—DRAMA see Jesus
Christ—Drama; Passion-plays

—PASSION—JUVENILE LITERATURE

London. Vita et Pax Convent School.
Children's Lent and Easter, written and illustrated by Vita et Pax, Benedictine Nuns of Cockfosters, London. Baltimore, Helicon ¡1965¡
1 v. (unpaged) col. illus. 24 cm.
BT400.L6 — j 232.9 — 65-16730

—PASSION—MANUSCRIPTS

Klemmt, Rolf, 1938–
Eine mittelhochdeutsche Evangeliensynopse der Passion Christi; Untersuchung und Text. ¡Heidelberg, 1964.
300 p. 2 facsims. 21 cm.
BT430.A32G4 1964 — 232.96 — 67-110232

Rozmyślania dominikańskie; ¡reprodukcja rękopisu¡ Wydali i opracowali Karol Górski i Władysław Kuraszkiewicz. Zofia Rozanow, opracowania ikonograficzne. Tadeusz Dobrzeniecki, wstęp komparatystyczny. ¡Wyd. 1.¡ Wrocław, Zakład Narodowy im. Ossolińskich, 1965–
v. illus. (part col.) facsims. 30 cm. (Instytut Badań Literackich Polskiej Akademii Nauk. Biblioteka pisarzów polskich. Seria A, nr 3)
BT430.R88 — 67-125128

—PASSION—MEDITATIONS

Alberione, Giacomo Giuseppe, 1884–
The paschal mystery and Christian living ¡by¡ James Alberione. Translated by the Daughters of St. Paul. ¡Boston, St. Paul Editions ¡1968¡
187 p. illus. 20 cm.
BT431.A413 — 232.96 — 68-28102

Bishop, Hugh, 1907–
The Man for us. London, British Broadcasting Corporation, 1968.
31 p. 21 cm. 2/6
BT431.B5 — 232.96 — B 68-11004 / 70-377371
SBN 563-07473-6

Calluf, Emir.
Lágrimas so meio-dia. ¡São Paulo, Edições Paulinas ¡1966¡
150 p. illus. 22 cm.
BT431.C27 — 68-79244

Edwards, David Lawrence.
God's cross in our world. Philadelphia, Westminster Press ¡1963¡
151 p. 19 cm.
[BT431] — 232.96 — 63-11084 ‡/CD
Printed for Card Div.

Gedda, Luigi.
Getsemani. Meditazioni per l'uomo d'oggi. ¡3. ed.¡ Milano, Massimo, 1968.
259 p. 18¼ cm. (Collana, "Compagni di viaggio," n. 16) 900
BT435.G4 1968 — 74-416043

Lønning, Per.
Pathways of the Passion; daily meditations for the Lenten season. Translated by J. Melvin Moe. Minneapolis, Augsburg Pub. House. ¡*1965¡
xi, 148 p. 21 cm.
BT431.L613 — 242.34 — 65-12133

Rahner, Karl, 1904–
Heilige Stunde und Passionsandacht. 4. Aufl. Freiburg, Herder ¡1965¡
62 p. 19 cm.
BT453.R53 1965 — 68-72848

Rahner, Karl, 1904–
Watch and pray with me. Translated by William V. Dych. New York, Herder and Herder ¡1966¡
63 p. 22 cm.
BT453.R313 — 232.96 — 66-13068

Target, George William.
We, the crucifiers, by G. W. Target. Grand Rapids, W. B. Eerdmans ¡1969, *1964¡
150 p. 19 cm. $1.95
BT431.T5 1969 — 242.3'5 — 69-12320

Wise, Charles C
Windows on the Passion ¡by¡ Charles C. Wise, Jr. Nashville, Abingdon Press ¡1967¡
143 p. 21 cm.
BT431.W5 — 242.35 — 67-11007

Wyon, Olive, 1890–
The grace of the Passion. Philadelphia, Fortress Press ¡1965, *1959¡
x, 93 p. 18 cm.
BT431.W9 1965 — 232.96 — 65-13405

—PASSION—MUSIC see Passion-
music

—PASSION—SERMONS

see also Good Friday sermons; Holy
Week sermons; Lenten sermons

Barrett, Charles Kingsley.
History and faith: the story of the Passion ¡by¡ C. K. Barrett. London, British Broadcasting Corporation, 1967.
40 p. 21 cm. 2/6
BV4298.B57 — 232.96 — B 67-7839 / 71-398409

Fryhling, Paul P
Prelude to the Cross, and other sermons, by Paul P. Fryhling. Grand Rapids, Baker Book House, 1965.
149 p. 20 cm.
BT431.F7 — 252.62 — 64-8347

Haushalter, Walter Milton, 1889–
The crucifixion of superiority, by Walter M. Haushalter. Philadelphia, Dorrance ¡1967¡
51 p. 20 cm.
BV95.H3 — 242.3'5 — 66-28861

Hedegård, David.
Smärtornas man. Passionsbetraktelser. Stockholm, EFS, 1967.
143 p. 20 cm. 13.75 skr
BT431.H39 — 68-91754

Lessmann, Paul G
The Lord's prayer and the Lord's Passion; Lenten sermons, by Paul G. Lessmann. Saint Louis, Concordia Pub. House ¡1965¡
100 p. 19 cm.
BV230.L43 — 242.722 — 66-12154

Melito, Saint, Bp. of Sardis, 2d cent.
Sur la Pâque et fragments ¡par¡ Méliton de Sardes. Introduction, texte critique, traduction et notes par Othmar Perler ... Paris, Éditions du Cerf, 1966.
287 p. 20 cm. (Sources chrétiennes, 123) 27 F.
BT430.M414 — 232.96 — 67-111378

Mithridates, Flavius Guillelmus Ramundus, fl. 1470–1483.
Flavius Mithridates Sermo de passione Domini. Edited with introd. and commentary by Chaim Wirszubski. Jerusalem, Israel Academy of Sciences and Humanities, 1963.
138 p. facsims. 25 cm. (Publications of the Israel Academy of Sciences and Humanities)
BT430.M57 — HE 65-359

Smith, Wilbur Moorehead, 1894– *comp.*
Great sermons on the death of Christ by celebrated preachers; with biographical sketches and bibliographies. Compiled Wilbur M. Smith. Natick, Mass., W. A. Wilde Co. ¡1965¡
244 p. 22 cm.
BT431.S6 — 232.963 — 65-12941

White, Jesse Eugene, 1926–
The drama of the cross, by J. Eugene White. Grand Rapids, Baker Book House ¡1968¡
111 p. 21 cm. 2.95
BT431.W43 — 232.963 — 68-31476

—PERIODICALS—INDEXES

Metzger, Bruce Manning, *ed.*
Index to periodical literature on Christ and the Gospels, compiled under the direction of Bruce M. Metzger. Leiden, E. J. Brill, 1966.
xxiii, 602 p. 25 cm. (New Testament tools and studies, v. 6)
Z7772.M1M4 — 016.226 — 66-6136

—PERSON AND OFFICES

Ainger, Geoffrey.
Jesus our contemporary. London, S. C. M. Press, 1967.
112 p. 18½ cm. (Living church books) 6/6
BT202.A35 — 232 — 67-86894

Ainger, Geoffrey.
Jesus our contemporary. New York, Seabury Press ¡1967¡
128 p. 22 cm.
BT202.A35 1967b — 232 — 67-91034

Audet, Jean Paul.
The Gospel project. Translated by Edmond Bonin. New York, Paulist Press ¡1969¡
v, 106 p. 19 cm. (Deus books) 1.25
BT202.A813 — 232 — 79-92991 MARC

Barrett, Charles Kingsley.
Jesus and the Gospel tradition ¡by¡ C. K. Barrett. London, S. P. C. K., 1967.
xi, 116 p. 22½ cm. 25/–
BT303.2.B3 — 232 — 67-101962

Barrett, Charles Kingsley.
Jesus and the Gospel tradition ¡by¡ C. K. Barrett. Philadelphia, Fortress Press, 1968 ¡*1967¡
BT303.2.B3 1968 — 232 — 68-10290

Besnard, Albert Marie.
Un certain Jésus ¡par¡ A.-M. Besnard o. p. ¡Paris, Éditions du Cerf, 1968.
112 p. 18 cm. 4.80 F
BT202.B42 — 232 — 68-112406

Blank, Josef, 1926–
Krisis; Untersuchungen zur johanneischen Christologie und Eschatologie. Freiburg im Breisgau, Lambertus-Verlag, 1964.
360 p. 24 cm.
BS2615.2.B53 — 73-392041

Boman, Thorleif.
Jesus, jødenes konge. Fantast eller realist? Oslo, Aschehoug, 1967.
140 p. 21 cm. 29.50 nkr (28.50 nkr)
BT202.B56 — N 67-47 / 71-378852

Bonnard, Pierre E.
La Sagesse en personne annoncée et venue: Jésus Christ ¡par¡ P.-E. Bonnard. Paris, Éditions du Cerf, 1966.
168 p. 23 cm. (Collection Lectio divina, 44) 14.20 F.
BS680.W6B6 — 220.81 — 67-83101

Bonsall, Henry Brash.
The person of Christ ¡by¡ H. Brash Bonsall; with foreword by F. F. Bruce. London, Christian Literature Crusade, 1967, i. e. 1968¡–
v. 23 cm. 18/– (v. 1)
BT202.B63 — 232 — 74-533727

Boros, Ladislaus, 1927–
God is with us; ¡translated from the German by R. A. Wilson¡. London, Burns & Oates, 1967.
xii, 110 p. 22 cm. 35/–
BT202.B6517 — 232 — 67-108680

Bousset, Wilhelm, 1865–1920.
Kyrios Christos; Geschichte des Christusglaubens von den Anfängen des Christentums bis Irenaeus. 6. Aufl. Göttingen, Vandenhoeck & Ruprecht ¡1967¡
xvii, 364 p. port. 24 cm.
BT198.B57 1967 — 68-136114

Breuning, Wilhelm.
Jesus Christus der Erlöser. Mainz, Matthias-Grünewald-Verlag ¡1968¡
147 p. 21 cm. (Unser Glaube; christliches Selbstverständnis heute, Bd. 4)
BT202.B7 — 79-357882

Būlus, Ilyās.
يسوع المسيح، شخصيته، عالمية ¡تأليف، بولس الياس البسري¡. الطبعة 2. بيروت، المطبعة الكاثوليكية ¡1966¡
381 p. 23 cm. £L 10.00
BT202.B8 1966 — PL 480: UAR-4446

Caemmerer, Richard Rudolph, 1904–
Earth with heaven; an essay in sayings of Jesus ¡by¡ Richard R. Caemmerer, Sr. St. Louis, Concordia Pub. House ¡1969¡
124 p. 21 cm. 2.75
BS2415.C32 — 232.95'4 — 69-13794

Campanella, Tommaso, 1568–1639.
Cristologia. Inediti. Testo critico e traduzione a cura di Romano Amerio. Roma, Centro internazionale di studi umanistici, 1958.
2 v. 25 cm. (His Theologicorum liber XVIII)
BT200.C3 — 75-386715

Fig. 29. Page from *Library of Congress Catalog–Books: Subjects.* (Note foreign-language entries.)

By checking the *National Union Catalog* for the period in which the printing occurred, you are able to locate the desired information. The key to those libraries having a copy of Inge's work is located under the entry as follows: CSt, AU, NjR, FTaSU, NBuC, MU, FU, KMK. These abbreviations stand for Stanford University (California); University of Alabama; Rutgers (New Jersey); Florida State University; University of Nebraska; University of Massachusetts; University of Florida; and Kansas State University.

But what do you do if there is no indication under an entry of where a copy may be obtained? Most of William Inge's other works in the illustration from the *National Union Catalog* appear without any indication of the libraries that might include a copy of his book(s).

A further key to libraries having a copy of Inge's work on English mystics is located at the bottom righthand corner of the entry—the number 69-17578. This is the Library of Congress order number and is primarily for librarians who may wish to order printed cards for this book from the Library of Congress. It serves another purpose, however, in that it directs researchers to library holdings from which the book may be obtained on inter-library loan.

For example, in the volumes at the end of the *National Union Catalog, 1968-1972* and in the *Register of Additional Locations, 1968-1972,* an entry will be found listing those libraries possessing a copy of Inge's book. In the front of the first volume there is an index explaining the abbreviations. CoU is the abbreviation for the University of Colorado; IU stands for University of Illinois; CoDMSC is Metropolitan State College, Denver. Each of these libraries has a copy of *Studies of English Mystics* and will be happy to make it available to you through inter-library loan. In fact, the *Register of Additional Locations* lists nine libraries possessing copies of Inge's book.

The illustration I have used was purposely obscure. If we can locate nine institutions of higher learning each possessing a copy of *Studies of English Mystics,* it will be far easier for you to locate something better known and more widely used. The principle for tracking down the source(s) from which a copy may be obtained, however, will be the same.

In this chapter we have covered a variety of themes of importance to researchers.

1. We began with the possible need to narrow down a topic. At the same time, we learned about using approved terminology if we are to obtain the best results from consultation of our library's book catalog.

2. We then used the subject heading(s) to find out what had been written on on our topic since 1950. The primary resource for this was the *Library of Congress Catalog—Books: Subjects.* The most recent publications since the last edition of the *Library of Congress Catalog* were traced through the latest edition of *Subject Guide to Books in Print.*

3. When a book you need is not in your own library you now know that, by consulting the *National Union Catalog* and the *Register of Additional*

Inge, George B.
see Order of Myths Society. Our book of state.
Mobile ₁Robert A. Sands Memorial Assoc.,
c1968₁

Inge, M Thomas, comp.
Agrarianism in American literature. Edited by
M. Thomas Inge. New York, Odyssey Press ₁1969₁
xx, 358 p. 21 cm. (Perspectives on American literature)
Includes bibliographical references.
1. American literature (Selections): Extracts, etc.) 2. Agricul-
ture—U. S.—Literary collections. I. Title.
PS509.A4 I 5   810.8'03   68-31706
                                            MARC

Inge, M. Thomas, ed.
see Faulkner, William, 1897-1962. A rose
for Emily. ₁Columbus, Ohio, Merrill ₁1970₁

Inge, M. Thomas, ed.
see Harris, George Washington, 1814-1869.
High times and hard times... ₁Nashville₁
Vanderbilt Univ. Press, 1967.

Inge, M. Thomas, ed.
see Wade, John Donald, 1892-   Augustus
Baldwin Longstreet... Athens, Univ. of
Georgia Press ₁1969₁

Inge, M. Thomas, joint author
see Young, Thomas Daniel, 1919-
Donald Davidson.   New York, Twayne
Publishers ₁c1971₁

Inge, Otis T
Research directed toward the development of
a low energy electron gun, by Otis T. Inge,
Leedy G. Ambrose ₁and₁ Roger C. Jones.
Bedford, Mass., Air Force Cambridge Research
Laboratories, Office of Aerospace Research,
U.S. Air Force, 1963.
v, 47, ₂—e p. illus. 29 cm. (AFCRL-63-
699)
"Final report."
Prepared by Melpar, Inc., Falls Church, Va.
1. Electron beams. 2. Electron tubes.
I. Ambrose, Leedy G., joint author. II. Jones,
Roger C., joint author. III. Title.
ViU   NⁱⁱC72-12342

Inge, William Motter.
Eleven short plays, by William Inge. ₁New York₁
Dramatists Play Service ₁1962₁
142 p. 20 cm.
CONTENTS.—To Bobolink, for her spirit.—People in the wind.—
A social event.—The boy in the basement.—The tiny closet.—Memory
of summer.—Bus Riley's back in town.—The rainy afternoon.—The
mall.—An incident at the Standish Arms.—The strains of triumph.
I. Title.
PS3517.N265A6 1962   812'.5'4   68-1699
IaU Wa MH RPB NcRS CSt

Inge, William Motter.
Good luck, Miss Wyckoff; a novel, by William Inge.
₁1st ed.₁ Boston, Little, Brown ₁1970₁
179 p. 21 cm. 4.95
I. Title.
PZ4.I45Go   813'.5'4   75-110260
₁PS3517.N265₁   MARC
MB TxFTC IaU CSt ViU WU KEmT FTaSU
MiEM GU NjP MH IaAS NjR MoSW

Inge, William Motter.
My son is a splendid driver; a novel by William Inge.
₁1st ed.₁ Boston, Little, Brown ₁1971₁
224 p. 21 cm. $5.95
I. Title.
PZ4.I45My   813'.5'4   79-147771
₁PS3517.N265M9₁   MARC
KyU

Inge, William Motter.
Two short plays: The call ₁and₁ A murder, by William
Inge. ₁New York, Dramatists Play Service ₁1968₁
46 p. 20 cm.
I. Title: The call. II. Title: A murder.
PS3517.N265T9   812'.5'4   78-17062
                                            MARC
DAU TxHU

Inge, William Ralph, 1860-1954.
Christian ethics and modern problems. Westport, Conn.,
Greenwood Press ₁1970₁
ix, 427 p. 23 cm.
Reprint of the 1930 ed.
1. Christian ethics. 2. Social problems.   I. Title.
BJ1251.I 54 1970   261   79-104263
ISBN 0-8371-8060-0   MARC

Inge, William Ralph, 1860-1954.
The church in the world; collected essays. Freeport,
N. Y., Books for Libraries Press ₁1969₁
xi, 275 p. 23 cm. (Essay index reprint series)
Reprint of the 1927 ed.
Bibliographical footnotes.
CONTENTS.—The condition of the Church of England.—The crisis
of Roman Catholicism.—The Quakers.—Hellenism in Christianity.—
Science and theology.—Science and ultimate truth.—Faith and rea-
son.—The training of the reason.
1. Religion—Addresses, essays, lectures.   I. Title.
BR85.I 6 1969   201   68-57324
                                            MARC

Inge, William Ralph, 1860-1954.
Hebrews; a little library of exposition with
new studies by W. R. Inge ₁and₁ H. L. Goudge.
Garden City, N. Y., Doubleday, Doran ₁n. d.₁
143 p.
1. Bible. N. T. Hebrews—Criticism,
interpretation, etc.   I. Goudge, Henry
Leighton, joint author.   II. Title.
CSaT   NUC68-72748

Inge, William Ralph, 1860-1954.
Lay thoughts of a dean. Freeport, N. Y., Books for Li-
braries Press ₁1972₁
vii, 366 p. 23 cm. (Essay index reprint series)
Reprint of the 1926 ed.
I. Title.
AC8.I 47 1971   824'.9'12   71-156663
ISBN 0-8360-2403-7   MARC

Inge, William Ralph, 1860-1954.
Mysticism in religion. ₁London₁ Rider
₁1969₁
222 p. 22 cm.
1. Mysticism.   I. Title.
IEdS   NUC70-81143

Inge, William Ralph, 1860-1954.
Our present discontents. Freeport, N. Y., Books for Li-
braries Press ₁1972₁
351 p. 22 cm. (Essay index reprint series)
"First published 1939."
I. Title.
AC8.I 49 1972   082   79-1343
ISBN 0-8360-2646-6   MARC

Inge, William Ralph, 1860-1954.
Outspoken essays. London, New York, Longmans, Green,
1919.
281 p. 23 cm.
Photo-offset. New York, Greenwood, 1968.
"All the essays in this volume, except the first, have appeared in
the Edinburgh review, the Quarterly review, or the Hibbert journal."
CONTENTS.— Our present discontents. — Patriotism. — The birth-
rate.—The future of the English race.—Bishop Gore and the Church
of England.—Roman Catholic modernism.—Cardinal Newman.—St.
Paul.—Institutionalism and mysticism.—The indictment against
Christianity.—Survival and immortality.
I. Title.
AC8.I 5 1968   082   68-8739

Inge, William Ralph, 1860-1954.
Outspoken essays (first series) Freeport, N. Y., Books
for Libraries Press ₁1971₁
281 p. 23 cm. (Essay index reprint series)
CONTENTS: Our present discontents.—Patriotism.—The birth-
rate.—The future of the English race.—Bishop Gore and the Church
of England.—Roman Catholic modernism.—Cardinal Newman.—St.
Paul.—Institutionalism and mysticism.—The indictment against
Christianity.—Survival and immortality.
I. Title.
AC8.I 5 1971   824'.9'12   75-156664
ISBN 0-8360-2404-5   MARC
KMKG

Inge, William Ralph, 1860-1954.
Outspoken essays (second series) New York, Greenwood
Press ₁1969₁
vii, 275 p. 23 cm.
Reprint of the 1922 ed.
CONTENTS.—Confessio fidei.—The state, visible and invisible: The-
ocracies. The Greek city state. The medieval ideal. The modern
god-state. Religion and the state.—The idea of progress.—The Vic-
torian age.—The white man and his rivals.—The dilemma of civiliza-
tion.—Eugenics.
I. Title.
AC8.I 52 1969   901.9'08   69-13947
                                            MARC
AU

Inge, William Ralph, 1860-1954.
Outspoken essays (second series). Freeport, N. Y., Books
for Libraries Press ₁1971₁
275 p. 23 cm. (Essay index reprint series)
Reprint of the 1922 ed.
CONTENTS.—The state, visible and invisible.—
The idea of progress.—The Victorian age.—The white man and his
rivals.—The dilemma of civilization.—Eugenics.
I. Title.
AC8.I 52 1971   824'.9'12   79-156665
ISBN 0-8360-2405-3   MARC

Inge, William Ralph, 1860-1954.
A pacifist in trouble. Freeport, N. Y., Books for Li-
braries Press ₁1971₁
xⁱⁱ p. 23 cm. (Essay index reprint series)
Reprint of the 1939 ed.
I. Title.
AC8.I 525 1971   082   75-152176
ISBN 0-8360-2192-3   MARC

Inge, William Ralph, 1860-1954.
The philosophy of Plotinus. ₁3d ed.₁ New York, Green-
wood Press, 1968.
2 v. 22 cm. (Gifford lectures, 1917-1918)
Reprint of the 1929 ed.
Bibliographical footnotes.
1. Plotinus.   I. Title.   (Series)
B693.Z7 I 5 1968   186'.4   68-8740

Inge, William Ralph, 1860-1954.
Studies of English mystics. Freeport, N. Y., Books for
Libraries Press ₁1969₁
vi, 233 p. 23 cm. (St. Margaret's lectures, 1905)
Essay index reprint series.
Reprint of the 1906 ed.
CONTENTS.—On the psychology of mysticism.—The Ancren rivie
and Julian of Norwich.—Walter Hylton.—William Law.—The mysti-
cism of Wordsworth.—The mysticism of Robert Browning.
1. Mysticism—Gt. Brit. 2. Mysticism in literature.   I. Title.
(Series)
BV5077.G7 I 6 1969   248.2'2'0922   69-17578
                                            MARC
CSt AU NjR FTaSU NBuC MU FU KMK

Inge, William Ralph, 1860-1954.
Talks in a free country. Freeport, N. Y., Books for Li-
braries Press ₁1972₁
196 p. 23 cm. (Essay index reprint series)
Reprint of the 1942 ed.
I. Title.
AC8.I 535 1972   824'.9'12   77-167365
ISBN 0-8360-2774-5   MARC

Inge, William Ralph, 1860-1954.
The Victorian Age. ₁Folcroft, Pa.₁ Folcroft Library
Editions, 1972.
54 p. 24 cm.
Original ed. issued as the 1922 Rede lecture.
1. Great Britain—History—Victoria, 1837-1901. 2. English litera-
ture—19th century—History and criticism.   I. Title. II. Series:
Rede lectures, 1922.
DA551.I 48 1972   914.2'03'81   72-7422
ISBN 0-8414-0380-5 (lib. bdg.)   MARC

Inge, William Ralph, 1860-1954.
Wit and wisdom of Dean Inge, selected and arr. by Sir
James Marchant. With a pref. by William Ralph Inge.
New York, Books for Libraries Press ₁1968₁
xii, 132 p. 23 cm. (Essay index reprint series)
Reprint of 1927 ed.
I. Marchant, Sir James, 1867-1956, ed. II. Title.
AC8.I 54 1968   081   68-16941
CSt MtU

Inge, William Ralph, 1860-1954, ed.
see Radhakrishnan ...   London, Allen &
Unwin; New York, Humanities P., 1968.

Inge, William Ralph, 1860-1954
see Twelve modern apostles and their creeds.
Freeport, N. Y., Books for Libraries Press
₁1968₁

Ingebo, Paul A
Effect of heavy late-fall precipitation on
runoff from a chaparral watershed.
₁Ft. Collins₁ 1969.
2 p. illus. (U.S. Rocky Mountain Forest
and Range Experiment Station. U. S. D. A.
Forest Service research note RM-132)
DNAL DAS   NUC70-7993

Ingeborg Bachmann. Eine Einführung. (2., erw. Aufl.)
München, Piper ₁1963₁.
59 p. front. 19 cm. DM 3.80
                                      (GDB 68-A30-158)
Bibliography of works by and about Ingeborg Bachmann: p. 54-
₁58₁.
1. Bachmann, Ingeborg, 1926-
PT2603.A147Z65 1963   70-354015
NcGU

Ingeborg Bachmann, ₁2. Aufl. München₁ Edition
Text+Kritik, Boorberg ₁1971₁
62 p. (Text+Kritik; Zeitschrift für Literatur, 6)
Cover title.
1. Bachmann, Ingeborg, 1926-   I. Text+
₁i. e. und₁ Kritik.
MH   NUC72-115817

Ingebrand, Hermann, 1938-
Interpretationen zur Kreuzzugslyrik Friedrichs von
Hausen, Albrechts von Johansdorf, Heinrichs von Rugge,
Hartmanns von Aue und Walthers von der Vogelweide.
₁n. p.₁ 1966.
241 p. 21 cm.
Inaug.-Diss.—Frankfurt am Main.
Vita.
Bibliography: p. 235-241.
1. German poetry—Middle High German—History and criticism.
2. Crusades—Poetry—History and criticism.   I. Title.
PT227.I 5   70-342648
CLU

69-17528 (Hayden) MnU-A UU CoU OU NIC WU ViU NbU WaU KU CoDMSC NNMM KyU MB OkU

69-17529 (Hanna) NSyU OkU MsU WU Wa CLU WaU NbU MiU FU OU UU KyU CaBVaU NbuC AAP IU RPB IdU GU KU LN MH GAT ViU MiEM NcRS NRU NBuU CoU FTaSU CoDCC ViBlbV CLSU TNJ-P OrPS NcU MoSW

69-17530 (Carson) MiU WaU UU NcD MnU LU CaOTP MU CU ICU NIC MiEM TxU MsU RPB ViU TU WU InU MsSM IU NbU CLU OU CLSU CaBVaU CtY NNC FU IaU IaAS OkU NSyU FMU KU NcU MoSW CoU Wa GU AU TNJ OrPS MB NBuU AAP OrU IEN CoDCC-W NRU

69-17531 (Cerney) IU Wa MB

69-17532 (Daly) IU LN MB

69-17533 (Damaskin) FTaSU WU FU TU CLSU MnU IaU MoSW MU KU DP MiEM DNAL CaOTP NcRS OkU UU GAT NBuU OU MoU NjP CoU WaU CoFS AAP ViBlbV OKenU KyU NcU PSt IaAS GU

69-17534 (Brinton) CtY NSyU CLSU IEN UU Wa MB KU LU MsSM TU MoSW NBuU FTaSU KEmT

69-17535 (Bois) ICN IaU UU CaBVaU TxFTC CoDuF NcRS NIC OU NcU MB FU TNJ RPB CoU NcD TNJ-R CtY-D TxU NRU IU ScU AAP WU MH-AH TU InU MoU LU NSyU NcGU IaAS ViU MU KEmT CSt KU NjPT GU OkU N Wa NjP NjR MiEM KyLaCB IEG NBuU MoSW RP NBuC LN MiU FTaSU MSohG CMIG MoU WaU NN CtY

69-17536 (Astin) OrCS MiU UU NcRS DAU GAT TNJ FM MU OrU MiEM ICMcC InNd NBuU TNJ-P IEN NcD MtU CaOTP NN KyU InU ViU OkU MoU FTaSU MnU-L WU CLU RPB MB MsU CaBVaU LU NIC NjR NbU IaAS IU AAP CtY CoU MnU IaU FU CoDuF NRU N MH ICU KU NcU CLSU TxDaS FMU IU NSyU NNC MsSM

69-17537 (Baer) OU FTaSU MiU MnU MB NSyU MoSW CU FMU KyU NRU CaOTP OCH InU PSt KEmT MH CSt TxU OrU IEdS NcGU LU MiEM N CSt-H NNC NcRS IaAS NjR OrPS CMIG MoU OrCS WU DS OrU CLU MtU

69-17538 (Beizmann) CoGuW NSyU NcU CLU ICU CLSU MiEM MnU NcRS Wa NjR IaU ViU-M PSt CtY-M ICJ NcD OrPS InU WU

69-17539 (Bessom) PSt OU CSt UU NSyU MiU NIC WaU MoU KEmT MnU MU LN IaAS KyU IU OrPS OU CLU CoGrS OrU TxU CoU NbU MH WU LU MsSM FTaSU MoSW GU FMU MB ICU ViU CoDCC

69-17540 (Berke) CU NN TNJ GAT CtY-L UU IU GU-I, CU-AL NRU MiEM N NIC IaU NNC

69-17541 (Physiology) MiU NjP NNC-M CtY-W DAU WU MoU ViBlbV CU NIC IU OU DNI M CoU TNJ-M WaU MiEM RPB NjR MnU IaAS OrU CU-M MoSW IaU KyU NcRS OrU NbU CaBVaU ViU-M UU AAP FMU IaAS KU MU CSt GAT

69-17542 (Bloomgarden) DSI TU RP NcD TxU NcU MB LU MtU CU-M

69-17545 (Klopfl) MB Wa OU LU INS AU MsSM AAP

69-17546 (D'Angelo) NIC MoSW NBuU OkU WU MnU CSt NjR CU MtU KyU NRU MB TxU ICU PSt NbU MiEM IaAS NcD KU AU IaU CoU OU UU IU NcRS MsU CaBVaU NjP FMU ICU LU IdU RPB OrCS AAP NSyU TU MoU

69-17547 (Shevlin) NjR

69-17548 (Morsey) OrPS N CLSU NSyU CoGrS MtU MU NjR MsU MiEM CU TU MoSW OkU NbU FTaSU IaAS NjP MB InU CoU UU CLU WU IaU FMU Wa NRU KEmT NIC KyU CoGuW NBuC MoU FU NcD NcRS

69-17551 (Zolotow) OrPS NBuC CLSU

69-17551 (Zaidenberg) MB LN

69-17552 (Sargent) CU MB

69-17553 (Lawson) MB InU CU CLSU IEN

69-17554 (Ayling) RP

69-17555 (Chang) NbuU IU CtY-F UU FU ScU TNJ MeB CtY MtU CSt-H MH-BA WaU NbU NN GAT CoU MnU MU NcD DAU NcGU TxU RPB CU KEmT RP NjP GU NcU IaAS MiEM IaU ICU HU-FWC MH NNC CSt MoU CLSU AU OrCS MoSW NjP NRU NcRS IaU AAP FMU FTaSU TxFTC N OrPS KyU DS CaBVaU ViU LU DNAL TU OrU NjR WU DSI MsSM OU MsU

69-17556 (Chen) MiU CtY-F MiEM NbU WaU KU NN IU NjR MnU NIC WU DAU NBuU FMU MH FU OU TxU AU N OrU NcD OrPS NbU InU CU OrCS MnU-A CLSU FTaSU CSt KEmT GAT MH-BA ICU IaU RPB IaAS UU NcGU CU NcU CaBVaU NNC TNJ RP CoDuF MsSM MU NcRS KyU MeB NjP CLU CtY NSyU CoU TU ViU AAP MsU MoU IEN MH FM CaQMM CaOTP CoGuW

69-17557 (Gibbney) OU NIC CFS MU NcD CSt CtY NjP WU

69-17558 (Birney) TU MiU NNC OrU CLU UU IaAS CtY-D MU FMU CBGTU-S NjP MB MtU IEN NN

69-17560 (Bergman) CLU InU OrU DAU MU ViU N NjR KyU CSt MiU NbU NIC OU MU TxU MnU MoU TxFTC NRU CU NcU FU AAP MB MsU MH Wa MiEM NcGU RPB IdU ICU AU CtY MnHi NNC NjP MoSW

69-17561 (Mellon) TU GAT MoU NIC CBGTU AU ICU IEN NcRS OrCS NjP CaOTP CtY OkU NBuC NjR CSt MiU MB AAP NN NNC IaAS N IU

WaU KEmT InU OrPS RPB LN MnU MsSM MiEM CaBVaU MNtcA

69-17562 (Birkenhead) MtU NBuU CoU LN DAU NBuC NNC N IU

69-17563 (Boas) IaAS OkU TNJ OrCS NIC IU FMU RPB GAT LN NcRS InU GU

69-17564 (Bradford) TU CaBVaU InU GAT NBuC

69-17565 (Brooks) FTaSU RPB NBuC WaU UU MB TU GAT IaU LN

69-17566 (Brown) NcGU CoU N OrPS ScU TU UU KEmT LN CLU NBuC Wa

69-17567 (Buchan) TU IU CoU ScU ICU OrCS InU LN CU NIC MtU N NBuC GU TxU OrU TNJ GAT DAU

69-17568 (Burgess) MtU NNC MiEM CoU CaOTP IU LN CLU GAT DAU

69-17569 (Cahill) TNJ NBuC ViU GAT NNC

69-17570 (Clemen) OrU NNC GAT WaU FTaSU IU ScU LN TU GU MsU NjR TxU

69-17571 (Graham) MtU RPB LN OrCS MoU CoU TNJ CLU GAT MnU

69-17572 (Darwin) KyU MiU RPB IU NbU InU NcRS GAT DAU MiU LN NBuC CLU

69-17573 (Delany) LN ScU NbU GAT IU RPB N TxU CoDMSC TNJ-R WaU NcD IaU CaBVaU GU

69-17574 (Edwards) MtU LN CoU NSyU ScU IU NcRS GAT KMK RPB TNJ DAU NIC ICU OrCS

69-17575 (Faris) GAT LN TNJ ScU InU NbU NjR

69-17576 (Hind) MtU CaBVaU LN InU GAT DAU NNC OrCS

69-17577 (Hodgson) MtU DAU CoU ScU TNJ-R TxU RPB GU IU CoDMSC NNC FTaSU CLU GAT LN

69-17578 (Inge) CoU IU MnU CoDMSC AAP InU CLU GAT OrPS

69-17579 (Jesuit) TxU TU IU TxFTC ICLT ScU OrU CSt NcRS RPB MtU NbU NNC GU DAU MH MU ICU GAT TNJ NcD LN

69-17580 (Jones) CtY TU NIC AAP IU CoU ScU CLSU GAT CLU IaAS

69-17581 (Kernahan) CU IU LN CoU NIC InU TNJ TxU GU DAU OrCS CLSU MtU RPB NcD OrU NbU MiEM

69-17582 (London) IU CoU CBGTU OrCS NNC NBuU GAT KMK LU CLSU DAU LN NSyU

69-17583 (Lucas) GAT ScU IU LN GAT TNJ InU MtU RPB

69-17584 (Massey) IU LN NIC OrCS ScU InU NcRS GU RPB DAU LU CLSU KyU GAT

69-17585 (Moore) MtU OrU ScU WU NcRS NIC InU TNJ N DAU TxU GAT OrCS IaU NcD RP RPB

69-17586 (Morison) TU ICU IaU CoU GU-I, GAT CLSU

69-17587 (Routh) InU IU CoDuF MnU

69-17588 (Simonini) N MiEM IU InU NjR IaAS TxU CLU

69-17589 (Smith) KU IU NbU LN MtU N LU WaU DAU GAT

69-17590 (Strong) FU PSt CaBVaU

69-17591 (Thomas) LN ScU OrCS NNC GAT NIC OrPS

69-17592 (Toynbee) INS NBuU TU TxFTC OrCS GU MH RP CtY RPB CaOTP CLU CU MsSM DAU NIC CoDuF CSt NSyU

69-17593 (Van Dyke) MiEM GAT CSt NbU OrCS GU NBuU KMK UU ViU MtU NSyU CLU

69-17594 (Welch) INS MoU CaBVaU NbU NcRS CoDMSC IU MoSW LN MtU WaU N NBuC CoU FTaSU OU

69-17595 (Williams) TU IU GAT NbU NIC TNJ LN InU DAU

69-17596 (Institute) ViU NcGU LN IaU FU IU

69-17597 (Knudsen) IaU NBuU CBGTU NcD OU NIC NjR MoSW MnU GU-I, OkU N FTaSU KU KyU CLU MnU MiEM DHUD

69-17598 (Gram) TxFTC IU FU NIC CLU OU InU MB MH-BA CBGTU MiEM NjR ICU CtY

69-17599 (Pilarski) MnHi MU NBuC RP Wa

69-17600 (Vermandel) CaOTP

69-17601 (Sullivan) IaU MtU FU IEN NN RPB NIC TxFTC NSyU ScU TxU MiEM KEmT OrU IaAS LU MH CoDMSC AAP ViU NcRS MiU CU CLU IdU CLSU TU NRU FMU MoU CaBVaU NjP MnU GAT OkU N UU InU TNJ NbU NBuC NNC WU KU

69-17604 (Poole) N NcRS CSt WaU MiEM LN NcD ICU AU IU MB MoU

69-17605 (Symposium) MnU MtU CSt NjP GAT CaOTP WaU

69-17606 (Symposium) MoSW CSt CtY-KS CU MnU CaOTP WU PSt

69-17607 (International) WU MoSW RPB MiEM NBuU NRU NIC NjR MnU CSt IU NjP IEN CaBVaU WaU CLU

69-17610 (Interpretation) TNJ MH TxU CaBVaU GU N UU LU IEN OrPS NIC MU ICLT NbU NjP ScU FMU NcRS GAT NcU KyU MsSM TxFTC PSt CoGrS CoU MB NcGU CtY NjR WU NbUU IaAS MnU IEG MiU OrU KEmT CSt NRU NjPT FTaSU LN MiEM OkU MoU InU AAP NSyU ViU OU MoSW NcD MCF MBlS WaU ICU OrCS RPB

69-17611 (Malone) NjR NBuC

69-17612 (Lipscy) NNC IaAS CU NcRS InU NcU WU IEN NjR NIC MtU ViU CLSU CaBVaU ViBlbV GAT NbU ViU-L IU OrCS DNAL ICU MnU-A FTaSU MB CSt CLU

69-17613 (Gardner) LU NN

69-17614 (Vinck) MBtS InU IaU DNLM CBGTU OrCS OrSthM CSt LN CtY-D

69-17615 (Davis) CtY-D CU MU MoU MtU NcRS CoGrS IEN AAP PSt LU OrCS NcD CaBVaU NN IU ScU RP NNC NcU IaAS MnU NIC NcGU GAT NRU TNJ FU NBuC KU KyU CLSU

69-17616 (Reed) KyU CoAIC AU FU NcRS CaOTP IU TxDaM-P CLSU IaU MiEM TxU GAT MU

69-17617 (Aubrey) IUJ NjR IEN CSt MB MnU

69-17618 (Thomas) UU CSt TU OU CaBVaU MB AAP OkU IEN NIC CtY PSt NBu FTaSU IaU

69-17619 (Chancellor) IaAS NNC ICU CSt NBuU ViU TU IU TxU MtU NbU DeU IaU CoU GU NcGU NbU CLSU FTaSU OU AAP CLU

69-17620 (Helps) DAU NcRS TxU NbU KyU ICU MU IU OrPS AAP

69-17621 (Black) MsU FMU CoU WaU-L N NcD-L MoU NjR DAU MiEM NNC-L CLU MnU NcD WaU KyU InU MB GU FU MH IEN NBuU NIC NjP CaOTP NBuC NN TxU OrCS MiU IdU-I CU-AL NcU-L OrU-L ViBlbV MeB TxFTC CaBVaU ViU-L OkU ViU UU AU RPB OrPS KU

69-17622 (Beard) MsSM MiEM MnU MiU CU NNC InU UU CSt CaBVaU WaU MoU TxU CLU NIC CtY NjP NIC IU AU FMU KyU LU ViU IaU FU OrPS T IaAS N CoU MsU ViBlbV CLSU NRU FTaSU OkU OU RPB MH-BA NN GAT MB MH

69-17623 (Newby) DC MtU CLU TNJ RP CLSU MiU TxU IaU IU DHUD NjP AAP NIC GU OU MsSM MB UU InU ICU CBGTU-S NBuC CaOTP WU MH NbU IEN CaBVaU IaAS MnU-L KEmT GAT OrPS MoSW NN Wa CoLcC NSyU CoGrS MnU MiEM KyU

69-17624 (Wellborn) MiU ViBlbV DAU CaOTP FMU CoGrS MoU MnU NBuC InU CLU TxFTC ScCicL IaAS NcD GU CU CaBVaU OkU FTaSU NN IU NIC TU LU IEN TNJ N CBGTU KEmT

69-17625 (Atkins) NjP OU AAP IU CtY MiEM

69-17626 (Stump) MsSM CLSU DAU TxU NBuC CU GAT UU NRU ICLT CaBVaU NcD CLL InU MoU IaAS KEmT OkU OrPS NIC NbU IU IEN WU MiU AAP TU InU Wa MH NN NbU MiU CtY

69-17627 (Rubin) MU OrCS GAT ICN MnU OrU N NbU TNJ-P MiU NBuU IU NIC CtY MiEM NjP ScU InU IdU CaOTP NcRS IEN NN CSt DAU CLSU TNJ KyU NcU NcD NjR RPJCR OrPS LU FU PSt IaAS WaU MH AAP CLL AU FTaSU NRU UU GU TxFTC CU TxU OL Wa FMU RPB CoGrS CaBVaU KU WU KEmT ICU IaU MtU MoSW OkU MsU ViU MB NcGU LN NSyU MoU

69-17628 (Johnson) IU ICU NcRS InU MnU NcU MB TNJ MoU NIC

69-17629 (Etcherelli) KU KyU MoU NNC IaAS IaU GAT MoSW WU MiU MiEM FU CtY InU CU UU CaOTP IU MoU

69-17630 (LaPelt) InU NIC RPB MnU GU McH IU IEN ViBlbV NbU GU-I, NBuU LU MsU TxU MoSW DS KEmT N CaBVaU CoDuF NRU NcD CU MH NcU IaAS OrU CU-SC KU KyU MH MiU Wa CSt FMU NjR DHUD ICU InU UU OU NNC RP WaU MiEM NBuC FTaSU LN CaOTP NcGU OCIU OrPS OrCS OWotP MnU-A IdU CLSU PSt AU NSyU WU AU AAP CoGrS CtY NN TNJ CLU DGU DNAL MSM

69-17631 (Compton) MiEM NNC NjP GU

69-17632 (Goldstein) TU McB MiU CoU UU NBuC NSyU LU NjR MnU KyU CU ICU NN NbU OU CaBVaU CSt NjP FU NcU IaAS InU RPB FTaSU IU WU NcRS N IaU MB ViU MiEM CLSU OkU MsSM OrU KU CLU MH MU MsSM

69-17633 (Muenchi) MtU IU FMU LN NjR TxFTC AAP OrU NBuC TxU

69-17634 (Wiseman) MiEM TNJ-P Wa InU NbU FMU NBuC OKenU WU InU OrCS CoGuW LU MoU MnU-A RP AAP NcU MB NbU OU MnU

69-17635 (Magnaini) ICU LN NBuC WU NbU OL CoU WaU FTaSU AAP NSyU MB NBuU KyU CLSU MsSM Wa GU FMU OCIU OrCS CaBVaU OkU MiEM

69-17637 (Plano) GAT

69-17638 (Holm) MB

69-17639 (Stancy) LN NBuU

69-17640 (Beery) IEG GU

69-17641 (Anderson) InU CLU PSt N MB IU NcU Wa MH OrU NIC OU OO

69-17644 (U. S.) CtY OU InU OKentU MB MU

69-17646 (Ausabel) OrPS CU CaOTP TxU NIC MtU TNJ CLU MsSM CaBVaU FMU IaAS TU UU CLSU NBuC CoU AU NbU CoGrS IaU NNC KyU InU ViBlbV OkU NjR RPB KEmT MiU FU OU ICU KU NbU WaU

69-17647 (Atkinson) MtU NbU CaBVaU MnU NjR FL NbU NRU KU InU GAT CoU OrCS MiEM KyU CLU MoSW NcRS GU LU RP ViU AAP LN UU TU FTaSU IaU OU Wa MoU NIC WaU N FMU NcGU IaU OU MsSM MiU MB AU OkU CLSU NjP TxU

69-17648 (Brockett) FMU InU NcRS CSt UU N NNMM NjP NcD NcU ICU LN NNC TxU CaBVaU CLSU IaAS MoU MB TxU DAU CU GAT NN IU MtU OkU IaU NSyU Wa OU RPB FTaSU NbU RP LU OrPS CoDCC KU KyU OEac KEmT NIC MU MoSW OO

69-17649 (Scott) CU NcRS NjP

CoDBR — U. S. Bureau of Reclamation, Denver
CoDCC — Community College of Denver
CoDCC–A — —Auraria Campus
CoDCC–R — —Red Rocks Campus
CoDCC–W — Obsolete: see CoDCC–R
CoDGS — U. S. Geological Survey, Federal Center, Denver
CoDI — Iliff School of Theology, Denver
CoDM — Medical Society of the City and County of Denver
CoDMS — Colorado Military School, Denver
CoDMSC — Metropolitan State College of Denver
CoDPS — Denver Public Schools. Professional Library
CoDt — Temple Buell College, Denver (Formerly Colorado Woman's College)
CoDU — University of Denver
CoDU–L — —School of Law
CoDVA–M — U. S. Veterans Administration Hospital, Denver. Medical Library
CoDuF — Fort Lewis A. & M. College, Durango
CoFS — Colorado State University, Fort Collins
CoG — Colorado School of Mines, Golden
CoGD — Dow Chemical Co., Rocky Flats Plant Library, Golden
CoGJ — Jefferson County Public Library, Golden
CoGj — Mesa County Library, Grand Junction
CoGjM — Mesa College Library, Grand Junction
CoGrS — Colorado State College, Greeley
CoGuW — Western State College, Gunnison
CoHi — Colorado State Historical Society, Denver
CoLH — Loretto Heights College
CoLeC — Colorado Mountain College, Eastern Campus, Leadville
CoSsC — Colorado Alpine College, Steamboat Springs (Formerly Yampa Valley College)
CoU — University of Colorado, Boulder
CoU–M — —Medical Center, Denver

CONNECTICUT

Ct — Connecticut State Library, Hartford
CtHC — Hartford Seminary Foundation
CtHWa — Wadsworth Museum, Hartford
CtM — Russell Public Library, Middletown
CtMW — Obsolete: see CtW
CtNbP — New Britain Public Library
CtNlCG — U. S. Coast Guard Academy, New London
CtS — Stamford's Public Library (The Ferguson Library)
CtU — University of Connecticut, Storrs
CtW — Wesleyan University, Middletown
CtY — Yale University, New Haven
CtY–D — —Divinity School
CtY–E — —Economic Growth Center
CtY–KS — —Kline Science Library
CtY–L — —Law Library
CtY–M — —Medical School
CtY–Mus — —School of Music

DISTRICT OF COLUMBIA
(Washington Metropolitan Area)

DA — Obsolete: see DNAL
DAFM — Obsolete: see DNLM
DAIA — American Institute of Architects Library
DARI — Africa Department of CARA (Center for Applied Research in the Apostolate, Inc.)
DAS — U. S. Dept. of Commerce. Environmental Science Services Administration. Atmospheric Sciences Library, Silver Spring, Md.
DAU — American University Library
DBB — U. S. Bureau of the Budget Library
DBC — U. S. Bureau of the Census Library
DBRE — Bureau of Railway Economics Library of the Association of American Railroads
DBS — National Bureau of Standards
DC — U. S. Dept. of Commerce Library
DCC — Chamber of Commerce of the United States Library
DCU — Catholic University
DDHC — Dunbarton College of Holy Cross
DDO — Dumbarton Oaks Research Library of Harvard University
DES — U. S. Engineer School Library, Ft. Belvoir, Va.
DFAO — Food and Agriculture Organization of the United Nations, North American Regional Office
DFG — Freer Gallery of Art Library
DFR — Board of Governors of the Federal Reserve System
DFo — Folger Shakespeare Library
DGC — Gallaudet College Library
DGU — Georgetown University Library
DGU–M — —Medical, Dental and Nursing Library
DGW — George Washington University Library
DGW–M — —Medical Library
DH — Obsolete: see DNIH
DHEW — U. S. Dept. of Health, Education, and Welfare Library
DHHF — Obsolete: see DHUD
DHUD — U. S. Dept. of Housing and Urban Development Library (Formerly U. S. Housing and Home Finance Agency Library)
DHN — Holy Name College Library
DHU — Howard University Library
DI — U. S. Dept. of Interior Library
DI–GS — —Geological Survey Library
DL — U. S. Dept. of Labor Library
DLC — U. S. Library of Congress
DLC–P4 — —Priority Four Collection
DME — U. S. Dept. of Commerce. National Oceanic and Atmospheric Administration. Marine and Earth Sciences Library, Rockville, Md.
DN — U. S. Dept. of the Navy Library
DN–HO — —Naval Oceanographic Office Library
DN–MHi — —U. S. Marine Corps Historical Library
DN–NW — —Bureau of Naval Weapons Library
DN–Ob — —Naval Observatory Library
DNAL — National Agricultural Library
DNGA — National Gallery of Art Library
DNIH — National Institutes of Health Library, Bethesda, Md.
DNLM — National Library of Medicine, Bethesda, Md.
DP — U. S. Patent Office Library
DPAHO — Pan American Health Organization, Pan American Sanitary Bureau
DPO — U. S. Post Office Dept. Library
DPR — U. S. Public Roads Bureau Library
DPU — Pan American Union Library
DS — U. S. Dept. of State Library
DSI — Smithsonian Institution Library (Includes collections in the National Air Museum, Astrophysical Observatory, Bureau of American Ethnology, National Collection of Fine Arts, National Museum, Division of Radiation and Organisms and National Zoological Park Libraries)
DSI–GA — Obsolete: see DNGA
DStPC — Saint Paul's College Library
DT — U. S. Dept. of the Treasury Library
DWB — Obsolete: see DAS
DWBI — World Bank—International Bank of Reconstruction and Development
DWHO–PSB — Obsolete: see DPAHO
DWT — Wesley Theological Seminary

DELAWARE

DeGE — Eleutherian Mills Historical Library, Greenville
DeU — University of Delaware, Newark
DeWH — Hercules Powder Company, Experiment Station, Wilmington
DeWI — Wilmington Institute Free Library and the New Castle County Free Library
DeWint — Henry Francis DuPont Winterthur Museum, Winterthur

FLORIDA

FBrU — Florida Atlantic University, Boca Raton
FM — Miami Public Library
FMU — University of Miami, Coral Gables
FSN — New College, Sarasota
FTS — University of South Florida, Tampa
FTaSU — Florida State University, Tallahassee
FU — University of Florida, Gainesville
FU–HC — —J. Hillis Miller Health Center
FU–L — —Law Library

GEORGIA
ATLANTA

G — Georgia State Library
GA — Atlanta Public Library
GAA — Atlanta Arts Alliance, Haverty Library, Atlanta

Fig. 32. Page from index of *Register of Additional Locations* (key to abbreviations).

Locations, you could ascertain which libraries have a copy.

The ease with which you can now begin to gather data and do your research—not to mention the time you will save—should begin to pay dividends in qualitatively better reports and greater depth in your research assignments.

ASSIGNMENT

In preparation for what is to follow, become familiar with the following resource tools:

- *Index to Religious Periodical Literature*
- *Religious Index One: Periodicals*
- *Religious and Theological Abstracts*
- *New Testament Abstracts*
- *Old Testament Abstracts.*

1. What is the difference between an index and an abstract?

2. How extensive is the coverage of the literature of each of the resource tools mentioned above? (Check a listing of those journals indexed or abstracted by the editors.) Are all the essays in a particular journal included, or only those selected by the editors? (Check an issue of *Biblical Viewpoint, Bibliotheca Sacra, Journal of Psychology and Theology.* How many of their articles were included in the index? Can you discern why some articles were omitted from an index by the editors?) Which seminary journals may have been omitted altogether (e.g., *Grace Theological Journal, Presbuterion, Seminary Review)?* In which other source might these journals be indexed?

3. How well are we able to achieve "bibliographic control" of periodical literature by using the resource tools we have studied? (I.e., What years do they cover? What are their known strengths? Can we compensate for any weaknesses by consulting other sources?)

11

SPECIFIC RESOURCE TOOLS: INDICES AND ABSTRACTS PART 1

Frederick Jackson Turner in his insightful book *The Frontier in American History* described the evolving values that he believed have been characteristic of past generations of Americans. Those values include a deeply ingrained sense of personal freedom, strong determination, rugged individualism, an inquisitive nature, and the ability to develop creative solutions to perplexing problems.

It was Frederick Turner's belief that those values were in large measure lost when the frontier closed and that that loss signalled an end to the "American way of life."

I believe those values characterizing Americans in years past have not been lost. Change in the way we live has not eliminated the desire for personal freedom, or the sense of determination that impelled men forward, or the rugged individualism, or the desire to pursue new areas of knowledge, or the creativity by which problems are solved. To be sure, the process of socialization has tended to breed conformity, but those same pressures were present in the days of the early frontier, only in different ways. History records only the exploits of the bold and the daring, not the work done by the timid and the retiring. The "maverick" quality still is present in America, but is evident in less dramatic ways.

One of the areas of American life that demands the characteristics so aptly described by Turner in *The Frontier in American History* is research, and all the values mentioned above must be inherent in the researcher if he is to be successful.

During my years in seminary I ran the bookstore. One day a friend of mine came in to idle away some time. As we greeted each other I noticed that he looked exhausted, and I asked how he was feeling. Leaning on the counter he told me that he had just spent three months—fourteen hours a day, six days a week—looking at the index in the back of every theological journal in the library to see if any of the journals contained articles dealing with the topic of his dissertation.

I lamely offered a few words of encouragement and my friend, after browsing through some new books that had just been unpacked, left for the snackroom next door. His dilemma stayed with me and provided much of the motivation for my studies in library science. Later on this incident sparked the development of a practical course that would meet students' needs by taking the tedium out of research without slighting the demands of academic scholarship.

Of course, since this conversation in the bookstore twenty years ago many new, innovative indices and abstracts have been published. They make the task of research much easier than it once was.

But someone will object: "I'm not engaged in dissertation research. Why should I concern myself with information contained in a multitude of journal articles?"

Being able to interact with the thinking of the finest intellects in this and other countries is a privilege that we should not take lightly. We may not agree with all that these writers have to say, but if we are to make any advances for the cause of Christ in this generation, we must be aware of the contribution of others.

Second, by mastering a few basic resource tools, our own research time will be reduced considerably. Indices and abstracts are designed to spare us the time that otherwise would be spent in checking the contents of each annual volume of each journal.

In this connection, your experience may be similar to that of my elder son, Allan. In his last semester as an undergraduate pre-law student at Whittier College, California, he was required to write a major term paper on "Search and Seizure and the Fourth Amendment." It was to be a well-researched paper replete with citations of recent case histories.

Allan spent a fruitless day going from the card catalog to the stacks and, in the course of twelve hours, checked every book in the library having "search and seizure" as a subject heading. The result was about as much information as could be stuffed into an olive without overlapping the sides.

When we discussed his dilemma that same night after dinner, we decided that anything germane to his topic would more likely be found in journal articles. Over the weekend we went to the library of California State University, Fullerton. By checking an index to law journals for the most recent two years, he found enough resource material for his term project. The next three weeks were spent in the library reading the articles and writing his paper.

The point I wish to make is this: The amount of time Allan spent consulting the index and locating the articles was less than two hours. A knowledge of indices and their use, regardless of whether one is an undergraduate or a graduate student, considerably reduces the time spent searching for information.

DEFINITIONS

The *Random House Dictionary* defines an index as a "more or less detailed alphabetical listing of names, places, and topics along with the numbers of the pages on which they are mentioned or discussed."

This is the kind of index with which most of us are familiar. It appears in the back of a book or set of books and alerts us to places where we are likely to find the information we seek.

Specialized indices, however, are different. They deal with a general topic (e.g., "Religion") and then, in an *alphabetically arranged subject index*, list those journal articles or festschrift essays that pertain to the topic. Usually the index covers a set period of time and, in the case of most modern ones, is published either annually or biennially.

An abstract is similar to an index. It, too, lists articles and essays under specific subject headings. The basic difference is that a work like *Religious and Theological Abstracts* provides a brief summary of the article or essay. This synopsis of the content of the article is helpful to you in determining whether the article is worth locating.

IMPORTANT RESOURCE TOOLS

Our discussion of important indices and abstracts begins with the following:
- *Index to Religious Periodical Literature*
- *Religious Index One: Periodicals*
- *Elenchus Bibliographicus Biblicus*
- *Religious and Theological Abstracts*
- *New Testament Abstracts*
- *Old Testament Abstracts*
- *Ephemerides Theological Louvaineses*
- *Christian Periodical Index*
- *Index to Jewish Periodicals*
- *Guide to Social Science and Religion in Periodical Literature.*

Index to Religious Periodical Literature (1949-76) is a semiannual index with biennial cumulations. It has long been regarded as one of the most important resource tools for theological research. The IRPL originally indexed only 31 journals, but the coverage increased to 58 in 1955-56, 113 in 1965-66, and 203 in 1975-76.

Essays dealing with aspects of church history, the history of religions, sociology, psychology of religion, the humanities, and current events are given a prominent place in IRPL. Church music and counseling, however, are also fairly represented.

IRPL places its emphasis primarily on English-language periodicals, although about twenty-five percent of those indexed bear foreign titles. Many of those foreign titles, however, have essays in English in every issue.

Protestant, Catholic, and Jewish journals are included without religious bias. Later volumes were divided into three sections: A *Subject Index* that adheres closely to the approved subject headings of the Library of Congress, an *Author Index* that includes a brief abstract of the article, and a *Book Review Index* listing alphabetically by author those works that received scholarly review during the preceding two years.

Journal articles on different books of the Bible (or parts of books of the Bible) are arranged under "Bible. (OT)" or "Bible. (N.T.)." To find an article dealing with Paul's thought in Romans 5:12-21, the investigator will need to check the entries in IRPL under "Bible. (N.T.) Romans" and then look down the entries for those articles discussing chapter 5.

Nearly all denominations are represented in IRPL. In recent years, however, with the emphasis moving away from organizations and focusing more on people, greater stress seems to have been placed on pastoral and social issues.

In summation, IRPL is indispensable to one's research. However, with its discontinuation in 1976, the American Theological Library Association began publishing two related works, *Religious Index One: Periodicals* (RIO) and *Religious Index Two: Multi-Author Works* (RIT), which includes festschriften and other collections of essays.

Religious Index One: Periodicals (1977-present) is published semiannually with biennial cumulations and continues the same kind of excellent coverage given for researchers in IRPL.

RIO regularly indexes about 210 journals, each biennial issue contains more than 10,000 entries included under approximately 24,000 subject headings. About 4,000 abstracts of articles are included in the author index.

Elenchus Bibliographicus Biblicus (1968-present) is primarily a guide for those engaged in biblical studies and, although prepared and edited by Catholic scholars in the Pontifical Biblical Institute, Rome, its scope transcends denominational boundaries.

From its early ninety-five page format in 1920, when it was a part of *Biblica* (1920-68), *Elenchus* has emerged as the most important and most comprehensive bibliographical resource tool available. References to books, periodicals, book reviews, and even some unpublished dissertations are included. Since Vatican II, *Elenchus* has consistently manifested an unbiased denominational approach, with many Protestant works included.

Even though the system of classification is in Latin, it does not take a

BIBLE. NEW TESTAMENT. (Books and parts)

Acts

Chapters 13-28 (cont)

Die Bedeutung des Apostelkonzils für Paulus. T.Holtz.
NovTest 16:110-48 Ap'74

Le discours à l'Aréopage, Actes 17:22-31, et son arrière-
plan biblique [bibliog] A.M.Dubarle. RSciPhTh 57:
576-610 O'73

Das letzte Wort der Apostelgeschichte [Acts 28:31] G.Del-
ling. NovTest 15 no 3:193-204 '73

Relationship of Galatians 2:1-10 and Acts 15:1-35; two
neglected arguments. R.H.Stein. JEvangThS 17:239-
42 Fall'74

Targumic parallels to Acts 13:18 and Didache 14:3. R.P.
Gordon. NovTest 16:285-9 O'74

Epistles of Paul

Apostelbrief und apostolische Rede/Zum Formular
frühchristlicher Briefe. K.Berger. ZNeutW 65 no 3-4:
190-231 '74

Computer analysis and the Pauline corpus. J.R.Moore.
BibSac 130:41-9 Ja-Mr'73

Glossolalia and other spiritual gifts in a New Testament
perspective. D.M.Smith. Interp 28:307-20 Jl'74

Irénée et la canonicité des Epîtres pauliniennes. P.Nautin.
RHistRel 182:113-30 O'72

Liebe, die sich der Wahrheit freut [reprint] E.Käsemann.
EvangTh 33:447-57 S-O'73

Mantel und Schriften, 2 Tim 4:13; zur Interpretation einer
persönlichen Notiz in den Pastoralbriefen. P.Tummer.
BibZ ns18 no 2:193-207 '74

New wine in old wine skins. IV. Leaven [Gal 5:9, I Cor
5:6] C.L.Mitton. ExposT 84:339-43 Ag'73

Papias; polemicist against whom? [prologue of Exposition
of the oracles of the Lord] C.M.Nielsen. ThSt 35:529-
35 S'74

Ein Paulustext aus Burgund. H.J.Frede. Bib 54 no 4:516-
36 '73

P46, the Pauline canon? J.D.Quinn. CathBibQ 36:379-85
Jl'74

Some considerations about attempts at statistical analysis
of the Pauline corpus. J.J.O'Rourke. CathBibQ 35:
483-90 O'73

Thanksgiving and the gospel in Paul. P.T.O'Brien. NTSt
21:144-55 O'74

Visit talk in New Testament letters. T.Y.Mullins.
CathBibQ 35:350-8 Jl'73

see also
Paul, Saint, Apostle

Commentaries

Marius Victorinus commentateur de saint Paul; les citations bibliques dans le De incarnatione de saint
Athanase. E.Des Places. Bib 55 no 1:83-7 '74

Romans

Die Botschaft des Römerbriefs. W.G.Kümmel. ThLit 99:
481-8 Jl'74

Charismatische Erscheinungen bei der Erbauung der
Gemeinde. K.Gábriš. ComVia 16 no 3:147-62 '73

Colloque exégétique sur l'Épître aux Romains. J.Gribo-
mont. Iren 45 no 4:501-2 '72

Erbarmen mit den Juden! Zu einer historisch-mate-
rialistischen Paulusdeutung. G.Klein. EvangTh 34:
201-18 Mr-Ap'74

False presuppositions in the study of Romans[with reply by
R.J.Karris] K.P.Donfried. CathBibQ 36:332-58 Jl'74

Formgeschichtliche und inhaltliche Probleme in den
Werken des jungen Melanchthon; ein neuer Zugang zu
seinen Bibelarbeiten und Disputationsthesen. L.C.
Green. ZKirchG 84 no 1:30-43 '73

God's righteousness shall prevail. J.L.Price. Interp 28:
259-80 Jl'74

Israel unter dem Ruf Gottes, Röm 9-11. D.Zeller.
IntKathZ no 4:289-301 Jl-Ag'73

Der Jude Paulus und die deutsche neutestamentliche Wis-
senschaft; zu Günter Kleins Rezension der Schrift von
F.W.Marquardt, Die Juden im Römerbrief. H.Gollwit-
zer, M.Palmer and V.Schliski. EvangTh 34:276-304
My-Je'74

Leid, Kreuz und Eschaton; die Peristasenkataloge als Merk-
male paulinischer theologia crucis und Eschatologie.
W.Schrage. EvangTh 34:141-75 Mr-Ap'74

Pistis in Romans. J.J.O'Rourke. CathBibQ 35:188-94 Ap
'73

Revolution, religion, and Romans [preprint] L.M.Starkey.
RelLife 42:334-43 Aut'73

Rom 14:1-15:13 and the occasion of Romans. R.J.Karris.
CathBibQ 35:155-78 Ap'73

Saint Paul and natural law. D.Greenwood. BibThBul 1:
262-79 O'71

Structuralist approach to Paul's Old Testament hermeneutic.
D.O.Via. Interp 28:201-20 Ap'74

Valentinian claim to esoteric exegesis of Romans as basis
for anthropological theory. E.H.Pagels. VigChr 26 no
4:241-58 '72

Why did Paul write Romans? W.S.Campbell. ExposT 85:
264-9 Je'74

·Commentaries

Magna pars iustitiae, velle esse iustum; eine augustinische
Sentens und Luthers Römerbriefvorlesung. M.Lindhardt.
StudTh 27 no 2:127-49 '73

Peter Martyr on Romans. M.W.Anderson. ScotJTh 26:
401-20 N'73

Chapters 1-4

Echtheitskritische Überlegungen zur Interpolations-
hypothese von Römer 2:16. H.Saake. NTSt 19:486-9 Jl
'73

Jesus as hilasterion in Romans 3:25. D.Greenwood.
BibThBul 3:316-22 O'73

Jesus - flesh and spirit; an exposition of Romans 1:3-4.
J.D.G.Dunn. JThSt ns24:40-68 Ap'73

Jødernes fortrin; en undersøgelse af Rom 3:1-9. K.Drejer-
gaard. DTTid 36 no 2:81-101 '73

Natural knowledge of God in Romans; patristic and medieval interpretation. W.Vandermarck. ThSt 34:36-52 Mr
'73

Noch einmal Römer 1:21-32. G.Bouwman. Bib 54 no 3:
411-4 '73

Paul's concept of justification, and some recent interpretations of Romans 3:21-31. W.A.Maier. Spfdr 37:248-
64 Mr'74

Studies in Romans. S.L.Johnson.
Pt 5: The Judgment of God. BibSac 130:24-34 Ja-Mr
'73
Pt 6: Rite versus righteousness. BibSac 130:151-63
Ap-Je'73
Pt 7: The Jews and the oracles of God. BibSac 130:
235-49 Jl-S'73
Pt 8: Divine faithfulness, Divine judgment, and the
problem of antinomianism. BibSac 130:329-37 O-D'73
Pt 9: The universality of sin. BibSac 131:163-72 Ap-
Je'74

Translation of Romans 1:17; a basic motif in Paulinism.
W.B.Wallis. JEvangThS 16:17-23 Wint'73

Chapters 5-8

Original sin reappraised [Rom 5:12-21] L.Sabourin.
BibThBul 3:51-81 F'73

Theological structure of Romans 5:12. A.J.M.Wedder-
burn. NTSt 19:339-54 Ap'73

Chapters 9-11

Hardness of heart according to biblical perspective [Ex 3:
14f, Isa 6, Rom 9-11, etc] L.J.Kuyper. ScotJTh 27:
459-74 N'74

Oracle in Romans 11:4. A.T.Hanson. NTSt 19:300-2 Ap
'73

Chapters 12-16

Analysis of Romans 13:8-10. A.L.Bencze. NTSt 20:90-2
O'73

An antiphonal litany from Romans 13 and Revelation 13;
prepared by S.Shoemaker. ChrCris 33:109 Je 11 '73

Christian and violence; some biblical and historical perspectives on violence and the ministry to those who employ it [Mk 12, Rom 13] D.Little. ChSoc 64:5-15 Mr-
Ap'74

New context for Romans 13. M.Borg. NTSt 19:205-18 Ja
'73

Fig. 33. Page from *Index to Religious Periodical Literature.*

genius to realize that "Archaelogia biblica" is "Biblical archaeology," "Bibliographia" is "Bibliography," and "Textus et Vers." is "Texts and Versions," et cetera. Furthermore, an increasing number of English-language works are being included in *Elenchus*, although emphasis still is placed on contributions written in French and German. In all, about 1,500 separate sources are cited, and any who are in doubt about where to look for information can begin by consulting the general index ("Index Generalis").

Bibliographical essays are included at the beginning of a volume. These immediately place the researcher in touch with the most up-to-date information available. One of the major drawbacks in using *Elenchus*, however, is the time lag between the writing of an article and its appearance in an issue of *Elenchus*. At present, that interval is about two years.

In order to close the gap, researchers should have access to Dallas Theological Seminary's *Mosher Periodical Index*. Published monthly, this index is more comprehensive in its coverage than IRPL or RIO, and keeps the researcher in touch with the relevant, scholarly information found in a variety of periodicals and journals.

Religious and Theological Abstracts (1958-present) is published quarterly. This nonsectarian abstracting service covers about 170 primarily English-language journals and arranges the material under five broad divisions: biblical, theological, historical, practical, and sociological. Each of those divisions is further subdivided (e.g., "theological" contains sections on philosophy, prolegomena, dogmatics, history of doctrines, and ethics).

RTA consistently has provided researchers with a variety of information drawn from fields as varied as archaeology and Christian education, philology and contemporary theology, evangelism and church management, apologetics and cross-cultural anthropology, mysticism and the application of ethics to life. What it lacks in quantity it attempts to make up for in quality.

Annual cumulated subject, author, and Scripture indices, with a listing of journals and their addresses, are appended.

New Testament Abstracts (1956-present) is published three times a year with an annual index of principal Scripture passages covered in the various articles, and separate indices of authors, book reviews, and book notices. This abstracting service currently covers approximately 400 scholarly journals dealing with the various areas of New Testament study.

The product of Roman Catholic scholarship, *New Testament Abstracts* is generally unbiased, is international in scope, and provides critiques in English of articles written in other languages.

A cumulative index to volumes one to fifteen (1956-71) was published in 1974.

All things considered, this is a valuable supplement to the bibliographies published by B. M. Metzger, and A. J. and M. B. Mattill (see Chapter 12)—*Index to Periodical Literature on Christ and the Gospels, Index to Periodical Literature on the Apostle Paul,* and *A Classified Bibliography of*

Literature on the Acts of the Apostles—all of which treated periodical literature up to the 1960s.

Old Testament Abstracts (1978-present) is also published three times a year, is likewise unbiased, and regularly directs those interested in Old Testament research to journal articles covering everything from "Archaeology, Epigraphy [and] Philology," through critical studies on select passages of Scripture, to an evaluation of the "Intertestamental and Apocrypha[l]" literature. In all, about 230 journals are indexed, and the concise abstract accompanying each entry will be of inestimable value to the researcher.

Book notices are also included in a section following the periodical abstracts. The critique given each book varies from about 600-2,000 words.

Indices to authors, Scripture texts, Semitic words, and the periodicals abstracted completes this resource tool.

Ephemerides Theological Louvanienses (1924-present) is published quarterly. A section of this journal entitled "Elenchus Bibliographicus" ("Bibliographical Record") provides one of the most complete references to contemporary theological literature available. Material is classified under the following headings: general, historical, religious, Old Testament, New Testament, and theology (with subdivisions in five categories). Numerous English titles are included. An author index, which appears in the final issue each year, completes this handy compilation.

Although recent issues of "Elenchus Bibliographicus" manifest more of an ecumenical approach, researchers will detect a Roman Catholic bias in some of the pre-Vatican II volumes. Works treating the Reformation and contemporary trends in Protestant theology are to be found throughout, although in earlier volumes they appear under the subject heading "Christianis separatis."

In contrast to *Elenchus Bibliographicus Biblicus*, in which the emphasis was primarily biblical, *Ephemerides* is of particular value as a theological resource. Its use is hampered by two factors: (1) the lack of a proper subject index, and (2) a lamentable time-lag between an article's appearing in print and its inclusion in "Elenchus Bibliographicus." At present, that time-lag is about eighteen months to two years, which makes recourse to the *Mosher Periodical Index* essential.

Christian Periodical Index (1961-present) is issued quarterly with annual and quinquennial cumulations. This index provides researchers with information to evangelical articles in magazines and journals that may have been overlooked by the other indexing and abstracting agencies.

The more than fifty periodicals indexed are in general more popular in nature than those found in IRPL or RIO and, were it not for CPI, we would not have access to them.

Index to Jewish Periodical Literature (1963-present) is an author and subject index to select American and Anglo-Jewish journals of interest to those engaged in the study of (or those desiring a better understanding of) the way in which contemporary Jews view the situation in the Middle East. Included in this index, along with studies of biblical texts, are articles on Jewish feasts, involvement in politics, and relief work.

A scholarly work of related interest is *Kiryat Sepher,* published by Jewish National and University Library, Jerusalem. This annotated index contains entries relating to published bibliographies, textual studies, Rabbinic literature, philological studies, and miscellany.

Guide to Social Science and Religion in Periodical Literature (1964-present) is published quarterly with annual and biennial cumulations. It provides access to magazines and journals of an interdenominational or non-denominational nature that may not have come to the attention of other agencies.

With volumes two to four (1965-68), the name was changed to a *Guide to Religious and Semi-Religious Periodical Literature.*

ASSIGNMENT

1. *Locate the Business Periodical Index* in either your institution's library or a public library. Peruse the topics under A-F of the alphabet, and make a list of those subjects having a bearing on the administration of the church.

2. Imagine that you have been placed in charge of the preschool department of your church. What information can you find in *Education Index* that will help you (a) understand this age group, (b) minister to their needs, and (c) be able to provide meaningful handcraft materials to occupy their attention?

3. Check the *Inventory of Marriage and Family Literature* and focus on those areas that deal with the influence of parents (both fathers and mothers) on their children (sons as well as daughters). What does this teach about the importance of diadic communication?

12

SPECIFIC RESOURCE TOOLS: INDICES AND ABSTRACTS PART 2

When the apostle Paul first wrote the Christians at Thessalonica, he concluded his letter with a series of admonitions. Among those words of parting counsel was, "But examine everything carefully; hold fast to that which is good" (1 Thess. 5:21).

His instruction is simple; its practice is difficult. Even though many believe that God is the author of all truth, culling the "good" from secular sources can be a threatening experience.

There is much to be gained from the research of others, and the better we know our Bibles, the easier will be the task of discerning and holding fast to that which is good.

Realizing the need for discernment, therefore, and in true submission to the guidance of the Holy Spirit, let us look at the areas of theological investigation that can be enriched through the practical application of truth from related disciplines. In doing so, we will again consider indices and abstracts and focus on the following specific areas of investigation:

- Administration
- Counseling
- Education
- History
- Marriage and the Family
- Philosophy
- Sociology and the humanities.

For the sake of students doing advanced research, we will conclude this chapter with a brief introduction to computer terminals, from which printed bibliographies may be obtained.

ADMINISTRATION

Secular principles for getting things done do not always mesh with the teaching contained in the Word of God. A synthesis can be achieved, however, as is illustrated in *Nehemiah and the Dynamics of Effective Leadership* (1976). Primacy was given to the Scriptures, and secular theories were integrated into the study only where they were found to be in harmony with the biblical text.

In the administration of the church and in the training of young people for positions of authority, in planning ahead and organizing one's time, in leading meetings and working with other people—a great deal of valid information can be found in *Business Periodical Index*.

Business Periodical Index (1958-present) is an annual and is arranged alphabetically with author and subject entries appearing together. Bibliographical articles are listed under the name of the biographee. "See" references guide the researcher from a term not used as an approved subject heading to one that is approved. "See also" references guide the user from one approved subject heading to another. Approximately 260 professional journals, magazines, and trade papers are indexed regularly.

The value of BPI to those preparing for, or already in, Christian work is that it contains a gold mine of information on topics as interrelated to the ministry of the church, the running of educational institutions, or the work of missions as assessing a person's ability, keeping proper records, efficient administrative practice, understanding the dynamics of decision-making, the principles of executive leadership, the place of women in administration and management, wise advertising, corporate leadership, communication, community development, et cetera.

Students researching the administration of a local church will find a wealth of insightful material in each cumulated volume. The secular material presented may not always parallel the teaching of the Word of God, and where it differs from the biblical model, reference to BPI will nearly always provide illustrations of those companies or individuals who adhered to man-made theories and failed.

COUNSELING

Few challenges can compare with the ministry of helps, and few areas of the pastor's work demand greater understanding and flexibility than counseling. A knowledge of personality is essential, and some awareness of human stages of development, pathology, and different therapeutic skills are essential.

When it comes to specifics, the issues a pastor may encounter may range all the way from adolescent rebellion to Zen Buddhism, alcoholism to withdrawal, states of anxiety to various forms of repression, defense mechanisms to transference, depression to sublimation, escapism to reaction formation, frustration to projection, hostility to negativism, and intellectualization to masochism. The counselor, therefore, soon becomes aware of his need for a high level of technical expertise. The question of the moment then is, Where can he find a competent discussion of the issue?

It may seem strange, but one of the best sources of scholarly information is *Cumulated Index Medicus* (1950-present). CIM contains information about journal articles written by psychiatrists (and a few psychologists). In these articles researchers will find various modes of counseling discussed, together with various approaches to specific problems.

CIM is published annually and is an extensive, multi-volume index arranged in accordance with a comprehensive system of subject headings. It includes book reviews and an extensive author index.

Although most of the entries in CIM have nothing whatever to do with counseling, psychiatry has long been associated with the medical profession. Extensive coverage, therefore, is devoted to counseling, and researchers will find scholarly articles on the therapeutic treatment of alcoholism, biofeedback, work with terminally ill patients, family therapy, problems experienced by people in midlife crisis or old age (with special consideration being given physiological and psychological issues), a variety of sexual dysfunctions, the care and rehabilitation of the disabled, homosexuality, and many other topics that can be traced easily through the subject index.

In addition, articles written by outstanding physicians such as C. Everett Koop (on abortion) or Ralph Byron (on counseling cancer patients and their families) may be traced through the author index.

Another source of information that counselors may find helpful is *Psychological Abstracts* (1927-present). Issued monthly with annual cumulations, PA is arranged according to broad subject categories: general, methodology and research technology, experimental psychology, animal psychology, and social psychology. Subject and author indices appear at the end of each volume.

Bibliographic control in psychology is fairly good because, prior to PA, *Psychological Index* (1894-1935) was being published by the Psychological Review Company in Princeton, New Jersey. There is obviously some overlap, but for all practical purposes coverage of the literature extends from 1894 to the present.

The easiest way to use PA is through the *Cumulated Subject Index to Psychological Abstracts* (1960), which covers all the annual volumes from 1927-60. Since 1966 regular quinquennial subject cumulations have been published.

The writings of authors from Sigmund Freud to James Dobson can be traced through the *Author Index to Psychological Index, 1894-1935, Psychological Abstracts, 1927-1958*, and the quinquennial author indices to PA.

There is one glaring weakness to PA, however, and that is the "selective indexing" of journal articles, which means nearly two-thirds of the articles from journals listed in PA are not even indexed. In spite of this weakness, PA is still worth consulting.

EDUCATION

Not to be ignored by those interested in Christian education is *Education Index* (1929-present). Although concentrating most attention on preschool, elementary, secondary, and higher education, a vast array of material is also included on school administration and supervision, vocational counseling, teaching methods, curriculum development, the use of audiovisual aids, the importance of the library, psychology and mental health, the teachings of linguistics and mathematics, special education, and the ever-present issue of accreditation.

Those involved with Christian day schools as well as those preparing to teach on a graduate level will find added stimulus from their consultation of *Education Index*. Furthermore, viable research done in the areas of belief and values, the interplay between moral development and true maturity, and the enhancement of one's identity through teaching/learning experiences, can all be traced with relative ease.

An index to book reviews concludes this important work.

HISTORY

An awareness of the historical setting in which people lived and moved can enrich our appreciation of what they did. King David, for example, built for himself a palace in Jerusalem. What was it like? How was it furnished? Was it a luxurious and awe-inspiring edifice? Would it have rivaled the palatial extravagance of the Borghese Villa in Rome or the splendor of Hampton Court near London? (See articles in general encyclopedias or the art section of your public library.) Were the ceramic utensils David used comparable to the workmanship of artisans in Crete or Rhodes? If there were differences in ornamentation and design, what were they?

Matters of historical importance impinge on all disciplines. For example, What educational principles did Alcuin use that brought about the Carolingian renaissance? How did the struggle for spiritual and political freedom affect the Huguenots? Why did the Anabaptists prefer martyrdom to renouncing their beliefs? And in more recent times, How has a new awareness of human dignity brought changes to American foreign policy as well as the delegation of responsibility to nationals by many missionary organizations?

Two important works are deserving of repeated consultation. Those are

220

EDUCATION INDEX

COMMUNICATION—*Continued*

Anecdotes, facetiae, satire, etc.
Trial of Sir Realism: a question of freedom. D. S. Bagley, 3d. il J Creative Behav 12 no3: 193-201 '78

Bibliography
Book reviews; ed. by H. E. Hill. See issues of Educational communications and technology journal
Book reviews; ed. by J. Stewart. See issues of Quarterly journal of speech
Book reviews; ed. by D. E. Williams. See issues of Southern speech communication journal
Research abstracts; ed. by D. P. Ely. See issues of Educational communication and technology journal

Content analysis
See Content analysis (communication)

International aspects
International commission for the study of communication problems. S. MacBride. Convergence 11 nos3-4:108-10 '78
World communication; symposium. bibl il J Comm 28:140-93 Aut '78

Political aspects
Campaign '76; communication studies of the presidential campaign; symposium; ed. by S. L. Becker and S. Kraus. bibl Comm Monogr 45:265-388 N '78
Challenge to the rule of minimum effect: a case study of the in man-out man strategy. J. T. Kitchens and B. Stiteler. bibl South Speech Comm J 44:176-90 Wint '79
Covering the political campaign; symposium. bibl il J Comm 28:80-138 Aut '78
Freedom and responsibility in First amendment theory; defamation law and media credibility. D. M. Hunsaker. bibl Q J Speech 65:25-35 F '79

Psychological aspects
Community size as a predictor of development of communication apprehension: replication and extension. J. C. McCroskey and V. P. Richmond. bibl Comm Educ 27:212-19 S '78
Decoding effects of cognitive complexity, tolerance of ambiguity, and verbal-nonverbal inconsistency. B. B. Domangue. bibl J Personal 46:519-35 S '78
Development of listener abilities in communication: how children deal with ambiguous information. M. Ironsmith and G. J. Whitehurst. bibl Child Devel 49:348-52 Je '78
Differential sensitivity to contradictory communication as a function of age and culture. K. W. McCluskey and D. C. Albas. bibl J Cross-Cult Psychol 9:167-78 Je '78
Double-bind theory; some current implications for child psychiatry. J. H. Weakland. bibl J Am Acad Child Psych 18:54-66 Wint '79
From the interactional view; interview; ed. by C. Wilder. P. Watzlawick. J Comm 28:35-45 Aut '78
Roles of egocentrism and of weakness in comparing in children's explanations of communication failure. E. J. Robinson and W. P. Robinson. bibl J Exper Child Psychol 26:147-60 Ag '78

Research
Some thoughts on correspondence between saying and doing. A. C. Israel. bibl J App Behav Anal 11:271-6 Summ '78

Research
See Communications research

Social aspects
Awareness of tornadoes; the importance of an historic event. P. O. Hanson and others. maps J Geog 78:22-5 Ja '79
Communicating education information to Anglo and Hispanic populations. S. L. Lauricella and E. D. Edington. Educ Comm & Tech J 27:54-7 Spr '79
Communication: message senders and receivers. E. L. Boyer. Comm Educ 27:271-6 N '78
Communication, social change and development. P. Hurst. il Educ Broad Int 11:104-7 S '78
Communications and society. G. V. Flannery and others. bibl Assn Sup & Curric Devel Yrbk 1978:29-67
Jacques Ellul's contributions to critical media theory. C. G. Christians and M. R. Real. bibl J Comm 29:83-93 Wint '79
Language and counseling. E. R. Gerler, jr. bibl Personnel & Guid J 56:496-9 Ap '78
Language, communication and the curriculum. J Gammage. bibl New Univ Q 32:353-68 Summ '78
Meeting the needs of today's youth. M. A. Ruebel. USA Today 107:11 Ap '79
New approaches to development; symposium. bibl il J Comm 28:63-90 Wint '78; Reply. R. F. Jacobson. 28:223-5 Aut '78
Off the cuff; on communication. A. Fuglesang. il Educ Broad Int 11:4-6 Mr '78
Our communication heritage: the genetic tie that binds. M. Osborn. bibl South Speech Comm J 44:147-58 Wint '79

Problems in assessing functional communication. C. E. Larson. bibl Comm Educ 27:304-9 N '78
Role-taking; a measure of communication development. J. L. McCaleb and D. L. Korman. bibl Eng J 67:41-5 O '78
Sequential analysis of social interaction. D. E. Hewes. bibl Q J Speech 65:56-73 F '79
Social need or sacred cow? a sociological perspective. H. Mendelsohn. J Comm 28:30-5 Spr '78
Social perspective-taking ability, cognitive complexity and listener-adapted communication in early and late adolescence. E. M. Ritter. bibl Comm Monogr 46:40-51 Mr '79
Theatre as communication. P. P. Gillespie. South Speech Comm J 44:167-75 Wint '79

Teaching
See Communication education

Tests and scales
Attentiveness as a style of communication: a structural analysis. R. W. Norton and L. S. Pettegrew. bibl Comm Monogr 46:13-26 Mr '79

COMMUNICATION, Nonverbal
Age changes in nonverbal decoding as a function of increasing amounts of information. B. M. DePaulo and R. Rosenthal. bibl J Exper Child Psychol 26:280-7 O '78
Beyond words; influence of nonverbal behavior of female job applicants in the employment interview. D. M. Young and others. bibl Personnel & Guid J 57:346-50 Mr '79
Children's use of head orientation and eye contact in making attributions of affiliation. R. Abramovitch and E. M. Daly. Child Devel 49:519-22 Je '78
Comparison of professional versus student ratings of job interviewee behavior. T. V. McGovern and others. J Counsel Psychol 26:176-9 Mr '79
Decoding effects of cognitive complexity, tolerance of ambiguity, and verbal-nonverbal inconsistency. B. B. Domangue. bibl J Personal 46:519-35 S '78
Effect of witnessing consequences on the behavioral recordings of experimental observers. F. C. Harris and A. R. Ciminero. bibl J App Behav Anal 11:513-21 Wint '78
Effects of eye contact and social status on the perception of a job applicant in an employment interviewing situation. R. Tessler and L. Sushelsky. bibl J Voc Behav 13:338-47 D '78
Encoding of nonverbal behavior by high-achieving and low-achieving children. V. L. Allen and M. L. Atkinson. bibl J Educ Psychol 70:298-305 Je '78
Formal, informal and technical aspects of nonverbal communication within the sport complex. E. Orr and B. C. Pelton. Phys Educ 35:36-8 F '78
Integration of mothers' referential speech with joint play. D. J. Messer. bibl Child Devel 49:781-7 S '78
Interviewer evaluations of interviewee nonverbal behavior. T. V. McGovern and H. E. A. Tinsley. bibl J Voc Behav 13:163-71 O '78
Job interview; body language and perceptions of potential effectiveness. J. H. Sterrett. bibl J App Psychol 63:388-90 Je '78
Laboratory study of the effects of varying levels of counselor eye contact on client-focused and problem-focused counseling styles. B. M. Tipton and R. A. Rymer. J Counsel Psychol 25:200-4 My '78
Language and hand; the dimension of referential competence. W. Bucci and N. Freedman. bibl il J Personal 46:594-622 D '78
Manual communication for the severely handicapped; an assessment and instructional strategy. C. Salisbury and others. Educ & Train Men Retard 13:393-7 D '78
Mother's eye; for better or for worse. A. Riess. bibl Psychoanal Stud Child 33:381-403 '78
Nonverbal behavior in the classroom. H. W. Richey and M. H. Richey. bibl Psychol Sch 15:571-6 O '78
Nonverbal coaching behavior. L. E. Armstrong. il Coach & Athlete 41:20 Ag/S '78
Nonverbal communication; I see what you say. J. W. Stewig. bibl Lang Arts 56:150-5 F '79
Nonverbal communication: information and application for counselors. S. Schlesinger. bibl Personnel & Guid J 57:183-7 D '78
Nonverbal communication of affect in interracial dyads. R. S. Feldman and L. F. Donohoe. bibl J Educ Psychol 70:979-87 D '78
Nonverbal communication: the unworded message. J. A. Manos. Bus Educ Forum 33:27-30 Mr '79
Nonverbal cues as indicators of verbal dissembling. R. S. Feldman and others. bibl Am Educ Res J 15:217-31 Spr '78
Nonverbal patterns in youth culture. R. L. French. il Phys Educ Lead 35:541-6 Ap '78
Patterns of touching between preschool children and male and female teachers. V. P. Perdue and J. M. Connor. bibl Child Devel 49:1258-62 D '78

Fig. 34. Page from *Education Index.*

Historical Abstracts: Bibliography of the World's Periodical Literature (1955-present) and *America: History and Life* (1964-present).

Historical Abstracts regularly provides brief summations of the contents of journal articles from about 1,300 journals. The material is arranged by subject, topic, and "area or country" of the world. Missiologists should not ignore the up-to-date data on the peoples and places that might be a special interest to them or their missions.

Issued quarterly in two parts with annual cumulations, *Historical Abstracts* deals with modern history, 1450-1914 (Part A), and twentieth-century history (Part B). The arrangement of each volume is by topic with further subdivisions and subject refinement. Bibliographic articles on a particular country or area are placed within the appropriate geographic division. Within each division the sequence is alphabetical by author.

A subject index and a list of the periodicals concludes each volume.

America: History and Life provides coverage to about 3,000 American and foreign journal articles each year. Arranged in broad subject divisions, and with a detailed table of contents, *America* is a quick way to review what has been written on different topics of interest to the researcher.

By means of these works, access can be obtained to the events of man's past as well as the present, and information of importance to research in the social and natural sciences, current events, literature, religion, political science, and different ethnic groups.

MARRIAGE AND THE FAMILY

Of great importance in the life of the church and the nation is the family. Changes, however, are taking place rapidly. The "nuclear family" of the 1960s has now given way to "dual career families," and who can predict what lies in store for the family in the future.

Literature on marriage and the family has assumed "Himalayan" proportions. As formidable as it appears, it can easily be reduced to manageable size by using the following resource tools.

The International Bibliography of Research in Marriage and the Family, 1900-1964, edited by J. Aldous and R. Hill (1967), is designed to facilitate high quality research. (Because this work is part of a continuing index to marriage and family literature it is included here.) This retrospective index identifies the topics that have been empirically investigated by competent specialists, classifies and summarizes the findings, identifies the theoretical approaches used by marriage and family counselors, establishes the major concepts meriting investigation, and organizes the findings into an inter-related set of hypotheses and propositions.

A Keyword-in-Context (KWIC) index makes reference to the literature of more than six decades easy and efficient. The symbols at the end of each line (e.g., **KIRKC-39-MAF**, see line one of the accompanying illustration) of the

```
FEMINISM IN RELATION TO MARITAL ADJUSTMENT.# A METHODOLOGICA  KIRKC -39-MAF
 INDIRECT ASSESSMENT OF MARITAL ADJUSTMENT.# A USE OF IMAGIN  FRUMRM-53-UIR
S IN MATE SELECTION AND MARITAL ADJUSTMENT.# APPLICABILITY O  KALLFJ-52-ATS
AL INTERESTS CRUCIAL TO MARITAL ADJUSTMENT.# COMMUN           FRUMRM-54-CIC
 SCHEDULE IN PREDICTING MARITAL ADJUSTMENT.# COMPARATIVE USE  SKIDRA-51-CUC
L AND SEXUAL ASPECTS OF MARITAL ADJUSTMENT.# EXTENT OF SPOUS  THOMB -55-ESA
LY INTERESTS CRUCIAL TO MARITAL ADJUSTMENT.# FAMI             FRUMRM-53-FIC
RS IN THE PREDICTION OF MARITAL ADJUSTMENT.# GROUP STRUCTURE  LITWE -60-GSI
OF EARLY EXPERIENCES ON MARITAL ADJUSTMENT.# INFLUENCE        PIERMW-47-IEE
TS OF RECENT STUDIES IN MARITAL ADJUSTMENT.# METHODOLOGY AND  TERMLM-39-MRR
TTRACTIVENESS, AGE, AND MARITAL ADJUSTMENT.# PHYSICAL A       KIRKC -51-PAA
SELF CONCEPT IN STUDENT MARITAL ADJUSTMENT.# ROLE OF THE      ALLEFD-62-RSC
LECTED URBAN FACTORS IN MARITAL ADJUSTMENT.# SE               WILLRC-53-SUF
LITY FACTORS RELATED TO MARITAL ADJUSTMENT.# SOCIAL CLASS AN  ROTHJ -51-SCS
 THE PSYCHOPATHOLOGY OF MARITAL ADJUSTMENT.# SOME OF          PRATGK-30-PMA
 INDIRECT ASSESSMENT OF MARITAL ADJUSTMENT.# THE              FRUMRM-52-IAM
EXUAL BEHAVIOR ON TOTAL MARITAL ADJUSTMENT.# THE INFLUENCE O  THOMB -63-MSB
 INDIRECT ASSESSMENT OF MARITAL ADJUSTMENT.# THE KIRKPATRICK  FRUMRM-53-KSF
 AND THE MEASUREMENT OF MARITAL ADJUSTMENT.# THE MARITAL ROL  HURVN -60-MRI
SYCHOLOGICAL FACTORS IN MARITAL ADJUSTMENT.# THE MEASUREMENT  HARRMR-54-PMA
NMENT.# MATE SELECTION, MARITAL ADJUSTMENT, AND SYMBOLIC ENV  TROSJ -64-MSA
HE INTERRELATIONSHIP OF MARITAL ADJUSTMENT, FERTILITY CONTRO  REEDRB-47-IMA
SIZE AS A FACTOR IN THE MARITAL ADJUSTMENTS OF COLLEGE COUPL  CHRIHT-52-FSF
ES OF TWO GENERATIONS.# MARITAL AND FAMILY ADJUSTMENT IN RUR  SHEEA -49-MFA
  WORKERS, MARCH, 1960.# MARITAL AND FAMILY CHARACTERISTICS O  SCHIJ -61-MFC
  WORKERS.• MARCH 1963.# MARITAL AND FAMILY CHARACTERISTICS O  PERRVC-64-MFC
ISH WOMAN.# THE SEXUAL, MARITAL AND FAMILY RELATIONSHIPS OF   CHESE -57-SMF
RAPHY.# THE RELATION OF MARITAL AND FAMILY STATUS TO MENTAL   FRUMRM-61-RMF
                    OR.# MARITAL AND NONMARITAL SEXUAL BEHAVI  EHRMW -64-MNS
FACTORS RELATED TO COED MARITAL ASPIRATIONS.# SOME            BELLRR-62-CMA
TUDY OF SOME ASPECTS OF MARITAL BEHAVIOR AS RELATED TO RELIG  SAMEJA-58-SSA
ASKAN ESKIMO SEXUAL AND MARITAL BEHAVIOR.# NORTH AL           SPENRF-59-AES
  PERSONALITY NEEDS AND MARITAL CHOICE.#                      STRAA -47-PNM
   ADOLESCENT VALUES IN MARITAL CHOICE.#                      ZUBRF -59-AVM
OF PARENTAL IMAGES UPON MARITAL CHOICE.# THE INFLUENCE        STRAA -46-IPI
.# THE TREATMENT OF PRE MARITAL COITUS IN ,,MARRIAGE AND THE  REISIL-57-TPC
REPANCIES REGARDING PRE MARITAL COITUS IN THREE WESTERN CULT  CHRIHT-62-VBD
ED BY SELF AND SPOUSE.# MARITAL COMPATIBILITY AS RELATED TO   KELLEL-41-MCR
TION OF SOME ASPECTS OF MARITAL COMPATIBILITY BY MEANS OF TH  BRICB -61-PAM
 PERSONALITY FACTORS IN MARITAL COMPATIBILITY.  I.#          TERMLM-35-PFM
# FACTORS AFFECTING THE MARITAL CONDITION OF THE POPULATION.  OGBUWF-23-FAM
                        MARITAL CONDITION.#                   SMITTL-52-MC
      TES.# FAMILIES AND MARITAL CONDITIONS IN THE UNITED STA  ANON  -32-FMC
HANGES.# SEX RATIOS AND MARITAL CONDITIONS OF THE ADULT POPU  DUNCOD-33-SRM
ON BETWEEN INSANITY AND MARITAL CONDITIONS.# RELATI           GAUDFJ-35-RIM
THE INTERACTION BETWEEN MARITAL CONFLICT AND ALCOHOLISM AS S  BALLRG-59-IAM
ING FAMILIES.# AREAS OF MARITAL CONFLICT IN SUCCESSFULLY AND  MITCHE-62-AMC
DNESS OF ALCOHOLISM AND MARITAL CONFLICT. INTERPERSONAL PERC  MITCHE-59-IAM
             # WOMEN IN MARITAL CONFLICT.• A CASEWORK STUDY.  HOLLF -49-WMC
DNESS OF ALCOHOLISM AND MARITAL CONFLICT.• THE INTERACTION B  BALLRG-59-IAM
DNESS OF ALCOHOLISM AND MARITAL CONFLICT.• 2. THE INTERACTIO  BULLSC-59-IAM
         THE ECHO OF MARITAL CONFLICT.#                       GREEKA-63-EMC
NALITY AS A FUNCTION OF MARITAL CONFLICT.# IMPRESSIONS OF PE  PRESMG-52-IPF
NT STATUS OF MOTHER AND MARITAL CONFLICT, PERMANENCE, AND HA  NYE FI-59-ESM
UNCTIONAL PSYCHOLOGY OF MARITAL CONFLICTS.# ON THE F          CANZW -62-FPM
S AND THE RESOLUTION OF MARITAL CONFLICTS.# VALUE ANALYSI     FOLSJK-60-VAR
     SOME ASPECTS OF MARITAL CONSENSUS.#                      NIMKMF-58-AMC
            ME.# THE MARITAL CONTEXT OF AN ANXIETY SYNDRO     FRY WF-62-MCA
     /JAMAICA/.# THE MARITAL CONTEXT OF FERTILITY CONTROL     STYCJM-64-MCF
   THE MANAGEMENT OF MARITAL COUNSELING CASES.#               SHOLHS-64-MCC
  VALUE CONGERIES AND MARITAL COUNSELING.#                    MARSDC-53-VMC
ISTENING AS A METHOD IN MARITAL COUNSELING.# CREATIVE L       DICKRL-50-CLM
Y JOINT INTERVIEWING IN MARITAL COUNSELING.# FOUR WA          GULLEN-62-FJI
OF GENERAL SEMANTICS IN MARITAL COUNSELING.# USE              MCLED -43-GSM
     PSYCHOTHERAPY OF MARITAL COUPLES.#                       CARREJ-63-PMC
      WAY OF LIFE AND MARITAL CRISIS.#                        GERFE -51-WLM
ENIC WOMEN.• STUDIES IN MARITAL CRISIS.# SCHIZOPHR            SAMPH -64-SW
EMOTIONAL BACKGROUND OF MARITAL DIFFICULTIES.# THE            MCLEHV-41-EBM
Y.# A STUDY OF CASES OF MARITAL DIFFICULTY REFERRED BY A FAM  WIGGRM-39-SMD
ARD WIFE-S EMPLOYMENT.# MARITAL DISAGREEMENT IN WORKING WIFE  GIANA -57-MDW
 SOME OF THE SOURCES OF MARITAL DISCONTENT.#                  GLUEB3-55-MD
TIVENESS OF CASEWORK IN MARITAL DISCORD WITH ALCOHOL.# EFFEC  BALDDS-47-ECM
          FACTORS IN MARITAL DISCORD.#                        SENOAE-57-FMD
  THE CAUSES OF MODERN MARITAL DISCORD.#                      UNGERV-37-CMM
ERSON TEST IN A CASE OF MARITAL DISCORD.# THE USE OF THE HOU  BUCKJN-50-HTP
ERNAL OVER PROTECTION.# MARITAL DISHARMONY AS A FACTOR IN TH  LOWEM -32-MDF
S OF HUSBAND AND WIFE.# MARITAL DISHARMONY.• CONCURRENT ANAL  GREEBL-60-MDC
THE SAME PSYCHIATRIST.# MARITAL DISHARMONY.• CONCURRENT THER  SOLOAP-63-MDC
        DRINKING AND MARITAL DISRUPTION.#                     KEPHWM-54-DMD
 OCCUPATIONAL LEVEL AND MARITAL DISRUPTION.#                  KEPHWM-55-OLM
ITY AND DIVORCE.# TOTAL MARITAL DISSOLUTIONS IN THE UNITED S  JACOPH-49-TMD
EN FAMILIES INCREASED.• MARITAL DISSOULTIONS BY DEATH AND DI  ANON  -49-BFI
           EN WOMEN.# MARITAL DISTURBANCES IN A GROUP OF T    MENGH -48-MDG
MARITAL ADJUSTMENT WITH MARITAL EDUCATION, RELIGIOUS ACTIVIT  CURRC -47-AMA
 LEADING TO BREAKDOWN.# MARITAL FAILURE AND DURATION.• FURTH  THOMJL-53-MFD
THE MENTAL HOSPITAL AND MARITAL FAMILY TIES.#                 SAMPH -61-MHM
# SCHIZOPHRENIA AND THE MARITAL FAMILY.• ACCOMMODATIONS TO S  TOWNRD-62-SMF
# SCHIZOPHRENIA AND THE MARITAL FAMILY.• IDENTIFICATION CRIS  TOWNRD-61-SMF
   ON THE VARIATION OF MARITAL FERTILITY IN FINLAND.#         HARTT -60-VMF

          DEGREES OF MARITAL HAPPINESS.#                      USHIY -54-C
   FACTORS ACTING ON MARITAL HAPPINESS.#                      HUJIA -55-F
       PREDICTION OF MARITAL HAPPINESS.#                      SHIKH -56-P
 WEIGHTS FOR PREDICTING MARITAL HAPPINESS.# CONCERNING THE V  KELLEL-39-Y
BETWEEN RESEMBLANCE AND MARITAL HAPPINESS.# CORRELATION       WILLS -30-C
PERSONAL PERCEPTION AND MARITAL HAPPINESS.# INTER             DYMOR -54-I
S ON THE MEASUREMENT OF MARITAL HAPPINESS.# NOTE              ROLLJM-61-I
SYCHOLOGICAL FACTORS IN MARITAL HAPPINESS.# P                 TERMLM-38-F
SYCHOLOGICAL FACTORS IN MARITAL HAPPINESS.# P                 HOLLHL-39-P
PTION OF THE SPOUSE AND MARITAL HAPPINESS.# THE RELATION OF   DYMOR -53-R
ND URBAN WOMEN APPRAISE MARITAL HAPPINESS.# TWO GENERATIONS   LANDPH-51-T
          ILDREN.# MARITAL HISTORY OF FORMER PROBLEM CH        ROBILM-59-F
     MEDICAL ASPECTS OF MARITAL INCOMPATIBILITY.#              STANWR-38-
ON OF ATTITUDES TOWARDS MARITAL INFIDELITY.# A CROSS CULTURA  CHRIHT-62-C
 THEORY OF EPAINOGAMY.# MARITAL INSTABILITY AMONG THE KPELLE  GIBBJL-63-M
 BASED ON CENSUS DATA.# MARITAL INSTABILITY AND ITS RELATION  HILLKG-62
HEIR CHILD-S BEHAVIOR.# MARITAL INTEGRATION AND PARENTS- AGR  FARBB -59
ARENT CHILD RELATIONS.# MARITAL INTEGRATION AS A FACTOR IN P  FARBB -62-M
          AN INDEX OF MARITAL INTEGRATION.#                   FARBB -57-I
IMATES AND THE INDEX OF MARITAL INTEGRATION.# I.Q. EST        CAPORJ-64-I
 ROLE-TAKING.• THE YALE MARITAL INTERACTION BATTERY.# COUPLE  BUERJV-59-C
PARTNER.# EVALUATION OF MARITAL INTERACTION IN THE TREATMENT  FIBUEW-57-E
HIPS.# SADO MASOCHISTIC MARITAL INTERACTION.• MODEL FOR A CH  ATKIME-64-S
MATERNAL EMPLOYMENT AND MARITAL INTERACTION.• SOME CONTINGEN  NYE FI-61-
DELY HELD BELIEFS ABOUT MARITAL INTERACTION.# AN EMPIRICAL I  UDRYJR-61-E
 CONCEPTS AS RELATED TO MARITAL INTERACTION.# PERCEPTUAL CON  LUCKEB-61
 AND VOICE TOLERANCE IN MARITAL INTERACTION.# SPEECH THRESHO  SHIPG -60-S
E DIAGNOSIS OF NEUROTIC MARITAL INTERACTION.# TH              ACKENW-54-
NCONSCIOUS COLLUSION IN MARITAL INTERACTION.# U               ELLTBG-64-
ONSHIPS.# PSYCHOLOGY OF MARITAL LIFE.• A STUDY OF FAMILY REL  USHIY -44-
          HISTORY OF MARITAL LIFE.#                           IEMAS -52-
 ELEMENTS OF HARMONIOUS MARITAL LIFE.#                        MACKWQ-55-E
SES.# RECONCILIATION OF MARITAL MALADJUSTMENT.• AN ANALYSIS   HIXEER-31-
   NEW ORIENTATIONS ON MARITAL MALADJUSTMENT.#                MATHVD-63-
SYCHOLOGICAL FACTORS IN MARITAL MALADJUSTMENT.# THE MEASUREM  HARRM -56-M
                        MARITAL MALADJUSTMENTS.#              TERHWB-31-
OCATION.# VARIATIONS IN MARITAL NEEDS WITH AGE, SEX, MARITAL  LAWGMC-55-
INTERFAITH MARRIAGE AND MARITAL OUTCOME.#                     HEISJS-61-I
OF THE KAISER METHOD TO MARITAL PAIRS.# APPLICATION           MITCHE-63-A
PATHOLOGIC REACTIONS OF MARITAL PARTNERS TO IMPROVEMENT OF P  KOHLRN-62
JOINT INTERVIEWING WITH MARITAL PARTNERS.#                    WEISM -64-J
LLEGE STUDENTS IN THEIR MARITAL PARTNERS.# A STUDY OF CERTAI  SINGBN-64-S
REATMENT TECHNIQUE WITH MARITAL PARTNERS.# JOINT INTERVIEWIN  GEISJ -60-
WIVES- REPORTS OF THEIR MARITAL PARTNERS- PREFERRED FREQUENC  WALLP -58
 RELIGIOUS PRACTICE AND MARITAL PATTERNS IN PUERTO RICO.#     DOMED -59
IN SEARCH OF A MOTHER,, MARITAL PATTERNS.# ONE TYPE OF THE ,  MARTPA-62-O
    THE GOLD CASE.• A MARITAL PROBLEM.#                       GOMBMR-46-
                  THE MARITAL PROBLEM.#                       KHALA -59
HIGH SCHOOL MARRIAGES.# MARITAL PROBLEMS AND SATISFACTION IN  INSERA-62-
  SOME ASPECTS OF THE MARITAL PROBLEMS OF THE ELDERLY.#       BERIMN-62-A
     PSYCHIATRY AND MARITAL PROBLEMS.#                        MUDDEH-55-P
        A SURVEY OF MARITAL PROBLEMS.#                        KONDT -57
IMENTAL TECHNIQUES WITH MARITAL PROBLEMS.# EXPER              RUTLAL-58-
Y ORIENTED TREATMENT OF MARITAL PROBLEMS.# FAMIL              GOMBMR-56-
ENTION AND TREATMENT OF MARITAL PROBLEMS.# SOME REFLECTIONS   WILSAT-49-
.• AN ITALIAN EXAMPLE.# MARITAL PROPERTY CONSIDERATIONS AMON  PITKDS-60-
           SOCIETY.# MARITAL PROPERTY RIGHTS IN BILATERAL     BENER -36-M
    THE DURATION OF MARITAL RELATIONS AND FERTILITY.#         OKAZA -56-D
CONDITIONS IN /AFRICAN/ MARITAL RELATIONS AND PARENTAL DUTIE  KRIGEJ-36-C
 OF FAMILY LIFE.# EXTRA MARITAL RELATIONS IN THE FELLOW EMPL  REINJD-45
OF FAMILY STRUCTURE AND MARITAL RELATIONS IN THE U.S.S.R.# S  SIMIND-58-P
WN IN THEIR FOLK LORE.# MARITAL RELATIONS OF THE HAUSAS /WLS  TREMAJ-14-
ALE SEXUAL RESPONSE AND MARITAL RELATIONS.# FEM               ELLIA -54-
HE EMOTIONAL ECONOMY OF MARITAL RELATIONS.# T                 FOOTNN-54-E
JUSTMENT.# CONTRASTS IN MARITAL RELATIONSHIP IMPINGING ON CH  BARUDW-38-C
ION AND ISOLATION.# THE MARITAL RELATIONSHIP OF PARENTS OF E  VOGEEF-60-M
ORING THE EFFECT OF THE MARITAL RELATIONSHIP ON CHILD FUNCTI  WEISI -63-
  THE DYNAMICS OF THE MARITAL RELATIONSHIP.#                  STONA -53-D
         PATTERNS OF MARITAL RELATIONSHIP.#                   SARWGJ-63-P
TIGATION INTO /INDIA-S/ MARITAL RELATIONSHIP.# A PSYCHOLOGIC  PAREU -54-PI
          VILLAGE.# MARITAL RELATIONSHIPS IN A TRINIDAD       RODMH -61-
RETE APARTMENT HOUSES.# MARITAL RELATIONSHIPS OF COUPLES LIV  MASUK -58-M
                        MARITAL RELATIONSHIPS OF PRISONERS.#  ZEMAE -58-M
ARCHY IN THE FAMILY AND MARITAL RELATIONSHIPS OF THE MINANG   MAREJV-60-D
                        MARITAL RELATIONSHIPS.#               YAMAT -56-F
FUNCTIONS OF FAMILY AND MARITAL RELATIONSHIPS.# A STUDY CONC  YAMAT -54-SC
 THE WIFE-S MIND IN THE MARITAL RELATIONSHIPS.# ON ,,IF SO,,  DOI M -57-
E DEPENDENT VARIABLE IN MARITAL RESEARCH.# TH                 NYE FI-59-D
  ETHNIC ENDOGAMY.# PRE MARITAL RESIDENTIAL PROPINQUITY AND   KENNRJ-43-P
 MARITAL ADJUSTMENT AND MARITAL ROLE DEFINITIONS OF HUSBANDS  AXELLJ-63-M
ORK AIMED AT SUPPORTING MARITAL ROLE REVERSAL.# CASEW         VESPS -62
    SEX OF CHILDREN.# MARITAL ROLE TENSIONS AND NUMBER AND    FARBB -
                  T.# MARITAL ROLES AND MARRIAGE ADJUSTMEN    LU  YC-52-
                  T.# MARITAL ROLES AND MARRIAGE ADJUSTMEN    YICHL -52-M
      CONCEPTIONS OF MARITAL ROLES BY STATUS GROUPS.#         MOTZAB-50-CM
ARITAL ADJUSTMENT.# THE MARITAL ROLES INVENTORY AND THE MEAS  HURVN -60-MRI
IN ATTITUDES TOWARD THE MARITAL ROLES OF HUSBAND AND WIFE.#   JACOAH-51-CA
                        MARITAL ROLES OF THE RETIRED AGED.#   LIPMA -60-MR
    THE COMPONENTS OF MARITAL ROLES.#                         HURVN -61-C
```

Fig. 35. Page from *The International Bibliography of Research in Marriage and the Family, 1900-1964*. (See KIRKC -39 -MAF, top entry, left column.)

KWIC index are explained in the "Complete Reference List." In the case cited above, KIRKC is identified as "Kirkpatrick, 6." The number 39 refers to the 1939 volume of the *American Sociological Review* (no. 4, pp. 325-34), and MAF is for the title of the article, "A Methodological Analysis of Feminism in Relation to Marital Adjustment."

Following upon the success of the first volume, Joan Aldous and Nancy Dahl teamed up to provide a second bibliographic index to literature produced between 1965 and 1972. This index exceeds 1,500 pages and continues the same excellent coverage found in volume one.

A change of title occurred with the publication of volume three, *The Inventory of Marriage and Family Literature*, edited by D. H. L. Olson and N. S. Dahl (1973-present), which has now become a biennial cumulation of articles by subject, author, and Keyword-in-Title.

Not all journals are fully indexed, with the result that certain excellent biblical and/or theological approaches to marriage and the family must be traced through other sources. All things considered, however, there is not a finer index to the periodical literature on the family than this one supplied by the Family Social Science Department of the University of Minnesota. Those engaged in pastoral counseling will find it most helpful.

The quarterly *Child Development Abstracts and Bibliography* (1927-present) was initially issued in the form of mimeographed sheets that grouped the literature on child development under five broad categories. This important abstract is now published by the Society for Research in Child Development, University of Chicago.

Information in CDAB is gleaned from the finest professional journals, and critical reviews of important books are included. A cumulated author and subject index concludes each annual issue.

The arrangement of CDAB is by topic, with each entry assigned a number. Browsing through an issue should spark off ideas for a score of research papers, in which secular research can be compared with the teaching of Scriptures.

PHILOSOPHY

For comprehensive coverage of "all major American and British philosophical periodicals, selected journals in other languages, and related interdisciplinary publications," there is nothing in English equal to *The Philosopher's Index* (1967-present). Published quarterly with annual cumulations, this index provides researchers with access to information contained in nearly 300 different journals.

The arrangement of the index is by subject (with extensive sections on God, human nature, religious experience, values, etc.), and then by author. Since 1969 abstracts have been included for many of the more important articles by different authors.

SOCIOLOGY AND THE HUMANITIES

Of considerable value to those engaged in applying theological truths to life is the *Social Sciences and Humanities Index* (1907-1974), which in its author and subject arrangement follows a single alphabetical sequence and enables researchers to find strategic articles in the fields of anthropology, archaeology, classical literature, economics, geography, history, philosophy, political science, religion, and related subjects.

In 1974 *Social Sciences and Humanities Index* divided into two: *Social Sciences Index* (1974-present) and *Humanities Index* (1974-present).

Published quarterly with annual cumulations, *Social Sciences Index* increased from 186 to 263 the number of journals in its coverage. "See also" references abound, and researchers will find in each volume information relating to the religious life of high school students, the effects of "birth order" on siblings, the application of Kohlberg's theories to the development of moral values, as well as the broad, general headings of child, family, father, mother, et cetera.

An index to book reviews is located at the end of each volume.

Humanities Index added 143 new titles to its coverage of journals, making a total of 260 periodicals indexed. "Religion and Theology" is included among its broad subdivisions. Published quarterly with annual cumulations, stress is laid primarily upon American history, literature, and culture, and the student of social mores will have many sources from which to draw.

An index of book reviews concludes each annual volume.

Another work that may prove useful is *Public Affairs Information Service* (1915-present). Issued twice a month with three quarterly cumulations and an annual cumulation, PAIS readily provides access to information obtained from about 1,400 periodicals, books, pamphlets, and other information of a contemporary nature.

With its emphasis on economic trends and public affairs, PAIS is of value to theologians and pastors for its international studies, statistics, information on developing countries, the incidence of divorce, education, family life, different kinds of impingements upon human freedom, the growth of various religions and cults, information about a variety of professions, the study of various age groups, data about women's rights, and details about ethnic groups.

Although often ignored by those in Christian circles, PAIS is filled with usable material.

A work of related significance is *Sociological Abstracts* (1952-present), which is published five times a year with annual cumulation. SA records journal articles under 30 topics (e.g., methodology and research technology, sociology, history and theory, social psychology, group interactions, etc.). Subject, author, and source indices enhance its usefulness. Access to information in SA is more easily obtained through a computer search.

Markov, Georgi
    Assassination
  It happens here. Economist 268:30 S 23 '78
Markov processes
  Effects of variables using panel data: a review of techniques.
    B. C. McCullough. bibl Pub Opinion Q 42:199-220 Summ
    '78
  Finite automaton model of behavior and learning. G. E.
    Flueckiger. bibl Econ Inquiry 16:508-30 O '78
  Indicators of educational progress—a Markov chain approach
    applied to Swaziland. K. Geary. J Mod Afric Stud 16:141-51
    Mr '78
  Information theory and sequences of land use: an application.
    V. B. Robinson. bibl Prof Geog 30:174-9 My '78
  Market areas in product differentiated industries: some con-
    ceptual and empirical approaches. N. M. M. Dorward and
    M. J. Wise. bibl maps Econ Geog 54:26-39 Ja '78
  Markov model for the short-term retention of spatial location
    information. A. F. Healy. bibl J Verb Learn 17:295-308 Je
    '78
  Stochastic model of the adoption of microtechnology in rural
    Buganda. M. C. Robbins and L. C. Robbins. bibl Hum Org
    37:16-23 Spr '78
Markovits, Andrei S. and Kazarinov, Samantha
  Class conflict, capitalism, and social democracy: the case of
    migrant workers in the Federal Republic of Germany. Comp
    Pol 10:373-91 Ap '78
Markowitz, Hal. See Yanofsky, R. jt. auth.
Marks, Leonard H.
  Free press—an endangered species. Atlan Com Q 16:331-8
    Fall '78
Marks, Stephen
  Who says council housing costs more? New Statesm 96:459 O
    13 '78
Marks and Spencer, ltd
  M & S's message. Economist 267:104 My 27 '78
Marksmanship. See Shooting
Markus, Hazel
  Effect of mere presence on social facilitation: an unobtrusive
    test. bibl J Exp Soc Psychol 14:389-97 Jl '78
Markusen, Ann R. and Fastrup, Jerry
  Regional war for federal aid. Pub Interest no53:87-99 Fall '78
Marland, Gregg and Rotty, Ralph M.
  Question mark over coal: pollution, politics, and CO₂. Futures
    10:21-30 F '78
Marlowe, Roy H. and others
  Severe classroom behavior problems: teachers or counsellors.
    bibl J App Behav Anal 11:53-66 Spr '78
Marmalade
  Oringe rindes. H. Spurling. New Statesm 95:130 Ja 27 '78
Marmor, Michael
  Heat wave mortality in nursing homes. bibl Environ Res 17:-
    102-15 Ag '78
Marmurek, Harvey H. C. See Johnson, N. F. jt. auth.
Marmurek, Harvey H. C. and others
  Presentation mode and repetition effects in free recall. bibl Am
    J Psychol 91:483-90 S '78
Maroldo, Georgette K.
  Zoos worldwide as settings for psychological research: a sur-
    vey. Am Psychol 33:1000-4 N '78
Maroldo, Georgette K. and Flachmeier, L. C.
  Machiavellianism, external control, and cognitive style of
    American and West German co-eds. bibl Psychol Rept 42:-
    1315-17 Je pt2 '78
Maroldo, Georgette K. and Parker, Joan
  Zoos as settings for psychological research: a preliminary sur-
    vey. Am Psychol 33:88 Ja '78
Maronites
  Take an old man; Lebanon. Economist 268:62-3 Jl 1 '78
Maroons
  See also
  Saramacca (Surinamese people)
Marotz-Baden, Ramona and Tallman, Irving
  Parental aspirations and expectations for daughters and sons:
    a comparative analysis. bibl Adolescence 13:251-68 Summ
    '78
Marquand, David
  Towards a Europe of the parties. Pol Q 49:425-45 O '78
Márquez Uría, María C. See González Morales, M. R. jt. auth.
Marquis, M. Susan. See Newhouse, J. P. jt. auth.
Marquit, Erwin
  Dialectics of motion in continuous and discrete spaces. Sci &
    Soc 42:410-25 Wint '78-79
  Nicolaus and Marx's method of scientific theory in the Grun-
    drisse. Sci & Soc 41:465-76 Wint '77-78
Marr, Warren, 2d
  NAACP in Senegal. il Crisis 85:61-3 F '78
Marr, William and Percy, Michael
  Government and the rate of Canadian prairie settlement. bibl
    Can J Econ 11:757-67 N '78

Marr, William L.
  On bonuses to end job discrimination; comment. Am J Econ
    & Sociol 37:102-5 Ja '78
Marriage
  Kinship and mode of production. J. Siskind. bibl Am Anthrop
    80:860-72 D '78
  See also
  Bride price
  Civil marriage
  Common law marriage
  Divorce
  Domestic relations
  Endogamy and exogamy
  Family
  Family life education
  Housewives
  Husband and wife
  Intermarriage of races
  Marital satisfaction
  Marital status
  Married women
  Mate selection
  Parenthood
  Polyandry
  Remarriage
  Remarriage (Church of England)
  Residence (kinship)
    Economic aspects
  Towards a marriage between economics and anthropology and
    a general theory of marriage. A. Grossbard. bibl Am Econ
    R Pa & Proc 68:33-7 My '78
    Prohibited degrees
  See Marriage law
    Statistics
  Age, biological factors, and socioeconomic determinants of
    fertility: a new measure of cumulative fertility for use in the
    empirical analysis of family size. B. Boulier and M. R. Ro-
    senzweig. bibl Demography 15:487-97 N '78
    Africa, Western
  Parenthood, marriage and fertility in west Africa. M. Fortes.
    bibl J Develop Stud 14:121-49 Jl '78
    Bougainville, Papua-New Guinea
  See also
  Nagovisi (Papua-New Guinea people)—Marriage
    China
  On a bicycle for two. Ma Chu. Far E Econ R 100:20 My 5 '78
    Dominican Republic
  La dispensa borra consanguinidad: preferred consanguineal
    marriage in a Dominican peasant community. M. Vázquez-
    Geffroy. Caribbean Stud 16:232-9 Jl '76
    England
    History
  Modes of reproduction. A. Macfarlane. bibl J Develop Stud
    14:100-20 Jl '78
    Himalayan region
  See also
  Pahari (Himalayan people)—Marriage
    Iceland
  Domestic cycle in modern Iceland. G. W. Rich. bibl J Marr &
    Fam 40:173-83 F '78
    India
  Inbreeding in Tamil Nadu, south India. P. S. S. Rao and S. G.
    Inbaraj. bibl Soc Biol 24:281-8 Wint '77
    Iran
    Public opinion
  Sex and parental education as determinants of marital aspira-
    tions and attitudes of a group of Iranian youth. A. H. Mehr-
    yar and G. A. Tashakkori. J Marr & Fam 40:629-37 Ag '78
    Ireland
    History
  Age, region, and marriage in post-famine Ireland: an empirical
    examination. E. E. McKenna. Econ Hist R s2 31:238-56 My
    '78
    Jamaica
  Residence, kinship, and mating as survival strategies: a West
    Indian example. T. L. Whitehead. bibl J Marr & Fam 40:817-
    28 N '78
  Value assertion and stratification: religion and marriage in
    rural Jamaica. M. M. J. Fischer. bibl Caribbean Stud 14:7-37
    Ap; 7-35 O '74
    Japan
  Interpersonal values of marital partners. R. Schwab and E.
    Schwab, jr. J Soc Psychol 104:157-63 Ap '78
    Nepal
  Marriage by exchange in east Nepal. P. H. Prindle. bibl An-
    thropos 73 no 1-2:133-40 '78
    New Hebrides
  Courts and courtship in a new Hebridean society. W. Rodman
    and M. Rodman. bibl Oceania 49:35-45 S '78
    Nigeria
  See also
  Fulahs (African people)—Marriage

Fig. 36. Page from *Social Sciences Index.*

CHRISTIANITY in literature—*Continued*
Metamorphoses of Moria: structure and meaning in The praise of Folly. W. A. Rebhorn. PMLA 89:463-76 My '74
Myth and style in Djuna Barnes's Nightwood. E. Gunn. Mod Fict Stud 19:545-55 Wint '73-74
Mythic components in Dryden's Hind and panther. M. Duggan. Comp Lit 26:110-23 Spr '74
New interpretation of the A and B text of Piers Plowman [review article] D. C. Fowler. Mod Philol 71:393-404 My '74
New light on The excursion. A. G. Hill. Ariel 5:37-47 Ap '74
Oskar Panizza's first and last books: a study in late nineteenth-century poetry. P. D. G. Brown. Germ R 48:269-87 N '73
Parody of medieval music in the Miller's tale. J. M. Gellrich. J Eng & Germ Philol 73:176-83 Ap '74
Pauline old man in Flannery O'Connor's The comforts of home. J. R. Millichap. Stud Short Fict 11:96-9 Wint '74
Rabbit redux: time/order/God. W. Falke. Mod Fict Stud 20:59-75 Spr '74
Reckoning with Boccaccio's questioni d'amore. V. Kirkham. MLN 89:47-59 Ja '74
Redemption of King Lear. P. T. Roberts, jr. Renascence 26:189-206 Summ '74
Religious musicals of Jean Racine. F. H. Londré. bibl Thought 49:156-86 Je '74
Ronsard's cosmic warfare: an interpretation of his Hymnes and Discours. W. Calin. Symposium 28:101-18 Summ '74
Ruth, Milton, and Keats's Ode to a nightingale. V. J. Lams, jr. Mod Lang Q 34:417-35 D '73
Spanish tragedy and the theatre of God's judgments. J. S. Colley. Pa Lang & Lit 10:241-53 Summ '74
Spenser and the Renaissance ideal of Christian heroism. M. West. PMLA 88:1013-32 O '73
Spenser's Amoretti and the art of the liturgy. W. C. Johnson. Stud Eng Lit 14:47-61 Wint '74
Theme of spiritual progression in Voss. J. Beston and R. M. Beston. Ariel 5:99-114 Jl '74
Two worlds of La ninfa del cielo. D. H. Darst. Hispan R 42:209-20 Spr '74
Uncle Tom and Archy Moore: the antislavery novel as ideological symbol. E. Brandstadter. Am Q 26:160-75 My '74
Updike's Couples: squeak in the night. P. Backscheider and N. Backscheider. Mod Fict Stud 20:45-52 Spr '74
Violence and belief in Mauriac and O'Connor. J. M. Mellard. Renascence 26:158-68 Spr '74
W. H. Auden: poet of parables. C. Baker. Theol Today 30:414-17 Ja '74
Waste land manuscript. L. Gordon. Am Lit 45:557-70 Ja '74
Wife of Bath's uncharitable offerings. R. L. Hoffman. Eng Lang Notes 11:165-7 Mr '74
Womanliness in the Man of Law's tale. S. Delany. Chaucer R 9:63-72 Summ '74
World is half the devil's: cold-warmth imagery in Paradise lost. L. Kuby. ELH 41:182-91 Summ '74
Wreck of the Deutschland and the dynamic sublime. J. Bump. ELH 41:106-29 Spr '74
See also
Calvinism in literature
Catholic church in literature
Jesus Christ in literature
Puritans in literature
Theology and literature
CHRISTIANS in Africa
Christianity in independent Africa. A. Hastings. Afric Affairs 73:229-33 Ap '74
CHRISTIANS in Rome
Christians and the Roman army AD 173-337. J. Helgeland. Church Hist 43:149-63+ Je '74
Gibbon and the Christian soldier: tonal manipulation as moral judgment. G. L. Veth. Stud Eng Lit 14:449-57 Summ '74
CHRISTIE, Agatha
Quite a nice run [Mousetrap] E. Shorter. Drama no 112:51-3 Spr '74
CHRISTMAS
Songs and music
See Christmas music
England
So there it was. . .merry Christmas. M. Coveney. il Plays & Players 21:46-7 F '74
Finland
Song of Tapani in Finnish Christmas celebration. I. Rank. il Western Folklore 33:133-57 Ap '74

CHRISTMAS carols
In hoc anni circulo. A. Hughes. Mus Q 60:37-45 Ja '71
CHRISTMAS music
Song of Tapani in Finnish Christmas celebration. I. Rank. il Western Folklore 33:133-57 Ap '74
CHRISTMAS plays, Medieval
See also
Mumming plays
CHRISTOFFERSON, Thomas R.
Urbanization and political change: the political transformation of Marseille under the Second republic. Historian 36:189-206 F '74
CHRISTOLOGY. *See* Jesus Christ
CHRISTOPHER, Georgia B.
In Arcadia, Calvin: a study of nature in Henry Vaughan. Stud Philol 70:408-26 O '73
CHRISTOS paschon. *See* Christus patiens (mystery)
CHRISTUS patiens (mystery)
Christos paschon and the Byzantine theater. S. Sticca. Comp Drama 8:13-44 Spr '74
CHRONICLE of current events (periodical)
See Khronika tekushchikh sobytii
CHRONICLES, Book of. *See* Bible. Old Testament—Chronicles
CHRONICLES and chroniclers, Medieval
See also
Bede, The Venerable, Saint
Gregory's chronicle
Pseudo-Turpin
CHRONOGRAMS
See also
Anagrams
CHRONOLOGY
See also
Dendrochronology
Time
CHRONOLOGY, Biblical. *See* Bible. Old Testament—Chronology
CHRONOLOGY, Ecclesiastical
See also
Church calendar
CHRONOLOGY, Hebrew
See also
Calendar, Jewish
Jews—History—Chronology
CHRONOLOGY, Historical
See also
Archaeology—Methodology—Dating methods
Radiocarbon dating
also subhead History—Chronology under the following subjects
Africa
Africa, East
Africa, North
Asia Minor
Athens
English language
German language
Greece
Jews
Literature
Mayas
Rome
Rome—Colonies and provinces
Zambia
CHRONOLOGY, Hittite
Some unusual Hittite expressions for the time of day. C. Carter. Am Orient Soc J 94:138-9 Ja '74
CHRONOLOGY, Literary. *See* Bibliography—Date of editions; Literature—History—Chronology
CHRONOLOGY, Maya
See also
Mayas—History—Chronology
CHRONOLOGY in literature. *See* Time in literature
CHRYSOSTOMUS, Dio. *See* Dio Cocceianus, Chrysostomus, of Prusa
CHU, Hsi
Reconstituting the Confucian tradition [review article] W. M. Tu. J Asian Stud 33:441-54 My '74
CHU, Raymond W. H. and Uyenaka, Shuzo
East Asian library collection in the University of Toronto. Pac Affairs 46:548-56 Wint '73-74
CHUBB, Jehangir N.
Commitment and justification: a new look at the ontological argument. Int Philos Q 13:335-46 S '73
CHUDAKOV, Alexander. *See* Chudakov, M. jt. auth.
CHUDAKOV, Marietta, and Chudakov, Alexander
And then there was the novelette. Sov Lit no2:132-8 '74
CHUKOVSKII, Kornei Ivanovich, 1882-1969
Young Kornei Chukovsky (1905-1914) a liberal critic in search of cultural unity. J. Brooks. Russian R 33:50-62 Ja '74
CHUMASHAN languages
Sibilants in Ventureño. J. P. Harrington. Int J Am Ling 40:1-9 Ja '74

Fig. 37. Page from *Humanities Index*.

COMPUTER SEARCHES

With the advent of computers, researchers in many academic institutions now have "online" retrieval services to data bases in various parts of the United States. One of the most popular is the Lockheed Corporation's DIALOG—an information retrieval system situated in Palo Alto, California. By using an online service, a researcher can obtain a computer-produced bibliography that might otherwise take him many hours to accumulate.

Begun in 1969, DIALOG is now the largest system of its kind anywhere in the world. Its resources exceed forty million individual records and more are being added every year. Data available through this service includes technical reports, conference papers, newspapers, journal and magazine articles, statistics, et cetera. Although the initial emphasis was placed on education and science, data bases have now been added in business, financial management, current affairs, the whole area of the social sciences, law, medicine, the arts, and humanities.

Data bases of interest to students of theology, and particularly those pursuing studies toward a doctorate are ADD (American Doctoral Dissertations); AMERICA: HISTORY AND LIFE; DAI (Dissertation Abstracts International); ERIC (Educational Resources Information Center); HISTORICAL ABSTRACTS; MEDLARS and MEDLINE (two sources that provide prompt access to the kind of counseling material found in *Cumulative Index Medicus*); PAIS (Public Affairs Information Service, including the PAIS Bulletin, Foreign Language Index, and PAIS International); PASAR (Psychological Abstracts Search and Retrieval); PHILOSOPHER'S INDEX, POPULATION BIBLIOGRAPHY; SOCIAL SCISEARCH (Social Sciences Citation Index); SOCIOLOGICAL ABSTRACTS; and several hundred other nondatabase facilities from which bibliographies may be obtained with a COM (Computer Output Microfilm) form.

Costs for each printout are nominal when compared with the time saved.

Coupled with the DIALOG information retrieval system is a DIALOG online ordering service called DIALORDER. This service applies to documents located through searching any of DIALOG's bibliographic files as well as to documents that preceded the establishment of the data base.

The ease with which orders can be placed and the value of the service (particularly where hard-to-locate items are concerned) is truly exceptional. For information required by DIALORDER to obtain data, you may write: DIALOG, 3460 Hillview Avenue, Palo Alto, Calif. 94304.

The following quotation comes from DIALOG's prospectus: "The DIALORDER service is provided for your convenience and there are no additional DIALOG charges for the use of the service other than the connect time associated with the file within which the order is prepared and issued. You will be billed directly by the supplier for your requests; DIALOG is only the messenger conveyor."

Costs, of course, will vary from one supplier to another, depending on the nature and the amount of information requested.

As we turn our attention to a few of the data bases, we find that ERIC, for example, has an extensive file on educational materials drawn from *Resources in Education* and *Current Index to Journals in Education.*

ERIC regularly adds information from more than 700 scholarly journals, and coverage includes career education, counseling, early childhood education, educational management, handicapped and gifted children, higher education, information resources, reading and communication skills, social studies, teacher education, tests, and test measurement and evaluation.

SOCIAL SCISEARCH, the international, multi-disciplinary index to information in the social and behavior sciences, indexes and cross references material on the basis of footnote citations.

Students doing advanced research have come to appreciate SSCI, and the ease with which its information can be provided via SOCIAL SCISEARCH is truly amazing. Subject areas covered include anthropology, area studies, business management, communication, educational research, geography, history, international relations, philosophy, political science, psychology, and sociology.

The wealth of resource material will be of particular significance to missiologists and those involved in church growth studies both at home and abroad.

PASAR, the data base to *Psychological Abstracts,* is limited to the disciplines growing out of a study of man—applied psychology, communication, educational research, geography, history, international relations, philosphy, political science, psychology, and sociology. Relatively little is included on the theory and practice of counseling. Although PASAR regularly indexes over 900 journals and makes reference to more than 1,500 books, technical reports, and monographs, it may not provide the researcher with the information he needs when it comes to the problems of socialization and tensions of family living.

COMPREHENSIVE DISSERTATION ABSTRACTS is a definitive subject, title, and author guide to virtually every dissertation accepted by an accredited institution since 1861. Professional degrees (e.g., M.D., J.D.) and honorary degrees (e.g., D.D., LL.D.) are not included. Theologically related areas have been included, however, and in recent years Xerox University Microfilms has published a special booklet containing information about D.Min. and D. Miss. degrees as well as the traditional Th.D. and Ph.D. degrees. Data contained in the CDA computer banks has therefore increased and now includes a wide variety of information.

SOCIOLOGICAL ABSTRACTS is devoted to covering the world's literature in sociology and related disciplines. Over 1,200 journals and other serial publications are scanned each year. These provide the researcher with access to original research, book reviews, discussions, monographs, conference reports, debates, and case studies.

PAIS INTERNATIONAL covers the whole range of the social sciences with emphasis on contemporary public issues. Because the scope is worldwide and foreign language works are included, PAIS may prove helpful to those who find themselves working in other countries and other cultures.

PAIS indexes over 1,200 journals and 8,000 monographs per year, and includes within its scope business, public administration, international relations, sociology, and demography.

Although the use of data bases can facilitate research, there is more to the successful use of one of the DIALOG files than might at first be apparent.

First, the researcher would do well to write out a descriptive statement of his proposed research, including synonyms or other descriptive phrases so that these "catch terms" may elicit from the data base as much information as possible. To aid the inquirer, many data bases publish a thesaurus listing their special subject headings and approved synonyms.

Second, if the research is going to include the writings of a person, this should be included so that material written by or about this individual may be included in the computer search.

The more time spent amplifying and refining one's descriptive statement of proposed research, the more finely focused and accurate will be the information secured via the printout.

Third, having thoroughly defined your proposed research, the next step is to consult the reference librarian or computer specialist in your institution (or one nearby your campus offering this service) to discuss with him or her the most helpful computer bank to tap into (e.g., PASAR, SOCIAL SCISEARCH, or both). Once your selection has been made, the computer operator will enter the necessary information and in anything from a day to four weeks, your printed bibliography should be available to you.

In a day of tremendous "knowledge explosion," obtaining information for your thesis or dissertation through computer data bases has become a necessity.

ASSIGNMENT

Choose a topic and consult the *Library of Congress Subject Guide* to ascertain the approved headings under which material is likely to be found. Now check the last five years of *Bibliography Index*, using each of the headings you have uncovered through the *Library of Congress Subject Guide*. Make a note of the entries and then try to locate the books or journals referred to. How extensive is each author's bibliography? If you were doing advanced research, how valuable would the data collected via these select bibliographies be to you?

13

BIBLIOGRAPHIES
PART 1

In Greek mythology, there is a story about a king of ancient Corinth named Sisyphus. Whatever his good points may have been, he is now remembered as one who was crafty and unscrupulous. One day he angered Zeus and was condemned to the Underworld where, as punishment for his crimes and deception, he was compelled forever to push a huge stone up a hill. As soon as he neared the summit, however, the stone would slip away from him and roll down the hill, whereupon Sisyphus would have to begin the task all over again.

Of all the labors bequeathed to mankind one of the most exacting, and one that requires much perseverance, is bibliographic research. Those who have prepared lengthy bibliographies know how demanding the task can be.

In a day of advanced specialization, published bibliographies are indispensable to research. The preparation of a subject bibliography, however, demands the integrated skill of men and women who are educators, librarians, and information specialists, plus hundreds of man-hours.

What follows in this chapter may be of greatest value to those working on a thesis or dissertation. However, because all students will be required to prepare at the very least a research paper, some awareness of the availability of bibliographies will doubtless proved beneficial.

With the publication of a bibliography (e.g., Wilbur M. Smith's A List of Bibliographies of Theological and Biblical Literature) some may question whether or not they need know anything about indices and abstracts. The obvious answer is, yes. This is because unless bibliographies are kept current with periodic supplements, they lose their value. Wilbur Smith's bibliography concluded in 1931. Only by using *Biblica* (later *Elenchus Bibliographicus Biblicus*) can we cover the intervening period between Dr. Smith's valuable list and IRPL and RIO.

GENERAL BIBLIOGRAPHIES

In 1939 Theodore Besterman published the first edition of his now famous *World Bibliography of Bibliographies* (4th ed., 5 vols., 1965-66). This vast and seemingly all-encompassing reference tool is international in scope and contains numerous entries that lead researchers to compilations of bibliographies. Entries are arranged alphabetically within each subject ("Theology" is found in vol. 4, pp. 6074-6121). One entry gleaned from Besterman's *Bibliography of Bibliographies* can lead to a source of several hundred references.

An equally valuable, though somewhat different, resource is *Bibliographic Index: A Cumulative Bibliography of Bibliographies* (1938-present). Published semi-annually since 1965 with annual cumulations, *Bibliographic Index* differs from Besterman's work in that it is the product of many people, concentrates on English-language works, and makes available to the researcher bibliographies at the end of journal articles and books.

This index is arranged alphabetically by subject only. Under each subject heading entries are arranged alphabetically by author. All subjects are covered, and each annual volume can lead investigators to secular as well as religious sources.

Of a more specific nature is John Graves Barrow's *A Bibliography of Bibliographies in Religion* (1955), a publication based on the author's 1930 Ph.D. dissertation at Yale. It lists separately published bibliographies by subject, and then chronologically from the fifteenth century to the twentieth. Author and subject indices are provided.

And, of course, there is Wilbur M. Smith's *A List of Bibliographies of Theological and Biblical Literature Published in Great Britain and America, 1595-1931; with Critical, Biographical and Bibliographical Notes* (1931) referred to above. Brief and purposely not comprehensive, this work covers areas such as church history, missions, religious education, and non-Christian religions. An author index is appended.

Also within the broad scope of religious studies is William J. Wainwright's *Philosophy of Religion: An Annotated Bibliography of Twentieth Century Writings in English* (1978), and the annotated index by Donald E. Capps, L. Rambo, and P. Ransohoff entitled *Psychology of Religion* (1976).

Wainwright's bibliography is intended for those in the "analytical tradition" who are primarily interested in the solution of philosophical problems rather than in the investigation of different systems of thought. His bibliography provides access to more than 1,100 resources under eight subdivisions. The annotations are extensive, in many instances taking up a full page.

Indices to authors, editors, and reviewers conclude the volume.

The work by Capps, Rambo, and Ransohoff begins with an introductory section followed by a treatment of the literature covering the dimensions of religion—mythological, ritual, experiential, dispositional, social, and directional. Publications cited include books and journal articles appearing since 1950, with the addition of important earlier works. Most book entries and those for articles of special merit or with nondescriptive titles are annotated.

SPECIAL BIBLIOGRAPHIES

Often overlooked in bibliographic searches are published holdings of specialized libraries. Those are numerous, and their number increases annually. For example, Union Theological Seminary in New York made available an *Alphabetical Arrangement of Main Entries from The Shelf List* (10 vols., 1960). In all, these volumes provide informative data to 191,000 monographs and sets of books. Those desiring a subject arrangement of books may wish to consult the *Shelf List of the Union Theological Seminary Library in New York City* (10 vols., 1960), which provides data about 203,000 separate titles.

As the focus of one's research narrows, specific attention can be focused on:

- Biblical studies
- Church history and the study of comparative religions
- Missions and ecumenics
- Philosophy
- Pastoral ministry

The works referred to will be representative of a vast reservoir of material to which new works are being added constantly. The first four areas will be treated in this chapter, and the section on pastoral topics in the next. Those wishing to supplement the material alluded to in the following pages or to find out what is available about denominational bibliographies are referred to John Bollier's *The Literature of Theology.*

BIBLICAL STUDIES

The American Baptist Seminary of the West published a work entitled *Tools of Biblical Interpretation: A Bibliographical Guide* (1968), containing bibliographic essays by the members of the faculty. A brief supplement covering publications issued between 1968 and 1970 appeared in 1980.

Another popular work rich in resources from the period of the Puritans to the nineteenth century is Charles Haddon Spurgeon's *Commenting and Commentaries* (1876/1969). In this work the famous British preacher draws attention to 1,437 commentaries covering the canonical books of the Old and New Testaments.

When it comes to the Old Testament, Brevard S. Childs has compiled a list of form critical and redaction critical works entitled *Old Testament Books for*

Pastor and Teacher (1977). (A work presently in progress is the *Index to English Periodical Literature on the Old Testament* by William G. Hupper. It is scheduled for publication in five volumes and will cover the period from 1800 to 1970.)

In England the Society for Old Testament Study has regularly issued a *Book List* (1945-present). These volumes include H. H. Rowley's *Eleven Years of Bible Bibliography* (1957), B. W. Anderson's *A Decade of Bible Bibliography* (1967), and P. R. Ackroyd's *Bible Bibliography, 1967-1973; Old Testament* (1974). Each work is replete with a scholarly critique, and combined they are most valuable.

Another important resource is the publication of the University of Chicago's *Catalog of the Oriental Institute Library* (16 vols., 1970), which alerts users to more than 50,000 items dealing with the art, literature, philology, history, science, and religious beliefs to those living in the countries composing the ancient Near East.

A supplementary *Catalog of the Middle Eastern Collection* was issued in 1977.

Of similar value is the University of London's *Library Catalogue of the School for Oriental and African Studies* (1963), with supplements issued every five years.

No survey on the literature of the Old Testament would be complete without some reference to the Septuagint. In this connection the *Classified Bibliography to the Septuagint,* compiled by S. P. Brock, C. T. Fritzsch, and S. Jellicoe (1973), evidences great care in the selection of materials for inclusion, yet succeeds in covering the period from 1860 to 1969. The compilers consulted nearly 200 sources and arranged the entries culled from those journals and scholarly monographs under specific subject headings. A comprehensive table of contents and index of authors indicates where data may be found.

As we consider the New Testament, we find numerous indices awaiting our attention. Bruce M. Metzger is to be complimented on being the prime mover behind the compilation of the *Index to Periodical Literature on Christ and the Gospels* (1966) and the *Index to Periodical Literature on the Apostle Paul* (1970). Both are part of the New Testament Tools and Studies series.

Probably as complete as a work such as this could be, the *Index to Periodical Literature on Christ and the Gospels* makes available a wealth of scholarly resource material from 160 periodicals in sixteen languages. Although recourse can always be made to IRPL and RIO for essays and articles from 1961 to the present, Metzger's work readily makes available information contained in journals published prior to 1961 (during the last century or the first half of this century). The format includes a detailed table of contents as well as helpful indices.

Following a similar format, the *Index to Periodical Literature on the Apostle Paul* provides access to a vast storehouse of literature drawn from more than 100 scholarly journals. The entries are arranged alphabetically by author under a comprehensive list of subjects. They cover historical, philological, theological, and ecclesiastical aspects of Paul's life and ministry.

First published in 1960, this bibliographic index also precedes IRPL and RIO in that it concentrates on essays written during the nineteenth century and the first five decades of this century. An author index is included.

A. J. and M. B. Mattill's *Classified Bibliography of Literature on the Acts of the Apostles* serves as a companion volume to the works by B. M. Metzger. This well-indexed, 6,646-entry bibliography includes material from 180 periodicals in all the major European languages. The researcher is introduced to a mind-boggling array of data that includes articles on textual criticism; philology; literary criticism; history; the theology of the early church and its leaders; character studies; chronology; archaeology; Roman laws, customs, and institutions; pseudepigraphal literature; et cetera. Preachers, researchers, and professors can all benefit from the use of this volume.

Other sources for the study of the books of the New Testament might well include Spurgeon's *Commenting and Commentaries* (1876/1969), John Coolidge Hurd's *Bibliography of New Testament Bibliographies* (1966), and the *Bibliography of New Testament Literature, 1900-1950*, by the faculty of the San Francisco Theological Seminary (1954). For resources published since those bibliographies were compiled, researchers should see *New Testament Abstracts*.

CHURCH HISTORY

Scripture, of course, is designed to form the basis of Christian belief. The study of church history and the different religions that have arisen, however, reveals that this basic principle has not always been followed. The "seed of the Word" has been sown, but there has also been a counter-sowing of "tares." Church history and a study of comparative religions, therefore, needs to be seen in the emerging sequence of the different movements and must be continually compared to the teaching of the Bible. History forms the backdrop for this kind of study, and historical sources must be included if our research into any facet of religious belief or practice is to have validity.

The bibliographies referred to in this section are only representative of the many available at the present time. For information since these works were published, reference can always be made to *Historical Abstracts*, IRPL, or RIO.

Of value in understanding pagan religion (but invariably misleading when applied to biblical Christianity) is the data to be found in *Psychoanalysis and Religion: A Bibliography* by Benjamin Beit-Hallahmi (1978). With significant sections on primitive religion, Greek religion and mythology, Islam, Buddhism, and Hinduism, this literary index can direct researchers to information about the underlying motivations found in specific religious beliefs and practices.

Trends in history can readily be traced through the American Historical Association's *Guide to Historical Literature*, edited by G. F. Howe et al (1961). This comprehensive, annotated guide to historical literature—from periodical and newspaper articles, books and book reviews, dissertations and encyclopedic articles—provides excellent coverage of the ancient and medieval periods.

Bruce M. Metzger, whose compiled bibliographies of essays on the gospels and the apostle Paul have already been noted, has provided another work to aid researchers in the study of the early Christian church. Entitled an *Index of Articles on the New Testament and the Early Church Published in Festschriften* (1951), and with a supplement added in 1955, this work succeeds in directing the scholar to a vast storehouse of easily overlooked material. The bibliographies at the end of these essays are very full and cannot help but aid one's research efforts.

Also of value in the study of the early church is *Bibliographia Patristicia: Internationale Patristische Bibliographie*, edited by W. Schallmelcher (1959-present). Published annually, this detailed index to the literature and religion, symbols and doctrine, people and practice of the period of the church Fathers, provides the user with access to information contained in about 900 scholarly journals in a variety of European languages.

In addition, the *International Bibliography of the History of Religions*, edited by S. H. Alich (1974-present), furnishes researchers with information about all the major religions of the Near East.

When it comes to the medieval period, the *Dictionary Catalog of the Library of the Pontifical Institute of Medieval Studies* of St. Michael's College, Toronto (5 vols. and supplement, 1972) provides investigators with access to a variety of source materials dealing with everything from religious ritual to religious paintings, from sacred music to the copying and preserving of sacred manuscripts, from court intrigue to Byzantine customs, from canon law to civil practice, and from vernacular literature to Bible translations.

The propagation of the gospel in England is chronicled in a series of bibliographies.

The first, a *Bibliography of British History; Tudor Period, 1485-1603*, edited by C. Read (1959), was first produced in 1933. Arranged under broad topics (e.g., political history, ecclesiastical history), it provides excellent coverage of the literature of the period. Some of the entries are annotated. This work is a *must* for the student of this era.

Likewise, the *Bibliography of British History; Stuart Period, 1603-1714*, edited by G. Davies and M. F. Keeler (1970), continues the admirable coverage provided in the earlier volume. In many instances the annotations are longer, and this work includes sections on the Angelican church and the place and influence of Jews in England during the seventeenth century.

Continuing coverage is contained in the *Bibliography of British History; the Eighteenth Century, 1714-1789*, edited by S. M. Pargellis and D. J.

Medley (1951). This bibliography is well-outlined and treats the Nonconformist movement in England. It also provides indispensable access to the material relating to social conditions in England (and elsewhere) during the time of Wesley and Whitefield.

Also of value is the *Bibliography of British History, 1789-1851*, edited by L. M. Brown and I. R. Christie (1977), which is replete with introductory essays, a chronicle of the expansion of the British Empire, and the rise and progress of missions.

Finally, there is the *Bibliography of British History, 1851-1914*, compiled and edited by H. J. Hanham (1976). This mammoth volume continues tracing the growth of the British Empire and deals primarily with England's era of power and influence. Interesting sections treat progress in industry, education, and the social sciences.

Where American history is concerned, few works can compare with the *Guide to the Study of the United States of America*, published by the General Reference and Bibliographic Division of the Library of Congress (1960), and the *Harvard Guide to American History*, by F. B. Freidel and R. K. Showman (revised ed., 1974).

The former work annotates most entries and provides a single author-title-subject index. The latter, following a series of introductory essays, helps researchers focus in on bibliographical data and personal records, specific areas of interest (e.g., interpretive accounts of American history), as well as regional, state, and local histories, special subjects (e.g., government, law, politics, economics, education, etc.), and a plethora of other topics. In all, over 400 journals are indexed, making this a most valuable resource.

MISSIONS AND ECUMENICS

Closely associated with the ministry of the church is the whole area of missions. Missionaries formerly did the work of evangelism, but today much more is required of them. A study of the culture of the people with which one will be working, together with an understanding of their history and beliefs, their method of socialization and leadership, economic practices and outlook on the future, are indispensable to one's preparation.

One of the most comprehensive collections of materials on Protestant missions, the *Dictionary Catalog of the Missionary Research Library* (17 vols., 1968), was accumulated by the Missionary Research Library in New York. This outstanding index to books has been located since 1929 on the campus of the Union Theological Seminary, New York. The catalog contains more than 100,000 entries and has author, title, and subject indices.

The Library of Congress, Africa Section, has published *Africa South of the Sahara: Index to Periodical Literature, 1900-1970* (4 vols., 1971), which makes accessible a vast amount of information on topics like ethnography, sociology, linguistics, and politics of all nations on the African continent. This work is a *must* for the missiologist.

Other related works include the *Cumulative Bibliography of African Studies,* published by the International African Institute, London (5 vols., 1973). Information is grouped under geographic areas, with subdivisions by subject, people, and language.

Then there is *The Howard University Bibliography of African and Afro-American Religious Studies,* prepared by Ethel L. Williams and C. F. Brown (1977). This provides access to about 13,000 primary and secondary sources. A helpful feature is the listing of approximately 230 American libraries where the information contained in this bibliography may be found.

The University of California, Berkeley, has published its *East Asia Library: Author-Title Catalog* (23 vols., 1968) by which it enables students of linguistics and Asian culture to have access to one of the largest collections of Chinese, Japanese, and Korean materials ever assembled. In addition, these volumes are filled with information relating to the religions of those peoples and communist influence in those countries.

A work of related significance is the *Cumulative Bibliography of Asian Studies, 1941-1965* (8 vols., 1965) with well over 100,000 entries, and the 1966-70 supplement (6 vols., 1972-73) of approximately 70,000 additional entries. These latter volumes have extensive sections devoted to Vietnam and Indochina.

Of a similar nature is the *Catalog of the Latin American Library of the Tulane University Library* in New Orleans (9 vols., 1970), with supplements appearing every two years.

This outstanding Latin American library was known until 1962 as the Middle American Research Institute Library. It was started in 1924 with the purchase of the William Gates Collection, which includes materials on Mexico, Central America, and the West Indies. Other private collections have since been added, and the *Catalog* now includes material for all of Latin America, most of which deals with the social sciences and humanities.

The *Catalog* is arranged in dictionary form but generally does not contain entries for newspapers, manuscripts, or maps, although main entries for Latin American materials now found in other divisions of the Tulane University Library are included.

Also of value is the *Index to Latin American Periodical Literature,* 1929-60 (8 vols., 1962), and the 1961-65 supplement. With preference given matters of cultural, economic, educational, historical, political, and social importance, this work can be of inestimable value to the D.Miss. candidate interested in the cross-cultural communication of the gospel

Finally, *Protestantism in Latin America: A Biblical Guide,* edited by J. H. Sinclair (1976), is a "made-for-missionaries" bibliography that includes resource and study tools, provides an introduction to sources of information on the customs and culture, and describes the history of those who have labored there for Christ since the first missions were established.

Bibliographies of the leading religions are legion. Two will suffice to illustrate the kind of works that are available.

First, *Studies of Chinese Religion: A Comprehensive and Classified Bibliography of Publications in English, French and German Through 1970,* compiled by L. G. Thompson (1976), contains entries arranged under 82 subject headings. The entries are not annotated; an author index is provided.

And *Index Islamicus, 1906-1955,* compiled by J. D. Pearson (1958), is a basic resource for the study of Islamic history and religion, ideology, and culture. Information is gleaned from about 510 periodicals, 120 festschrifts and more than 70 other works. It is kept up to date with quinquennial indexes to current literature.

Some missiologists will be interested in the ecumenical movement and the library holdings and publications of the World Council of Churches, Geneva, Switzerland. The following are a few of the works that missiologists may wish to consult.

The Library of the World Council of Churches published a *Classified Catalog of the Ecumenical Movement* (2 vols., 1972) listing approximately 52,000 books and pamphlets, 1,350 periodicals (750 current), and 6,500 boxes of archival materials. The ecumenical sections contain approximately 11,000 titles that are indexed in the *Classified Catalog,* arranged according to a modified Dewey Decimal system. The collection consists of the history of various ecumenical movements in the twentieth century, the history of the World Council of Churches (WCC) all reports and publications of its divisions, departments, et cetera since 1948, complete records of the four WCC Assemblies, records of World Confessional Families, publications of national and regional councils of churches, church union negotiations and surveys, Vatican II and non-Catholic reactions, all aspects of ecumenical theology (ecumenical literature is also included), and ecumenical biographies.

Other works of related significance include the brief but informative compilation by Paul A. Crow, Jr., *The Ecumenical Movement in Bibliographical Outline* (1965); *Laici in ecclesia* (1961), which lists books and other materials on the role of the laity in the life and mission of the church; and the *Internationale oekumenische Bibliographie. International Ecumenical Bibliography. Bibliographie Oecuménique Internationale. Bibliografia Ecuménica International* (1967-present), an annual that is published in German, English, French, and Italian and is one of the most comprehensive continuous classified bibliographies available.

PHILOSOPHY

Bibliographies on philosophy are fairly numerous. Richard De George has compiled a handy *Guide to Philosophical Bibliography and Research* (1971), in which he has listed important reference works for both the student and the more advanced scholar. The entries are grouped by the kind of material (i.e., dictionaries, encyclopedias, histories of philosophy, sources of information [e.g., bibliographies, and the standard editions and collected works of individual philosophers], bibliographies on specific subjects, and guides to writing and publishing, etc.). A brief introduction precedes the listing of source material in each section, and many of the entries are annotated.

Earlier, Henry J. Koren prepared an extensive work entitled *Research in Philosophy* (1966). This was preceded the year before by Charles L. Higgins's *Bibliography of Philosophy* (1965). The need for such compilations of material had been established by Wilhelm Totok in Europe, where he had published his *Handbuch der Geschichte der Philosophie* (1959), and where the French scholar Gilbert Varet had issued his *Manuel de bibliographie philosophique* (1956).

These works, however, may be viewed as valuable supplements to Herbert Guerry's *A Bibliography of Philosophical Bibliographies* (1977), which contains a listing of the compilations of competent scholars published between 1450 and 1974. The material is divided into two parts. Part 1 (entries 1-1395) contains a bibliographic index relating to the works of, and literature about, individual philosophers from the earliest times to the present. Part 2 (entries 1396-2353) contains a listing of bibliographies on philosophical topics. By using this valuable resource tool, researchers will be able to locate speedily and effortlessly a wealth of information on Plato or the development of his ideas, Kant and the formation of his thought, Descartes and the rise of the Cartesian school, et cetera. There is also information on other leading philosophers (e.g., Aristotle, Berkeley, Hegel, Hume, James Russell, Whitehead, etc.) and a useful listing of works by or about modern thinkers.

This bibliography does not replace the earlier philosophical works cited, but it does enhance the resource materials from which a student may cull his information.

In our next chapter we will consider bibliographies in the applied areas of the pastoral ministry.

ASSIGNMENT

What are congregations looking for in a pastor? Make a list of the skills and attributes they are seeking. Arrange the entries in their order of importance. Assuming that you are working on a graduate degree in this area, how would you go about gathering data? Prepare a brief bibliography on one of these areas: homiletics, pastoral administration, the Christian education program, counseling.

14

BIBLIOGRAPHIES PART 2

The pastoral ministry is one of the most varied and demanding of occupations. Often, as Dr. Earl D. Radmacher, president of the Western Conservative Baptist Theological Seminary, Portland, Oregon, has pointed out, the pastor is expected to be a "Jack-of-all-trades" and master of none.* He is required to preach and teach, counsel and visit, encourage and exhort, administrate and build, and if there is time left over, study the Word and pray, spend time with his family, and plan for the future.

Now, perhaps more so than at any time in the history of the Christian church, there is a need for a multiple staff ministry.

Whether or not there is a delegation of specific responsibilities to suitably trained individuals, the fact remains that it is the local church that is responsible for building up believers so they can do the work of the ministry—whether in some foreign land or within the United States (i.e., in the local community). The work of the church, therefore, involves both vertical and horizontal dimensions: worship and evangelism, praise and education. Professionally trained men and women, committed to the teaching of the Scriptures, yet trained in some specialized area (e.g., counseling, education, interracial ministry), need to work cooperatively in and through the church.

In this chapter, bibliographies dealing with the following areas of the church's ministry will be discussed:

- The pastor and the development of pastoral skills

*See "Pastor of all Trades," *The Christian Reader* 9, no. 6 (December 1971-January 1972), pp. 44-48.

- The ministry of music
- The ministry of education
- Ministry to ethnic groups
- The ministry of counseling.

Each of these areas is wide open for research, particularly on the part of those pursuing D. Min. degrees.

THE PASTOR AND THE DEVELOPMENT OF PASTORAL SKILLS

Pastors need to have, in addition to a mastery of Bible and theology, some knowledge of their own personality dynamics, some skill in communication, an understanding of their role as leaders of God's people, an awareness of the homiletic process, and the ability to develop groups of believers into nuclei of concern.

Pioneer work has been done by Robert J. Menges and James E. Dittes in *Psychological Studies of Clergymen: Abstracts of Research* (1965). In this interdenominational compilation of studies, those entering the ministry were assessed under certain significant headings: unique characteristics, effectiveness, mental health or illness, wives and family, et cetera. Now, however, other dimensions need to be added, and those areas are wide open for investigation and research.

Furthermore, many churches are expanding their ministries to include audiovisual means of sharing the gospel. *Communication: A Guide to Information Sources,* by George Gitter and R. Grunin (1980), provides excellent coverage for the study of mass media and cross-cultural communication, with special emphases placed on motivation, the use of television, and different aspects of journalism.

The whole area of leadership receives excellent handling by Ralph M. Stogdill, *Leadership Abstracts and Bibliography, 1904-1974* (1977). This annotated bibliography to more than 3,000 books and journal articles directs researchers to professional materials and makes available a vast resource of empirically verified data. It is well indexed and ideal for those studying leadership dynamics.

And then, of course, there is the pastor's pulpit ministry. *Recent Homiletic Thought: A Bibliography, 1935-1965,* edited by W. Toohey and W. D. Thompson (1967), begins with the year in which C. H. Dodd gave his lectures on "The Apostolic Preaching and Its Developments" at King's College, London. It then surveys ten different areas of the preacher's role and concludes with a bibliography. Each entry is annotated. A comprehensive list of theses and dissertations in the area of sermon preparation and delivery concludes the work. Interdenominational in scope, this compilation of materials is ecumenical in its content and coverage.

In Christian circles we make much of the church as the Body of Christ, and so we should. Believers are part of a select community. An understanding of how people function in groups, however, has only recently begun to engage the attention of those in the ministry. From a secular point of view *Group Behavior: A Guide to Information Sources,* by Gloria Behar Gottsegen (1979), can become the means of stimulating interaction that will then lead pastors to a better understanding of the dynamics of power, the leadership of groups, and the techniques of communication within a group.

THE MINISTRY OF MUSIC

The ministry of music is of vital importance if a church's "reasonable service of worship" is to be achieved. *Church Music, An International Bibliography,* by Richard Chaffey von Ende (1980), begins with an extensive subject guide to the contents of the book. Kinds of choral music are included, as well as the musical preferences and contributions of different denominations. Hymnals are discussed and ethnographic distinctives listed. All things considered, this a very complete bibliography.

Pastors desiring to trace some song for homiletic illustration will find *The Literature of American Music,* by David Horn (1977), and the *Popular Song Index,* by Patricia P. Havlice (1975, with its 1978 supplement), helpful resources. In addition, the *Bibliographic Guide to Music* (1975-present), an annual published by the New York Public Library and the Library of Congress, covers virtually all musical subjects, and the scores represent the broadest spectrum of musical style and history.

THE MINISTRY OF EDUCATION

Not to be ignored is the important ministry of education, which necessitates a knowledge of biblical principles of education, the history of education, and modern research in the field of education.

DeWitte Campbell Wyckoff's *Suggested Bibliography in Christian Education for Seminary and College Libraries* (1968) is kept up to date with irregular supplements and is probably the most extensive bibliography published on Christian education.

The *Bibliography of American Educational History,* by Francesco Cordasco and William W. Brickman (1975), gives evidence of a high degree of professional competence. It should be consulted regularly by all those preparing for a ministry in the classroom, regardless of whether their sphere of operation is a Christian grade school or a university.

The *Bibliographic Guide to Educational Research,* by Dorothea M. Berry (1975), contains more than 500 references (with descriptive annotations) to a variety of literature. This work is often useful to teachers as well as advanced students. The section on "Special Types of Materials" promises something for Sunday school teachers and directors of Christian education who may be able to take ideas from the secular arena and adapt them for use in the church.

And not to be ignored is the *Dictionary Catalog of the Teachers College*

Library, Columbia University, New York (35 vols., 1970), which is kept current with frequent supplements.

Providing access to approximately 470,000 books, current and past journals, and a variety of audiovisual materials in the numerous special fields of education and related areas, this catalog is about as broad in its coverage as one could desire. The sections dealing with American elementary and secondary education are exceptionally comprehensive, consisting of original documents, historical and contemporary textbooks, early catalogs and histories of academies and schools, courses of study, surveys, and administrative reports of school systems for all of the states and many major cities.

MINISTRY TO ETHNIC GROUPS

The church's ministry to ethnic groups has long been ignored. It can be enhanced, however, by consulting a *Comprehensive Bibliography for the Study of American Minorities,* by Wayne Charles Miller et al (2 vols., 1976), which covers nearly all ethnic groups that have sought solace in the United States. It describes their experiences, problems of adjustment, sociology, politics, religion, et cetera.

Other related works include a *Bibliography of American Ethnology,* by Marc Casman and Barry Klein (1976); the annual issue of *Bibliographic Guide to Black Studies* (1975-present); and *Reference Materials on Mexican Americans,* by Richard D. Woods (1976).

Also of importance is Lenwood G. Davis's *The Black Family in the United States: A Selected Bibliography of Annotated Books, Articles, and Dissertations on Black Families in America* (1978), which admirably fulfills its own subtitle.

THE MINISTRY OF COUNSELING

Finally, the ever-expanding area of pastoral counseling demands close attention. Concern shall be placed first on the skills needed to be a competent counselor, then on the family (including the children and the aged). After this we shall deal with specific works treating the place and plight of women, and finally specific kinds of counseling—abortion, alcoholism, drug abuse, euthanasia, homosexuality, rape, and suicide—shall be discussed.

In *Counseling: A Bibliography (with Annotations),* Ruth St. J. Freedman and H. A. Freedman (1964) provide guidance for lawyers, doctors, clergymen, teachers, social workers, psychologists and psychiatrists, and all others engaged in counseling, so that quality interaction may triumph over mere quantity. Their approach and the resources they cite are at once suggestive and stimulating. Sections two ("Religion [Clergy]") and eight ("Marriage Counseling") will amply reward the pastor's time. IRPL and RIO can be used to trace material from 1965 to the present.

Where the family is concerned, the two-volume work by the Wakefield Washington Associates, Inc., entitled *Family Research: A Source Book,*

Analysis, and Guide to Federal Funding (1979) is the outgrowth of years of sociological research, and it catalogs the kind of work being done by federal agencies. It also is suggestive of many areas of investigation that doctoral students in D.Min. programs in marriage and family ministries might adapt profitably to the local church.

As we turn from the family as a whole to consider the child as an individual, the *Bibliography of Child Psychiatry and Child Mental Health, With a Selected List of Films,* edited by Irving N. Berlin (1976), shows why national interest is being focused on the plight of children. This bibliography offers comprehensive coverage on a plethora of topics of interest to pastors as well as parents—topics such as the stages of child development, birth order, the preschool years, school "phobia," the latency years, adolescence, fear of failure, depression, obsessive-compulsive disorders, hyperactivity, antisocial behavior, illnesses necessitating hospitalization, and even death and dying.

Information published since 1976 can be obtained by consulting CDAB.

In addition, Hazel B. Benson's *Behavior Modification and the Child: An Annotated Bibliography* (1979), a companion volume to *The Gifted Student* by J. Laubenfels and *Child Abuse and Neglect* by B. J. Dalisch, covers a wide variety of childhood problems from toilet training to drug abuse, and thumb sucking to pyromania. The kind of counsel offered, however, will need to be augmented with biblical principles if it is to have any lasting effect.

Also of value is Andrew and Rhoda Garoogian's *Child Care Issues for Parents and Society: A Guide to Information Sources* (1977). With the coverage of subjects similar to Benson's *Bibliography of Child Psychiatry,* this work concentrates more on those events and circumstances associated with a child's growth and development than with the treatment of pathology. Its goal is to support and strengthen the family, and as such it will be of value to those in the church who work with families.

Of importance when working with senior citizens is *Aging: Its History and Literature,* by Joseph T. Freeman (1979), which not only provides a historical perspective on gerontology and geriatrics, but also lists journals on the subject. From this volume pastors and church workers may glean ideas on how to make the aged feel a useful part of the local community.

Death and Dying: A Bibliography (1950-1974) by G. Howard Poteet (1976) attempts to cover every aspect of thanatology and permits the whole subject to come "out of the closet." This bibliography shows the vast amount of empirical research on death that has been generated over the last quarter century. A supplementary volume focusing specifically on suicide, and covering the same 1950-74 time period, was published in 1978.

In recent years considerable attention has focused on women, so much so that entire bibliographies on the subject now are needed.

Albert Krichmar, in *The Women's Movement in the Seventies: An International English-Language Bibliography* (1977), deals with the quest for status on the part of women in all parts of the world. He includes religious, psychological, philosophical, and sociological information in his coverage. The book is well indexed.

Virginia R. Terris's *Woman in America: A guide to Information Sources* (1980) covers the role, image, and status of women in American history, literature, education, and society. Due consideration is given women in minority groups as well as those in the professions. Each entry is annotated.

A work of related significance is *Women: A Bibliography on Their Education and Careers* by Helen S. Astin, N. Suniewick, and S. Dweck (1974).

Of related interest is Carolyn Moss's *Bibliographic Guide to Self-disclosure Literature, 1956-1976,* (1977), which describes the research done in this area of human problems and suffering. It can provide a valuable source of material for pastoral counseling, or even on occasion, homiletic illustration.

SPECIFIC AREAS OF COUNSELING

Because of the rising incidence of divorce, doctoral students or pastors needing: (1) statistical information, (2) awareness of special clinics or organizations for helping those going through a divorce, or (3) data relating to child support or the effect of separation on the mental health of spouse and child will find their research needs met by Kenneth and Betty Sell's *Divorce in the United States, Canada, and Great Britain* (1978).

Mary K. Floyd's *Abortion Bibliography* (1970-present) annually culls information from a variety of medical, educational, legal, and social sources. It presents entries without annotation under both title and subject (sixty-three separate) headings. An author index concludes this valuable resource tool.

The *International Bibliography of Studies of Alcohol: Vol. 1, References, 1901-1950,* prepared by S. S. Jordy (1966), contains information arranged alphabetically by author under each year indicated in the title. This bibliography explores the rise of alcoholism in each country of the world, shows what governments, medical practitioners, and therapists are doing with those caught in the syndrome of its compulsive use, and provides information on the various techniques used with alcoholics. Volume two (1968) contains author and subject indices and is the only practical key to the reference volume. Volume three is a supplement covering the literature generated between 1951 and 1960.

Information on alcoholism and its treatment since 1960, although not as extensive as this bibliography, also may be obtained by consulting *Cumulative Index Medicus.*

Drug Abuse Bibliography, compiled by J. C. Advena (1971-present), indexes annually a vast amount of literature on drug abuse and contains information about nearly everything on this subject that the pastor or counselor may need to know.

Charles W. Triche III and his wife, Diane Samson Triche, have compiled *The Euthanasia Controversy, 1812-1974. A Bibliography with Select Anno-*

tations (1975), which is important for its historical perspective as well as its comprehensiveness. It includes sections on the law, pediatrics, suicide, the terminally ill, and war crimes.

Also of importance to the pastoral counselor is the issue of homosexuality. *Annotated Bibliography of Homosexuality* (2 vols., 1976), Vern L. Bullouch et al, and the work by M. S. Weinberg and A. P. Bell, *Homosexuality: An Annotated Bibliography* (1972), guide researchers to much of the literature generated since 1940. More recent studies may be located by consulting *Cumulative Index Medicus.*

In addition, William Parker's *Homosexuality: A Selective Bibliography of Over 3,000 Items* (1971) is an index to books, pamphlets and documents, theses and dissertations, periodical and newspaper articles, court cases, and data in medical journals. It is not annotated, but is easy to use and is well indexed. A sequel entitled *Homosexuality: Bibliography; Supplement, 1970-1975,* containing 3,136 entries, was published in 1977.

Rape and Rape-related Issues: An Annotated Bibliography by Elizabeth Jane Kemmer (1977) deals with the rising incidence of rape and directs pastors to sources explaining how to handle the crises, what professional help is available, and to whom to refer their counselee. This bibliography deals sensitively with the problem and covers all aspects of the crime.

In *Suicide: A Guide to Information Sources,* David Lester, Betty H. Sall, and Kenneth D. Sall (1980) contribute to the growing body of source materials on this topic. Their work is encyclopedic in its coverage and yet specific enough to tabulate and correlate the various kinds of people who attempt suicide with the kinds of therapy the counselor may employ.

As has been mentioned before, there are bibliographies on nearly every subject imaginable. They may be found in the card catalog of your library or the *Library of Congress Catalog—Books: Subjects* or *Subject Guide to Books in Print* by checking the approved subject heading for your topic. This will be followed by a dash and the word *bibliography.* For example, MARRIAGE—BIBLIOGRAPHY; SINGLE ADULTS—BIBLIOGRAPHY; YOUTH—BIBLIOGRAPHY.

Remember, a bibliography is supposed to be an unbiased list of materials from all available sources.

Assignment

Good research should include data collected from books, periodicals, and unpublished materials. By checking *Comprehensive Dissertation Index* locate as many works as you can dealing with: (1) God's image in man; and (2) the theology of either Charles Gore, Søren Kierkegaard, or Paul Tillich. Then look up the actual abstract of each dissertation in DAI. Take note of how the abstract has been prepared and the way in which each doctoral candidate has developed his theme.

15

UNPUBLISHED MATERIALS

Competent research must demonstrate an awareness of the scholarly investigations of others. This does not mean that a term paper must cite dissertations in the footnotes and bibliography. It does mean that students submitting theses and dissertations for advanced degrees should know of, and have interacted with, the scholarly work of others.

Unpublished materials can include papers read at the meetings of different societies (e.g., Evangelical Theological Society, Society for New Testament Studies, Society of Biblical Literature, etc.) that have not been made available in the journals of those societies. Such papers constitute a valuable resource and, in many instances, are included in the privately circulated proceedings of the society (e.g., proceedings of the annual meeting of the Christian Psychological Association, or the American Theological Library Association, etc.).

Because such papers can be traced through indices or abstracts or via computer searches, in this chapter we will focus our attention primarily on dissertations. These are the most likely resource to be consulted by students preparing theses or dissertations of their own.

To keep our own research in perspective, let us remember that competent research includes a consultation of the following sources:

- General reference works (e.g., encyclopedias and dictionaries pertaining to the subject under investigation)
- Scholarly books and monographs
- Journal articles (located through indices and abstracts)
- Unpublished materials.

We have worked successively through the available resources in the first three of these areas. Quite obviously, the more advanced the level of research, the greater will be the reliance upon scholarly journal articles and unpublished dissertations.

In the United States, we have excellent coverage of dissertations from 1861, when the first doctorates were awarded by Yale University, to the present.

By the turn of the century about 350 doctorates were awarded each year throughout the country. By 1950 the number had risen to about 6,000; in the 1970s the figure exceeded 35,000 annually. No figures are available for the 1980s, but educators are estimating that the number of earned doctorates will increase. Their "guesstimate" is probably accurate, for with the introduction of professional doctorates (e.g., D.A., D.B.A., D.Eng., D.F.A., D.L.S., D.Min., D.Miss., D.S.W., etc.) an increase seems inevitable.

The *List of American Doctoral Dissertations* (26 vols., 1913-40) was for many years one of the only sources of access to the literary output of advanced students. Then in 1934 *Doctoral Dissertations Accepted by American Universities* (1934-56) was published. DDAA followed a topical arrangement, with dissertations listed by university within each topical division, and made available a list of dissertations granted in the United States and Canada.

In 1957, Xerox University Microfilms in Ann Arbor, Michigan, began publishing *American Doctoral Dissertations* (1955-56—1969). The title of this work was initially *Index to American Doctoral Dissertations*, and with the publication of issue number 13 was changed to *Dissertation Abstracts*. From July 1969 onward, it became known as *Dissertation Abstracts International*.

The number of accredited universities and seminaries cooperating with Xerox University Microfilms in the publication of abstracts of dissertations has steadily increased and now exceeds 300. The dissertations submitted are microfilmed and are available for purchase from Xerox University Microfilms. For each dissertation an abstract is included in DAI, or reference is given to an individual university's series of abstracts. The main list is arranged alphabetically by subject field and then by university; each listing includes title, order number, author's name, university, date, name of supervisor, abstract, and number of pages. Each issue of DAI includes a subject index and an author index. Part two of issue number 12 (June) of each year since 1961-62 is a cumulated subject and author index for the year.

Beginning with volume twenty-seven, DAI began appearing in two separately bound sections each month: the humanities and social sciences (A); and the sciences and engineering (B). Author and subject indices for both parts originally appeared in each section with page references distinguished as A or B. Part two, number 12 annually continues to be the cumulative index for the volume and includes both sections. Beginning with volume thirty, the indices became mechanized using "keyword title indexes," and the cumulations for sections A and B were published separately.

The easiest way to check on what research has been done in an area of your interest is to consult *Comprehensive Dissertation Index, 1861-1972* (37 vols., 1973). This computer-produced index is arranged by key word(s) and author. If, for example, your research involves "ethics," by looking up the words *Ethic* and *Ethical* you will instantaneously be able to read off the dissertations having these words in the title. The same procedure applies if you are studying the life of Paul or some fact of Pauline doctrine.

Each entry in CDI contains the name of the successful doctoral candidate, the degree he received, the year in which it was conferred, and the name of the institution. At the end of each entry is a number, which is the key to the place where the author's abstract in DAI may be found. The same number must be cited when obtaining a photocopy or microfilm of the dissertation from Xerox University Microfilms.

CDI in effect supersedes the Library of Congress *List of American Doctoral Dissertations* and *Doctoral Dissertations Accepted by American Universities*. It provides an extensive, retrospective index to all dissertations conferred by American institutions since 1851.

Volume thirty-two of CDI is devoted to "Religion and Philosophy." Volumes thirty-three to thirty-seven contain an author index.

CDI is kept current with annual volumes listing the dissertations of those having earned doctorates during that year.

Xerox University Microfilms has also developed a computerized information retrieval system called DATRIX II. The DATRIX II data based now contains information on more than 500,000 doctoral dissertations received from accredited institutions in the United States. Information on new dissertations is entered into the data base as soon as it is received. An order form with directions relating to procedure and cost may be obtained from:

Xerox University Microfilms
300 North Zub Road
Ann Arbor, Mich. 48106

Researchers may wish to use CDI for older dissertations and utilize a computer search for the most recent works not yet in CDI.

Dissertations in progress may be traced through a journal entitled *Religious Studies Review* (1974-present), which regularly lists dissertation topics accepted for research.

Theses and dissertations submitted to universities overseas may be traced by consulting the *Index to Theses Accepted for Higher Degrees in the Universities of Great Britain and Ireland* (1953-present), *Deutsche National-bibliographie und Bibliographie des im· Ausland erschieneuen deutschsprachen Schriftums* (1968-present), *Jahresverzeichnis der deutschen Hochulschriften 1885/86* (1887-1936 and 1937-present), *Catalog des thèses et écris acadîmeques, 1884/85* (1884-1952), et cetera.

ESSENTIALIST

RELIGION AND THEOLOGY

ESSENTIALIST

IS DUNS SCOTUS AN **ESSENTIALIST**?— LINDBECK, GEORGE A. (PH D. 1955 YALE UNIVERSITY) W1955, p.7

EST-ELLE

L'EUCHARESTIE **EST-ELLE** NECESSAIRE AU SALUT— FORTIN, GUY (PH D 1948 UNIVERSITE LAVAL (CANADA)) 143p W1948, p 4

ESTERO

ABRAHAM GER - 'FORTALEZA DEL HEBRAISMO E CONFUSION DEL **ESTERO**'. A POLEMICAL TREATISE— DREYFUS, A. STANLEY (PH D 1951 HEBREW UNION COLLEGE) W1951, p.7

ESTHER

THE GREEK TEXT OF **ESTHER**— MOORE, CAREY ARMSTRONG (PH D 1965 THE JOHNS HOPKINS UNIVERSITY) 225p. 26/04, p 2357 65-06880

ESTRANGEMENT

SPIRITUAL **ESTRANGEMENT** IN CONTEMPORARY AMERICAN DRAMA— KINGSLEY, JAMES GORDON, JR (PH D 1965 NEW ORLEANS BAPTIST THEOLOGICAL SEMINARY) X1965, p 210

THE IDEA OF SELF-**ESTRANGEMENT** IN THE THOUGHT OF ERICH FROMM AND PAUL TILLICH A COMPARATIVE STUDY WITH EMPHASIS ON IMPLICATIONS FOR THEOLOGICAL METHOD — HAMMOND, GUYTON BOWERS (PH D 1962 VANDERBILT UNIVERSITY) 305p. 23/04, p.1433 62-04507

ETAPLES

THE CHURCH REFORM PRINCIPLES IN THE BIBLICAL WORKS OF JACQUES LEFEVRE D' **ETAPLES**— JORDAN, JAMES DANIEL, JR (PH D 1966 DUKE UNIVERSITY) 401p. 27/06-A, p.1914 66-12733

ETAT

ETAT DE L'EGLISE CATHOLIQUE OU DIOCESE DES ETATS-UNIS DE L'AMERIQUE SEPTENTRIONALE, PAR JEAN DILHET— BROWNE, PATRICK WILLIAM (PH D 1922 THE CATHOLIC UNIVERSITY OF AMERICA) 121p. L1922, p.35

ETATS-UNIS

RELATIONS DE MGR BRIAND ET DE MGR PLESSIS AVEC L'EGLISE DES **ETATS-UNIS** (1763-1825)— LAURENT, LAVAL (PH D 1944 THE CATHOLIC UNIVERSITY OF AMERICA) W1944, p 3

ETAT DE L'EGLISE CATHOLIQUE OU DIOCESE DES **ETATS-UNIS** DE L'AMERIQUE SEPTENTRIONALE, PAR JEAN DILHET— BROWNE, PATRICK WILLIAM (PH D 1922 THE CATHOLIC UNIVERSITY OF AMERICA) 121p. L1922, p.35

ETERNAL

THE DOCTRINE OF THE TRINITY FROM JONATHAN EDWARDS TO HORACE BUSHNELL A STUDY IN THE **ETERNAL** SONSHIP OF CHRIST— STEPHENS, BRUCE MILTON (PH D. 1970 DREW UNIVERSITY) 250p 31/06-A, p 3028 70-24591

RESURRECTION, IMMORTALITY, AND **ETERNAL** LIFE IN INTERTESTAMENTAL JUDAISM— NICKELSBURG, GEORGE WILLIAM ELMER, JR (PH D 1968 HARVARD UNIVERSITY) X1968, p 252

TEMPORAL AND **ETERNAL** FOUR PERSPECTIVES ON HUMAN DESTINY AND FULFILLMENT IN RECENT AMERICAN RELIGIOUS THOUGHT— GIBSON, RAYMOND EUGENE (PH D 1962 COLUMBIA UNIVERSITY) 299p 26/05, p 2890 65-12377

THE RELATIONSHIP OF DISPENSATIONALISM TO THE **ETERNAL** PURPOSE OF GOD— SAUCY ROBERT LLOYD (PH D 1961 DALLAS THEOLOGICAL SEMINARY) X1961, p 175

THE **ETERNAL** CONCEPT OF THE ATONEMENT IN THE THOUGHT OF CERTAIN CONTEMPORARY PROTESTANT THEOLOGIANS— AMBERSON, TALMADGE RICHARD (PH D 1961 SOUTHWESTERN BAPTIST THEOLOGICAL SEMINARY) X1961 p 177

A CRITICAL EDITION AND TRANSLATION OF 'THE **ETERNAL** LIFE' BY YEHIEL NISIM DA PISA— ROSENTHAL, GILBERT S (PH D 1960 JEWISH THEOLOGICAL SEMINARY OF AMERICA) X1960, p 167

AN INTERPRETATION OF **ETERNAL** LIFE IN THE FOURTH GOSPEL— STAGG, ROBERT WILLIAM (PH D 1960 NEW ORLEANS BAPTIST THEOLOGICAL SEMINARY) X1960, p 167

A CRITICAL EVALUATION OF THE DENIALS OF THE DOCTRINE OF **ETERNAL** PUNISHMENT IN CONTEMPORARY PROTESTANT THOUGHT— STUCKEY, JOHNIE R (PH D 1960 SOUTHWESTERN BAPTIST THEOLOGICAL SEMINARY) X1960, p 168

A COMPARATIVE STUDY OF THE JOHANNINE CONCEPT OF **ETERNAL** LIFE AND THE SYNOPTIC CONCEPT OF THE KINGDOM— PATTERSON, LEON BELL (PH D 1959 SOUTHWESTERN BAPTIST THEOLOGICAL SEMINARY) X1959, p 154

A COMPARATIVE STUDY OF PAUL'S TERM 'RIGHTEOUSNESS OF GOD' AND JOHN'S TERM '**ETERNAL** LIFE'— HESTER, JAMES B (PH D 1955 SOUTHWESTERN BAPTIST THEOLOGICAL SEMINARY) W1955, p 7

THE DOCTRINE OF **ETERNAL** PUNISHMENT AND MAN, AS CONTAINED IN THE WRITINGS OF GREGORY THE GREAT— FONASH, IGNATIUS (PH D 1952 THE CATHOLIC UNIVERSITY OF AMERICA) 222p W1952, p 4

KANT'S CONCEPTION OF **ETERNAL** PEACE AND ITS INFLUENCE DURING THE NINETEENTH CENTURY— FALK, HEINRICH W K (PH D 1952 UNIVERSITY OF SOUTHERN CALIFORNIA) 175p W1952, p 8

JUDAS ISCARIOT, A SCRIPTURAL AND THEOLOGICAL STUDY OF HIS PERSON, HIS DEEDS AND HIS **ETERNAL** LOT— HALAS, ROMAN B (PH D 1946 THE CATHOLIC UNIVERSITY OF AMERICA) W1946, p 2

A CRITICAL EXAMINATION OF THE DOCTRINE OF **ETERNAL** HELL— BELCASTRO, JOE (PH D 1942 THE SOUTHERN BAPTIST THEOLOGICAL SEMINARY) 201p W1942, p 5

THE CONCEPT OF **ETERNAL** LIFE IN THE GOSPEL OF ST JOHN— LYONS, DAMIAN B (PH D 1938 THE CATHOLIC UNIVERSITY OF AMERICA) W1938, p 3

THE CONCEPTION OF **ETERNAL** LIFE IN JOHN'S GOSPEL AND THE EPISTLES— GATES, SIDNEY A (PH D 1937 THE SOUTHERN BAPTIST THEOLOGICAL SEMINARY) W1937, p.4

ETERNITY

THE TIME-**ETERNITY** CORRELATION IN WESTERN THEOLOGY AN EXPLORATION OF METAPHYSICAL FOUNDATIONS— STHOMSETH, WALTER ANDREW (PH D 1961 YALE UNIVERSITY) X1961, p 178

SECURITY FOR **ETERNITY**— SAXE, RAYMOND H (PH D 1954 DALLAS THEOLOGICAL SEMINARY) W1954, p 5

KIERKEGAARD'S CONCEPTION OF THE MOMENT. AN INVESTIGATION INTO THE TIME-**ETERNITY** CONCEPT OF SOEREN KIERKEGAARD— DAANE, JAMES (PH D 1947 PRINCETON THEOLOGICAL SEMINARY) 187p W1947, p 4

THE CONCEPT OF **ETERNITY**— CAIRNS, GRACE E (PH D 1942 UNIVERSITY OF CHICAGO) W1942, p 4

ETHIC

THE SOCIAL **ETHIC** OF THE UNITED PRESBYTERIAN CHURCH IN THE UNITED STATES OF AMERICA AS FOUND IN THE SOCIAL PRONOUNCEMENTS OF THE GENERAL ASSEMBLY FOR THE 1960'S— MOORE, JAMES FORRESTER (PH D 1972 SAN FRANCISCO THEOLOGICAL SEMINARY) X1972, p 334

JOHN'S PERSECUTION **ETHIC** A STUDY IN THE FAREWELL DISCOURSE— RIGGS, DON RICHARD (PH D 1969 VANDERBILT UNIVERSITY) 245p 30/10-A, p 4538 70-05422

THE LUTHERAN **ETHIC** AND SOCIAL CHANGE— KERSTEN, LAWRENCE KENNETH (PH D 1968 WAYNE STATE UNIVERSITY) 603p 30/04-A, p 1625 69-14673

AN APPRAISAL OF THE HALLUCINOGENIC DRUGS FROM THE STANDPOINT OF A CHRISTIAN PERSON-AGAPEIC **ETHIC**— PROVONSHA, JACK WENDELL (PH D 1967 CLAREMONT GRADUATE SCHOOL) 361p 29/03-A, p 955 68-10533

A VISION OF THE KINGDOM OF GOD THE SOCIAL **ETHIC** OF FRIEDRICH CHRISTOPH OETINGER— YEIDE, HARRY ELWOOD, JR (PH D 1966 HARVARD UNIVERSITY) X1966, p 197

AN EXAMINATION AND ANALYSIS OF THE RELEVANCE OF THE CHRISTIAN **ETHIC** OF SEX WITH RESPECT TO PREMARITAL SEXUAL INTERCOURSE AN INQUIRY BASED ON THE THOUGHT OF REINHOLD NIEBUHR AND EMIL BRUNNER IN VIEW OF THE FINDINGS OF ALFRED KINSEY AND MARGARET MEAD— GRAHAM, LEROY STONEY (PH D 1965 DREW UNIVERSITY) 410p 26/05, p 2890 65-11327

ROOTED AND GROUNDED IN LOVE F. D MAURICE'S RELATIONAL **ETHIC** OF RECONCILIATION AND TRANSFORMATION— BARTH, EUGENE HOWARD (PH D 1965 PRINCETON UNIVERSITY) 490p 26/07, p 4097 65-13124

THE ELEMENT OF ACCOMMODATION IN THE BASIC SOCIAL **ETHIC** OF REINHOLD NIEBUHR— BARNES, E. WAYNE (PH D 1965 SOUTHWESTERN BAPTIST THEOLOGICAL SEMINARY) X1965, p 211

THE **ETHIC** OF JOHN BUNYAN— TRULL, JOE E. (PH D 1965 SOUTHWESTERN BAPTIST THEOLOGICAL SEMINARY) X1965, p 211

THE EMERGING GROUP **ETHIC** A CHRISTIAN APPRAISAL— WARE, BROWNING (PH D 1962 SOUTHWESTERN BAPTIST THEOLOGICAL SEMINARY) X1962, p 201

THE PROBLEM OF A 'TRINITARIAN' SOCIAL **ETHIC** A STUDY IN THE THEOLOGICAL FOUNDATIONS OF CHRISTIAN SOCIAL ETHICS WITH SPECIAL REFERENCE TO WERNER ELERT AND DIETRICH BONHOEFFER— SHERMAN, FRANKLIN EUGENE (PH D 1961 UNIVERSITY OF CHICAGO) X1961, p 175

TESTIMONY OF FAITH THE GENESIS OF LUTHER'S MARRIAGE **ETHIC** SEEN AGAINST THE BACKGROUND OF HIS EARLY THEOLOGICAL DEVELOPMENT (1517-1525)— LAZARETH, WILLIAM HENRY (PH D 1958 COLUMBIA UNIVERSITY) 364p 19/02, p 372 58-02595

THE PROBLEM OF THE DEVELOPMENT OF THE CHRISTIAN **ETHIC** IN JAPANESE CULTURE— HAYS, GEORGE H (PH D 1954 THE SOUTHERN BAPTIST THEOLOGICAL SEMINARY) W1954, p 6

THE RELIGIOUS **ETHIC** OF ST PAUL— CLELAND, JAMES T (PH D 1954 UNION THEOLOGICAL SEMINARY IN THE CITY OF NEW YORK) W1954, p 7

SOME ELEMENTS OF AN EVANGELICAL **ETHIC** WITH SPECIAL REFERENCE TO THE PROBLEM OF ORDER— MAGRUDER, NORVIN B (PH D 1953 THE SOUTHERN BAPTIST THEOLOGICAL SEMINARY) W1953, p 9

ETHICAL

TOWARD A PROTESTANT **ETHICAL** THEORY ON THE VOCATIONAL DILEMMA OF THE LATE ADOLESCENT— OLSON, RICHARD PAUL (PH D 1972 BOSTON UNIVERSITY) 335p 33/04-A, p 1824 72-25316

AN **ETHICAL** ANALYSIS OF AUSTRALIAN POLICIES IN DEVELOPMENT PARTNERSHIP AND IMMIGRATION RESTRICTION— PRESTON, NOEL WILLIAM (TH D 1972 BOSTON UNIVERSITY) 360p 33/05-A, p 2485 72-27998

FAITH AND COMMUNITY IN THE **ETHICAL** THEORY OF KARL RAHNER AND BERNARD LONERGAN — BOYLE, JOHN PHILLIPS (PH D 1972 FORDHAM UNIVERSITY) 338p 33/01-A, p 386 72-20554

ETHICAL FACTORS IN MANAGEMENT DECISION— ALEXANDER, JAMES EDWIN (D DIV 1972 VANDERBILT UNIVERSITY DIVINITY SCHOOL) 109p 33/04-A, p 1813 72-26068

THE METHODOLOGY OF 'NATURAL LAW' **ETHICAL** REASONING IN THE THEOLOGY OF KARL RAHNER, AND ITS SUPPLEMENTARY DEVELOPMENT USING THE LEGAL PHILOSOPHY OF LON L FULLER— BRESNAHAN, JAMES FRANCIS (PH D 1972 YALE UNIVERSITY) 668p 33/05-A, p 2478 72-29520

AN **ETHICAL** ANALYSIS OF DECISION-MAKING THE RESPONSE OF THE UNITED STATES SENATE TO THE NONPROLIFERATION TREATY— WELCH EDWIN HUGH (PH D 1971 BOSTON UNIVERSITY) 375p 32/04-A, p 2189 71-26500

THE COMMUNICATION OF **ETHICAL** INSIGHT TO MORAL AGENTS AN ASSESSMENT OF CONTEMPORARY THEOLOGICAL ETHICS — BACHMEYER, T J (PH D 1971 UNIVERSITY OF CHICAGO) X1971, p 343

THE INTELLECTUAL SOURCES OF THE **ETHICAL** THOUGHT OF MARTIN LUTHER KING, JR., AS TRACED IN HIS WRITINGS WITH SPECIAL REFERENCE TO THE BELOVED COMMUNITY— ZEPP, IRA GILBERT, JR (PH D 1971 ST MARY'S SEMINARY AND UNIVERSITY) 414p 32/07-A, p 4101 72-01159

RELIGIOUS AND **ETHICAL** SENSITIVITY AND ONTOLOGY IMPLICIT IN THE CONTENT AND STYLE OF SELECTED BLACK POETRY— PINKSTON, HAROLD EDWARD SR. (PH D 1971 TEMPLE UNIVERSITY) 369p. 32/06-A, p 3414 71-31047

THE SECULARIZATION OF AUTHORITY AN INQUIRY INTO THE CONTEMPORARY CRISIS OF AUTHORITY FROM A SOCIO-**ETHICAL** PERSPECTIVE— MAXEY, MARGARET NAN TERESA (TH D 1971 UNION THEOLOGICAL SEMINARY IN THE CITY OF NEW YORK) 330p 32/04-A, p 2182 71-26380

AN HISTORICAL AND **ETHICAL** EVALUATION OF SELECTIVE CONSCIENTIOUS OBJECTION IN THE UNITED STATES — ETTEN, THOMAS JAMES (S T D 1970 THE CATHOLIC UNIVERSITY OF AMERICA) 370p 31/08-A, p 4253 71-04357

THE EVOLUTION OF **ETHICAL** AND LEGAL CONCERN FOR THE PRISONER OF WAR — GRADY, ROBERT F. (S T D 1970 THE CATHOLIC UNIVERSITY OF AMERICA) 216p 31/07-A, p 3630 71-01459

EMMANUEL LEVINAS THE PROBLEM OF **ETHICAL** METAPHYSICS— WYSCHOGROD, EDITH (PH D 1970 COLUMBIA UNIVERSITY) 332p 31/09-A, p 4882 71-06279

CHRISTIAN ETHICS IN THE MUSLIM CONTEXT A STUDY OF THE THEOLOGICAL PRESUPPOSITIONS AND THE **ETHICAL** IMPLICATIONS OF THE THEOLOGICAL SUMMA OF ABU ISHAQ IBN AL-ASSAL— DOGHRAMJI, PETER BUTRUS (TH D 1970 PRINCETON THEOLOGICAL SEMINARY) 306p 31/08-A, p 4252 71-04997

SELECTIVE CONSCIENTIOUS OBJECTION AS AN **ETHICAL** APPROACH TO CHRISTIAN PARTICIPATION IN WARFARE— SIMMONS, PAUL DEWAYNE (TH D 1970 THE SOUTHERN BAPTIST THEOLOGICAL SEMINARY) 324p 31/01-A, p 459 70-12218

EMMANUEL LEVINAS THE PROBLEM OF **ETHICAL** METAPHYSICS— WYSCHOGROD, EDITH (PH D 1970 UNION THEOLOGICAL SEMINARY IN THE CITY OF NEW YORK) X1970, p 309

CLERICAL EXEMPTION FROM MILITARY TRAINING AND SERVICE HISTORICAL AND **ETHICAL** ANALYSIS— MESSER, DONALD EDWARD (PH D 1969 BOSTON UNIVERSITY) 436p 30/05-A, p 2136 69-18743

MAURICE AS MORALIST THE **ETHICAL** TEACHING OF FREDERICK DENISON MAURICE— MCCLAIN, FRANK MAULDIN (PH D 1969 CAMBRIDGE UNIVERSITY (GREAT BRITAIN)) 711p 33/05-A, p 2485 72-27893

CHRISTIAN FREEDOM AND **ETHICAL** DECISION IN THE THEOLOGY OF MARTIN LUTHER— MCINTYRE, RUSSELL LEONARD (TH D 1969 EMMANUEL COLL OF VICTORIA UNIV IN THE UNIV OF TORONTO (CANADA)) 299p 33/06-A, p 3018 70-20681

PREACHING AS **ETHICAL** ACTION A RESPONSE TO THE CONCENTRATION ON PREACHING IN BARTH AND BULTMANN FROM THE VIEWPOINT OF PRACTICAL THEOLOGY— JOHNSON, WILLIAM WALTER (TH D 1969 PRINCETON THEOLOGICAL SEMINARY) [illegible]p 30/07-A, p 3086 69-21918

TOWARD AN **ETHICAL** UNDERSTANDING OF LEISURE IN A TECHNOLOGICAL SOCIETY— DEVER, JOHN PRESTON (TH D 1969 THE SOUTHERN BAPTIST THEOLOGICAL SEMINARY) 274p 30/02-A, p 794 69-12296

ETHICAL CRITERIA FOR THE CHRISTIAN USE OF INCOME AND PROPERTY— SESSIONS, ROBERT PAUL (PH D 1968 BOSTON UNIVERSITY) 428p 29/07-A, p 2349 68-18120

THE LIMITED NUCLEAR TEST BAN AND THE CHURCHES—A POLITICAL AND **ETHICAL** ANALYSIS OF UNITED STATES ARMS CONTROL EFFORTS, 1958-1963— SAUNDERS, ALBERT CONRAD (PH D 1968 DUKE UNIVERSITY) 337p 29/12-A, p 4551 69-09464

A CHRISTIAN **ETHICAL** ANALYSIS OF REVOLUTION WITH SPECIAL REFERENCE TO THE WORLD CONFERENCE ON CHURCH AND SOCIETY GENEVA, SWITZERLAND, JULY 12-26, 1966— WILBANKS DANA WINSTON (PH D 1968 DUKE UNIVERSITY) 273p 29/12-A p 4552 69-09466

THE WORLD RULE OF LAW AS AN **ETHICAL** IDEA— BRYANT, ROBERT DAVID (TH D 1967 BOSTON UNIVERSITY) 403p 28/05-A, p 1886 67-14114

ETHICAL IMPLICATIONS OF THE DOCTRINE OF THE PRIESTHOOD OF BELIEVERS WITH SPECIAL REFERENCE TO BAPTISTS— CHANCE, JERRY MCAULEY (PH D 1967 NEW ORLEANS BAPTIST THEOLOGICAL SEMINARY) X1967, p 243

A STUDY TO DETERMINE THE ROLE OF THE **ETHICAL** AND SOCIO-CULTURAL BACKGROUND AS INFLUENCE FORCES IN THE RELIGIOUS EDUCATION OF BAPTIST STUDENTS OF MEXICAN DESCENT IN TEXAS— RIVAS, JOSE (PH D 1967 SOUTHWESTERN BAPTIST THEOLOGICAL SEMINARY) X1967, p 103

CONSCIENCE AND RESPONSIBILITY A STUDY IN CONTEMPORARY CHRISTIAN **ETHICAL** THEORY — MOUNT, CHARLES ERIC, JR (PH D 1966 DUKE UNIVERSITY) 236p 27/11-A, p 3925 67-06286

THE IDEA OF DIVINE EDUCATION A STUDY IN THE **ETHICAL** AND THE RELIGIOUS AS ORGANIZING THEMES FOR THE INTERPRETATION OF THE LIFE OF THE SELF IN KANT, SCHLEIERMACHER, AND KIERKEGAARD— DESPLAND, MICHEL SAMUEL (PH D 1966 HARVARD UNIVERSITY) X1966, p 197

A GESTALT ANALYSIS OF THE MORAL DATA AND CERTAIN OF ITS IMPLICATIONS FOR **ETHICAL** THEORY— DYCK, ARTHUR JAMES (PH D 1966 HARVARD UNIVERSITY) X1966, p 197

REACTIONS TO RELATIVISM AN INVESTIGATION INTO THE **ETHICAL** THOUGHT OF REINHOLD NIEBUHR AND DIETRICH BONHOEFFER — MEYERS, LEONARD LEE (PH D 1966 THE UNIVERSITY OF IOWA) 318p 27/09-A, p 3113 67-02652

THE **ETHICAL** SIGNIFICANCE OF ABRAHAM'S DOMESTIC AUTHORITY— STRINGFIELD, LEROY PELHAM (PH D 1966 NEW ORLEANS BAPTIST THEOLOGICAL SEMINARY) X1966, p 197

THE **ETHICAL** THOUGHT OF JOSEPH MARTIN DAWSON— DUNN, JAMES MILTON (PH D 1966 SOUTHWESTERN BAPTIST THEOLOGICAL SEMINARY) X1966, p 196

SOME **ETHICAL** ISSUES INVOLVED IN THE STATEMENTS OF REPRESENTATIVE RELIGIOUS BODIES ON THE ALLOCATION OF RESPONSIBILITY FOR SOCIAL WELFARE— HUNTER, JOHN WALTER (PH D 1965 BOSTON UNIVERSITY) 225p. 26/05, p 2893 65-11233

Fig. 38. Page from *Comprehensive Dissertation Index, 1861-1972*. (See entries ETHIC and ETHICAL, center column.)

PATTERNS

RELIGION AND THEOLOGY

PATTERNS

PATTERNS OF SACRALIZATION MARK TWAIN. FAULKNER, HEMINGWAY, AND UPDIKE— SCAFELLA, FRANK S., JR. (PH.D. 1972 UNIVERSITY OF CHICAGO) X1972

PATTERNS FOR PREACHING–A RHETORICAL ANALYSIS OF THE SERMONS OF PAUL IN ACTS 13, 17, AND 20— SUNUKJIAN, DONALD ROBERT (PH.D. 1972 DALLAS THEOLOGICAL SEMINARY) X1972, p.332

THE **PATTERNS** OF ULTIMACY OF SVAMI VIVEKANANDA— WILLIAMS, GEORGE MASON, JR (PH.D. 1972 THE UNIVERSITY OF IOWA) 234p. 32/12-A, p.7082 72-17619

SOME FACTORS ASSOCIATED WITH CLERGYMEN'S PROJECTED RESPONSES TO MENTAL HEALTH CONSULTATION WITH A FOCUS ON **PATTERNS** OF DEPENDENCY— STEWART, JOHN THOMAS (TH.D. 1971 BOSTON UNIVERSITY) 202p. 33/06-A, p.3021 72-28314

PRAYER **PATTERNS** OF MINISTERIAL COUPLES IN WORCESTER COUNTY, MASSACHUSETTS— MARTIN, RAY IVAN (TH.D. 1968 BOSTON UNIVERSITY) 188p. 29/06-A, p.1947 68-14685

PATTERNS OF EMPHASIS IN THE BEREAVEMENT MINISTRY OF PROTESTANT CLERGY— EVEREST, RUTHERFORD ELMER (PH.D. 1967 BOSTON UNIVERSITY) 271p. 28/05-A, p.1888 67-13294

ATTITUDE **PATTERNS** OF NEGRO MINISTERS EXPERIENCING DESEGREGATION IN THE NORTH CENTRAL JURISDICTION OF THE METHODIST CHURCH— RILEY, NEGAIL RUDOLPH (TH.D. 1967 BOSTON UNIVERSITY) 256p. 28/05-A, p.1893 67-14116

INDIVIDUAL AND COMMUNITY SOME **PATTERNS** IN THE ETHICS OF INTERTESTAMENTAL JUDAISM, HELLENISTIC PHILOSOPHY, AND EARLY CHRISTIANITY— PAULSEN, DAVID HAROLD (PH.D. 1967 UNIVERSITY OF CHICAGO) X1967, p.241

THE SCHOOL OF PROPHETS, A STUDY OF THE CULTURAL AND THEOLOGICAL **PATTERNS** IN THE ESTABLISHMENT AND EARLY DEVELOPMENT OF THE GERMAN REFORMED MISSION HOUSE IN WISCONSIN— ULRICH, REINHARD (PH.D. 1963 LUTHERAN SCHOOL OF THEOLOGY AT CHICAGO) X1963, p.177

CHANGING **PATTERNS** OF LEADERSHIP IN THE AMERICAN REFORM RABBINATE, 1890-1957— MARX, ROBERT JOSEPH (PH.D. 1958 YALE UNIVERSITY) 172p. X1958, p.140

PATTERNS OF ADJUSTMENT AMONG JEWISH STUDENTS IN MIDWESTERN UNIVERSITIES— TEITELBAUM, SAMUEL (PH.D. 1953 NORTHWESTERN UNIVERSITY) 267p. 14/01, p.195 00-06248

A STUDY OF CHANGES IN THE VALUE **PATTERNS** OF THE CHURCH OF THE BRETHREN— ESHLEMAN, ROBERT F. (PH.D. 1948 CORNELL UNIVERSITY) W1948, p.4

A STUDY OF THE DEVELOPMENT OF THE BASIC DOCTRINES AND INSTITUTIONAL **PATTERNS** IN THE CHURCH OF GOD (ANDERSON, INDIANA)— FORREST, AUBREY L. (PH.D. 1948 UNIVERSITY OF SOUTHERN CALIFORNIA) W1948, p.5

RELATIONS OF RELIGIOUS TRAINING AND LIFE **PATTERNS** TO THE ADULT RELIGIOUS LIFE. A STUDY OF THE RELATIVE SIGNIFICANCE OF RELIGIOUS TRAINING AND INFLUENCE AND OF CERTAIN EMOTIONAL AND BEHAVIOR PATTERNS FOR THE ADULT RELIGIOUS LIFE— WOODWARD, LUTHER ELLIS (PH.D. 1932 COLUMBIA UNIVERSITY) 75p. L1932, p.214

PAUL'S TERMS AS ILLUSTRATIONS AND **PATTERNS** RATHER THAN DOGMATIC CONCEPTS— DEXTER, DORA LUCINA (PH.D. 1931 BOSTON UNIVERSITY) S0822

PATTISON

THE EARLY CAREER OF MARK **PATTISON**— SNIEGOWSKI, DONALD CHESTER (PH.D. 1966 YALE UNIVERSITY) 192p. 27/01-A, p.247 66-04929

THE RELIGIOUS PHILOSOPHY OF ANDREW SETH PRINGLE-**PATTISON**— VANDER WAAL, JOHN ANTHONY (PH.D. 1953 COLUMBIA UNIVERSITY) 242p. 14/01, p.198 00-06727

THE THEISM OF ANDREW SETH PRINGLE-**PATTISON**— POLLOCK, JAMES R. (PH.D. 1938 YALE UNIVERSITY) W1938, p.4

PRINGLE-**PATTISON**'S IDEA OF GOD— GALLAGHER, DENIS M. (PH.D. 1933 THE CATHOLIC UNIVERSITY OF AMERICA) S0043

PAUL

THE CONDITIONS OF INTELLIGIBLE ANALOGICAL GOD-LANGUAGE IN THE THEOLOGIES OF **PAUL** TILLICH, ERIC MASCALL, AND KARL BARTH— TEMPELMAN, ANDREW D. (PH.D. 1972 UNIVERSITY OF CHICAGO) X1972

WAR IN A MORAL PERSPECTIVE A CRITICAL APPRAISAL OF THE VIEWS OF **PAUL** RAMSEY— O'CONNOR, DON THOMAS (PH.D. 1972 CLAREMONT GRADUATE SCHOOL) 352p. 33/05-A, p.2485 72-30547

PATTERNS FOR PREACHING–A RHETORICAL ANALYSIS OF THE SERMONS OF **PAUL** IN ACTS 13, 17, AND 20— SUNUKJIAN, DONALD ROBERT (PH.D. 1972 DALLAS THEOLOGICAL SEMINARY) X1972, p.332

PAUL TILLICH'S PROTESTANT PRINCIPLE AND CATHOLIC SUBSTANCE IN RECENT CATHOLIC THOUGHT— STURDIVANT, ROBERT VICTOR (PH.D. 1972 EMORY UNIVERSITY) 322p. 33/04-A, p.1829 72-25947

THE CENTRALITY AND SIGNIFICANCE OF THE CONCEPT OF ECSTASY IN THE THEOLOGY OF **PAUL** TILLICH— MUELLER, PHILIP JOHN (PH.D. 1972 FORDHAM UNIVERSITY) 333p. 33/01-A, p.393 72-20570

AN EVALUATION OF PROTESTANT PUBLIC EVANGELISM IN ARGENTINA COMPARED WITH **PAUL**'S METHODS AS THEY APPEAR IN THE NEW TESTAMENT— ARTEAGA, ANTONIO (PH.D. 1972 FULLER THEOLOGICAL SEMINARY) X1972, p.332

THE NATURE OF THEOLOGICAL ARGUMENT A STUDY OF **PAUL** TILLICH— SCHRADER, ROBERT WILLIAM (PH.D. 1972 HARVARD UNIVERSITY) X1972, p.333

PAUL RICOEUR'S PHILOSOPHY OF RELIGIOUS LANGUAGE INTERPRETED AS AN ALTERNATIVE TO ANTONY FLEW'S EMPIRICISTIC REJECTION OF RELIGIOUS LANGUAGE— ALEXANDER, RONALD (PH.D. 1972 LUTHERAN SCHOOL OF THEOLOGY AT CHICAGO) X1972, p.333

HISTORY AS SYMBOL IN THE THOUGHT OF **PAUL** TILLICH— STRUZYNSKI, ANTHONY (PH.D. 1972 UNIVERSITY OF NOTRE DAME) X1972, p.353

THE ROLE OF GENERAL REVELATION IN AMERICAN NEOORTHODOXY REINHOLD NIEBUHR, **PAUL** TILLICH, AND H. RICHARD NIEBUHR— TAYLOR, LARRY MICHAEL (PH.D. 1972 SOUTHWESTERN BAPTIST THEOLOGICAL SEMINARY) X1972

THE TWO-AGE DOCTRINE IN **PAUL** A STUDY OF PAULINE APOCALYPTIC— CAUDILL, EARL MADISON (PH.D. 1972 VANDERBILT UNIVERSITY) 385p. 33/04-A, p.1814 72-26094

THE PRACTICAL IMPLICATIONS OF **PAUL** TILLICH'S THEOLOGY FOR A DOCTRINE OF CHURCH RENEWAL— BOTTOMS, ROBERT GARVIN (D.MIN. 1972 VANDERBILT UNIVERSITY DIVINITY SCHOOL) 179p. 33/04-A, p.1813 72-26069

THE RELEVANCE OF THE REFORMED THOUGHT OF JUSTIFICATION FOR A CONTEMPORARY CHURCH AS ILLUSTRATED IN THE THINKING OF **PAUL** TILLICH— GIBBS, REAGAN PHILIP (D.DIV. 1972 VANDERBILT UNIVERSITY DIVINITY SCHOOL) 132p. 33/04-A, p.1817 72-26072

THE FEAR OF THE FUTURE AN ANALYSIS OF THE ESSENCE OF ANXIETY IN THE THOUGHT OF **PAUL** TILLICH AND SIGMUND FREUD— HENDRIX, HARVILLE (PH.D. 1971 UNIVERSITY OF CHICAGO) X1971, p.343

DEVELOPMENTAL PSYCHOLOGY AND MORAL ANTHROPOLOGY–SOME IMPLICATIONS IN THE WORK OF **PAUL** TILLICH AND ERIK ERIKSON— MADDOCK, JAMES (PH.D. 1971 UNIVERSITY OF CHICAGO) X1971, p.343

SYMBOLIC KNOWLEDGE IN ERNST CASSIRER AND **PAUL** TILLICH— ARNINK, DALE EDWIN (PH.D. 1971 CLAREMONT GRADUATE SCHOOL) 238p. 32/02-A, p.1062 71-21665

THE IMAGE OF **PAUL** IN THE BOOK OF ACTS— KAYAMA, HISAO (PH.D. 1971 CLAREMONT GRADUATE SCHOOL) 245p. 32/02-A, p.1064 71-21674

THE THEME OF UNITY IN THE THEOLOGY OF **PAUL** TILLICH EVALUATED ON THE BOUNDARY BETWEEN HIS THEOLOGY AND THE SCIENCE OF PERCY BRIDGMAN— WOODBURY, WILLIAM CLAIR (PH.D. 1971 DREW UNIVERSITY) 276p. 32/05-A, p.2796 71-29413

THE NORMATIVE ELEMENT IN **PAUL**'S THEOLOGIZING WHAT IT IS AND HOW IT FUNCTIONS— MYERS, WILLIAM ROBERT (PH.D. 1971 EMORY UNIVERSITY) 230p. 32/05-A, p.2790 71-27790

THE PLACE OF AESTHETICS IN THE THEOLOGY OF **PAUL** TILLICH— WEISBAKER, DIMIS TAYLOR (PH.D. 1971 EMORY UNIVERSITY) 184p. 32/04-A, p.2188 71-27803

PAUL TILLICH AND BONAVENTURE AN EVALUATION OF TILLICH'S CLAIM TO STAND IN THE AUGUSTINIAN-FRANCISCAN TRADITION— DOURLEY, JOHN PATRICK (PH.D. 1971 FORDHAM UNIVERSITY) 321p. 32/04-A, p.2176 71-26964

AN EVALUATION OF THE CONCEPT OF GUILT IN SELECTED WRITINGS OF **PAUL** TOURNIER— RYNBRANDT, THURMAN PHILIP (PH.D. 1971 FULLER THEOLOGICAL SEMINARY) X1971, p.343

CHRIST WITH OR WITHOUT GOD AND MYTHOLOGY AN ANALYSIS AND CRITIQUE OF THE THEOLOGICAL PROPOSALS AND DEBATE OF SCHUBERT OGDEN AND **PAUL** VAN BUREN— THOMSEN, MARK WILLIAM (PH.D. 1971 NORTHWESTERN UNIVERSITY) 239p. 32/06-A, p.3417 71-30969

'THE LAW OF CHRIST' A STUDY OF **PAUL**'S USE OF THE EXPRESSION IN GALATIANS 6.2— STOIKE, DONALD ALLEN (TH.D. 1971 SCHOOL OF THEOLOGY AT CLAREMONT) 276p. 32/06-A, p.3416 71-30520

PAUL'S USE OF THE EXPRESSION 'THE LAW OF CHRIST' IN GALATIANS 6:2— STUIKE, DONALD ALLEN (PH.D. 1971 SCHOOL OF THEOLOGY AT CLAREMONT) X1971, p.344

THE OPPONENTS OF **PAUL** IN GALATIA— HAWKINS, JOHN GALE (PH.D. 1971 YALE UNIVERSITY) 392p. 32/05-A, p.2785 71-28176

GRACE AND OBEDIENCE A STUDY OF THE IDEA OF MAN THAT UNDERLIES **PAUL**'S TEACHING ON SALVATION— JOHN, MATHEW P. (PH.D. 1970 UNIVERSITY OF CHICAGO) X1970, p.306

THE ESCHATOLOGICAL DESTINY OF THE INDIVIDUAL IN THE THOUGHT OF **PAUL** TILLICH— HARRIS, BOND (PH.D. 1970 DREW UNIVERSITY) 198p. 31/06-A, p.3018 70-24584

PAUL AND HIS SENSE OF MISSION A CRITIQUE OF JOHANNES MUNCK'S VIEW OF PAUL'S CONCEPTION OF HIS PLACE IN THE HISTORY OF REDEMPTION AS REVEALED IN ROMANS 9-11— BARTON, FREEMAN EARL (PH.D. 1970 THE UNIVERSITY OF IOWA) 183p. 31/03-A, p.1361 70-15580

THE ROMAN CATHOLIC RESPONSE TO THE WRITINGS OF **PAUL** BLANSHARD— MCNEARNEY, CLAYTON LEROY (PH.D. 1970 THE UNIVERSITY OF IOWA) 270p. 31/06-A, p.3022 70-23923

'HOMO RELIGIOSUS' A DOCTRINE OF MAN IN THE THOUGHT OF **PAUL** TILLICH— CROSBY, ISAAC (PH.D. 1970 UNION THEOLOGICAL SEMINARY IN VIRGINIA) X1970, p.309

THE FORM AND FUNCTION OF THE BODY OF THE GREEK LETTER A STUDY OF THE LETTER-BODY IN THE NON LITERARY PAPYRI AND IN **PAUL** THE APOSTLE— WHITE, JOHN LEE (PH.D. 1970 VANDERBILT UNIVERSITY) 169p. 31/06-A, p.3031 70-24899

THE CONCEPT OF REJOICING IN **PAUL** — WEBBER, ROBERT DUFF (PH.D. 1970 YALE UNIVERSITY) 401p. 32/01-A, p.531 71-17160

THE RELATIONSHIP OF CHRISTIANITY TO NON-CHRISTIAN RELIGIONS IN THE THEOLOGIES OF DANIEL T. NILES AND **PAUL** TILLICH— SNOWDEN, GLEN WENGER (TH.D. 1969 BOSTON UNIVERSITY) 328p. 30/10-A, p.4540 70-06681

PROVIDENCE AND EVIL. A STUDY BASED ON THE THOUGHT OF FRIEDRICH SCHLEIERMACHER AND **PAUL** TILLICH— MINTON, FRANK D. (PH.D. 1969 UNIVERSITY OF CHICAGO) X1969, p.280

A CORRELATION BETWEEN RELIGIOUS LANGUAGE AND AN UNDERSTANDING OF MAN A CONSTRUCTIVE INTERPRETATION OF THE THOUGHT OF **PAUL** RICOEUR— RASMUSSEN, DAVID MICHAEL (PH.D. 1969 UNIVERSITY OF CHICAGO) X1969, p.280

THE REFERENT OF GODLANGUAGE IN THE THOUGHT OF **PAUL** TILLICH— TARBOX, EVERETT JACOB, JR (PH.D. 1969 UNIVERSITY OF CHICAGO) X1969, p.280

THE NATURE OF BEING IN THE THOUGHT OF **PAUL** TILLICH AND MARTIN HEIDEGGER— VUNDERINK, RALPH WILLIAM (PH.D. 1969 UNIVERSITY OF CHICAGO) X1969, p.2

THE CONCEPT OF MULTIDIMENSIONAL UNITY IN **PAUL** TILLICH WITH OPERATIONAL IMPLICATIONS FOR INTERDISCIPLINARY METHODOLOGY— JACKSON, GEORGE ANDREW, JR (PH.D. 1969 CLAREMONT GRADUATE SCHOOL) 192p. 30/01-A, p.381 69-08935

TOWARDS A THEOLOGY OF EPHAPAX A COMPARISON OF THE CLAIMS MADE FOR THE CHRIST EVENT BY **PAUL** TILLICH AND GERHARD EBELING— ROSS, JAMES ROBERT (PH.D. 1969 EMORY UNIVERSITY) 284p. 30/10-A, p.4538 70-05752

THE THEOLOGICAL CONCEPT OF THE GOSPEL ACCORDING TO ST. **PAUL**— LAUNSTEIN, DONALD HUGH (PH.D. 1969 GRACE THEOLOGICAL SEMINARY AND COLLEGE) X1969, p.281

A SECULAR EUCHARIST **PAUL** TILLICH'S VIEW OF THE EUCHARIST AS A FOCUS FOR SECULARIZATION IN THEOLOGY— LONG, WIL (TH.D. 1969 GRADUATE THEOLOGICAL UNION) 252p. 30/07-A, p.3088 69-22083

THE SPIRIT AND THE AGE TO COME IN **PAUL**— EWERT, DAVID (PH.D. 1969 MC GILL UNIVERSITY (CANADA)) 30/07-A, p.3085

A COMPARATIVE STUDY OF PAULINE AND EARLY GNOSTIC LITERATURE DEMONSTRATING THAT **PAUL** WAS NOT PROTO-GNOSTIC— WILSON, JOHN HENRY (PH.D. 1969 MICHIGAN STATE UNIVERSITY) 226p. 30/06-A, p.2612 69-20957

PAUL'S IDEA OF GROWTH AND MATURITY REFLECTED IN THE TRAINING PROGRAM CURRENTLY SUGGESTED TO SOUTHERN BAPTIST CHURCHES— MURPHY, EARL LEE (PH.D. 1969 SOUTHWESTERN BAPTIST THEOLOGICAL SEMINARY) X1969, p.282

THE APPROACH OF **PAUL** S. MINEAR TO THE PROBLEM OF BIBLICAL SYMBOLISM— PETTY, JULIUS EUGENE (PH.D. 1969 SOUTHWESTERN BAPTIST THEOLOGICAL SEMINARY) X1969, p.282

PREACHING THE PRESENCE OF GOD BASED ON A CRITICAL STUDY OF THE SERMONS OF **PAUL** TILLICH, KARL BARTH AND HERBERT H. FARMER— NIEDENTHAL, MORRIS JEROME (TH.D. 1969 UNION THEOLOGICAL SEMINARY IN THE CITY OF NEW YORK) 269p. 30/05-A, p.2137 69-18149

FREEDOM FROM THE LAW **PAUL**'S DOCTRINE AND ITS ROLE IN THE EARLY CHURCH— FESPERMAN, FRANCIS IRVING (PH.D. 1969 VANDERBILT UNIVERSITY) 351p. 30/10-A, p.4533 70-05447

TELEOLOGICAL ASPECTS OF CREATION A COMPARISON OF THE CONCEPTS OF BEING AND MEANING IN THE THEOLOGIES OF JONATHAN EDWARDS AND **PAUL** TILLICH— HAND, JAMES ALBERT (PH.D. 1969 VANDERBILT UNIVERSITY) 488p. 30/02-A, p.796 69-13456

THE FUNCTION OF SPIRITUAL PRESENCE IN **PAUL** TILLICH'S THEOLOGY OF CULTURE— DYAL, ROBERT ALLISON (PH.D. 1968 BOSTON UNIVERSITY) X1968, p.251

CHRISTOLOGY IN THE THOUGHT OF NELS F. S. FERRE, W. NORMAN PITTENGER AND **PAUL** TILLICH— MINTER, DAVID CURTIS (PH.D. 1968 BOSTON UNIVERSITY) X1968, p.251

PAUL'S WEAKNESS A STUDY IN PAULINE POLEMICS (II CORINTHIANS 10-13)— HARADA, MAKOTO (PH.D. 1968 BOSTON UNIVERSITY) 269p. 29/07-A, p.2344 68-18162

CHRISTOLOGY IN THE THOUGHT OF NELS F. S. FERRE, W. NORMAN PITTENGER AND **PAUL** TILLICH— MINTER, DAVID CURTIS (PH.D. 1968 BOSTON UNIVERSITY) 292p. 29/07-A, p.2346 68-18163

A THEORY OF INTERPERSONAL MINISTRY BASED ON THE SYSTEMATIC THEOLOGY OF **PAUL** TILLICH AND THE PSYCHOLOGICAL THEORY OF HARRY STACK SULLIVAN— PATTON, JOHN HULL (PH.D. 1968 UNIVERSITY OF CHICAGO) X1968, p.251

ONTOLOGICAL AND THEOLOGICAL DIMENSIONS OF GOD IN THE THOUGHT OF **PAUL** TILLICH AND CHARLES HARTSHORNE— TOWNE, EDGAR A. (PH.D. 1968 UNIVERSITY OF CHICAGO) X1968, p.251

THE FAR SIDE OF DESPAIR SARTRE'S HIDDEN ETHICS AND THE DEATH OF GOD A LITERARY AND THEOLOGICAL STUDY OF JEAN **PAUL** SARTRE'S DRAMA— WILLIAMS, JOHN S. (PH.D. 1968 UNIVERSITY OF CHICAGO) X1968, p.251

THE SIGNIFICANCE OF THE PAROUSIA IN THE THEOLOGY OF **PAUL** A STUDY IN PAULINE ESCHATOLOGY— MAXWELL, DONALD MALCOLM (PH.D. 1968 DREW UNIVERSITY) 174p. 29/05-A, p.1593 68-15408

PAUL IN DIALOGUE AN EXEGETICAL STUDY OF II COR 2 14–7 4 IN THE LIGHT OF H. RICHARD NIEBUHR'S CONSTRUCT OF THE RESPONSIBLE SELF— MCKINNIS, RAY ALLEN (PH.D. 1968 DREW UNIVERSITY) 263p. 29/05-A, p.1593 68-15407

TOWARD A CONTEMPORARY CONSTRUCT OF PROVIDENCE AN ANALYSIS OF THE CONSTRUCT OF PROVIDENCE IN THE SYSTEMATIC THEOLOGY OF **PAUL** TILLICH AND THE NEOCLASSICAL METAPHYSICS OF CHARLES HARTSHORNE— CAVANAGH, RONALD RAYMOND (TH.D. 1968 GRADUATE THEOLOGICAL UNION) 393p. 30/02-A, p.793 69-12571

THE 'PNEUMATIKOS-PSUCHIKOS' TERMINOLOGY IN I CORINTHIANS A STUDY IN THE THEOLOGY OF THE CORINTHIAN OPPONENTS OF **PAUL** AND ITS RELATION TO GNOSTICISM— PEARSON, BIRGER ALBERT (PH.D. 1968 HARVARD UNIVERSITY) X1968, p.252

PAUL HENKEL, PIONEER LUTHERAN MISSIONARY— BAUR, RICHARD HAROLD (PH.D. 1968 THE UNIVERSITY OF IOWA) 211p. 29/06-A, p.1944 68-16782

THE CONCEPT OF PARTICIPATION IN **PAUL** TILLICH'S THOUGHT–WITH STUDIES IN ITS HISTORICAL BACKGROUND AND PRESENT SIGNIFICANCE— WETTSTEIN, ADELBERT ARNOLD (PH.D. 1968 MC GILL UNIVERSITY (CANADA)) 30/01-A, p.384

THE VALENTINIAN (GNOSTIC) USE OF THE LETTERS OF **PAUL**— STORY, GEOFFREY LEE, JR (PH.D. 1968 NORTHWESTERN UNIVERSITY) 359p. 29/07-A, p.2350 69-01951

THE MYSTICAL A PRIORI **PAUL** TILLICH'S CRITICAL PHENOMENOLOGY OF RELIGION— STREIKER, LOWELL DEAN (PH.D. 1968 PRINCETON UNIVERSITY) 332p. 29/08-A, p.2797 69-02785

Fig. 39. Page from *Comprehensive Dissertation Index*. (See entry PAUL, beginning bottom of left column.)

By way of review, the process we have followed for the gathering of data began with : (1) *general reference works,* followed by (2) *books,* (3) *periodical articles,* and (4) *unpublished materials.* We moved progressively from the general to the specific.

GENERAL REFERENCE WORKS Encyclopedias; Dictionaries; Yearbooks.	BOOKS AND MONOGRAPHS *L.C. Catalog— Books: Subjects; Subject Guide to Books in Print.*	PERIODICAL ARTICLES via Indices; Abstracts; Bibliographies.	UNPUBLISHED MATERIALS Proceedings of different societies; Dissertations.

The better known the subject, the less reliance there will be on general reference works. The less sophisticated the project, the less one need progress through the four successive steps outlined above.

Because this introduction to theological research is to be kept up to date with periodic revisions, I would like to ask readers to respond with criticisms and suggestions—information they feel can improve a later edition. Please write to this address:

Cyril J. Barber
P.O. Box 5181
Hacienda Heights,
Calif. 91745